Kamisama Kiss

24

Story & Art by
Julietta Suzuki

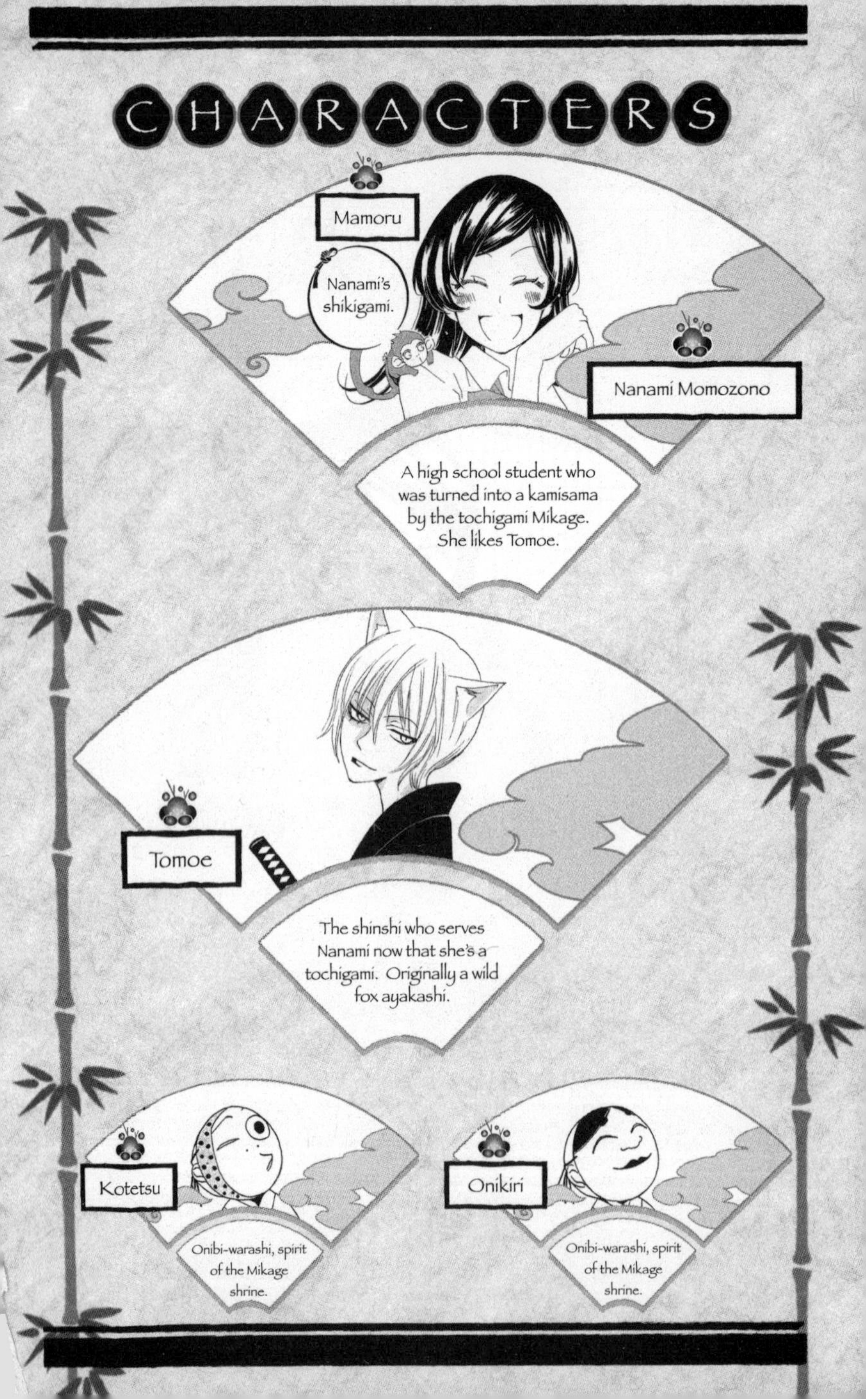
CHARACTERS
Mamoru
Nanami's shikigami.
Nanami Momozono
A high school student who was turned into a kamisama by the tochigami Mikage. She likes Tomoe.
Tomoe
The shinshi who serves Nanami now that she's a tochigami. Originally a wild fox ayakashi.
Kotetsu
Onibi-warashi, spirit of the Mikage shrine.
Onikiri
Onibi-warashi, spirit of the Mikage shrine.

Mizuki

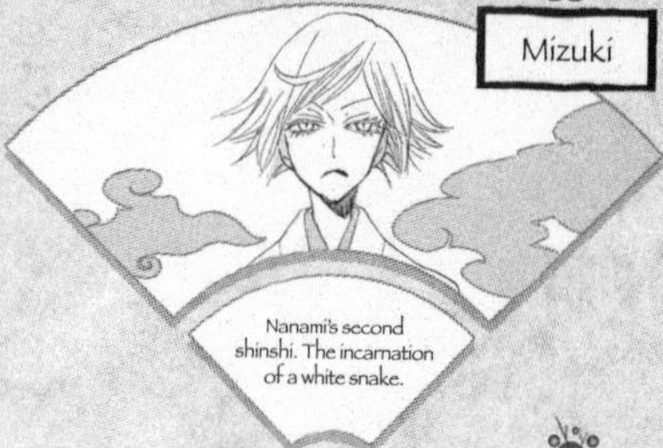

Nanami's second shinshi. The incarnation of a white snake.

Mikage

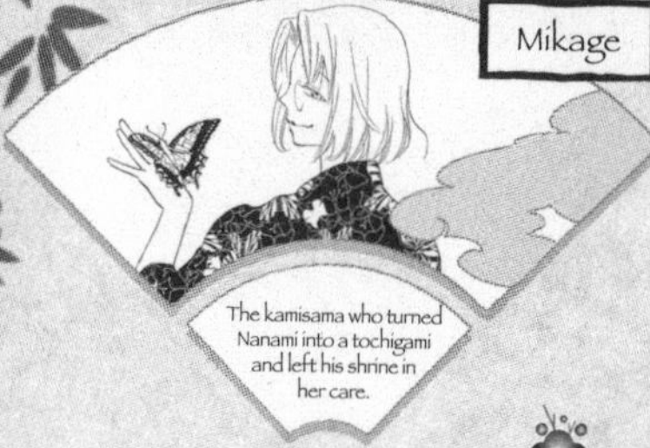

The kamisama who turned Nanami into a tochigami and left his shrine in her care.

Akura-oh

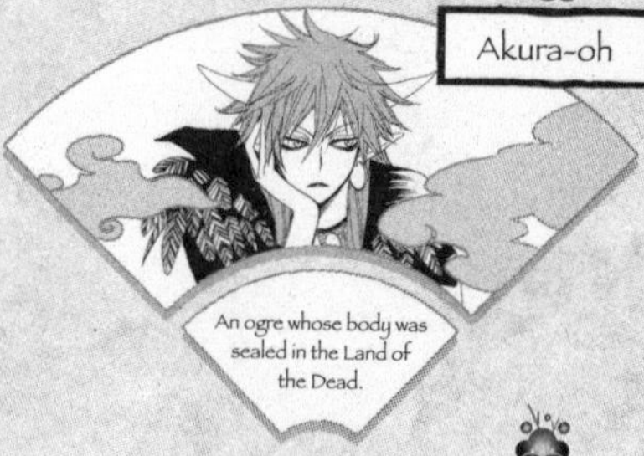

An ogre whose body was sealed in the Land of the Dead.

Yatori

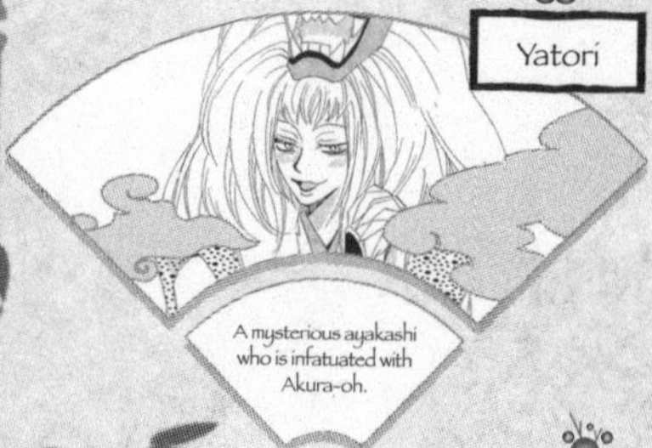

A mysterious ayakashi who is infatuated with Akura-oh.

Kirihito

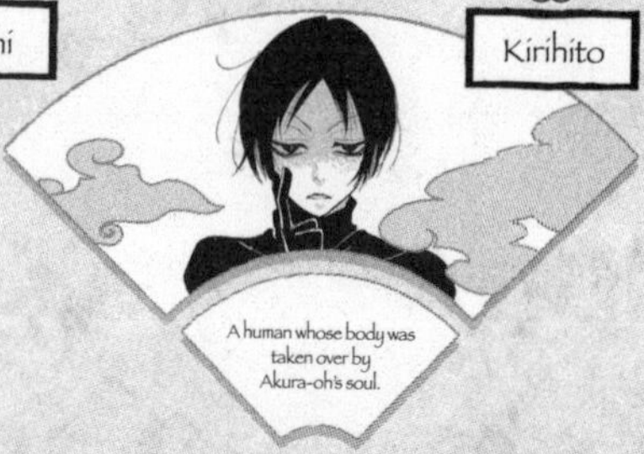

A human whose body was taken over by Akura-oh's soul.

Ôkuninushi

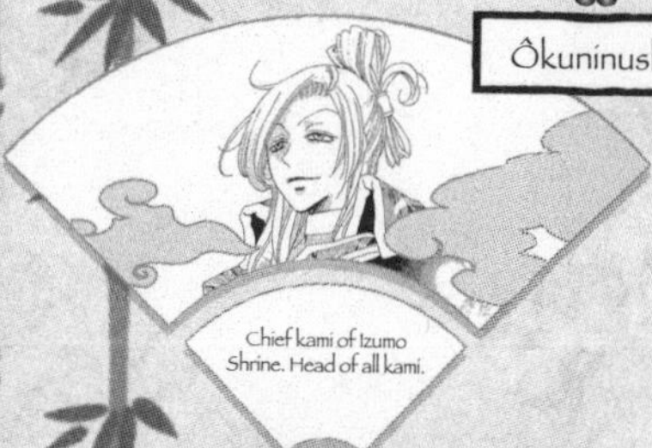

Chief kami of Izumo Shrine. Head of all kami.

Story so far

Nanami Momozono is a high school student who was evicted from her home when her dad skipped town.
She meets the tochigami Mikage at a park, and he leaves his shrine and his kami powers to her.
Now Nanami spends her days with Tomoe and Mizuki, her shinshi, and with Onikiri and Kotetsu, the onibi-warashi spirits of the shrine.
Nanami has been slowly gaining powers as kamisama through all sorts of other adventures. Nanami's and Tomoe's feelings for each other are finally out in the open and they have started to date!
Eventually Tomoe starts to think about becoming human so he can live his life with Nanami.
Meanwhile, Kirihito and Yatori head for the Mountain of Flames where Akura-oh's body is interred. But Kirihito dies while protecting his mother Ako. Yatori then becomes one with Akura-oh's body, just like he wanted...

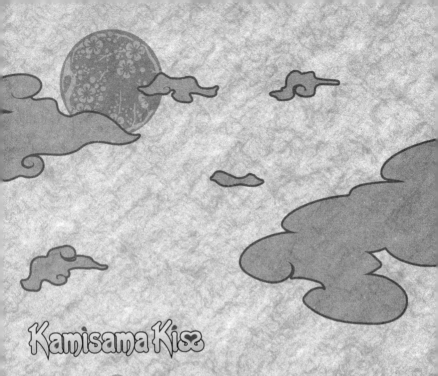

Kamisama Kiss

Volume 24
CONTENTS

Chapter 138

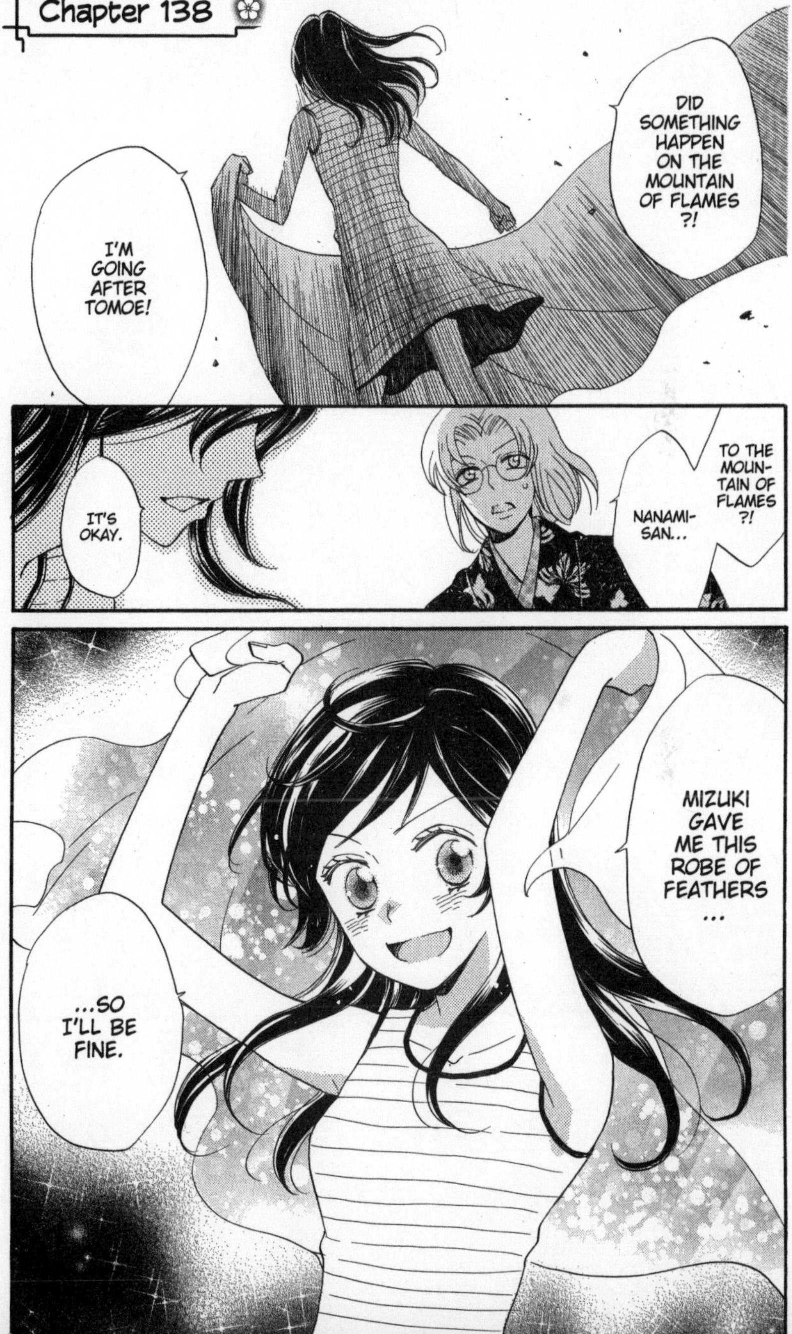
DID SOMETHING HAPPEN ON THE MOUNTAIN OF FLAMES ?!
I'M GOING AFTER TOMOE!
TO THE MOUN-TAIN OF FLAMES ?!
NANAMI-SAN...
IT'S OKAY.
MIZUKI GAVE ME THIS ROBE OF FEATHERS ...
...SO I'LL BE FINE.

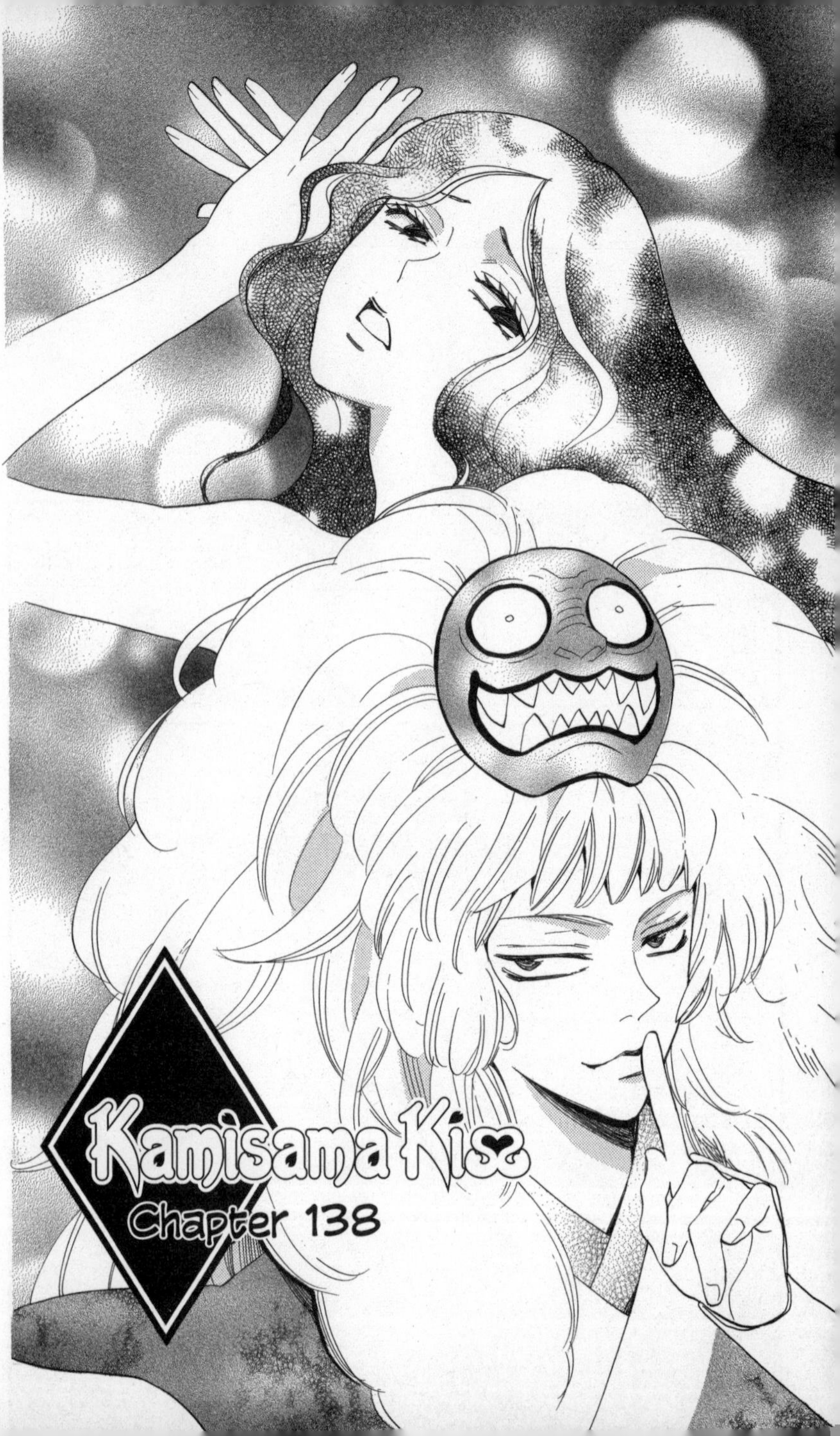
Kamisama Kiss
Chapter 138

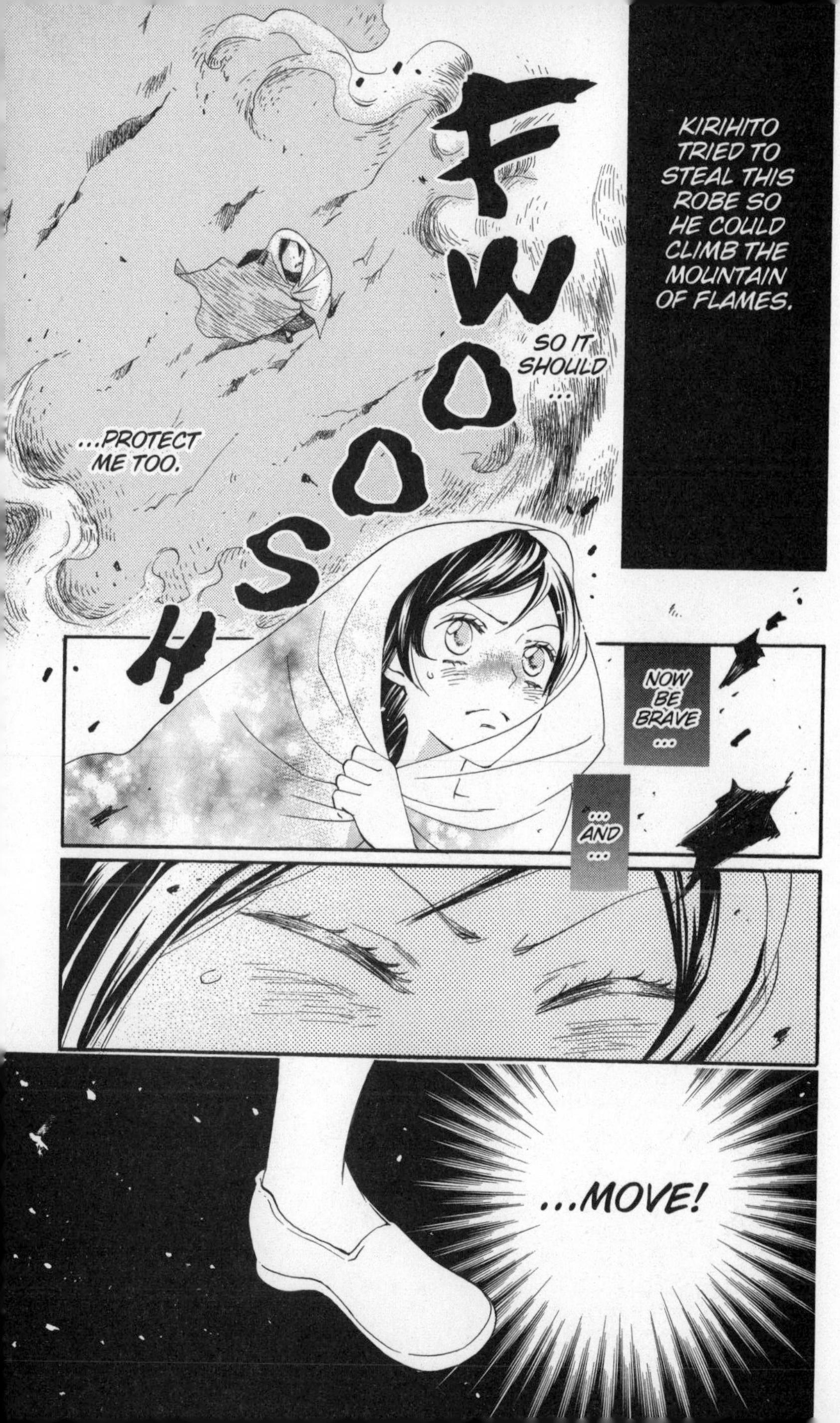
KIRIHITO TRIED TO STEAL THIS ROBE SO HE COULD CLIMB THE MOUNTAIN OF FLAMES.
FWOOSH
SO IT SHOULD ...
...PROTECT ME TOO.
NOW BE BRAVE ...
... AND ...
...MOVE!

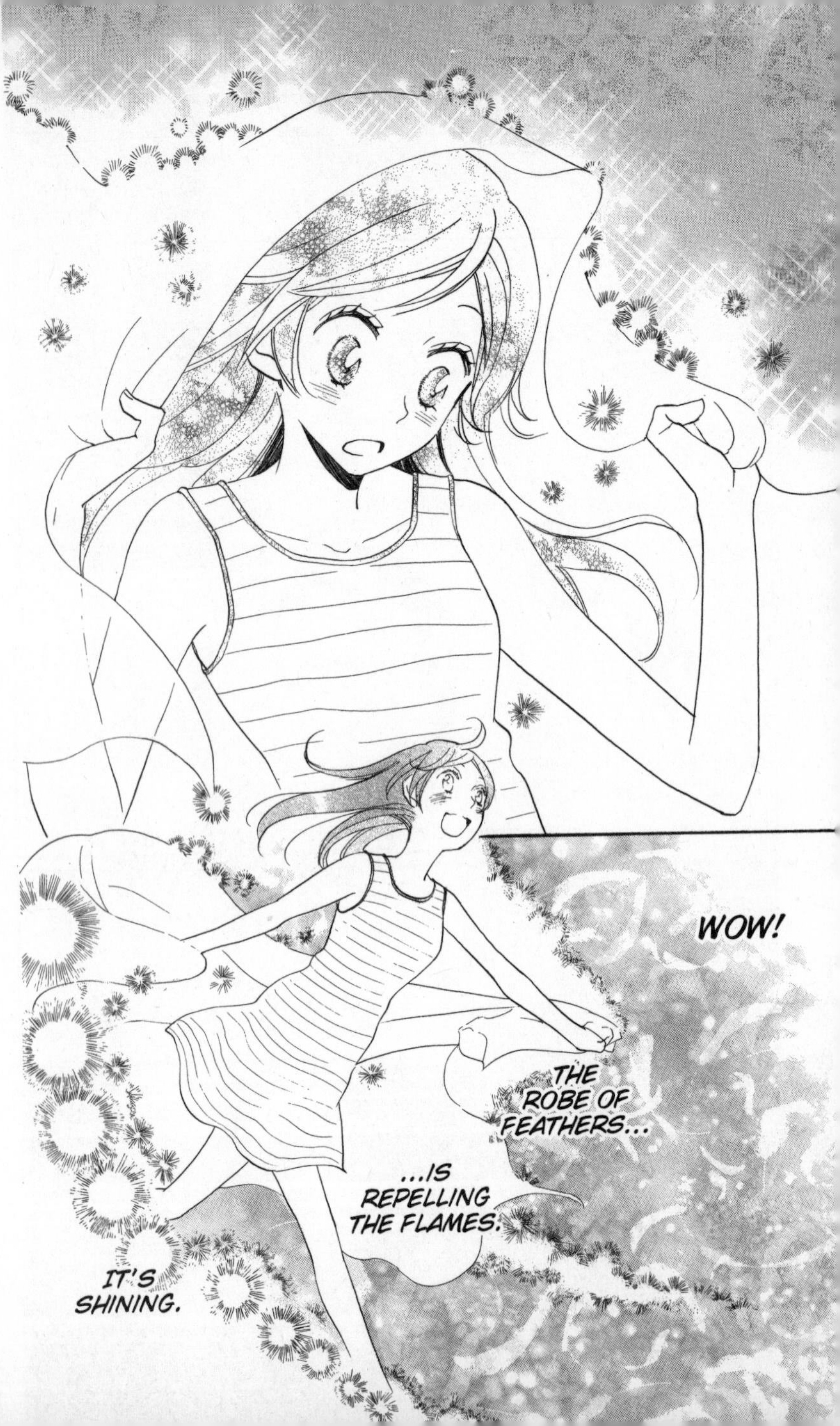
WOW!
THE ROBE OF FEATHERS...
...IS REPELLING THE FLAMES.
IT'S SHINING.

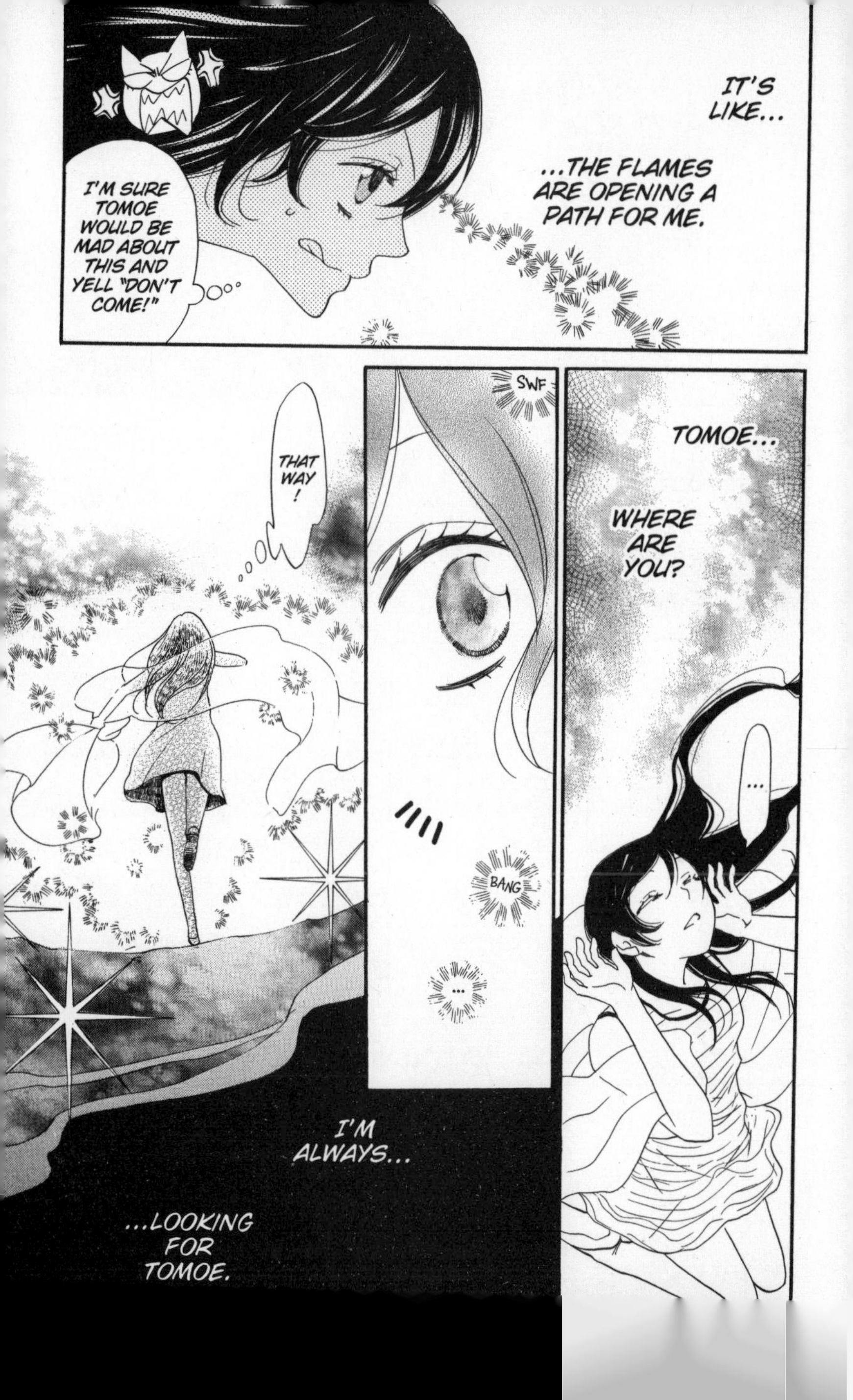
IT'S LIKE...
...THE FLAMES ARE OPENING A PATH FOR ME.
I'M SURE TOMOE WOULD BE MAD ABOUT THIS AND YELL "DON'T COME!"
TOMOE...
WHERE ARE YOU?
...
SWF
BANG
...
THAT WAY!
I'M ALWAYS...
...LOOKING FOR TOMOE.

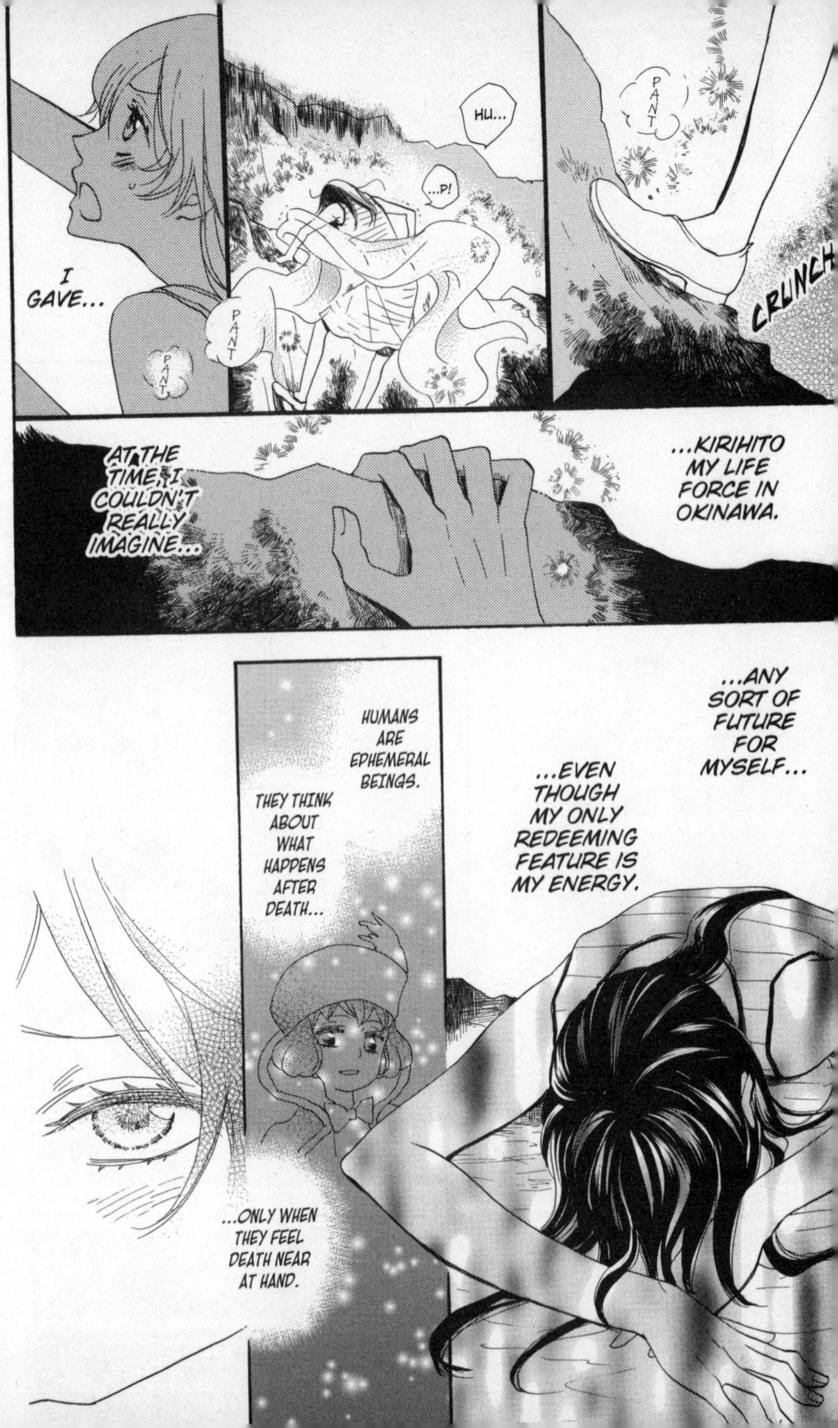
PANT
CRUNCH
HU...
...P!
PANT
I GAVE...
PANT
...KIRIHITO MY LIFE FORCE IN OKINAWA.
AT THE TIME, I COULDN'T REALLY IMAGINE...
...ANY SORT OF FUTURE FOR MYSELF...
...EVEN THOUGH MY ONLY REDEEMING FEATURE IS MY ENERGY.
HUMANS ARE EPHEMERAL BEINGS.
THEY THINK ABOUT WHAT HAPPENS AFTER DEATH...
...ONLY WHEN THEY FEEL DEATH NEAR AT HAND.

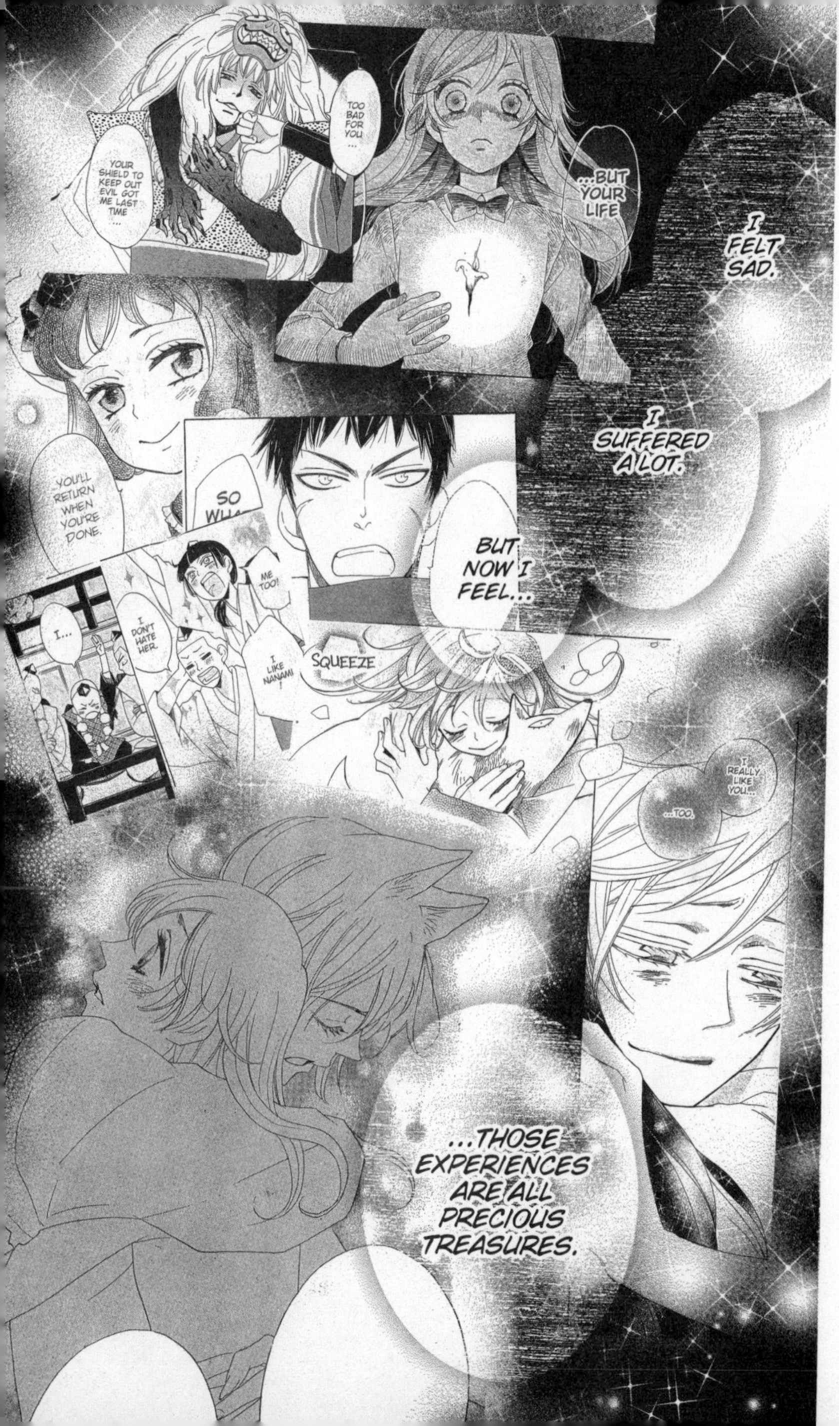
...BUT YOUR LIFE
TOO BAD FOR YOU...
YOUR SHIELD TO KEEP OUT EVIL GOT ME LAST TIME...
I FELT SAD.
I SUFFERED A LOT.
SO WHA...
YOU'LL RETURN WHEN YOU'RE DONE.
BUT NOW I FEEL...
SQUEEZE
I LIKE NANAMI!
ME TOO!
I DON'T HATE HER.
I...
I REALLY LIKE YOU...
...TOO.
...THOSE EXPERIENCES ARE ALL PRECIOUS TREASURES.

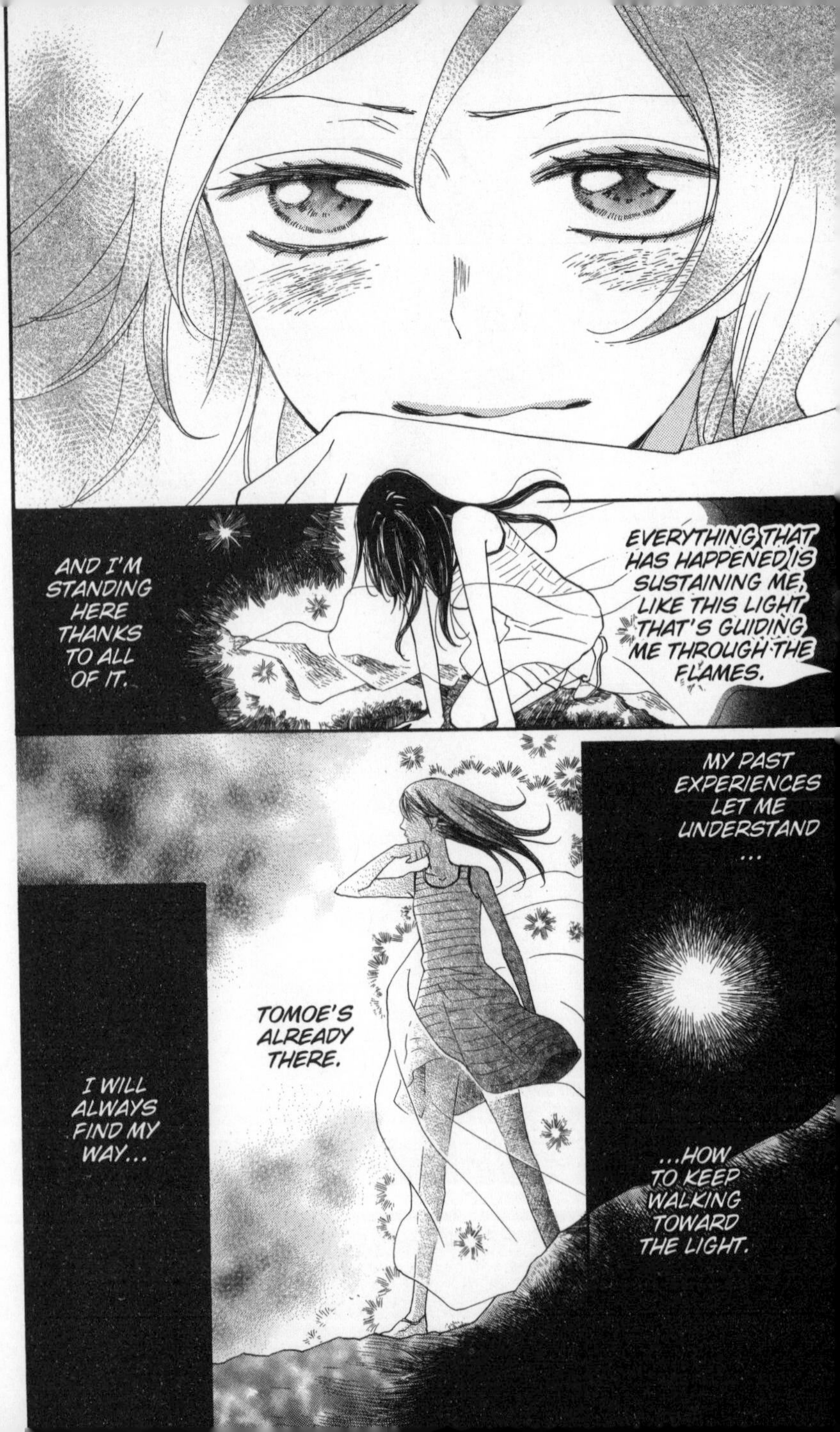
EVERYTHING THAT HAS HAPPENED IS SUSTAINING ME, LIKE THIS LIGHT THAT'S GUIDING ME THROUGH THE FLAMES.
AND I'M STANDING HERE THANKS TO ALL OF IT.
MY PAST EXPERIENCES LET ME UNDERSTAND ...
...HOW TO KEEP WALKING TOWARD THE LIGHT.
TOMOE'S ALREADY THERE.
I WILL ALWAYS FIND MY WAY...

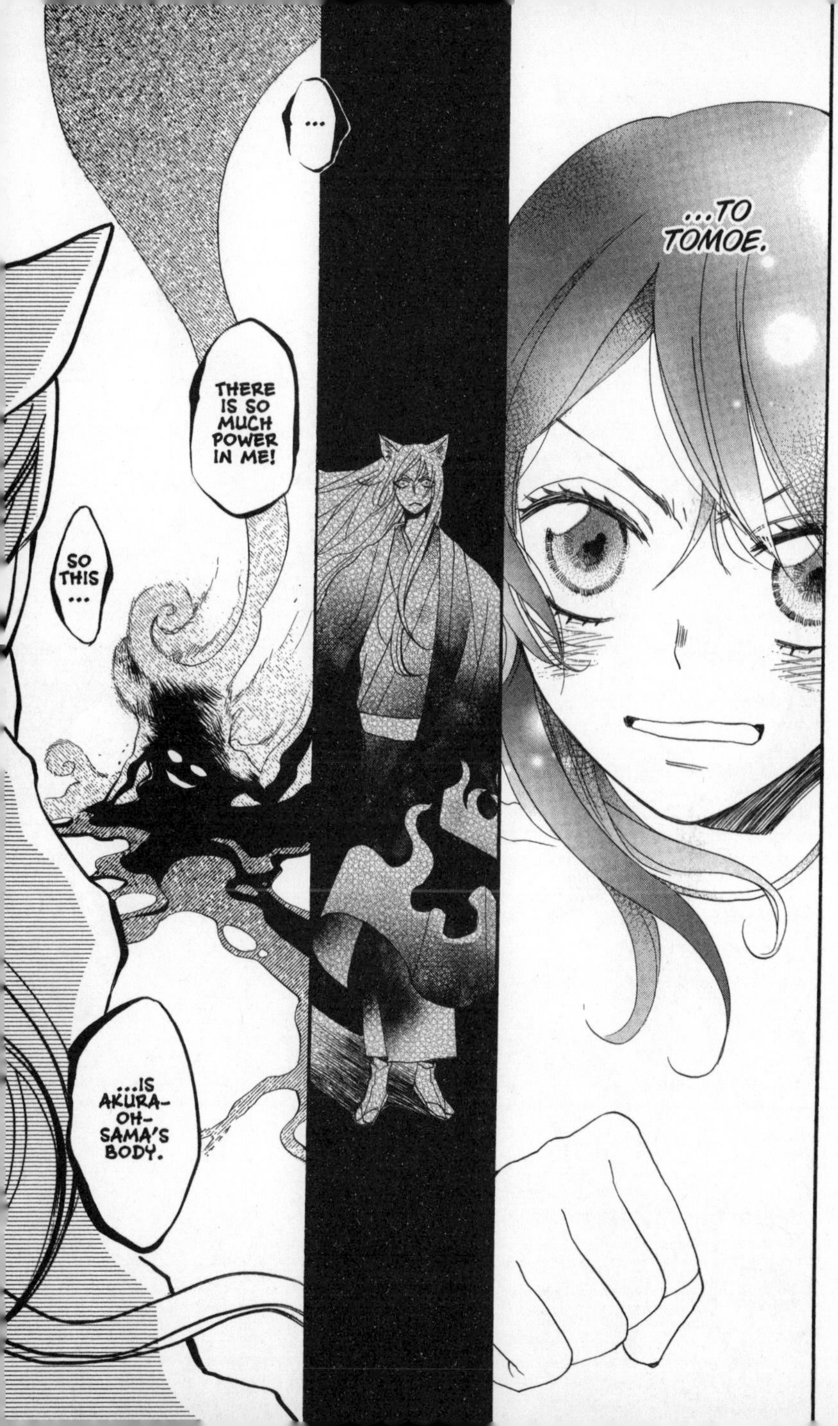
...TO TOMOE.
...
THERE IS SO MUCH POWER IN ME!
SO THIS ...
...IS AKURA-OH-SAMA'S BODY.

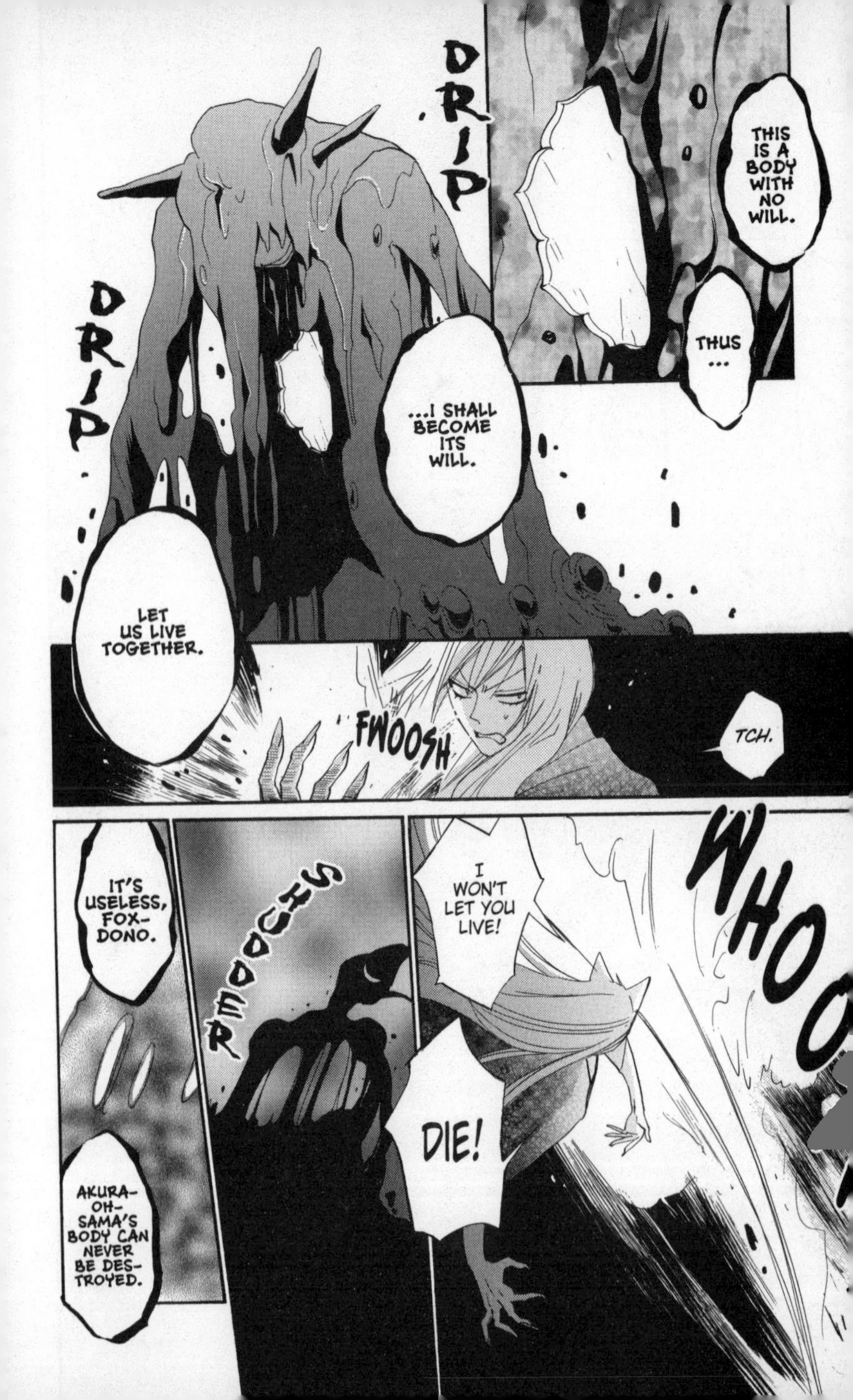
THIS IS A BODY WITH NO WILL.
THUS...
DRIP DRIP
...I SHALL BECOME ITS WILL.
DRIP DRIP
LET US LIVE TOGETHER.
TCH.
FWOOSH
WHOO
I WON'T LET YOU LIVE!
DIE!
SHUDDER
IT'S USELESS, FOX-DONO.
AKURA-OH-SAMA'S BODY CAN NEVER BE DESTROYED.

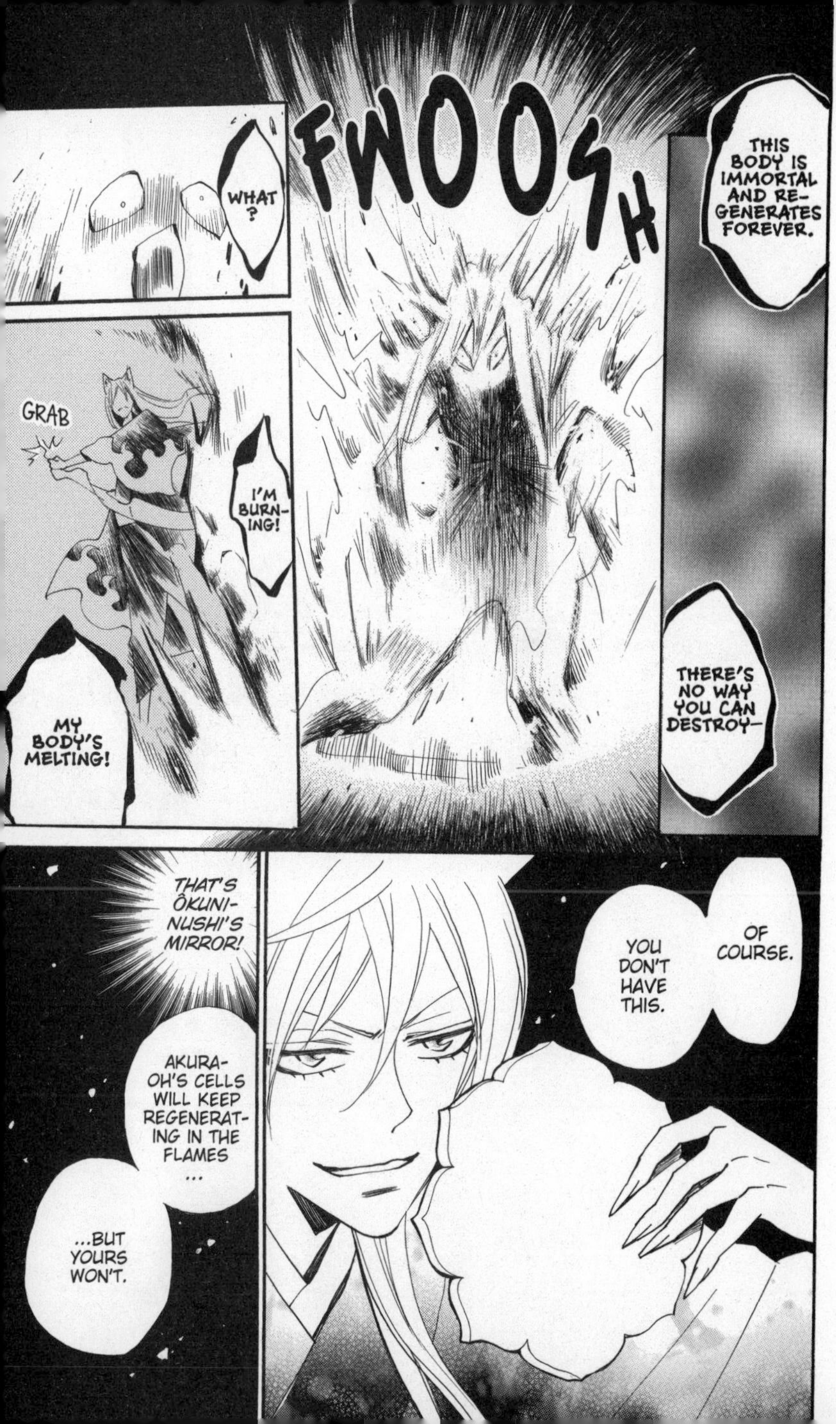
THIS BODY IS IMMORTAL AND REGENERATES FOREVER.
FWOOSH
THERE'S NO WAY YOU CAN DESTROY—
WHAT?
GRAB
I'M BURNING!
MY BODY'S MELTING!
OF COURSE.
YOU DON'T HAVE THIS.
AKURA-OH'S CELLS WILL KEEP REGENERATING IN THE FLAMES...
...BUT YOURS WON'T.
THAT'S ÔKUNINUSHI'S MIRROR!

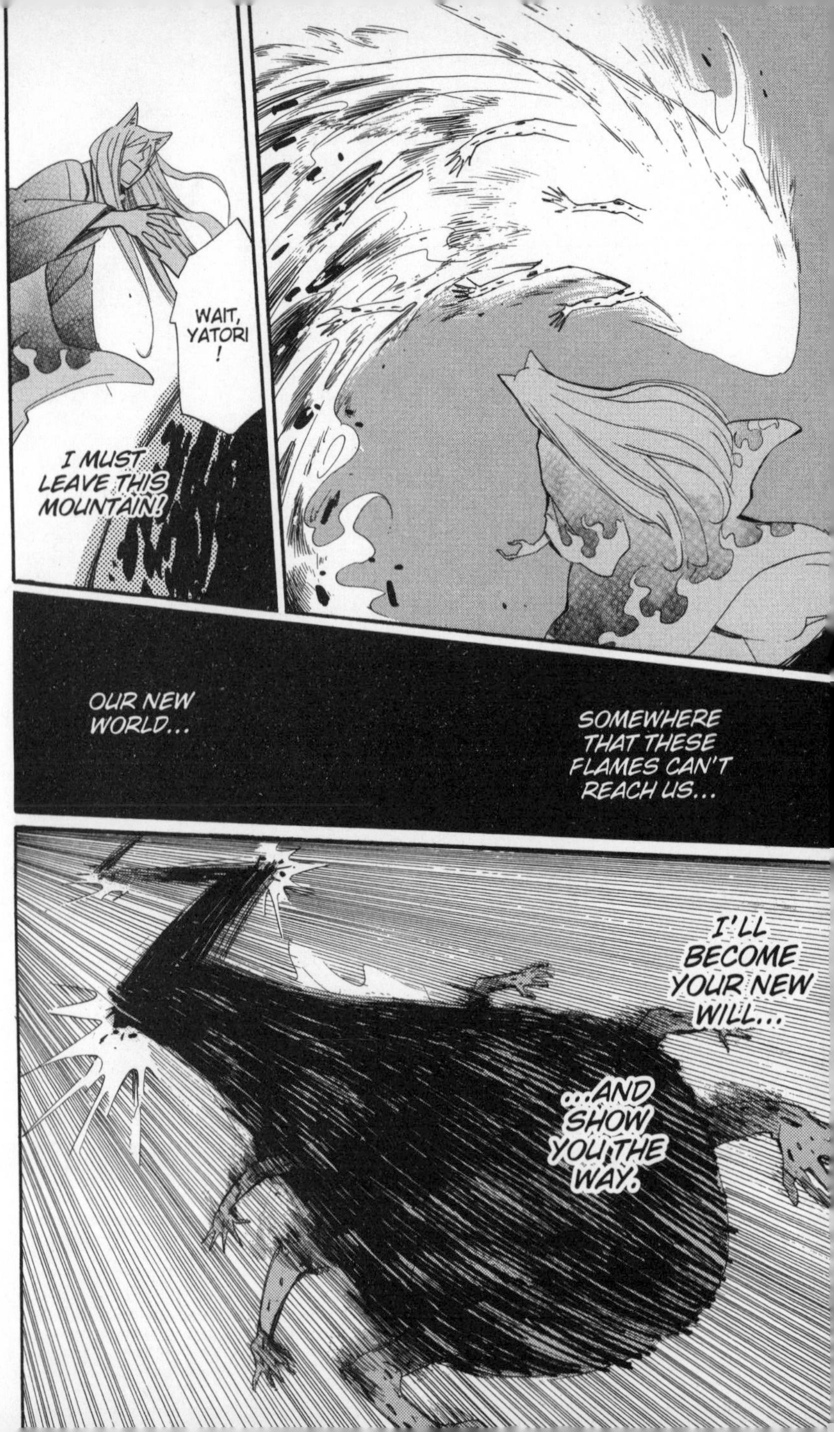
WAIT, YATORI!
I MUST LEAVE THIS MOUNTAIN!
SOMEWHERE THAT THESE FLAMES CAN'T REACH US...
OUR NEW WORLD...
I'LL BECOME YOUR NEW WILL...
...AND SHOW YOU THE WAY.

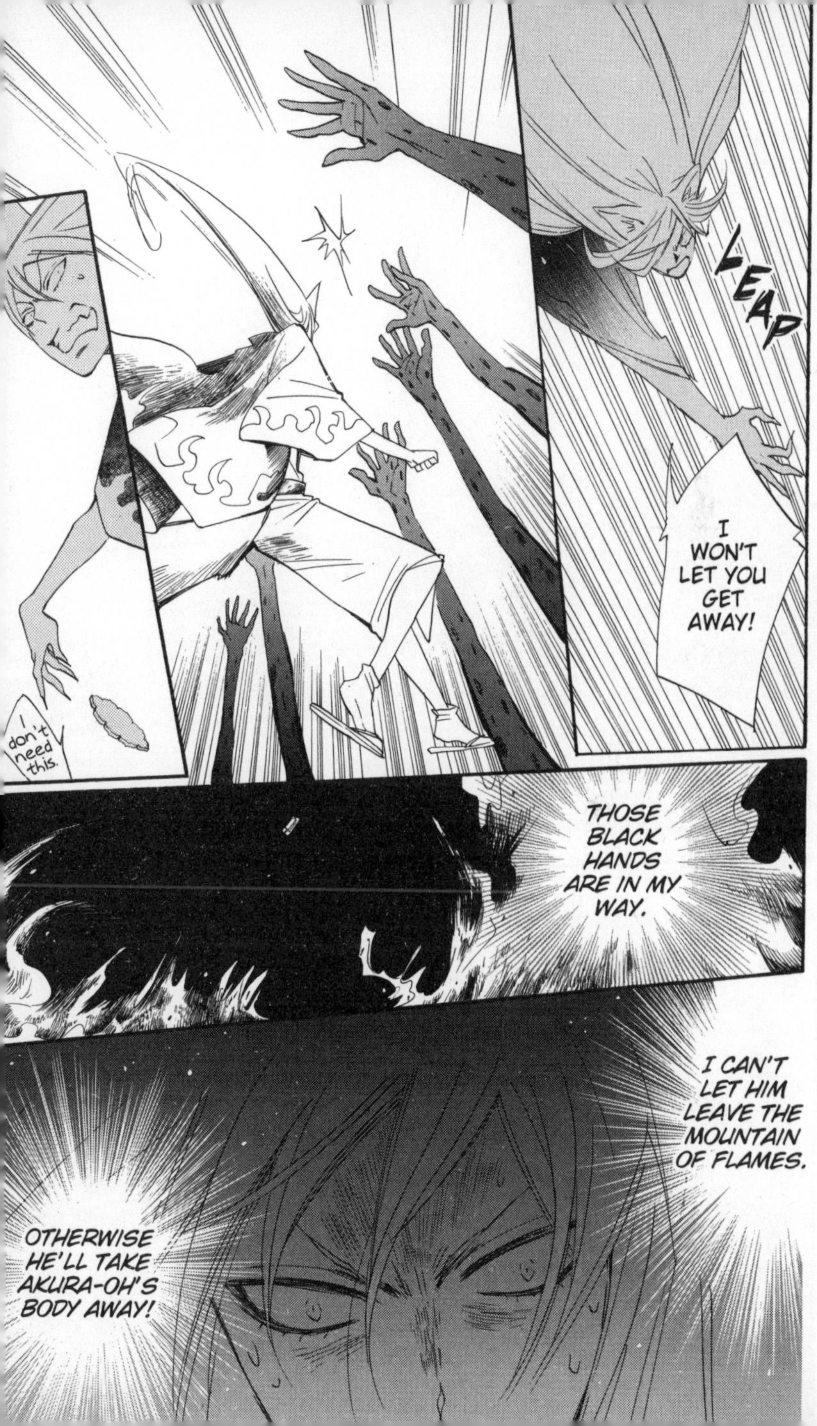
LEAP
I WON'T LET YOU GET AWAY!
I don't need this.
THOSE BLACK HANDS ARE IN MY WAY.
I CAN'T LET HIM LEAVE THE MOUNTAIN OF FLAMES.
OTHERWISE HE'LL TAKE AKURA-OH'S BODY AWAY!

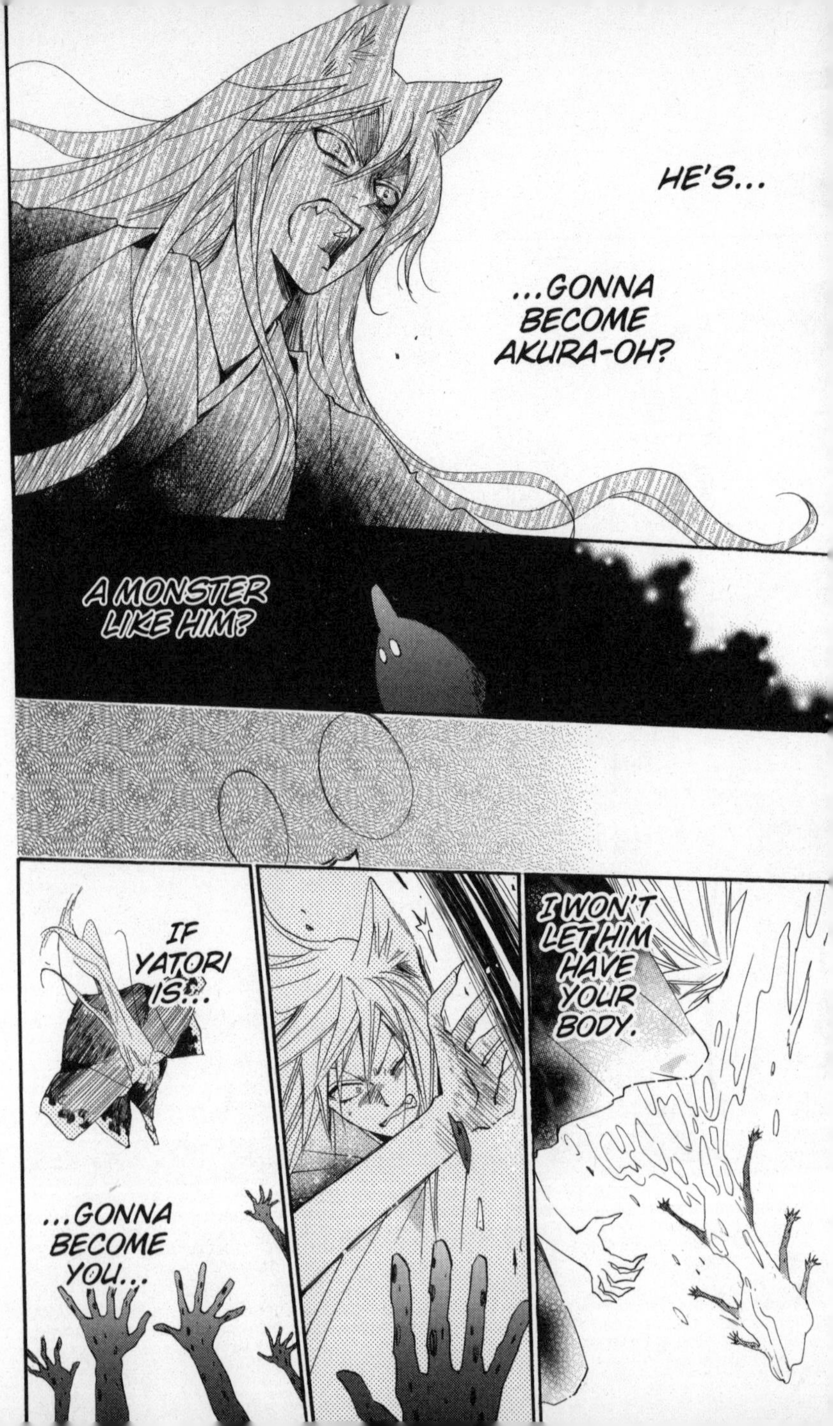
HE'S...
...GONNA BECOME AKURA-OH?
A MONSTER LIKE HIM?
I WON'T LET HIM HAVE YOUR BODY.
IF YATORI IS...
...GONNA BECOME YOU...

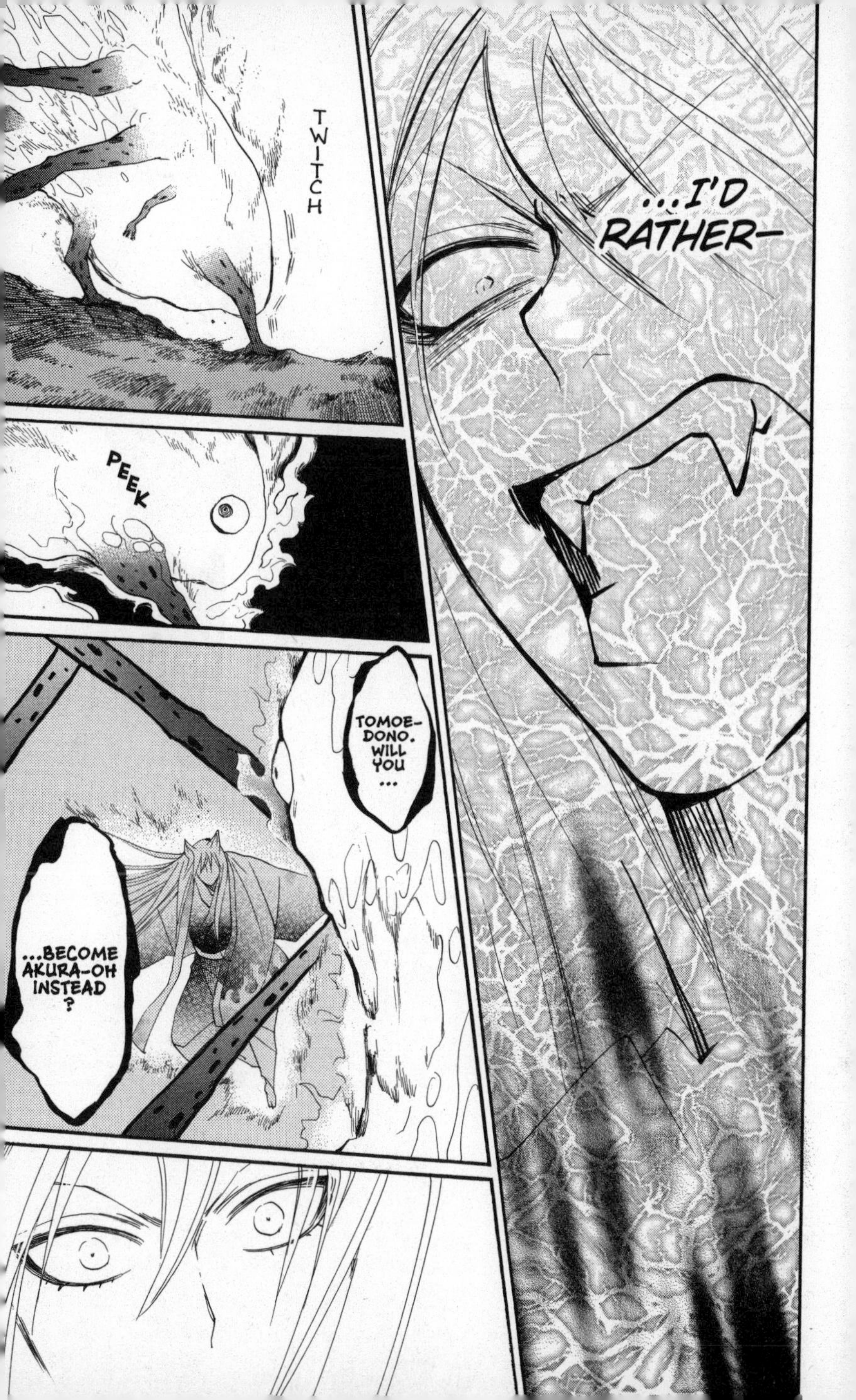
...I'D RATHER—
TWITCH
PEEK
TOMOE-DONO. WILL YOU ...
...BECOME AKURA-OH INSTEAD ?

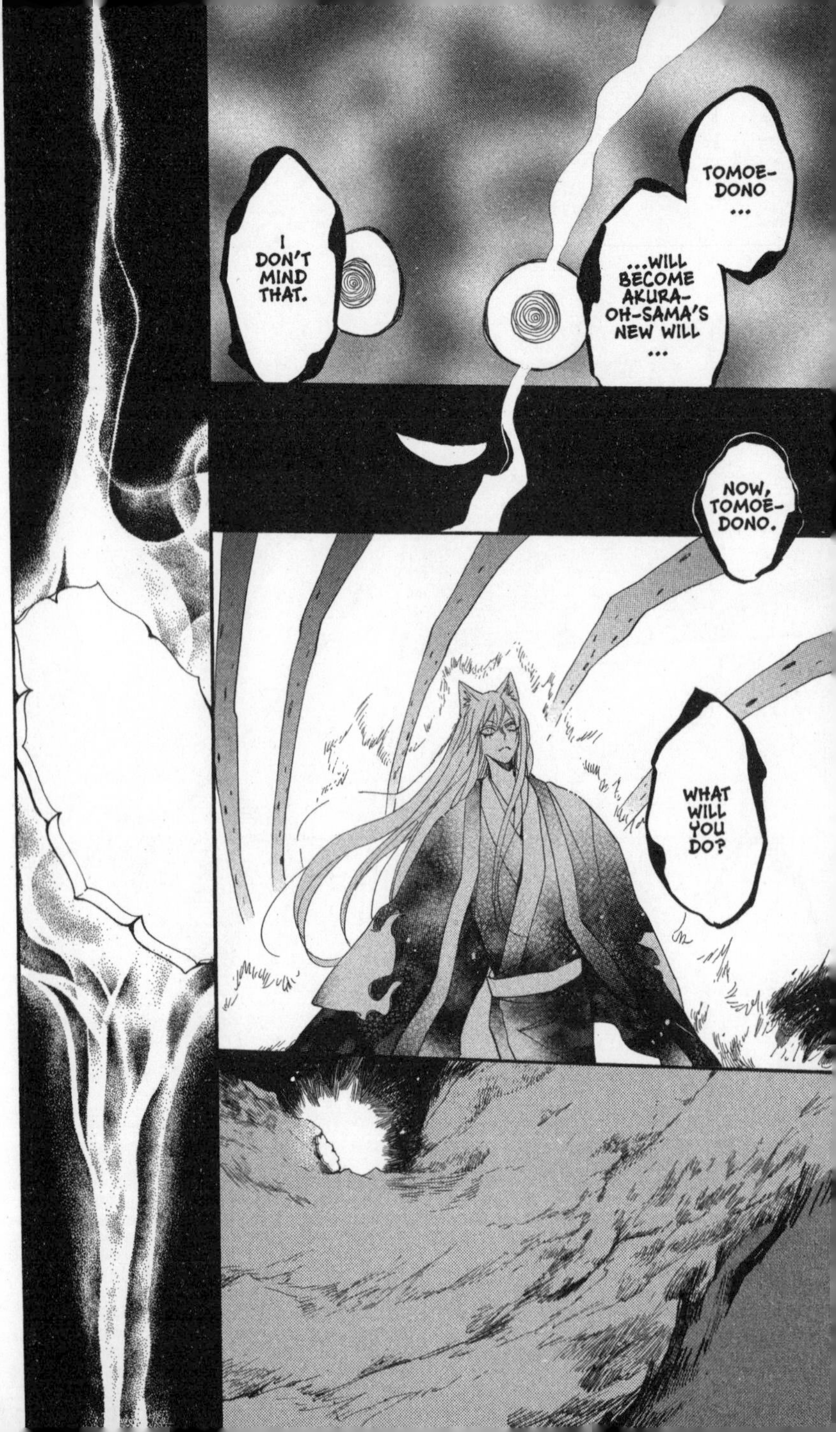
TOMOE-DONO ...
...WILL BECOME AKURA-OH-SAMA'S NEW WILL ...
I DON'T MIND THAT.
NOW, TOMOE-DONO.
WHAT WILL YOU DO?

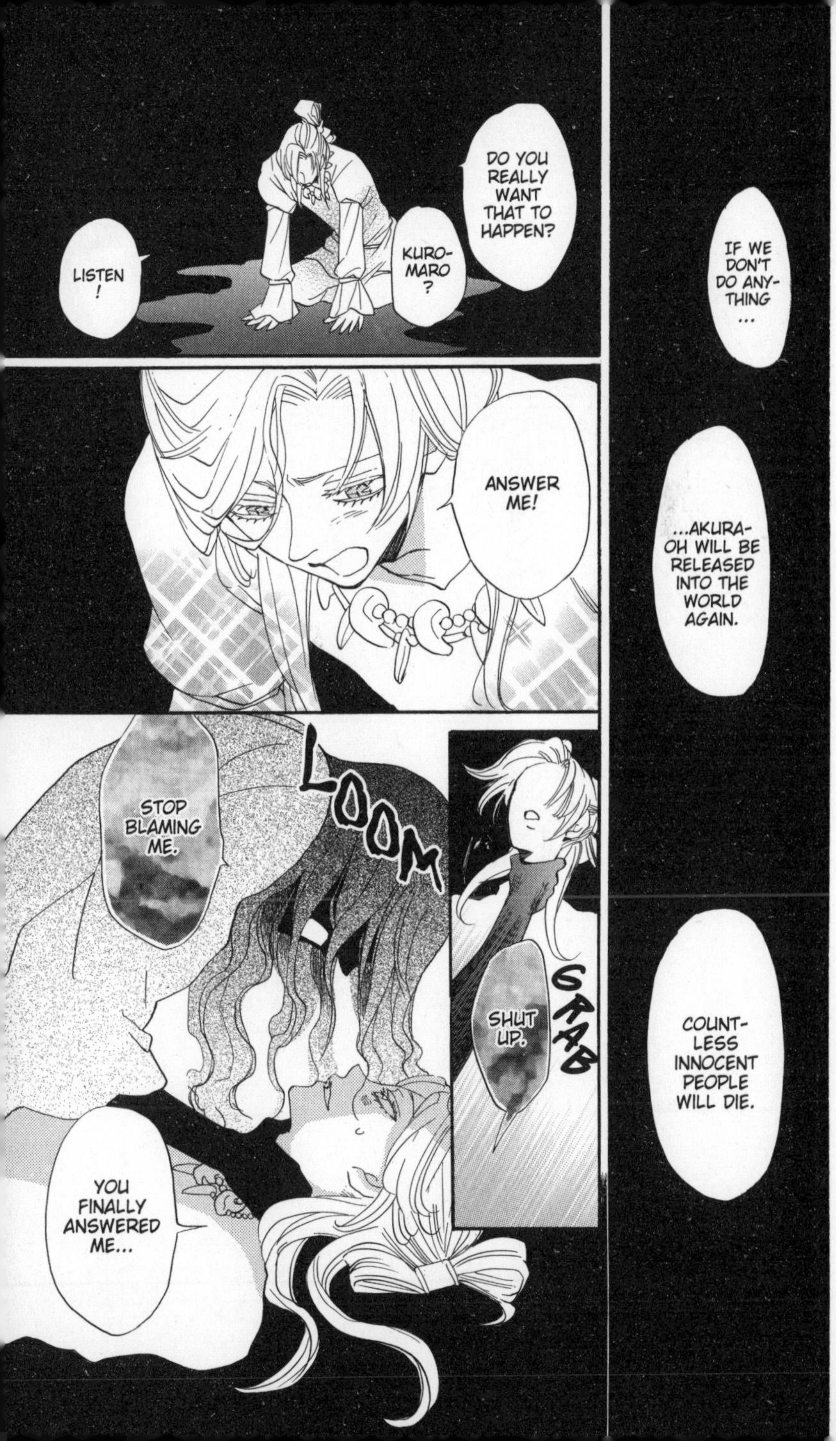
IF WE DON'T DO ANYTHING...
...AKURA-OH WILL BE RELEASED INTO THE WORLD AGAIN.
COUNTLESS INNOCENT PEOPLE WILL DIE.
DO YOU REALLY WANT THAT TO HAPPEN?
KURO-MARO?
LISTEN!
ANSWER ME!
GRAB
SHUT UP.
LOOM
STOP BLAMING ME.
YOU FINALLY ANSWERED ME...

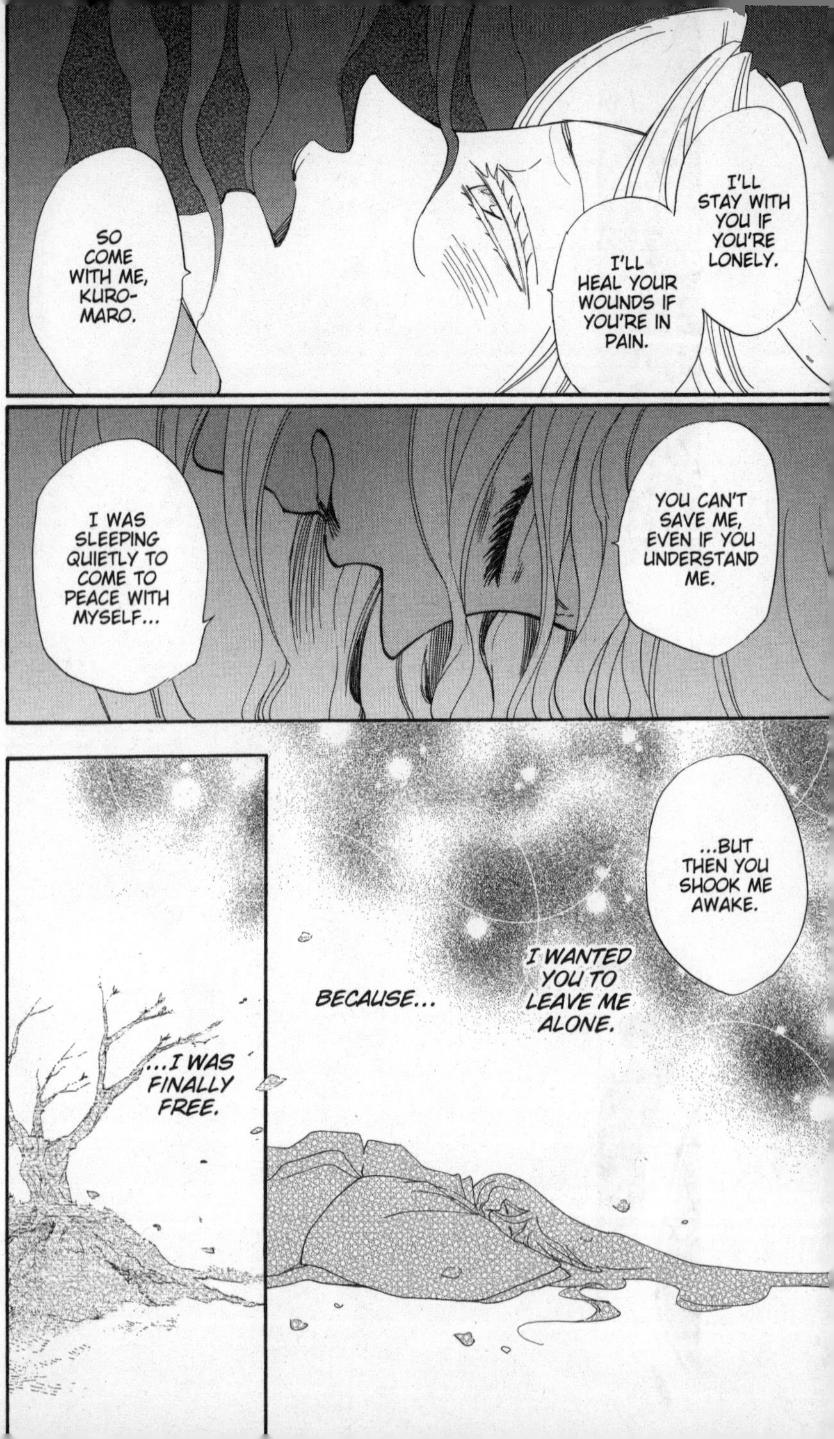
I'LL STAY WITH YOU IF YOU'RE LONELY.
I'LL HEAL YOUR WOUNDS IF YOU'RE IN PAIN.
SO COME WITH ME, KURO-MARO.
YOU CAN'T SAVE ME, EVEN IF YOU UNDERSTAND ME.
I WAS SLEEPING QUIETLY TO COME TO PEACE WITH MYSELF...
...BUT THEN YOU SHOOK ME AWAKE.
I WANTED YOU TO LEAVE ME ALONE.
BECAUSE...
...I WAS FINALLY FREE.

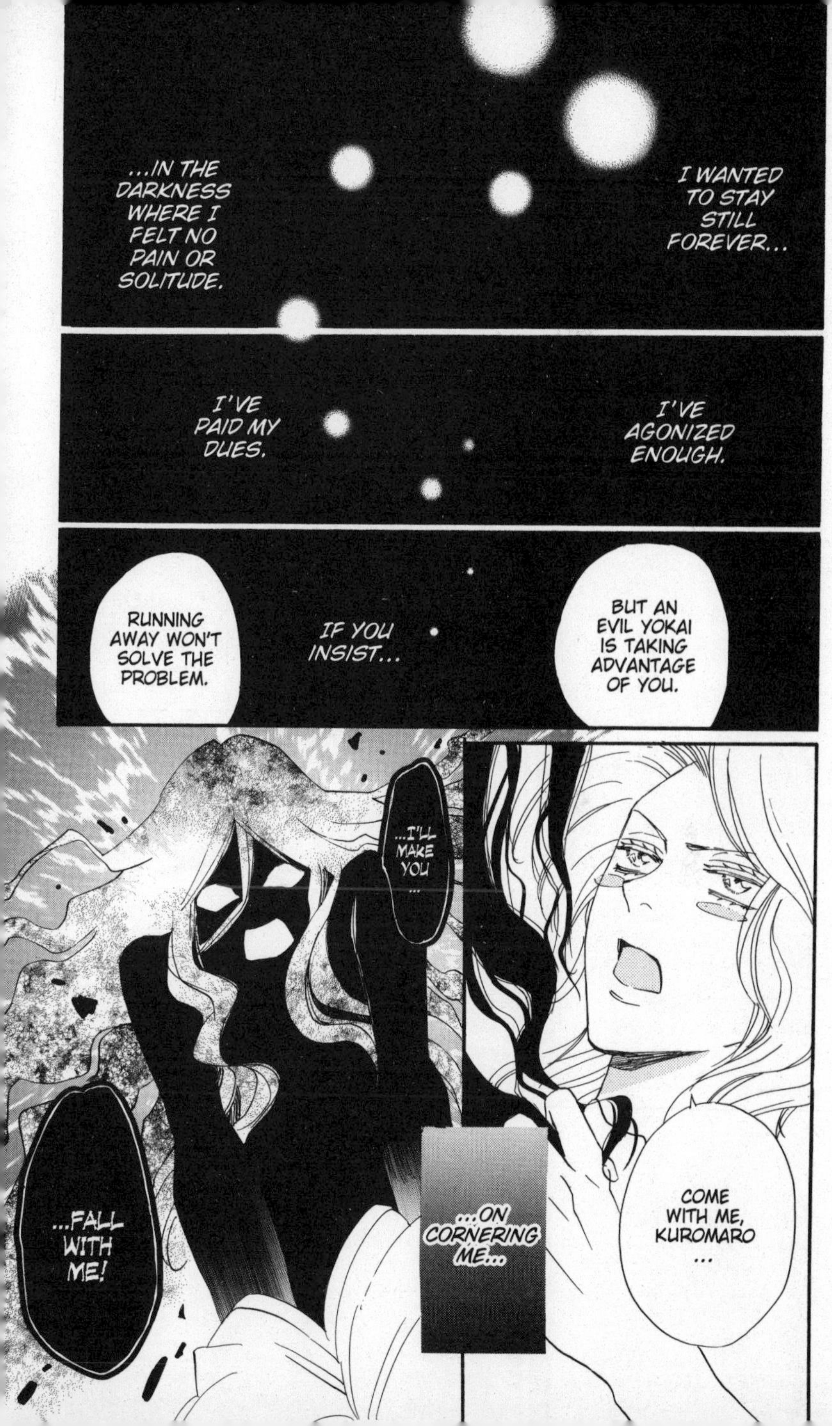
I WANTED TO STAY STILL FOREVER...
...IN THE DARKNESS WHERE I FELT NO PAIN OR SOLITUDE.
I'VE AGONIZED ENOUGH.
I'VE PAID MY DUES.
BUT AN EVIL YOKAI IS TAKING ADVANTAGE OF YOU.
IF YOU INSIST...
RUNNING AWAY WON'T SOLVE THE PROBLEM.
COME WITH ME, KUROMARO ...
...ON CORNERING ME...
...I'LL MAKE YOU ...
...FALL WITH ME!

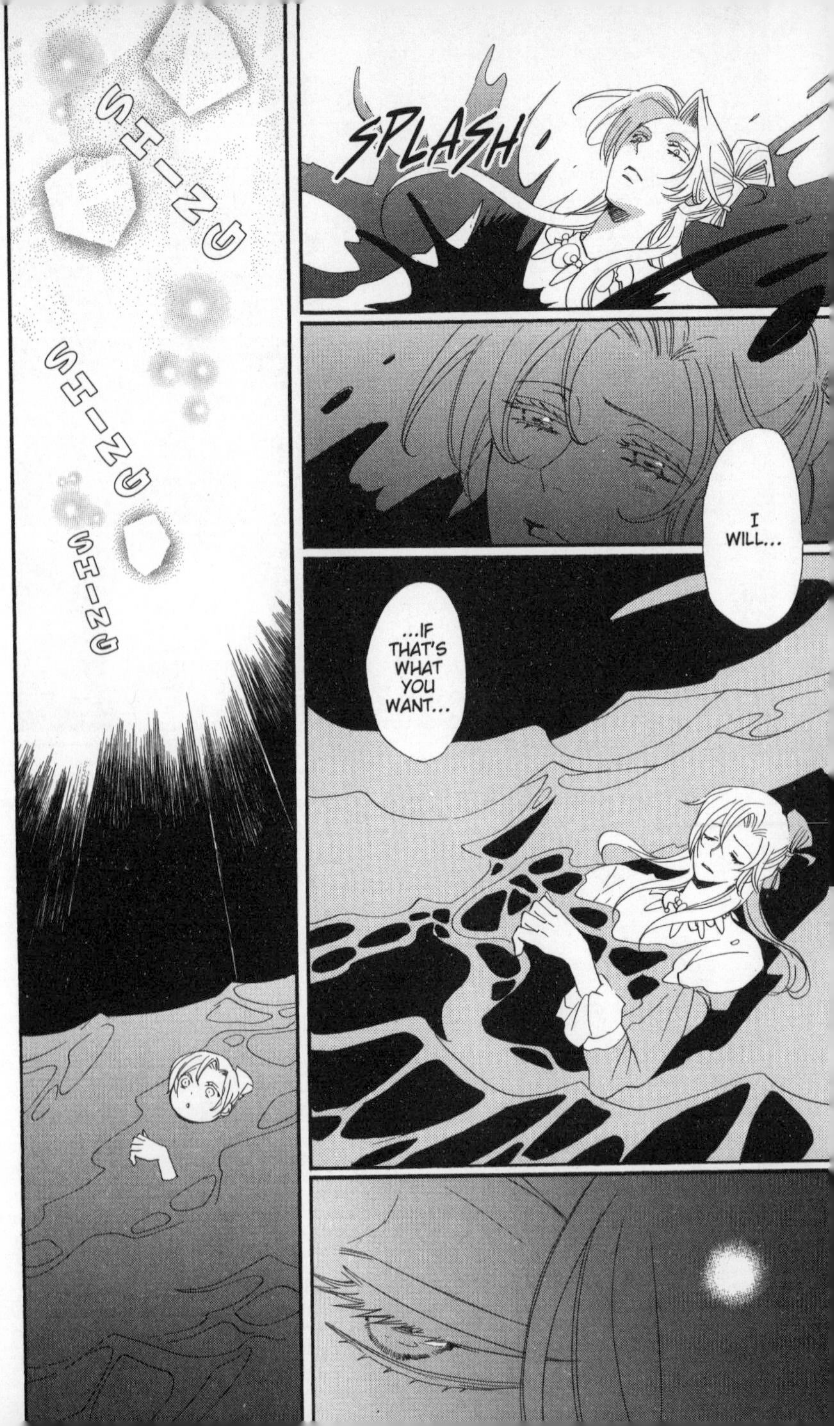
SPLASH
I WILL...
...IF THAT'S WHAT YOU WANT...
SHI-NG
SHI-NG
SHING

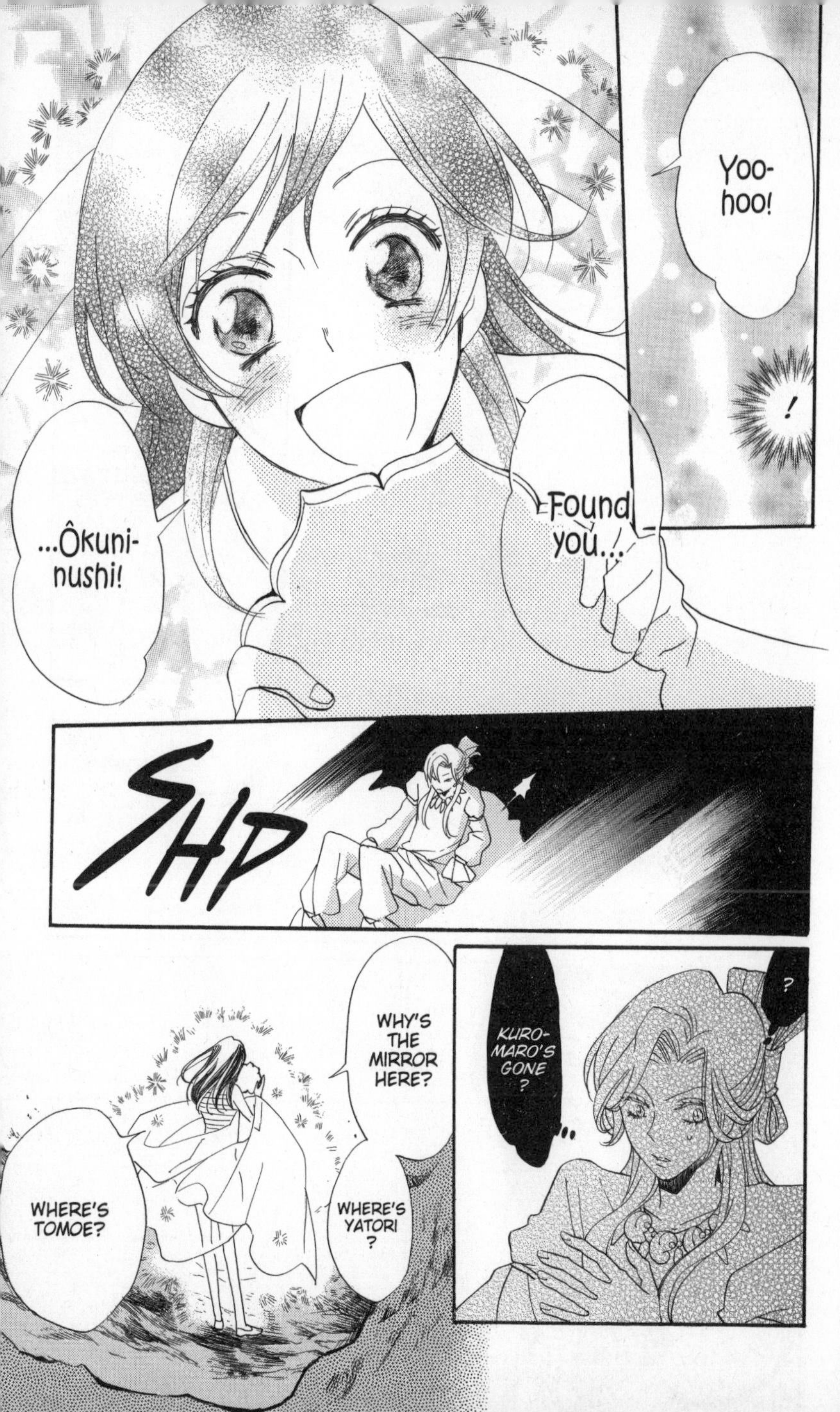
Yoo-hoo!
!
Found you...
...Ôkuni-nushi!
SHP
?
KURO-MARO'S GONE?
...
WHY'S THE MIRROR HERE?
WHERE'S YATORI?
WHERE'S TOMOE?

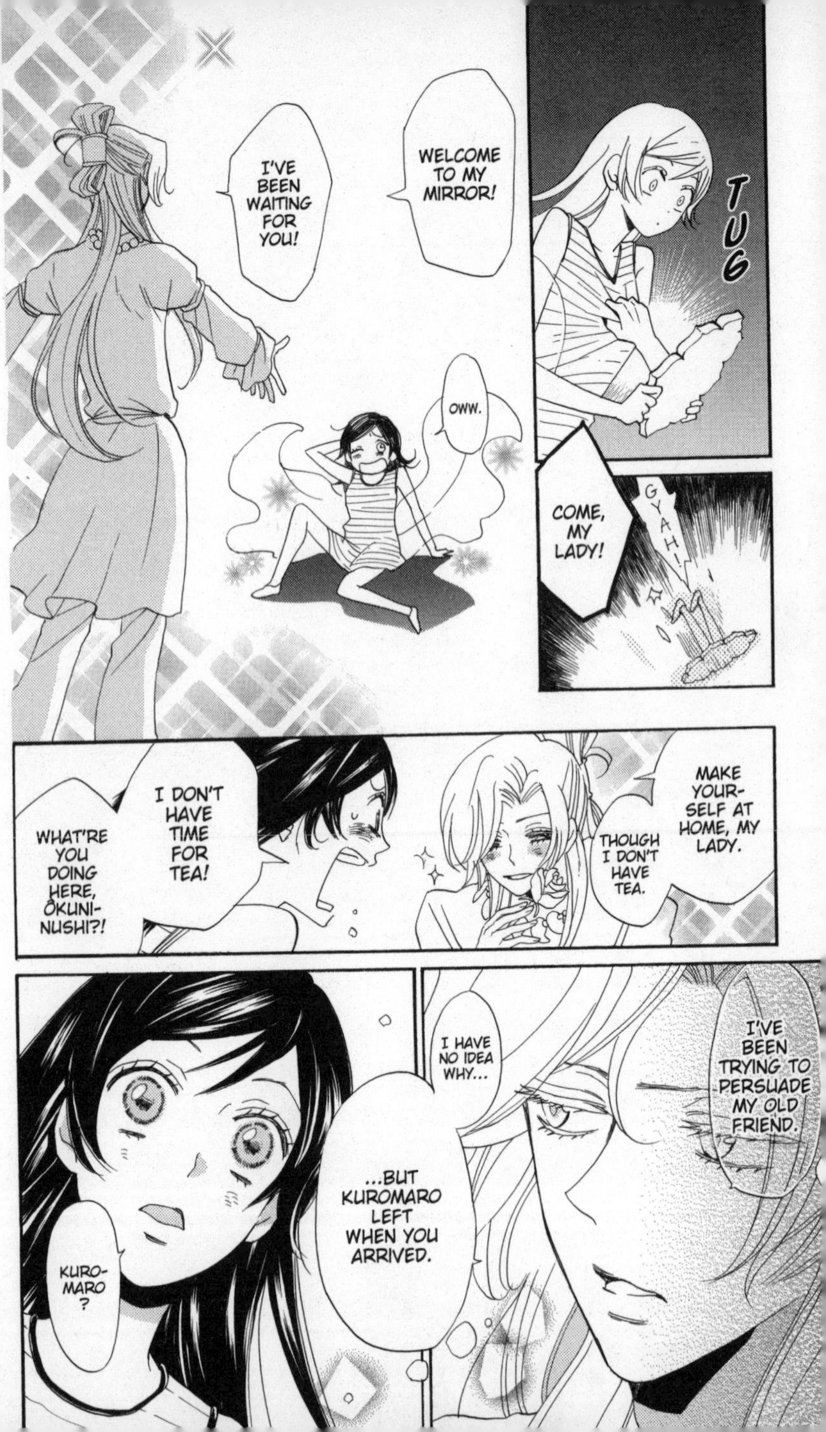
TUG
COME, MY LADY!
GYAH!
WELCOME TO MY MIRROR!
I'VE BEEN WAITING FOR YOU!
OWW.
MAKE YOURSELF AT HOME, MY LADY.
THOUGH I DON'T HAVE TEA.
I DON'T HAVE TIME FOR TEA!
WHAT'RE YOU DOING HERE, ŌKUNINUSHI?!
I'VE BEEN TRYING TO PERSUADE MY OLD FRIEND.
I HAVE NO IDEA WHY...
...BUT KUROMARO LEFT WHEN YOU ARRIVED.
KUROMARO?

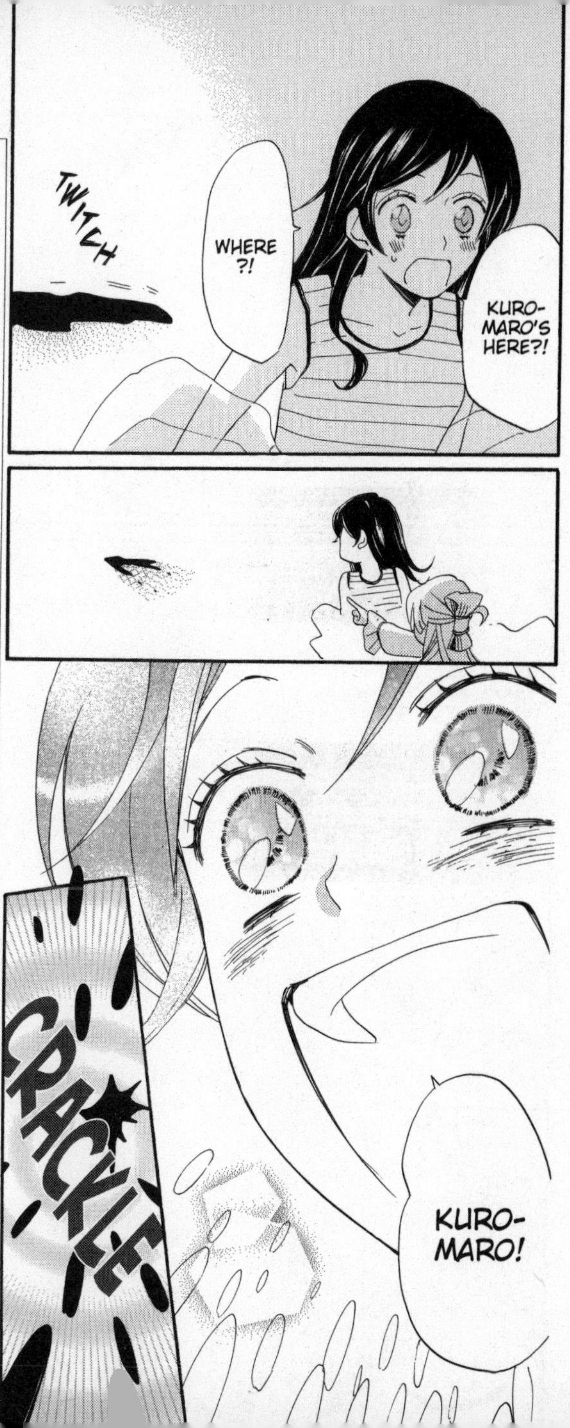
KURO-MARO'S HERE?!
WHERE ?!
TWITCH
KURO-MARO!
CRACKLE

Hello!

Thank you for picking up this volume of Kamisama Kiss!!

Volume 24 concludes the Akura-oh arc. Please enjoy it!

There're five sidebars this time, so read them all. ☺

Let's meet again in the fifth sidebar!

By Juli

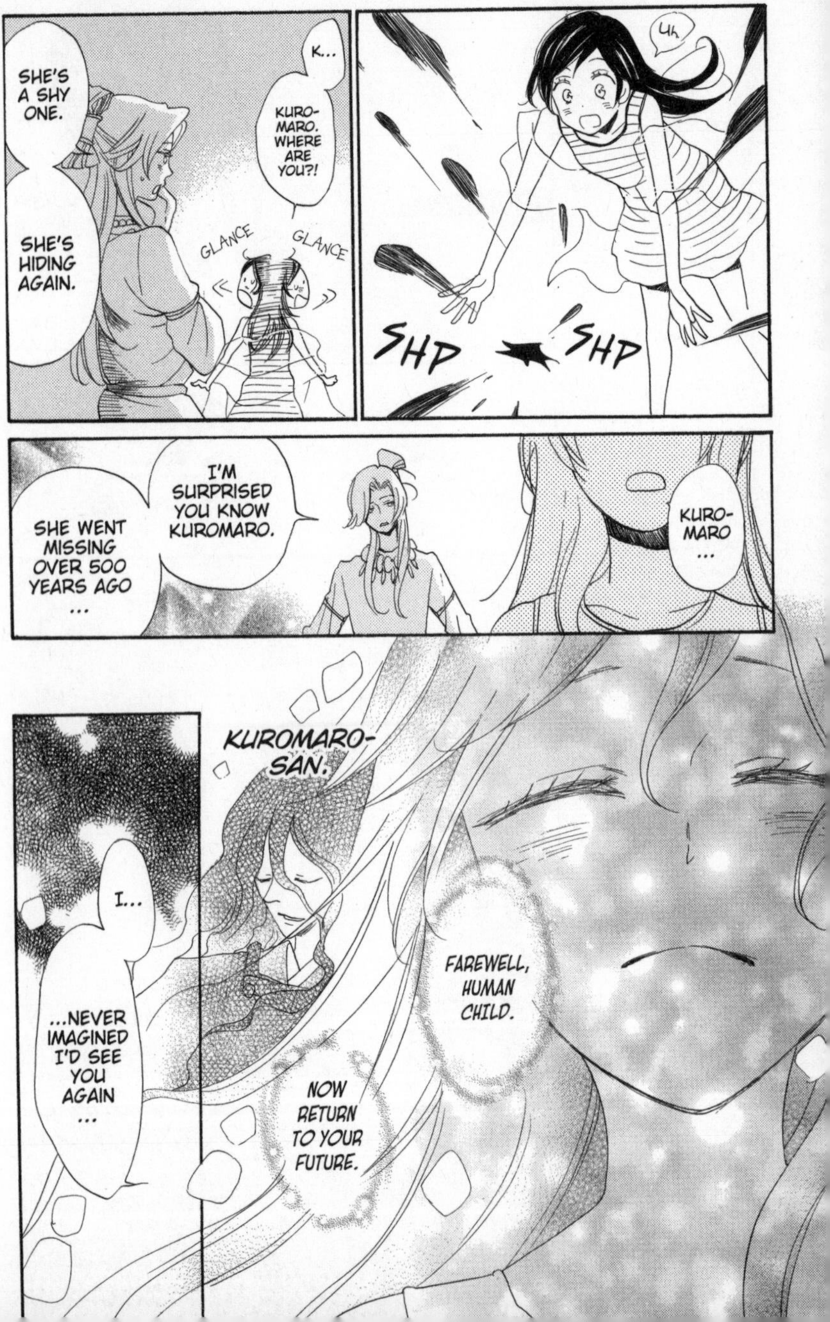
Uh
SHP
SHP
K...
KURO-MARO. WHERE ARE YOU?!
GLANCE
GLANCE
SHE'S A SHY ONE.
SHE'S HIDING AGAIN.
KURO-MARO ...
I'M SURPRISED YOU KNOW KUROMARO.
SHE WENT MISSING OVER 500 YEARS AGO ...
KUROMARO-SAN.
FAREWELL, HUMAN CHILD.
NOW RETURN TO YOUR FUTURE.
I...
...NEVER IMAGINED I'D SEE YOU AGAIN ...

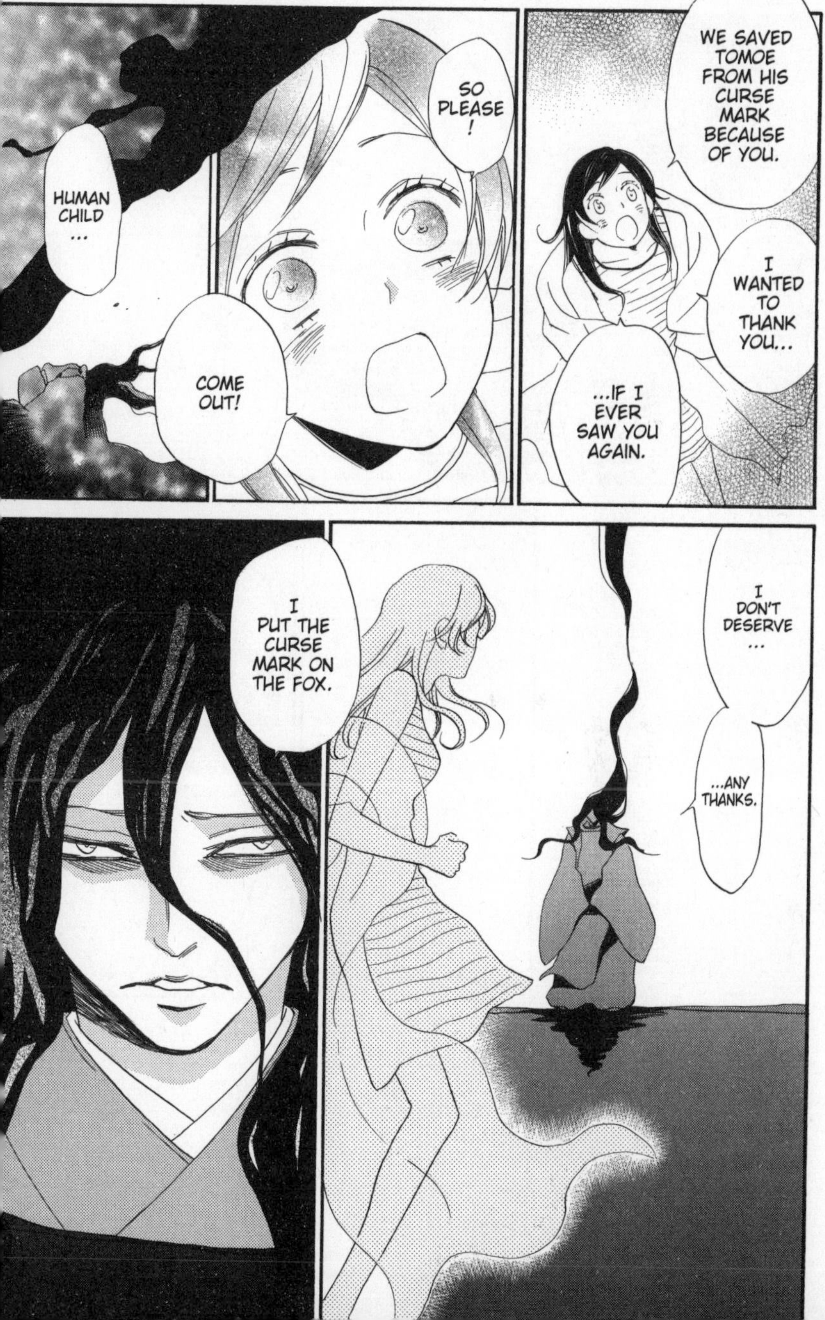
WE SAVED TOMOE FROM HIS CURSE MARK BECAUSE OF YOU.
I WANTED TO THANK YOU...
...IF I EVER SAW YOU AGAIN.
SO PLEASE!
COME OUT!
HUMAN CHILD...
I DON'T DESERVE...
...ANY THANKS.
I PUT THE CURSE MARK ON THE FOX.

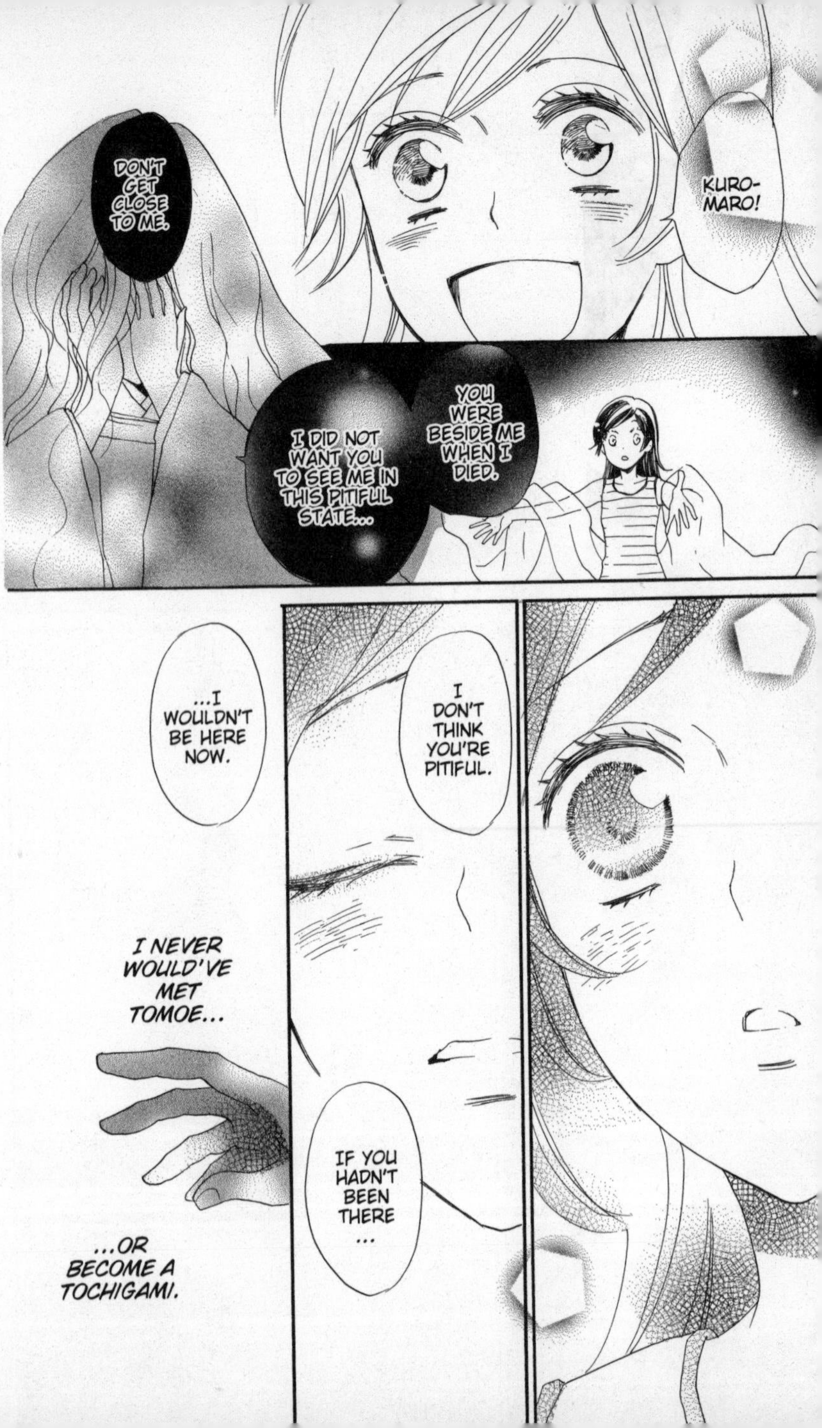
KURO-MARO!
DON'T GET CLOSE TO ME.
YOU WERE BESIDE ME WHEN I DIED.
I DID NOT WANT YOU TO SEE ME IN THIS PITIFUL STATE...
I DON'T THINK YOU'RE PITIFUL.
IF YOU HADN'T BEEN THERE...
...I WOULDN'T BE HERE NOW.
I NEVER WOULD'VE MET TOMOE...
...OR BECOME A TOCHIGAMI.

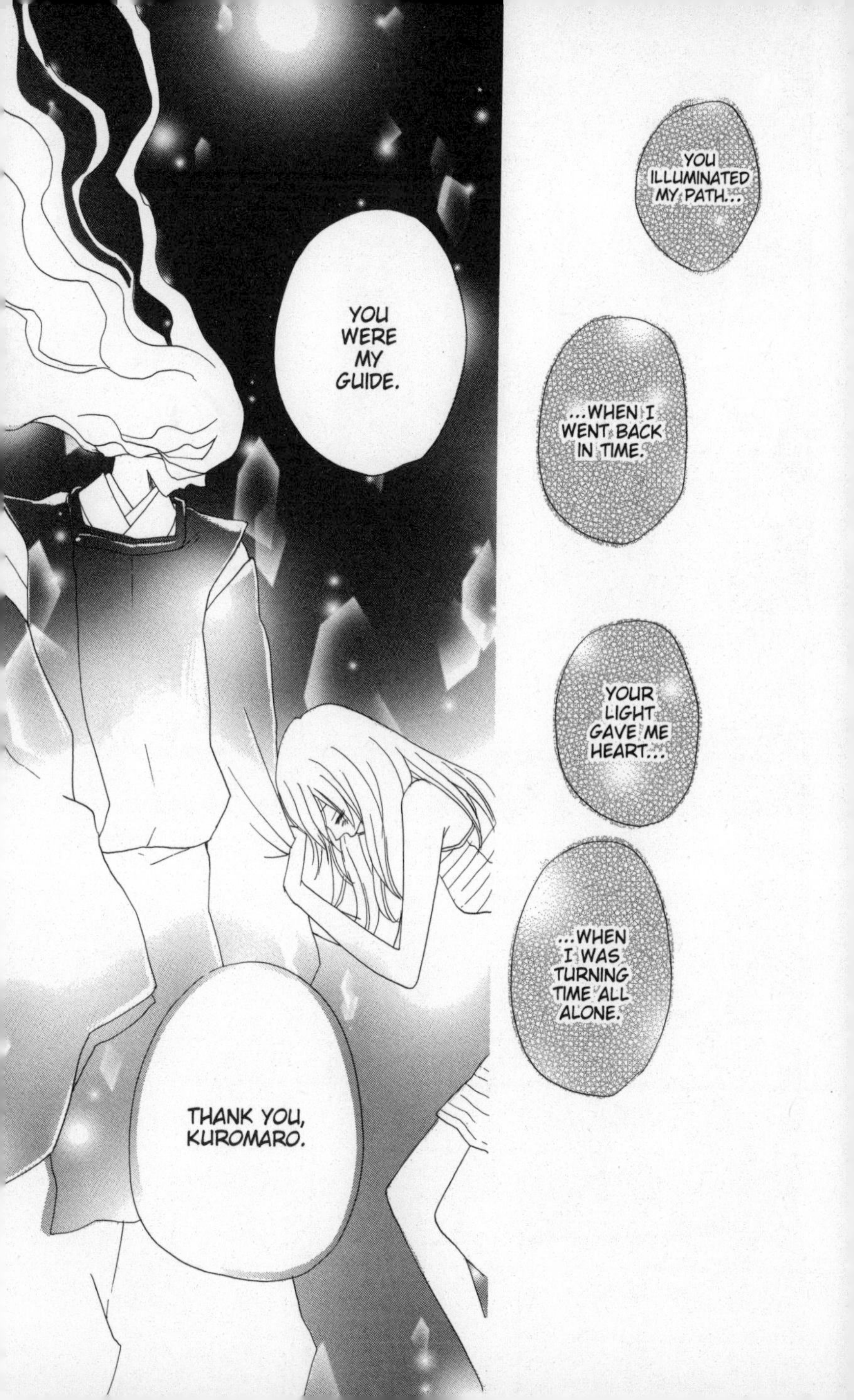
YOU ILLUMINATED MY PATH...
...WHEN I WENT BACK IN TIME.
YOUR LIGHT GAVE ME HEART...
...WHEN I WAS TURNING TIME ALL ALONE.
YOU WERE MY GUIDE.
THANK YOU, KUROMARO.

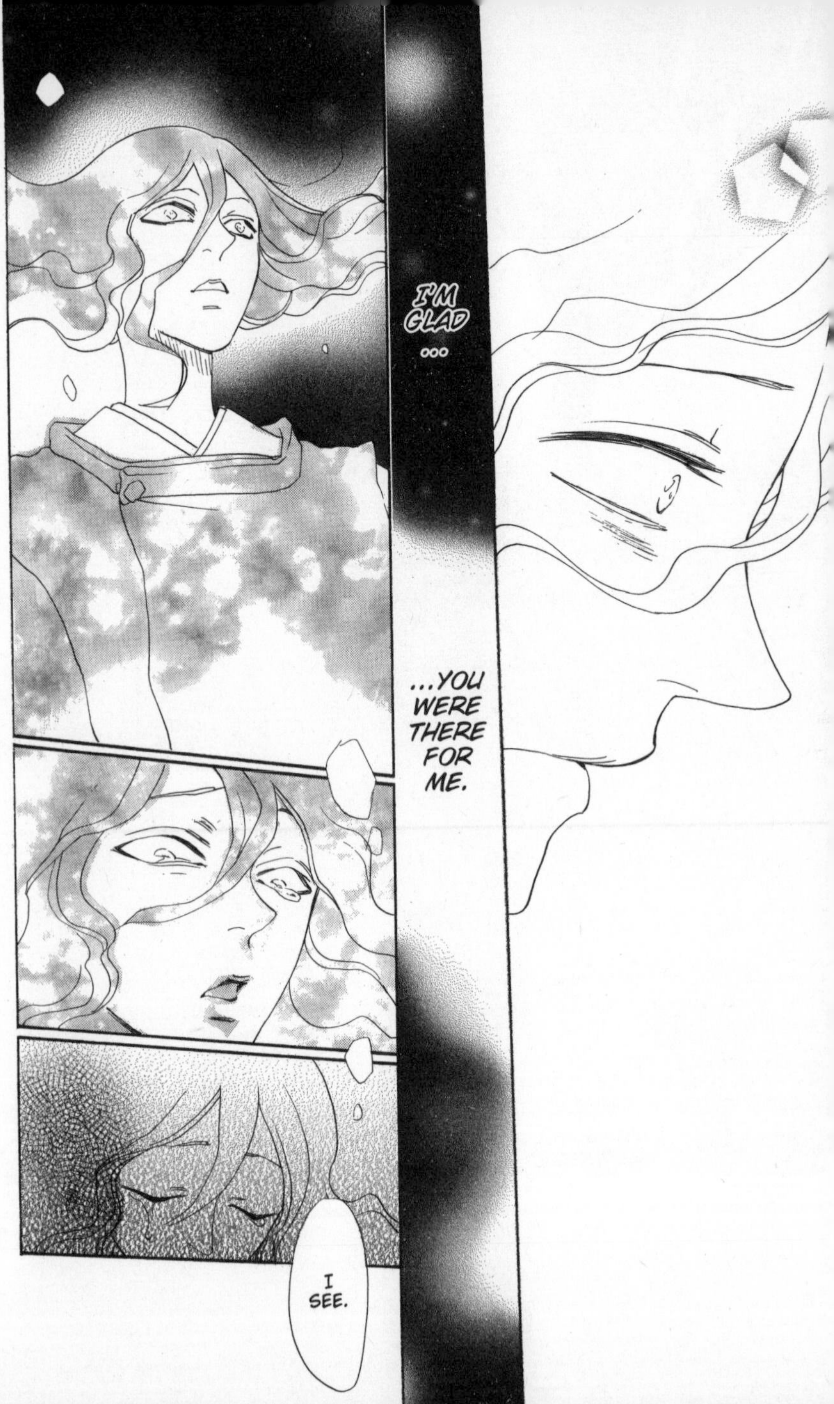
I'M GLAD...
...YOU WERE THERE FOR ME.
I SEE.

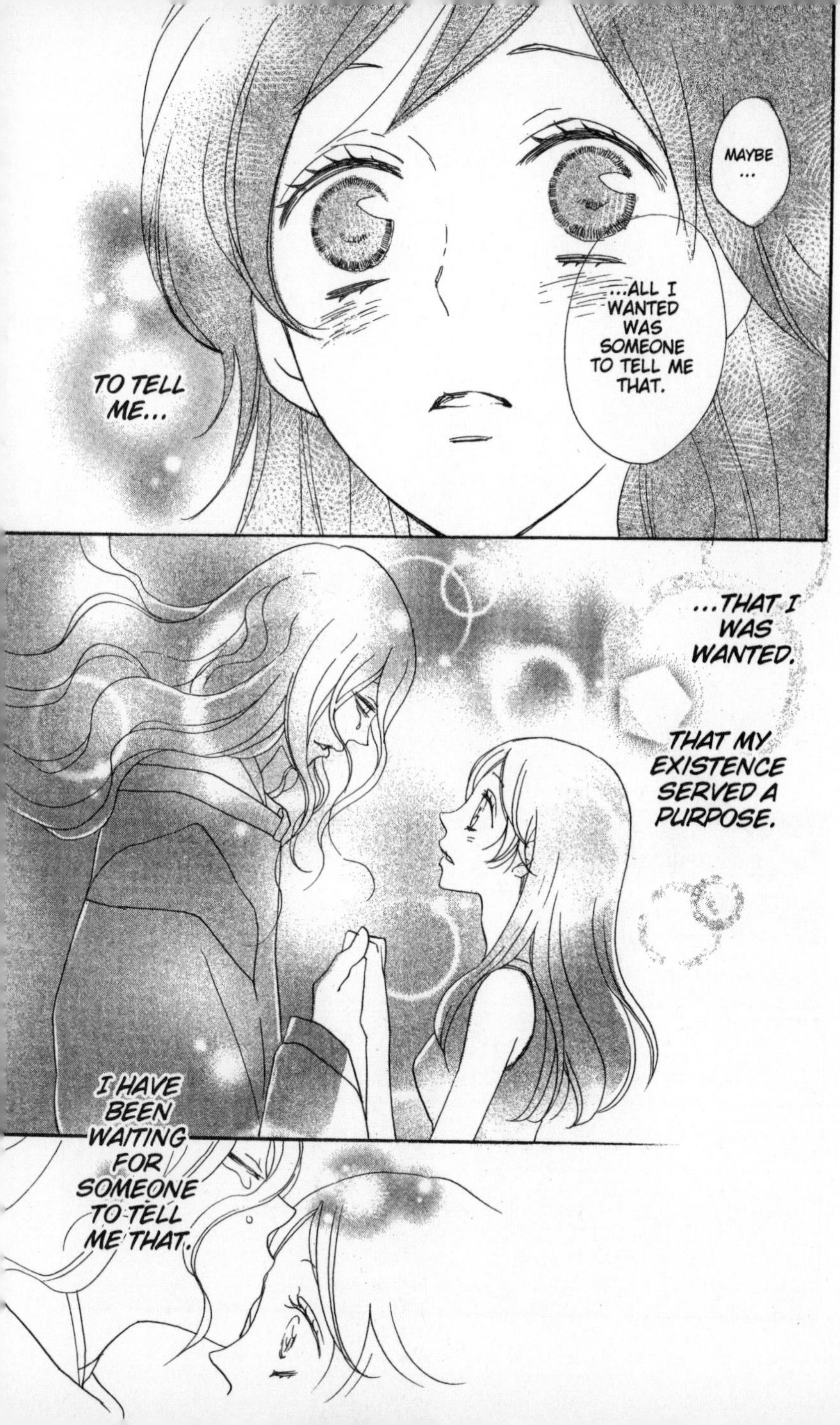
MAYBE ...
...ALL I WANTED WAS SOMEONE TO TELL ME THAT.
TO TELL ME...
...THAT I WAS WANTED.
THAT MY EXISTENCE SERVED A PURPOSE.
I HAVE BEEN WAITING FOR SOMEONE TO TELL ME THAT.

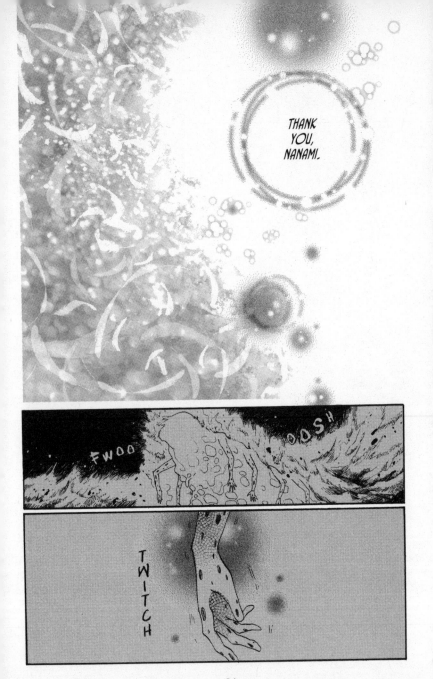

THANK
YOU,
NANAMI.

FWOO

OOSH

TWITCH

34

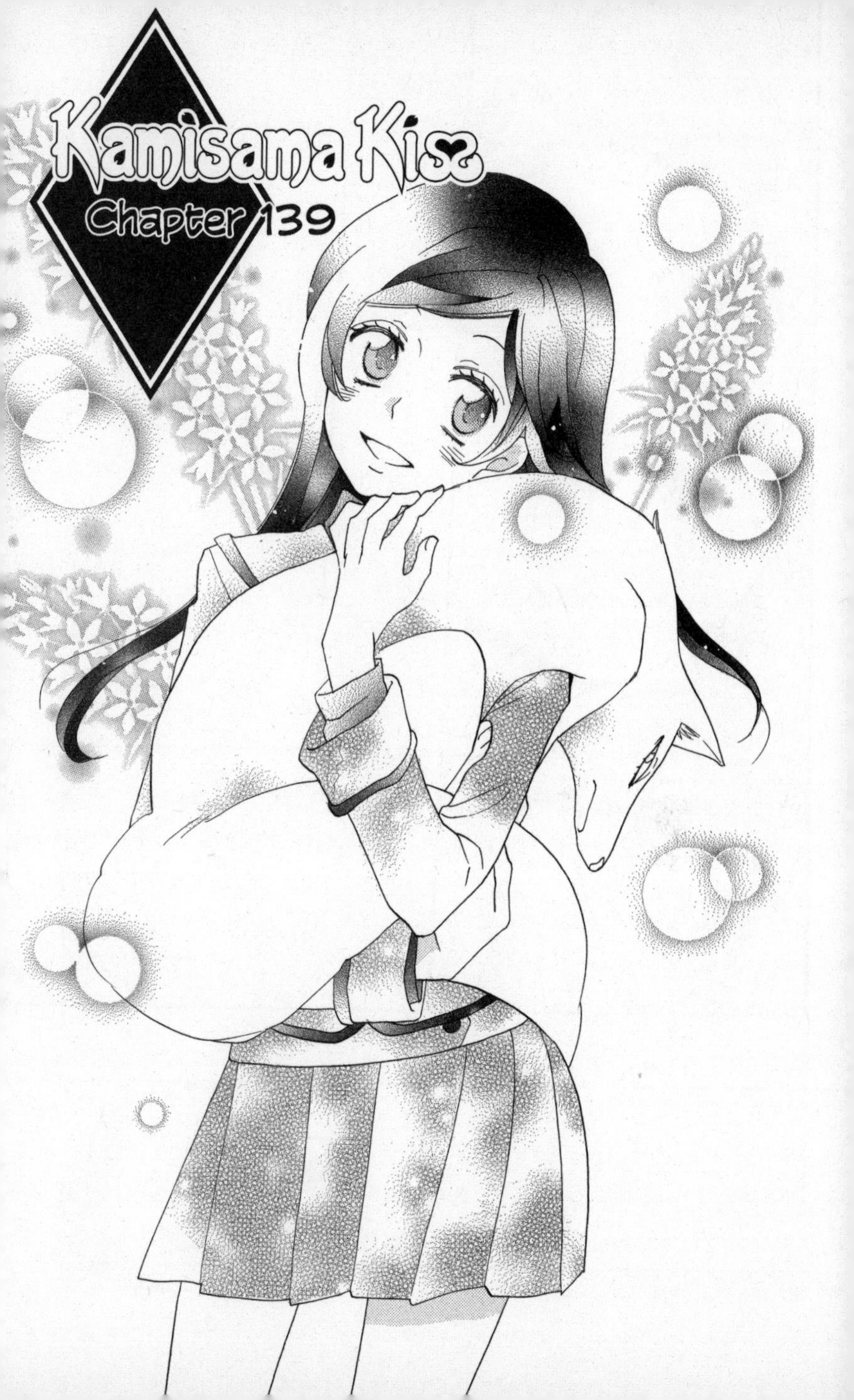
Kamisama Kiss
Chapter 139

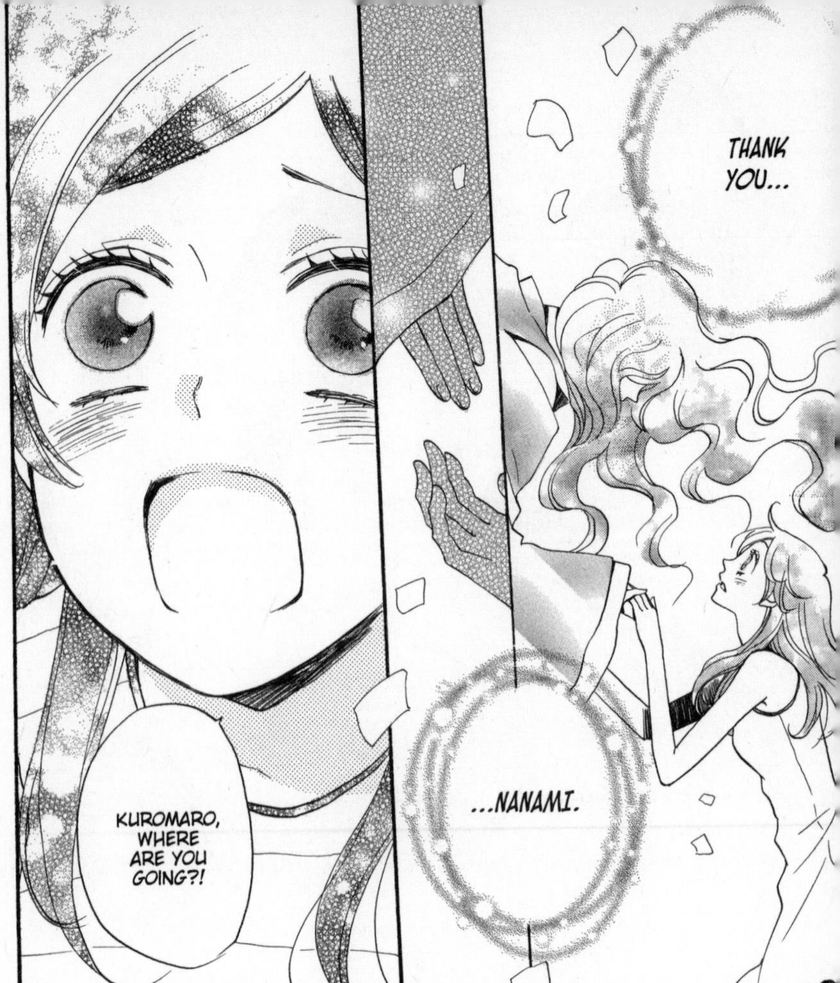
THANK YOU...
...NANAMI.
KUROMARO, WHERE ARE YOU GOING?!

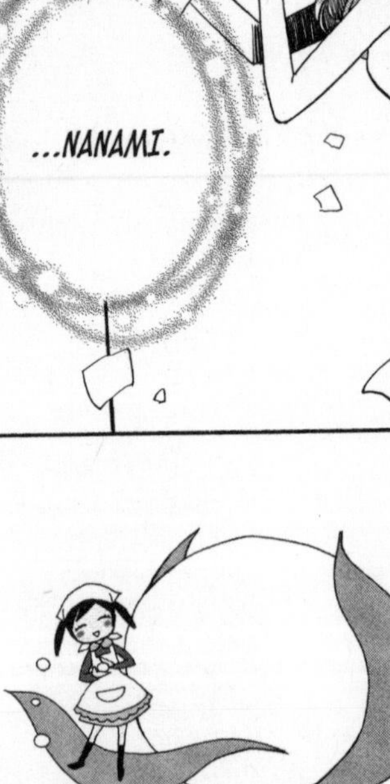

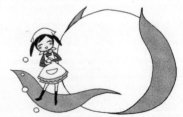

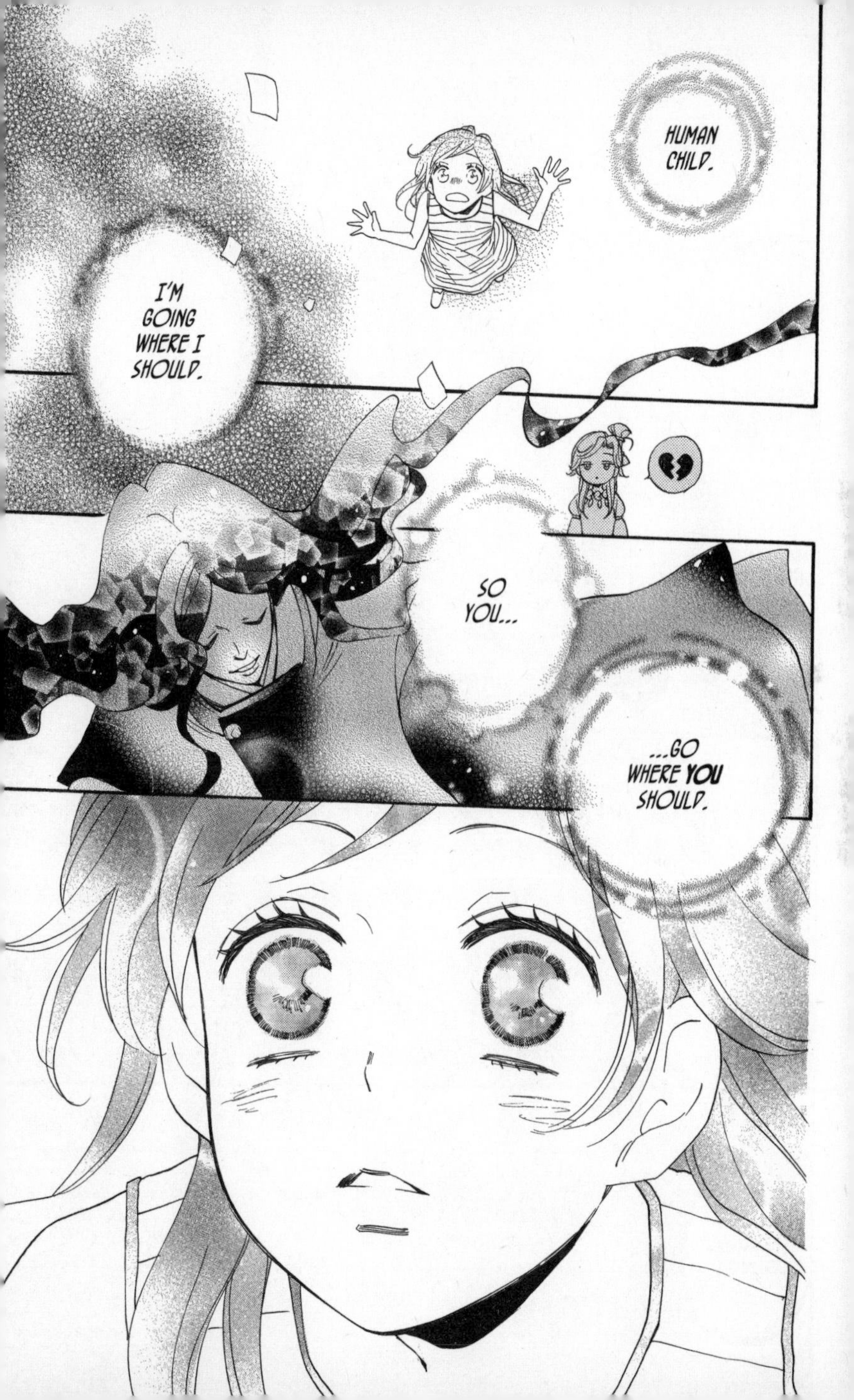
HUMAN CHILD.
I'M GOING WHERE I SHOULD.
SO YOU...
...GO WHERE YOU SHOULD.

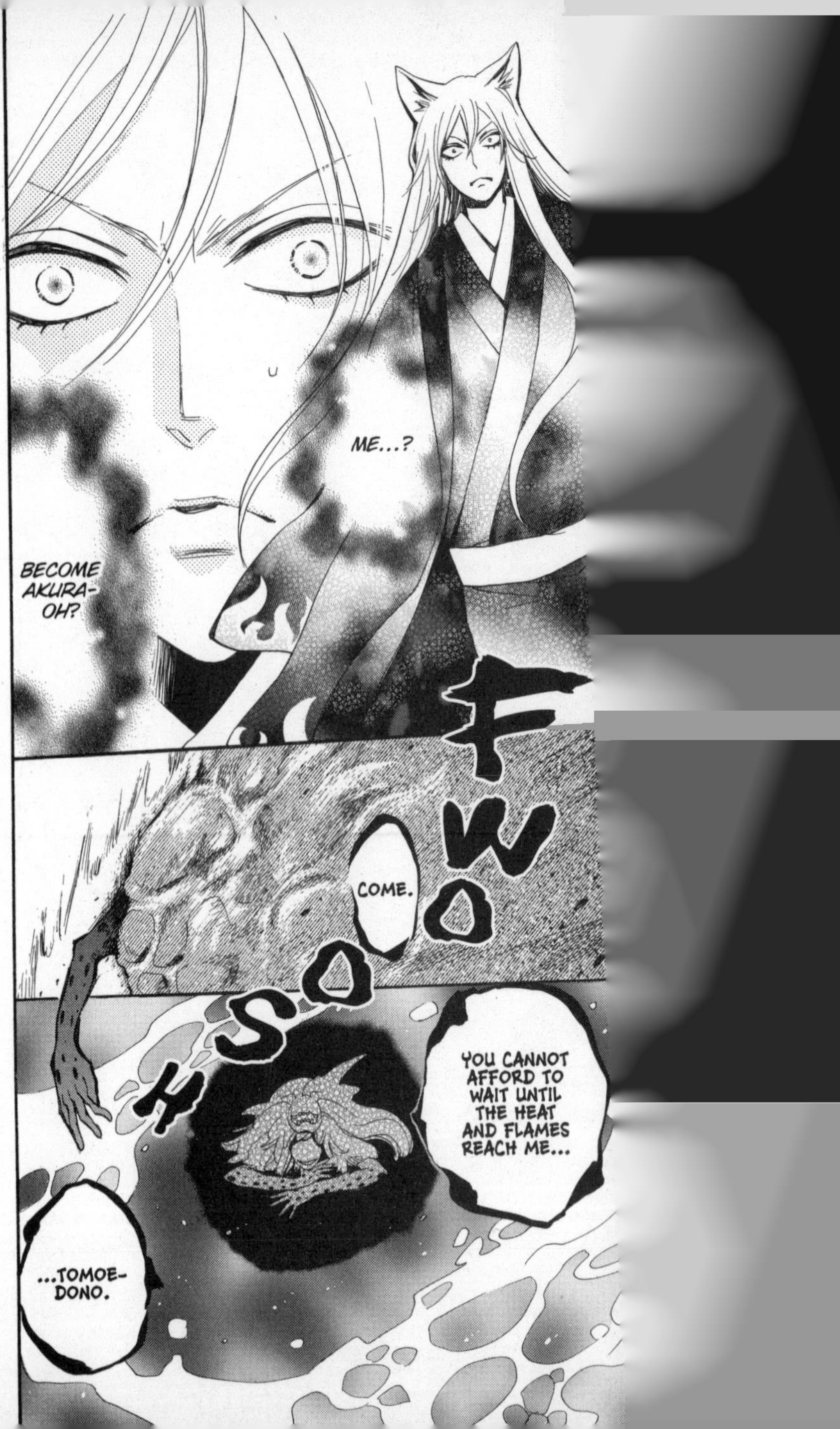
ME...?
BECOME AKURA-OH?
FWOOSH
COME.
YOU CANNOT AFFORD TO WAIT UNTIL THE HEAT AND FLAMES REACH ME...
...TOMOE-DONO.

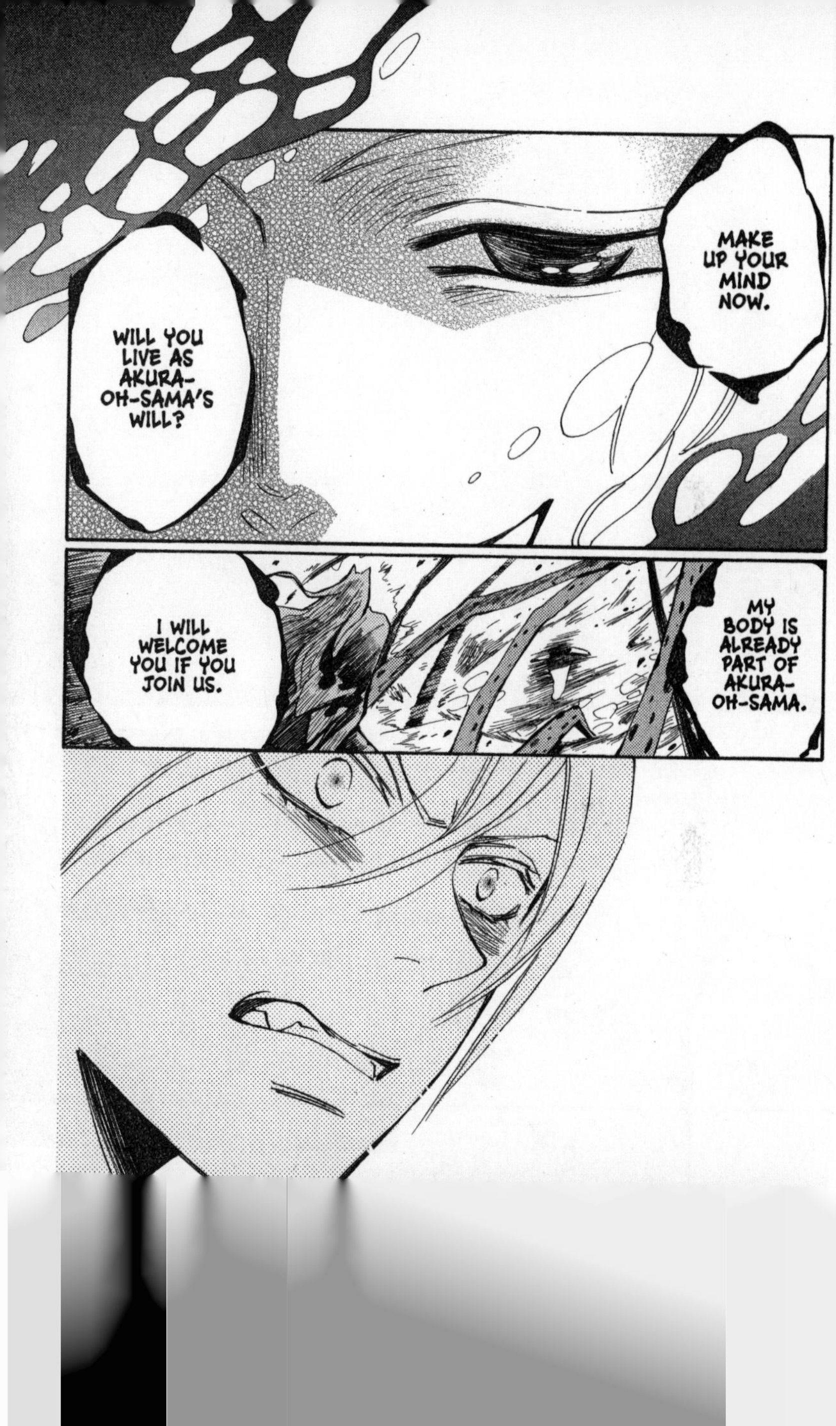
MAKE UP YOUR MIND NOW.
WILL YOU LIVE AS AKURA-OH-SAMA'S WILL?
MY BODY IS ALREADY PART OF AKURA-OH-SAMA.
I WILL WELCOME YOU IF YOU JOIN US.

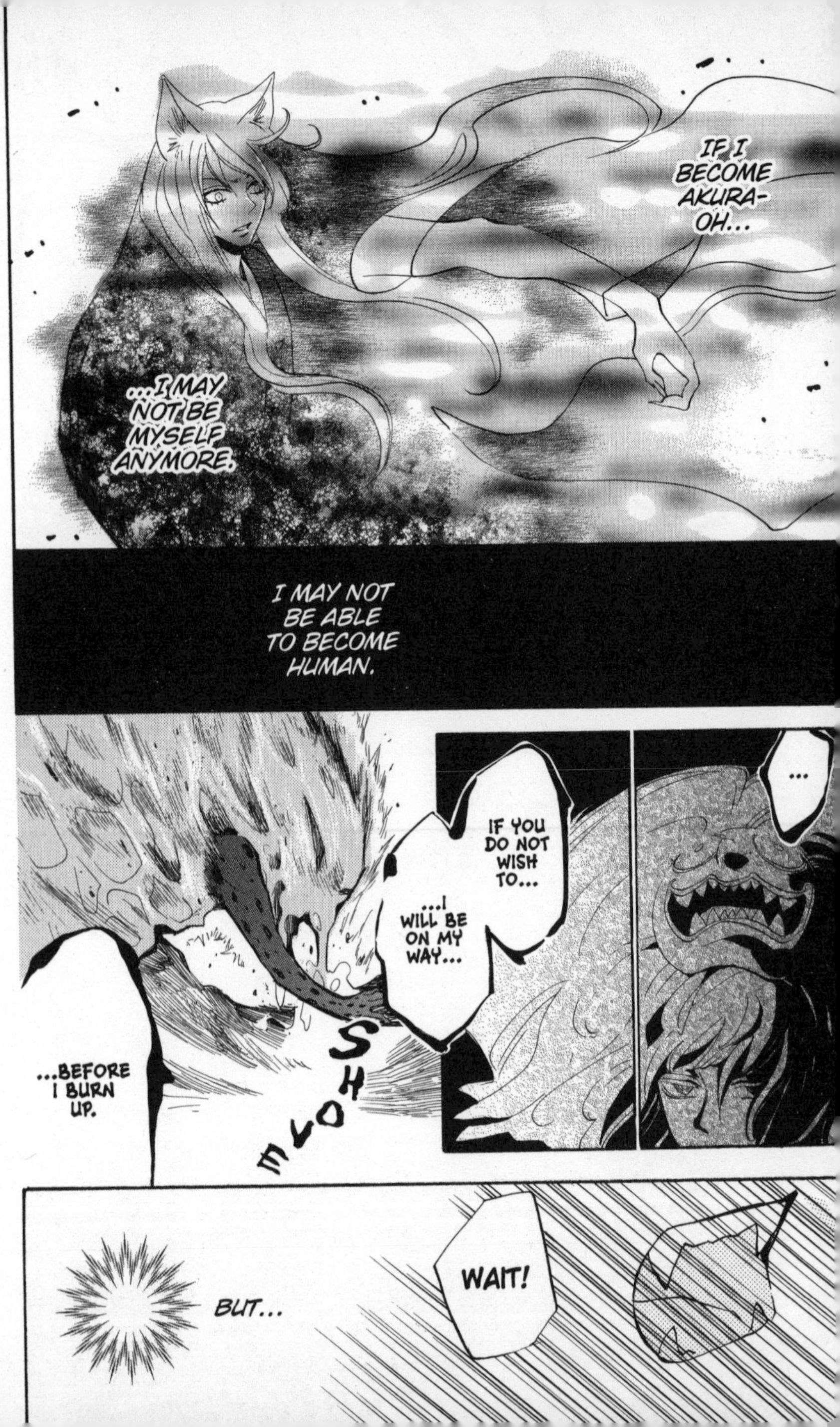
IF I BECOME AKURA-OH...
...I MAY NOT BE MYSELF ANYMORE.
I MAY NOT BE ABLE TO BECOME HUMAN.
...
IF YOU DO NOT WISH TO...
...I WILL BE ON MY WAY...
...BEFORE I BURN UP.
SHOVE
WAIT!
BUT...

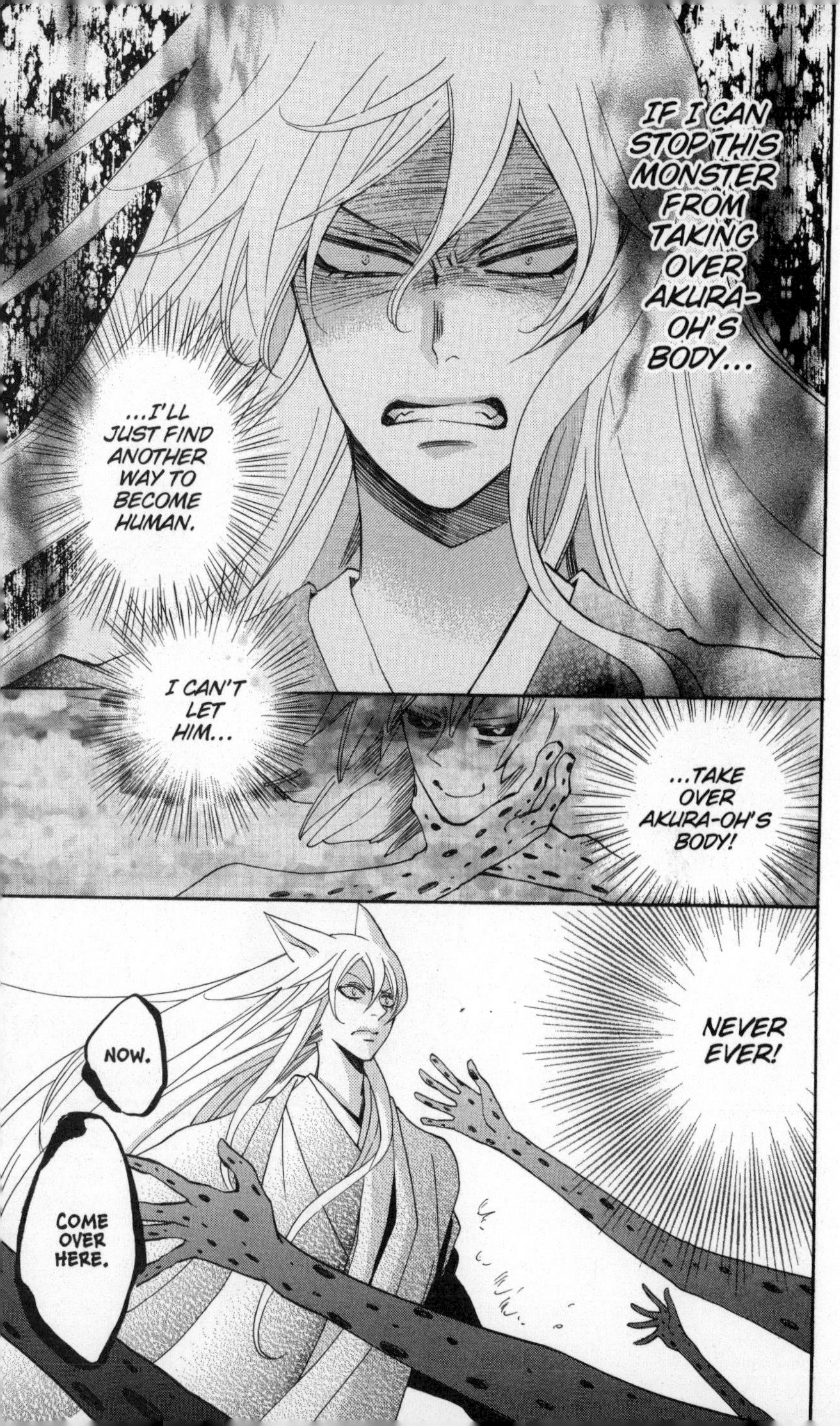
IF I CAN STOP THIS MONSTER FROM TAKING OVER AKURA-OH'S BODY...
...I'LL JUST FIND ANOTHER WAY TO BECOME HUMAN.
I CAN'T LET HIM...
...TAKE OVER AKURA-OH'S BODY!
NEVER EVER!
NOW.
COME OVER HERE.

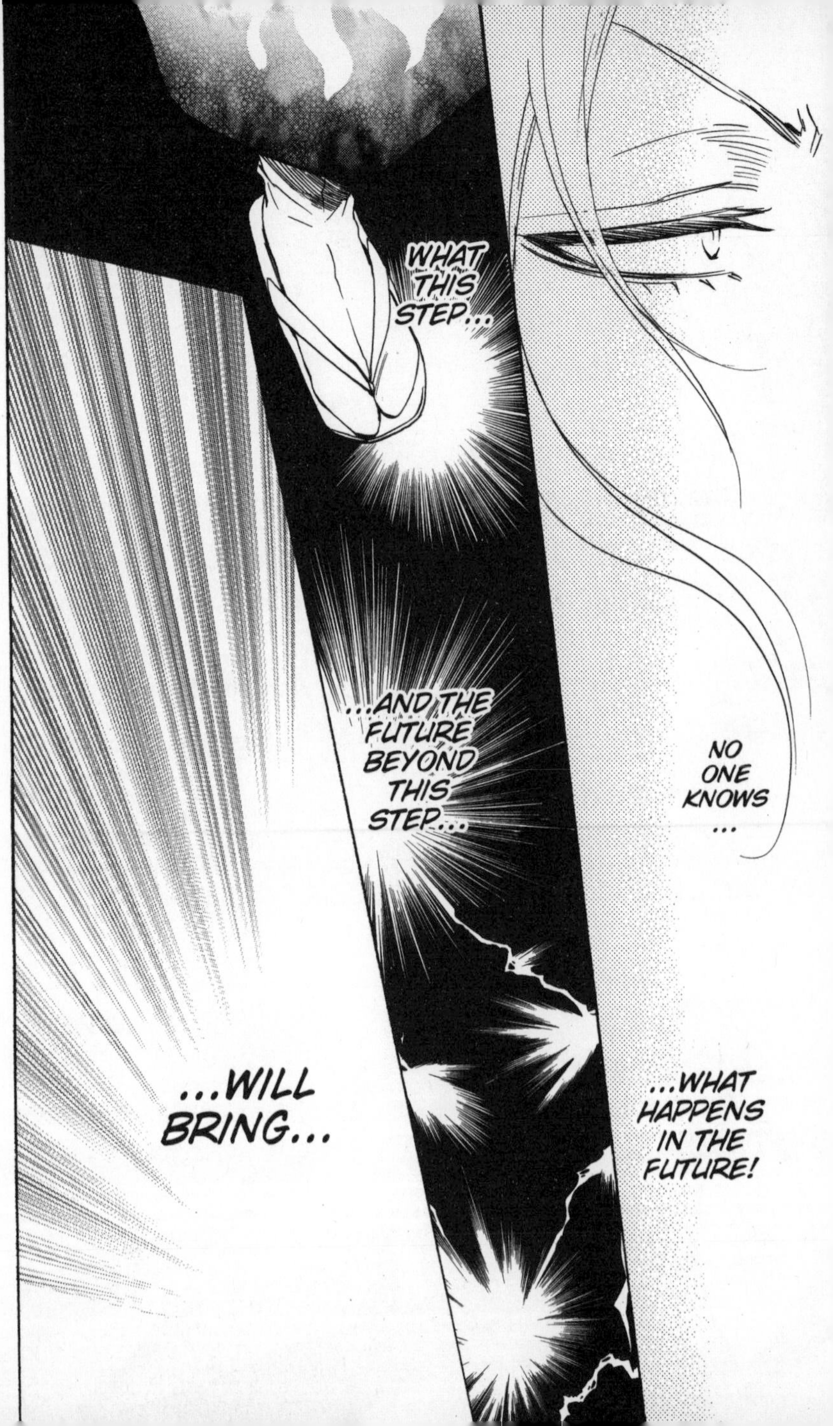
NO ONE KNOWS...
...WHAT HAPPENS IN THE FUTURE!
WHAT THIS STEP...
...AND THE FUTURE BEYOND THIS STEP...
...WILL BRING...

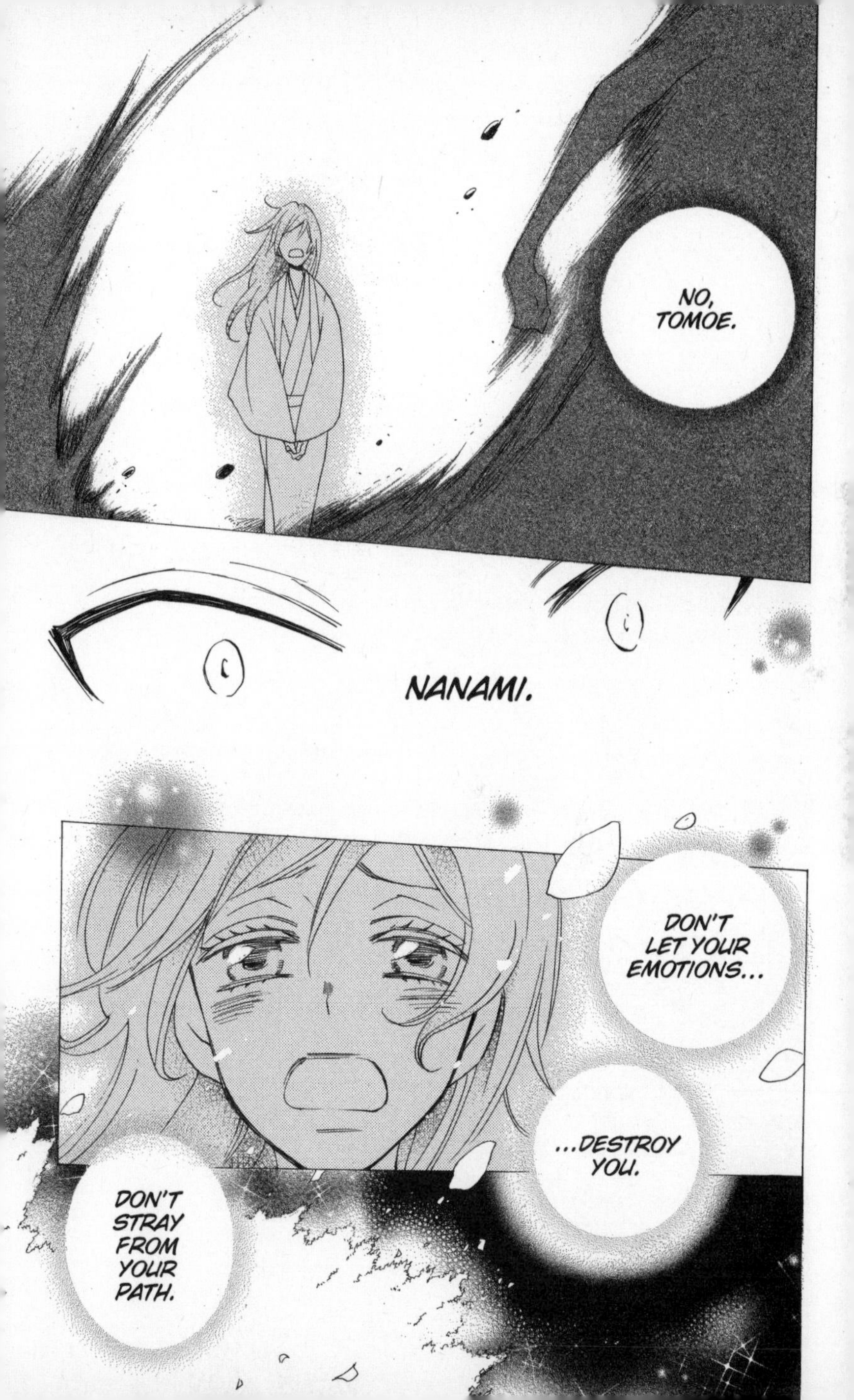
NO, TOMOE.
NANAMI.
DON'T LET YOUR EMOTIONS...
...DESTROY YOU.
DON'T STRAY FROM YOUR PATH.

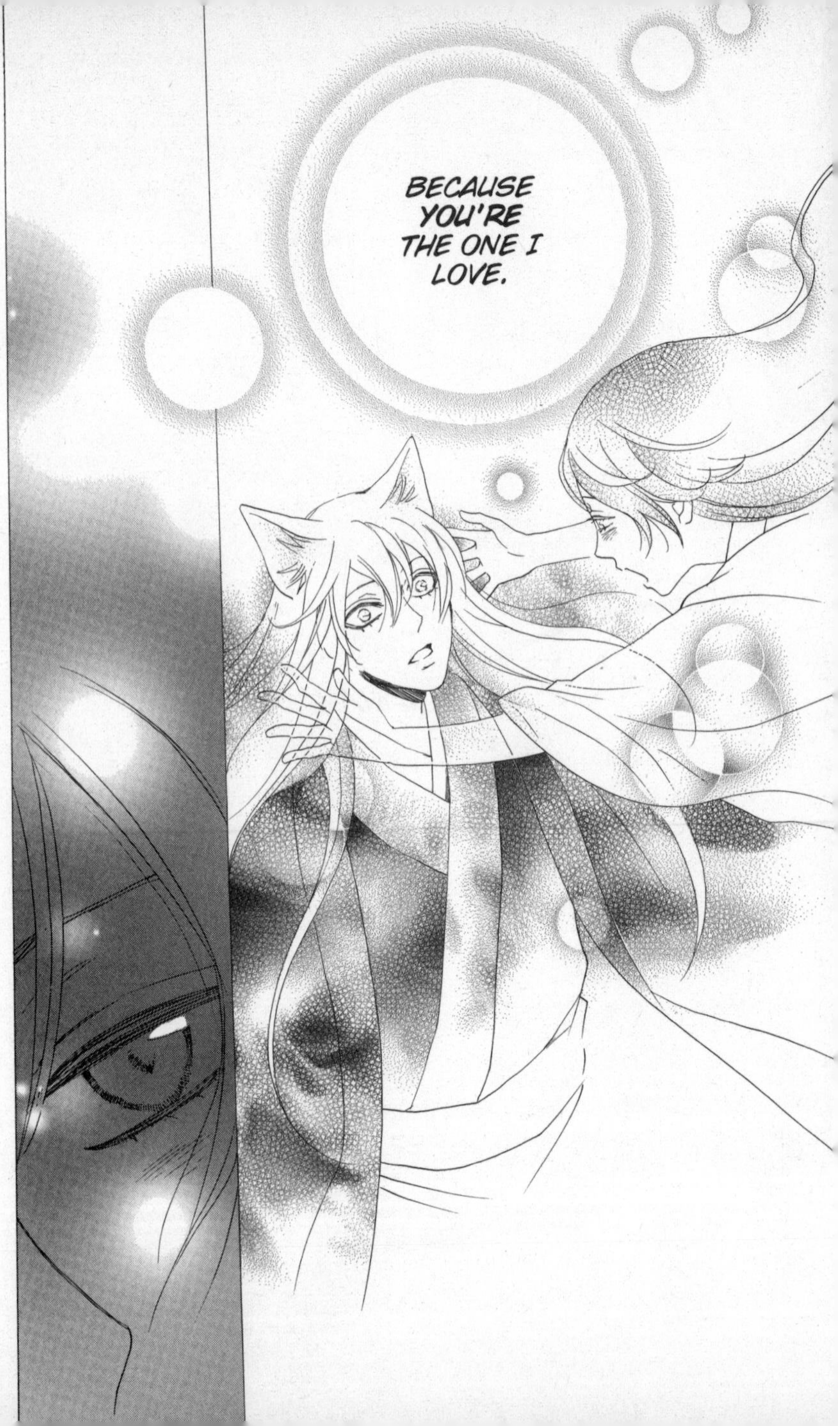
BECAUSE YOU'RE THE ONE I LOVE.

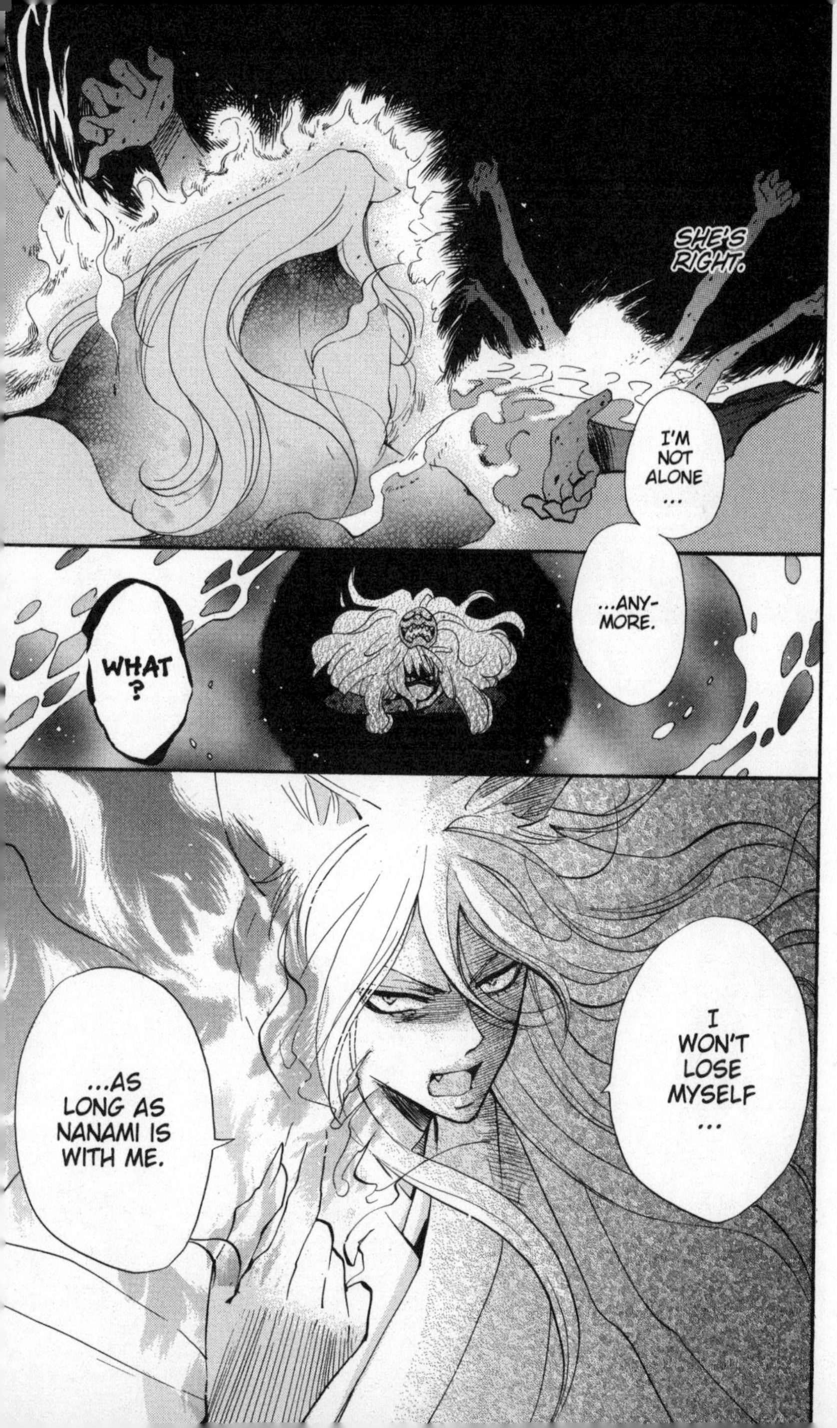
SHE'S RIGHT.
I'M NOT ALONE ...
...ANY-MORE.
WHAT?
I WON'T LOSE MYSELF ...
...AS LONG AS NANAMI IS WITH ME.

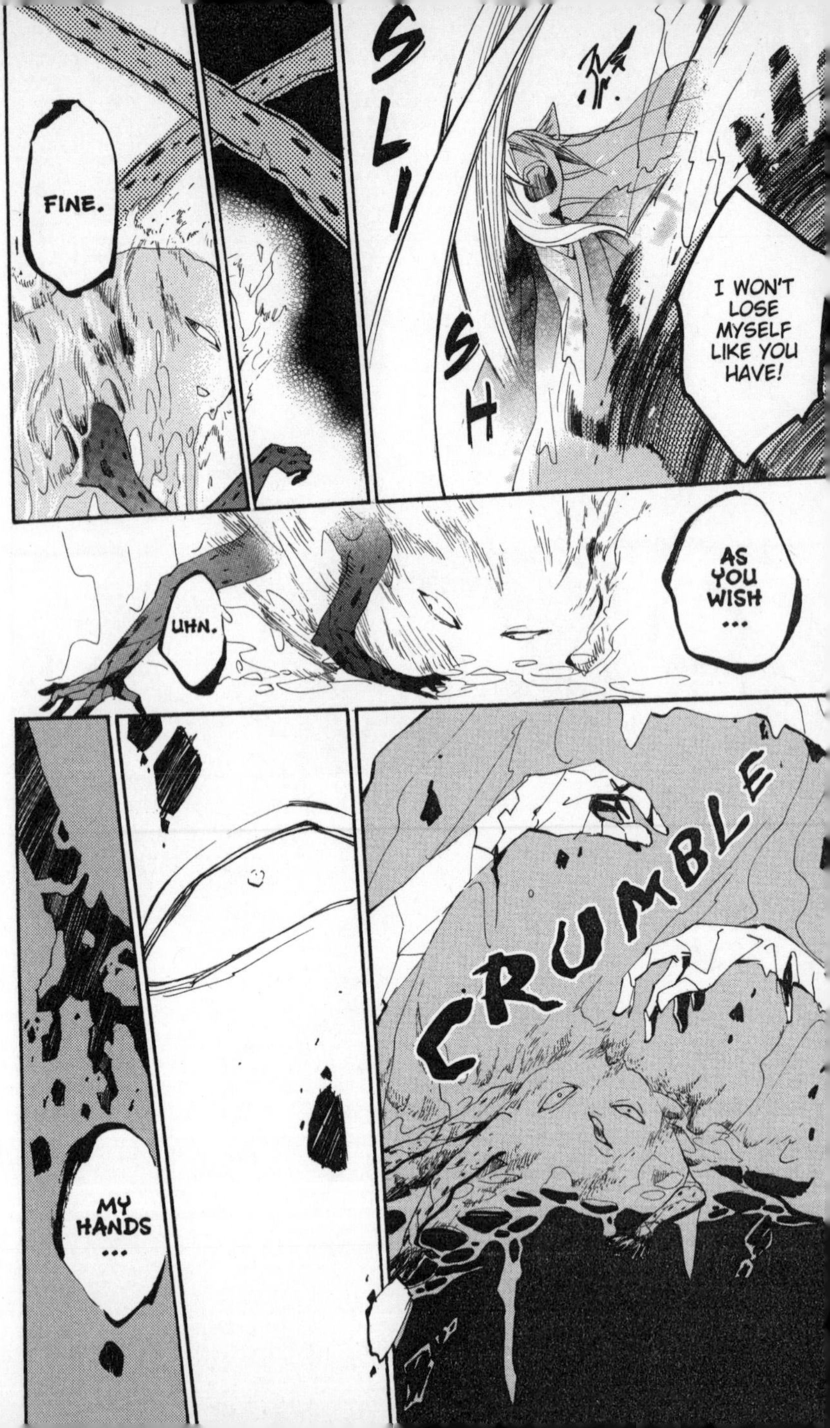
I WON'T LOSE MYSELF LIKE YOU HAVE!
SLISH
FINE.
AS YOU WISH...
UHN.
CRUMBLE
MY HANDS...

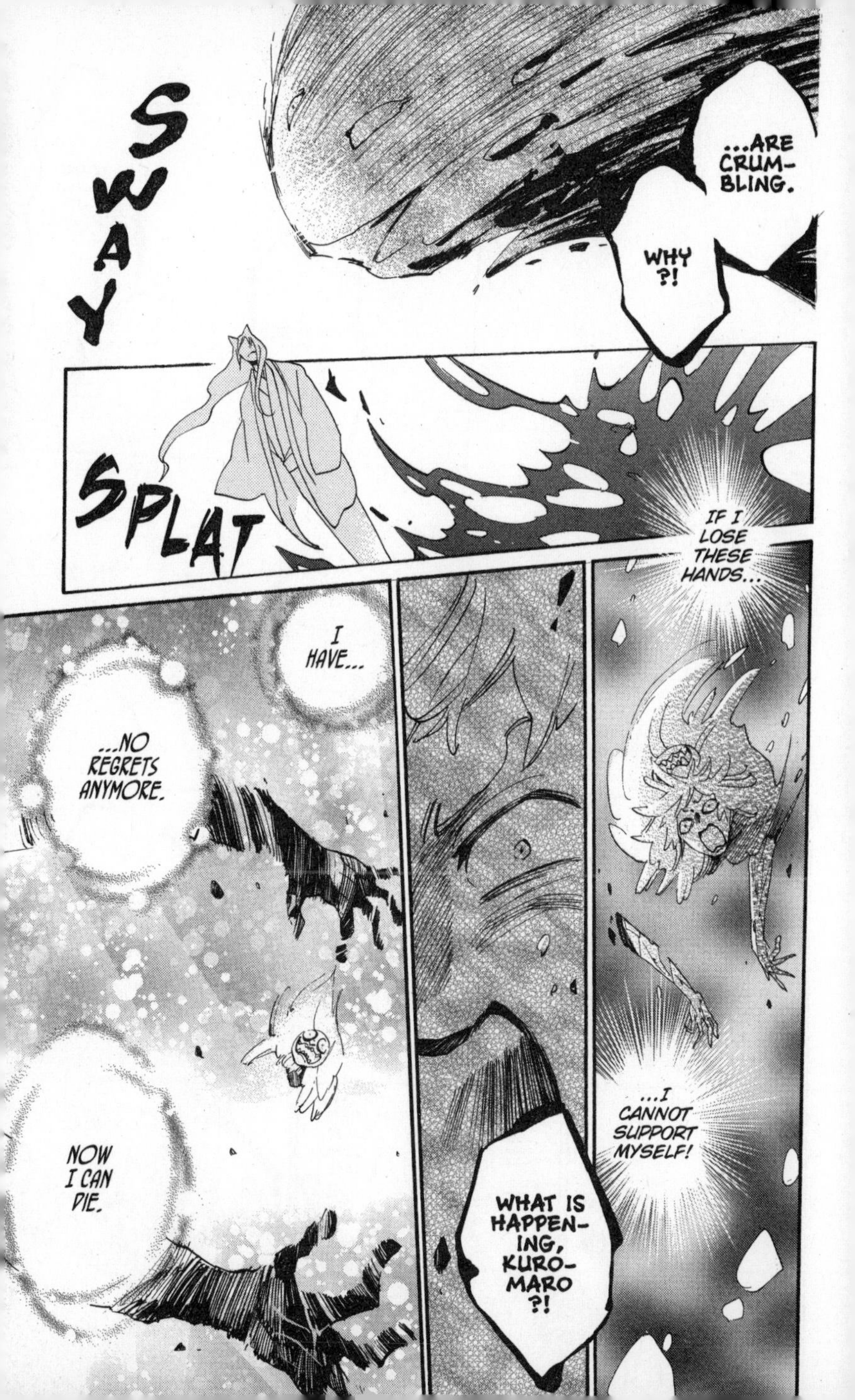
...ARE CRUM-BLING.
WHY?!
SWAY
SPLAT
IF I LOSE THESE HANDS...
...I CANNOT SUPPORT MYSELF!
WHAT IS HAPPEN-ING, KURO-MARO?!
I HAVE...
...NO REGRETS ANYMORE.
NOW I CAN DIE.

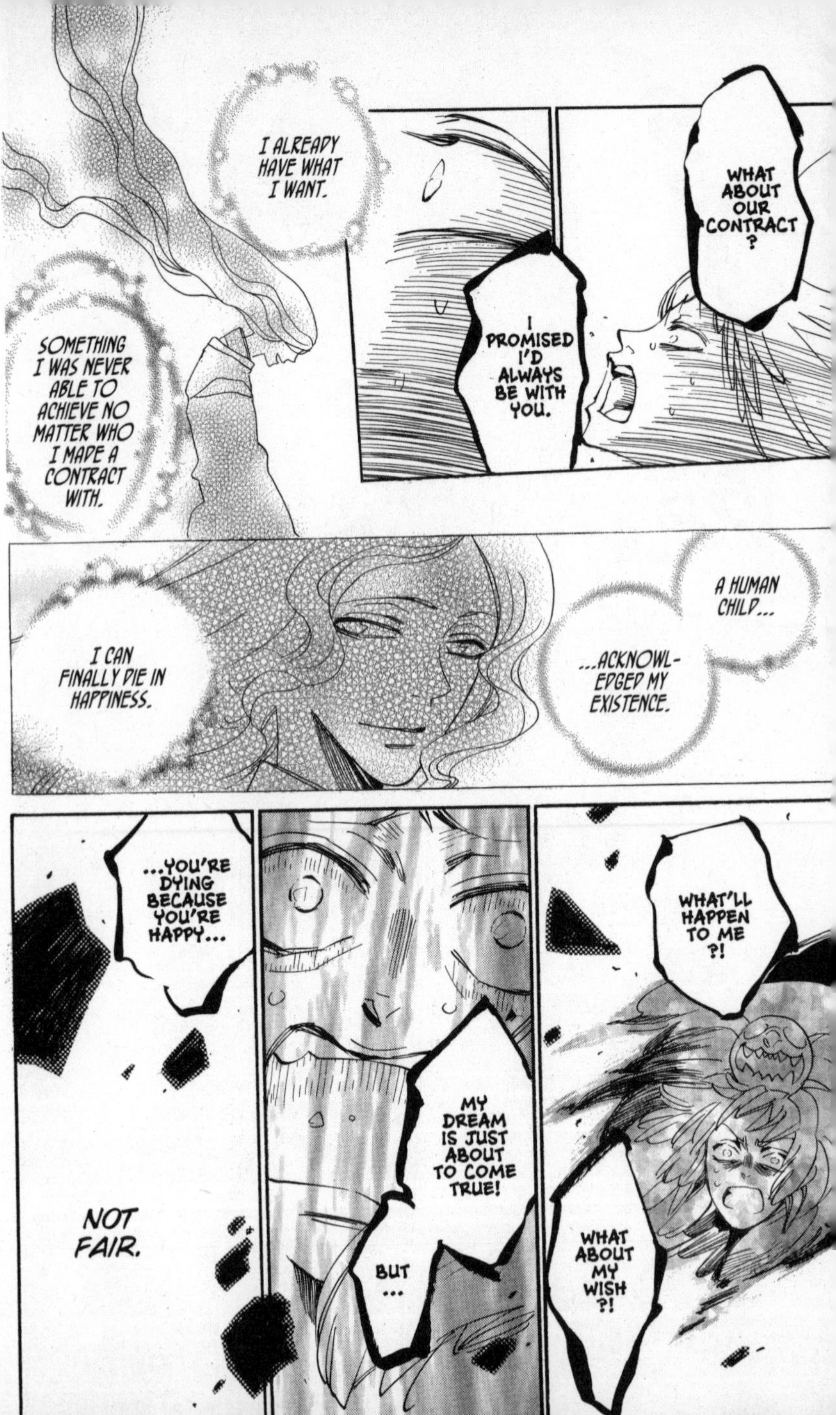
WHAT ABOUT OUR CONTRACT?
I PROMISED I'D ALWAYS BE WITH YOU.
I ALREADY HAVE WHAT I WANT.
SOMETHING I WAS NEVER ABLE TO ACHIEVE NO MATTER WHO I MADE A CONTRACT WITH.
A HUMAN CHILD...
...ACKNOWL-EDGED MY EXISTENCE.
I CAN FINALLY DIE IN HAPPINESS.
WHAT'LL HAPPEN TO ME?!
WHAT ABOUT MY WISH?!
MY DREAM IS JUST ABOUT TO COME TRUE!
BUT...
...YOU'RE DYING BECAUSE YOU'RE HAPPY...
NOT FAIR.

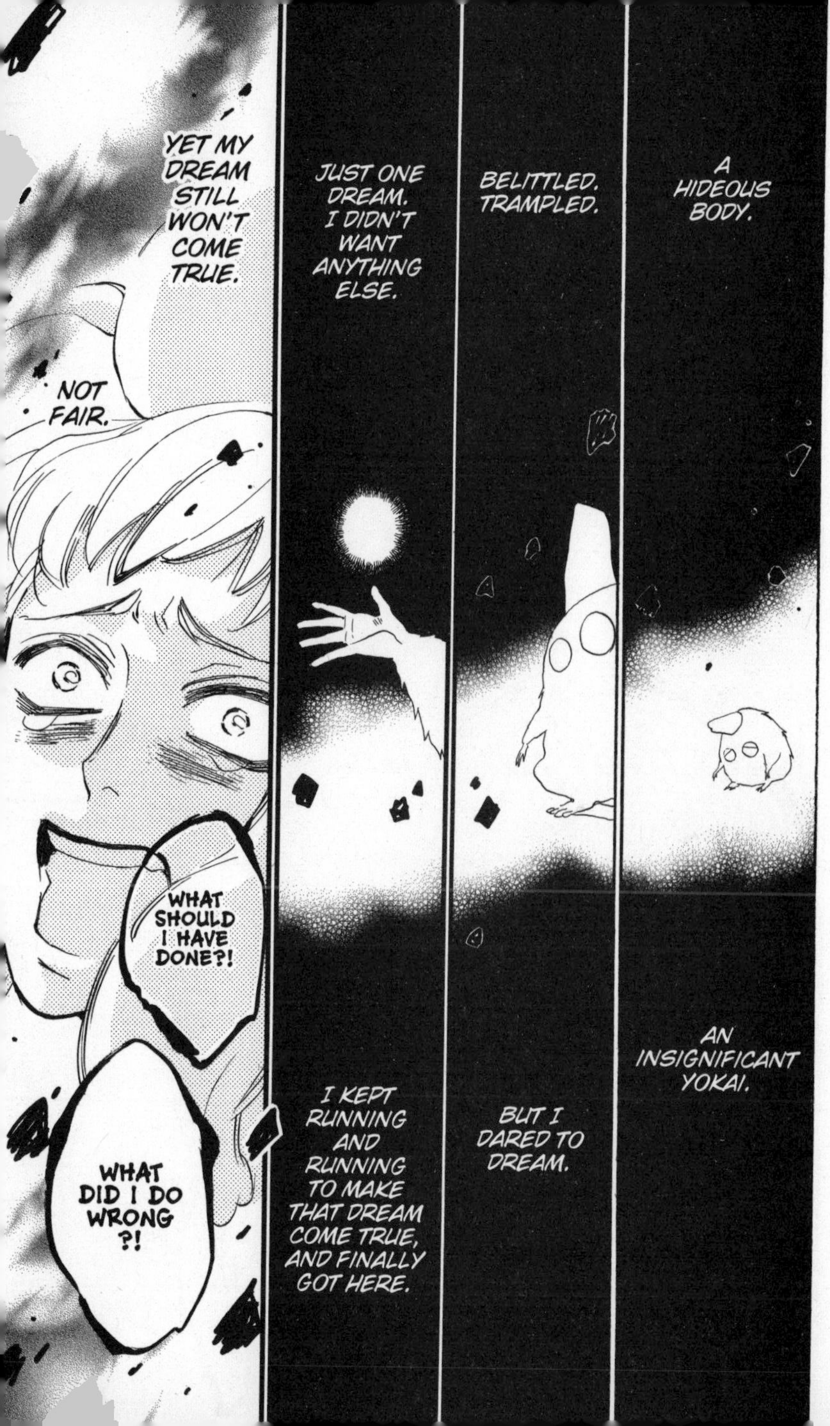
A HIDEOUS BODY.
AN INSIGNIFICANT YOKAI.
BELITTLED. TRAMPLED.
BUT I DARED TO DREAM.
JUST ONE DREAM. I DIDN'T WANT ANYTHING ELSE.
I KEPT RUNNING AND RUNNING TO MAKE THAT DREAM COME TRUE, AND FINALLY GOT HERE.
YET MY DREAM STILL WON'T COME TRUE.
NOT FAIR.
WHAT SHOULD I HAVE DONE?!
WHAT DID I DO WRONG?!

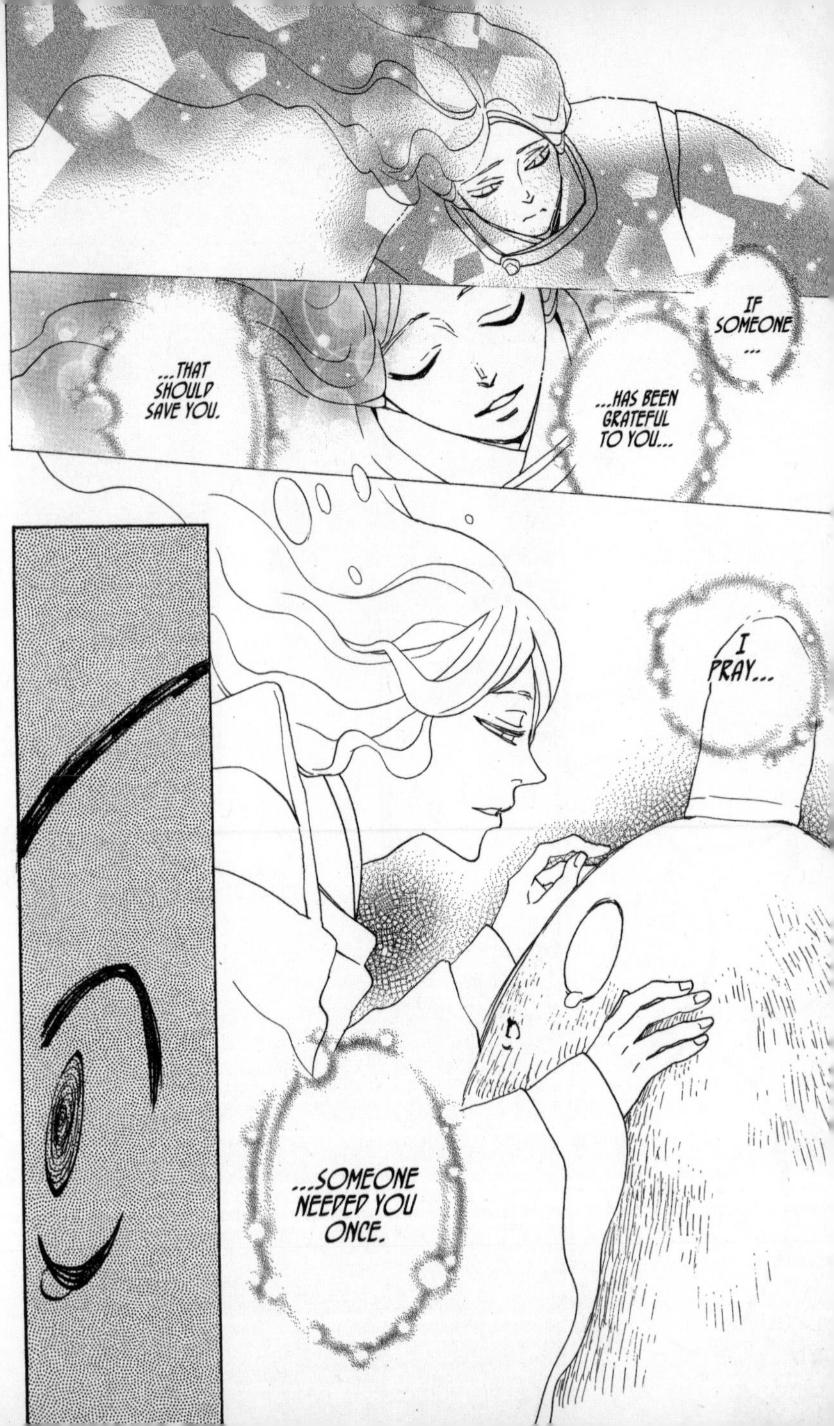
IF SOMEONE...
...HAS BEEN GRATEFUL TO YOU...
...THAT SHOULD SAVE YOU.
I PRAY...
...SOMEONE NEEDED YOU ONCE.

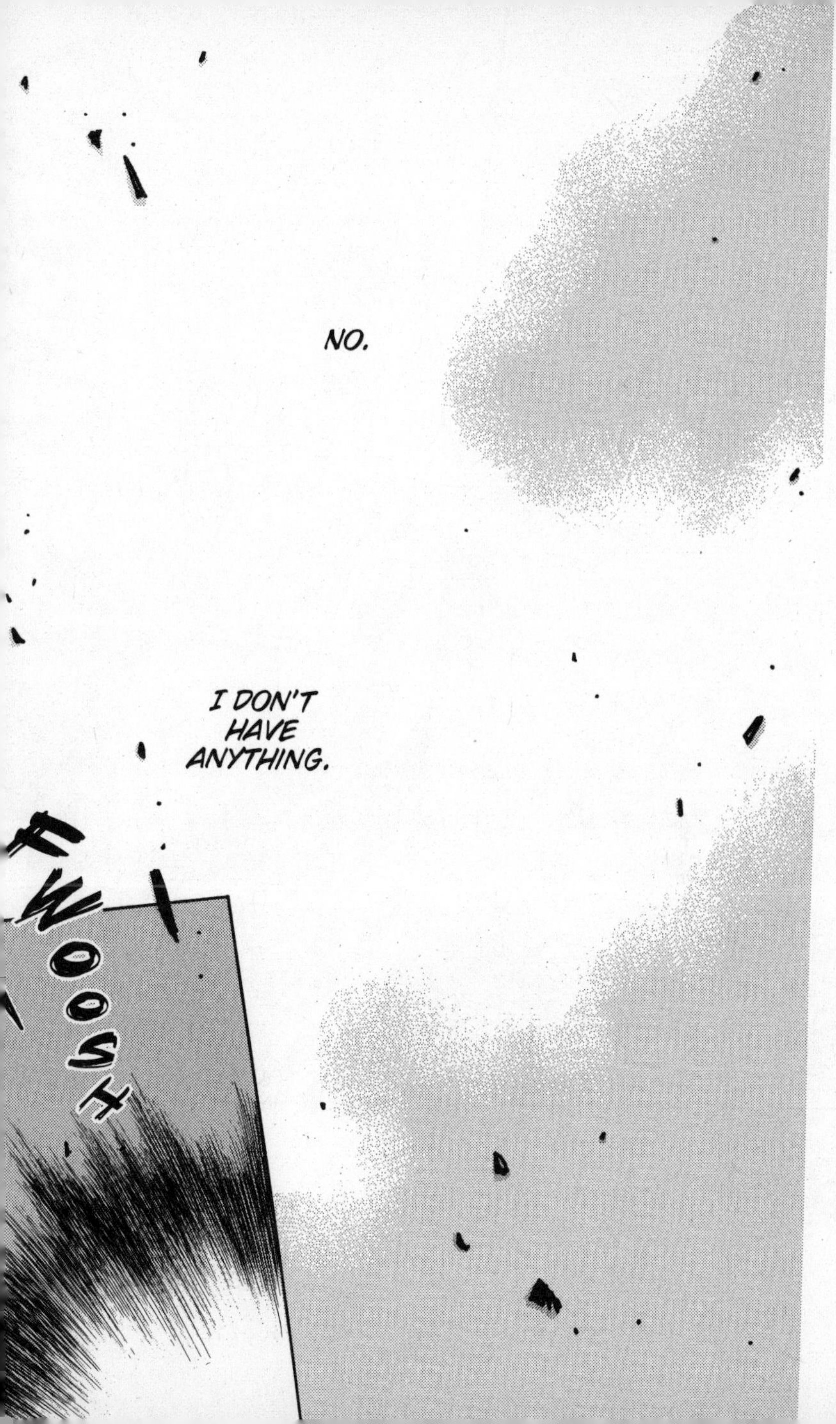
NO.
I DON'T HAVE ANYTHING.
FWOOSH

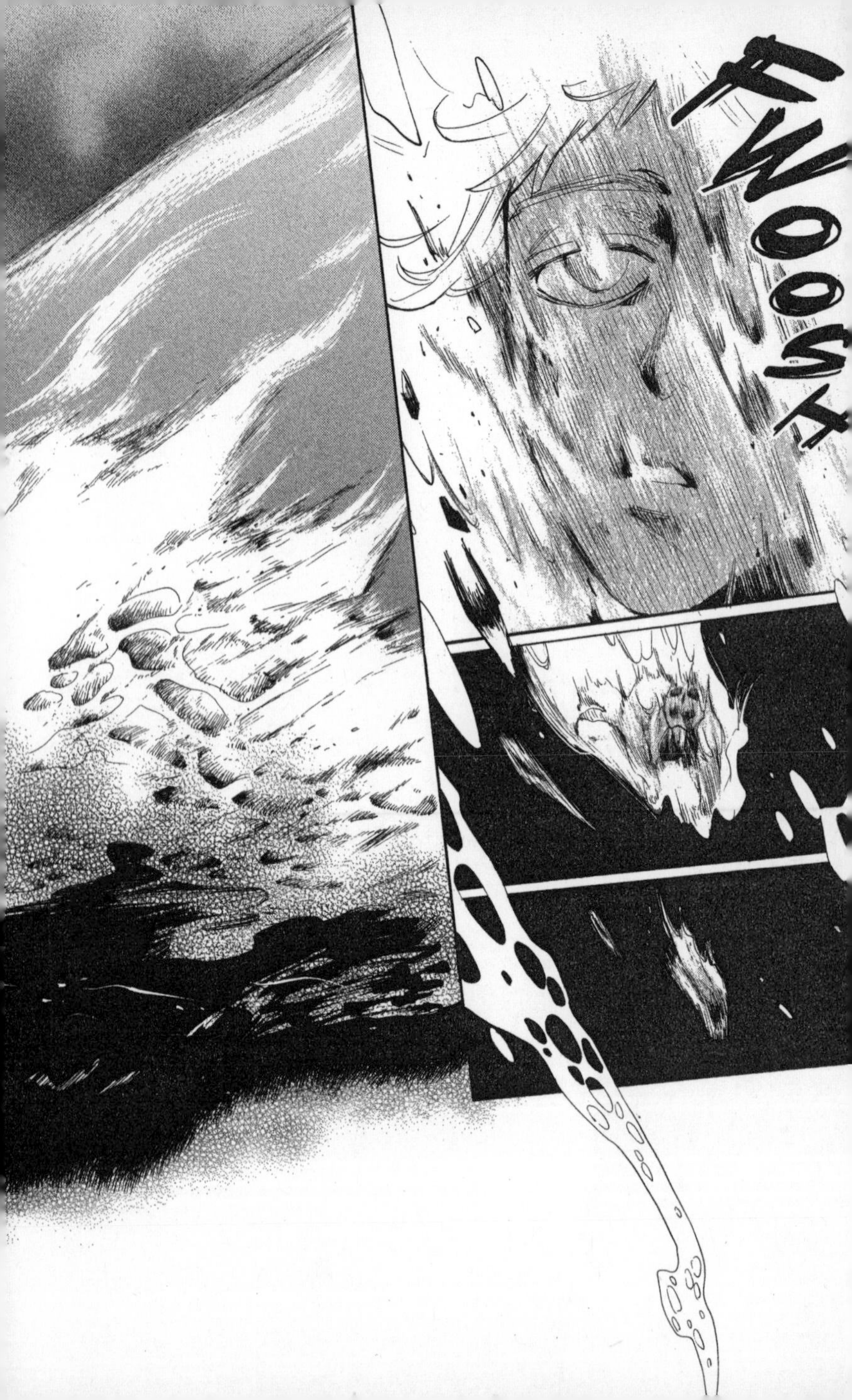
FWOOSH

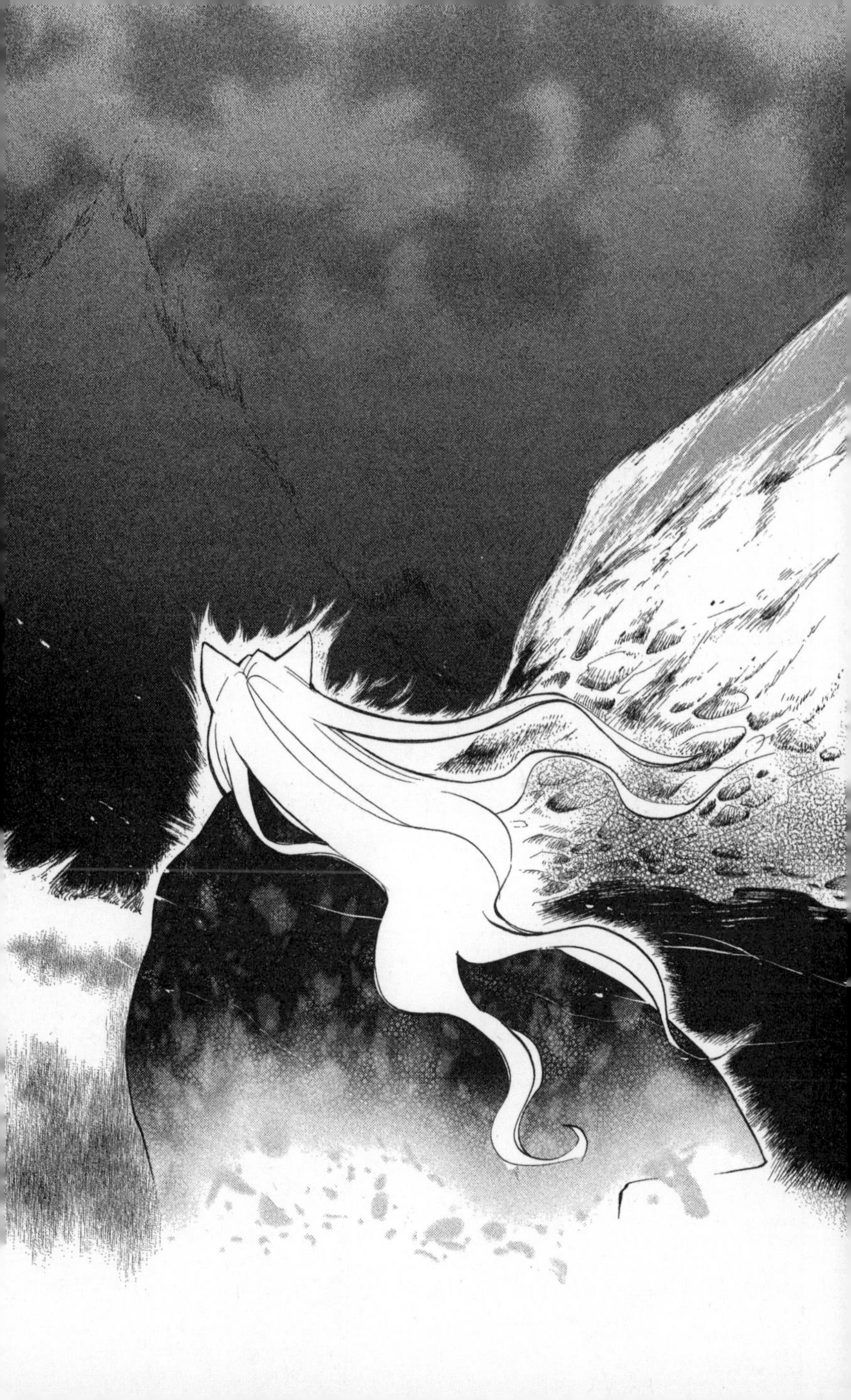

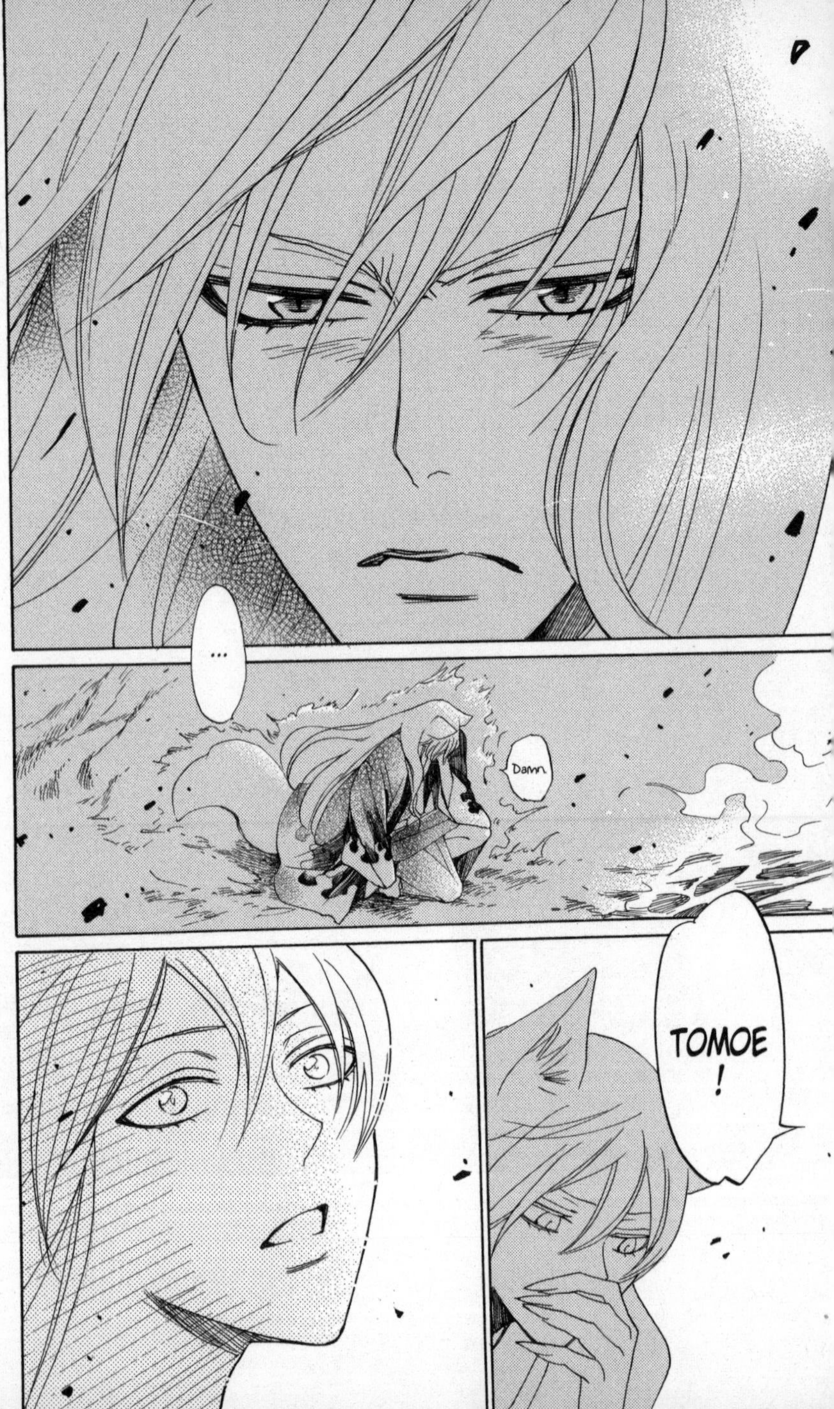
...
Damn.
TOMOE!

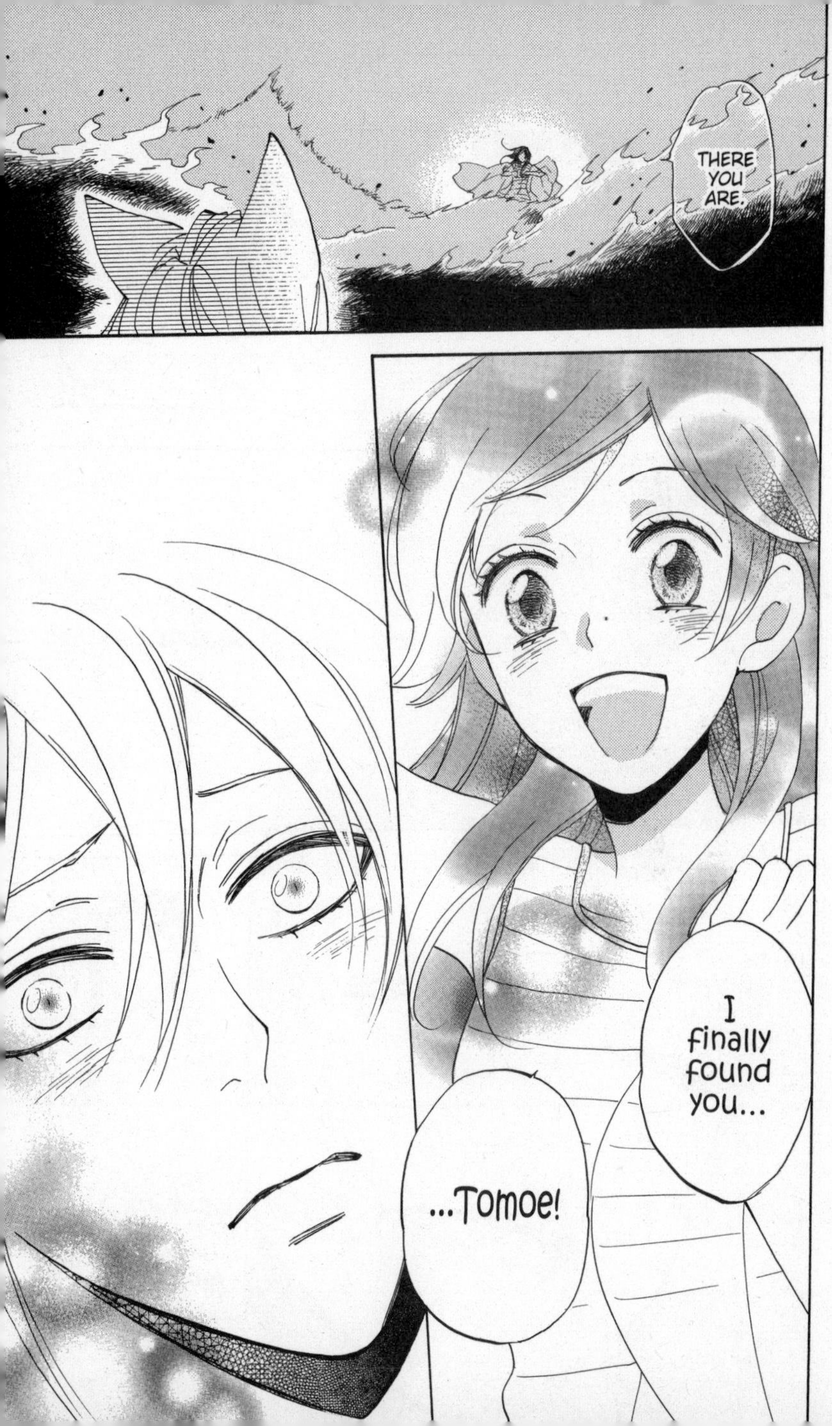
THERE YOU ARE.
I finally found you...
...Tomoe!

I'LL COME TO YOU.

TWITCH

DON'T.

HUP

I'LL COME TO YOU.

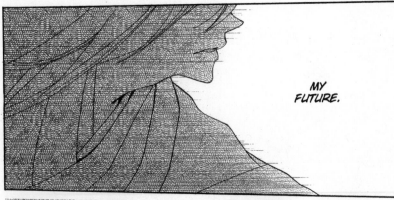

MY FUTURE.

THE LIGHT AT THE END OF MY PATH...

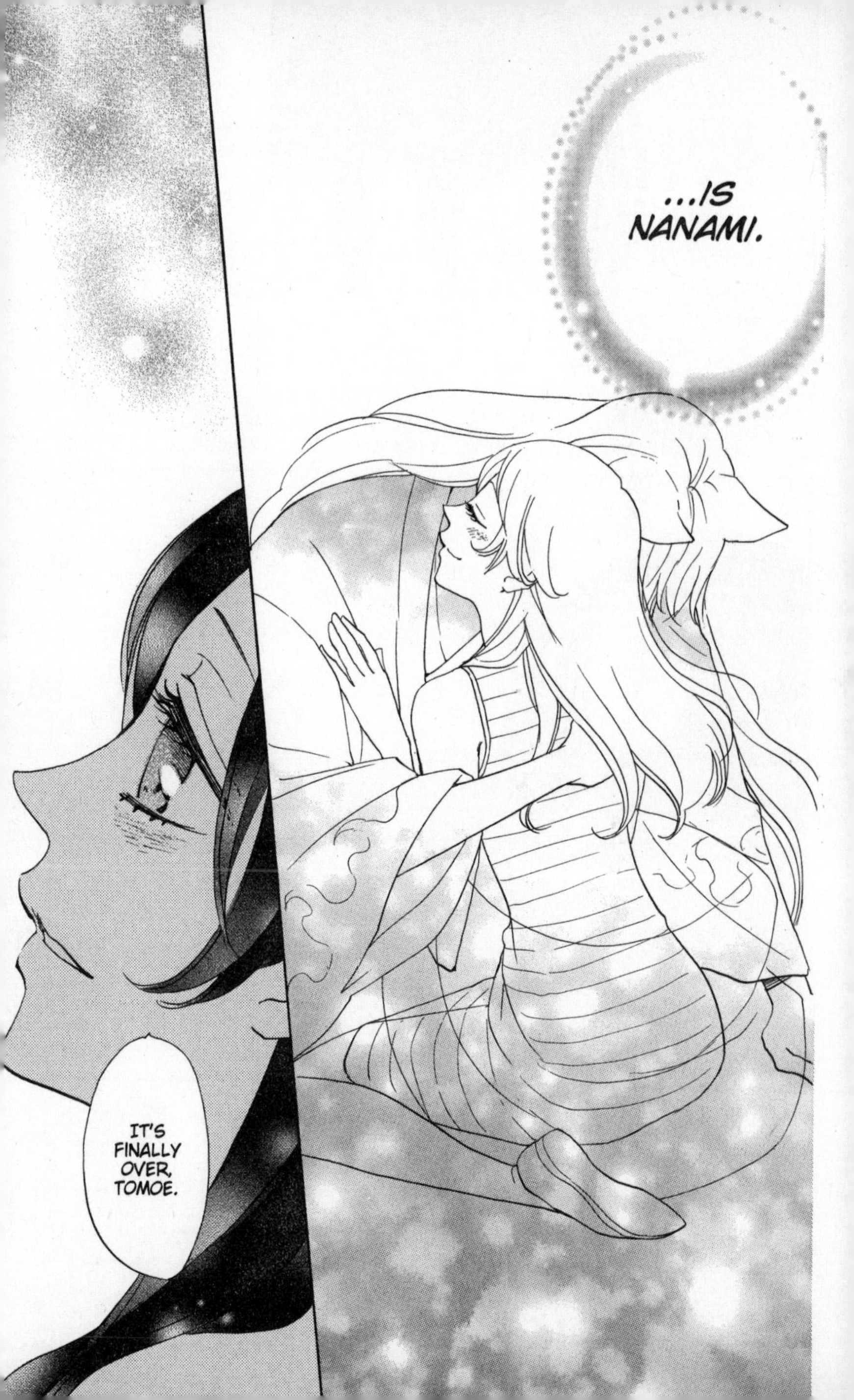
...IS NANAMI.
IT'S FINALLY OVER, TOMOE.

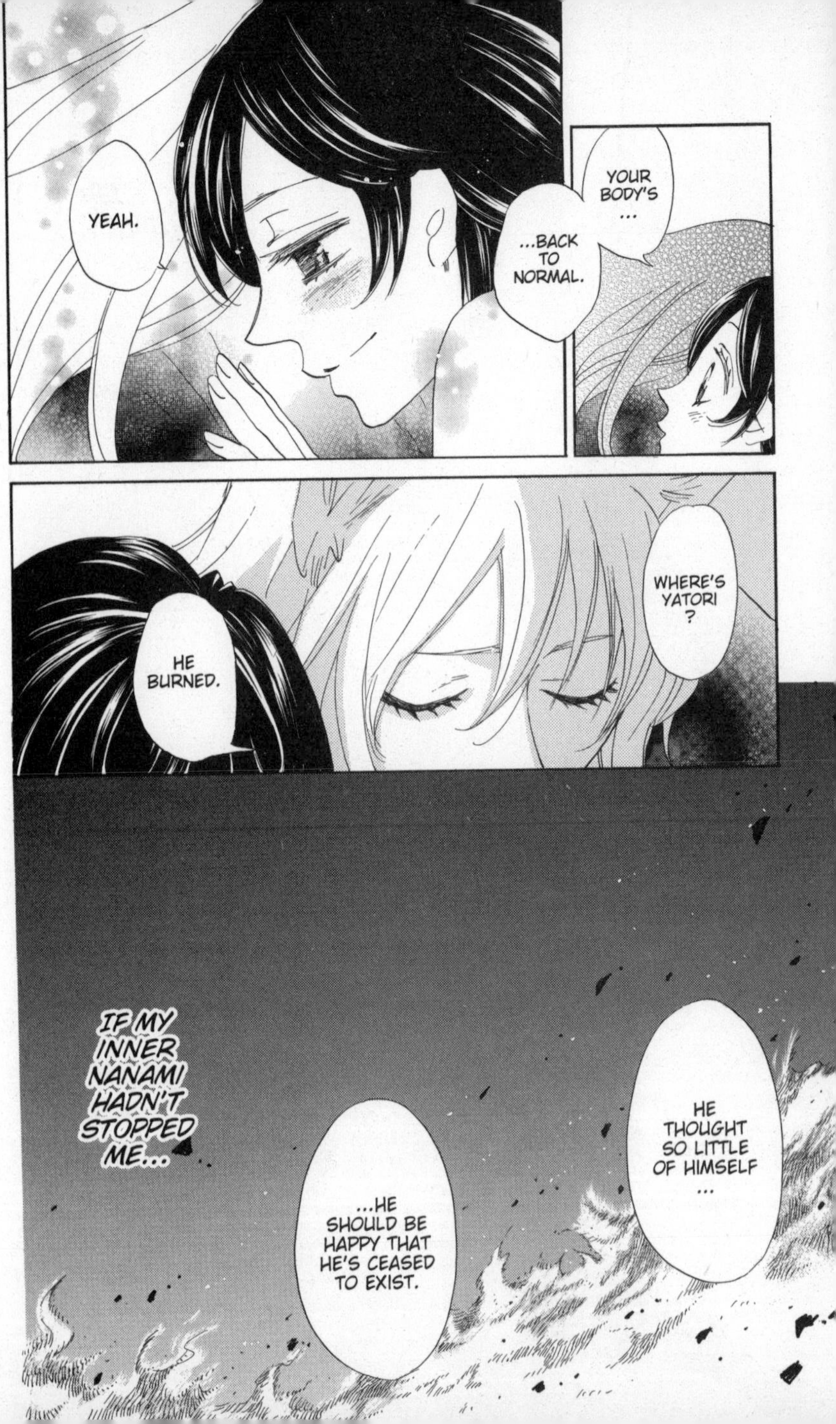
YOUR BODY'S ...
...BACK TO NORMAL.
YEAH.
WHERE'S YATORI ?
HE BURNED.
HE THOUGHT SO LITTLE OF HIMSELF ...
...HE SHOULD BE HAPPY THAT HE'S CEASED TO EXIST.
IF MY INNER NANAMI HADN'T STOPPED ME...

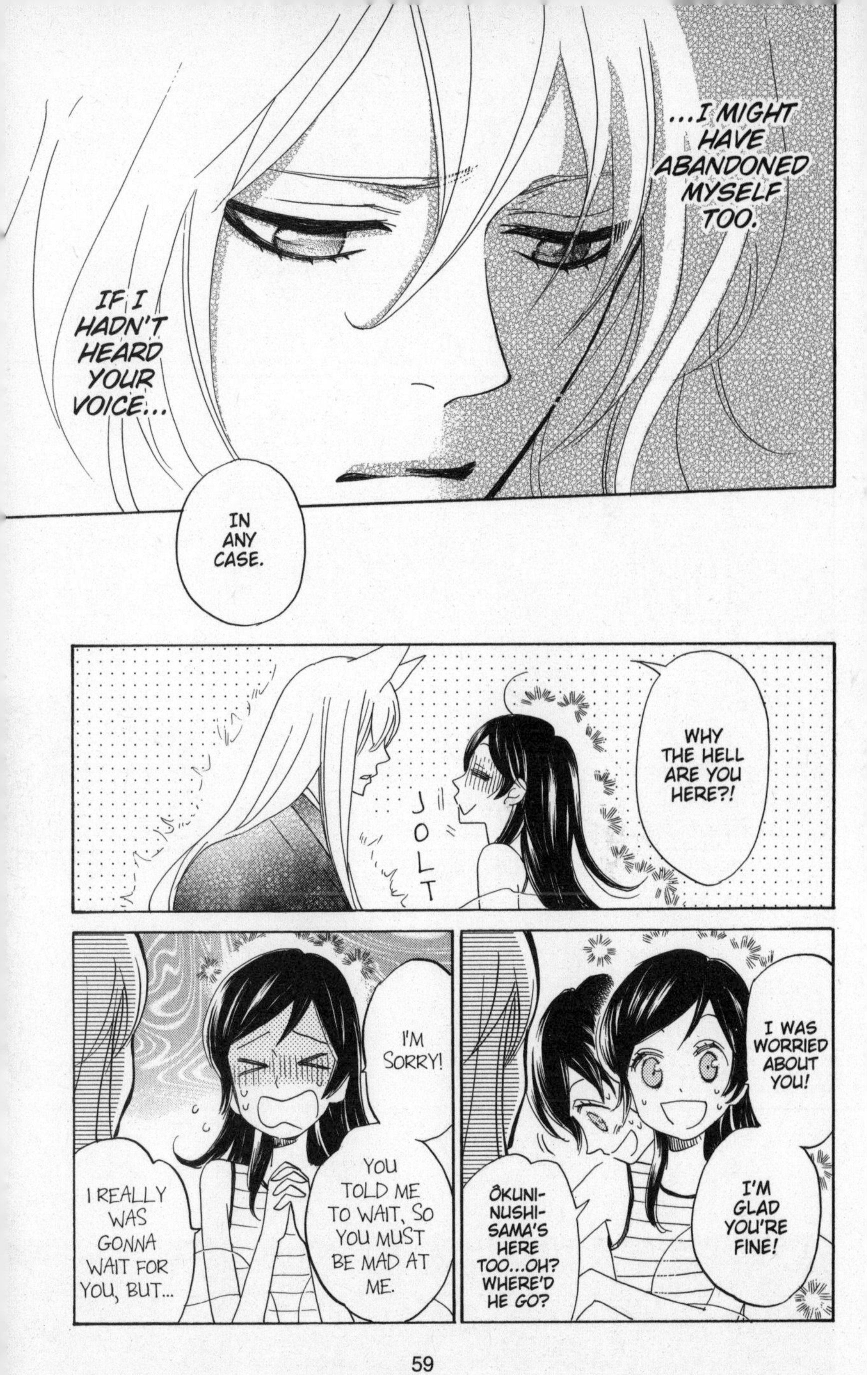
...I MIGHT HAVE ABANDONED MYSELF TOO.
IF I HADN'T HEARD YOUR VOICE...
IN ANY CASE.
WHY THE HELL ARE YOU HERE?!
JOLT
I WAS WORRIED ABOUT YOU!
I'M GLAD YOU'RE FINE!
ŌKUNI-NUSHI-SAMA'S HERE TOO...OH? WHERE'D HE GO?
I'M SORRY!
YOU TOLD ME TO WAIT, SO YOU MUST BE MAD AT ME.
I REALLY WAS GONNA WAIT FOR YOU, BUT...

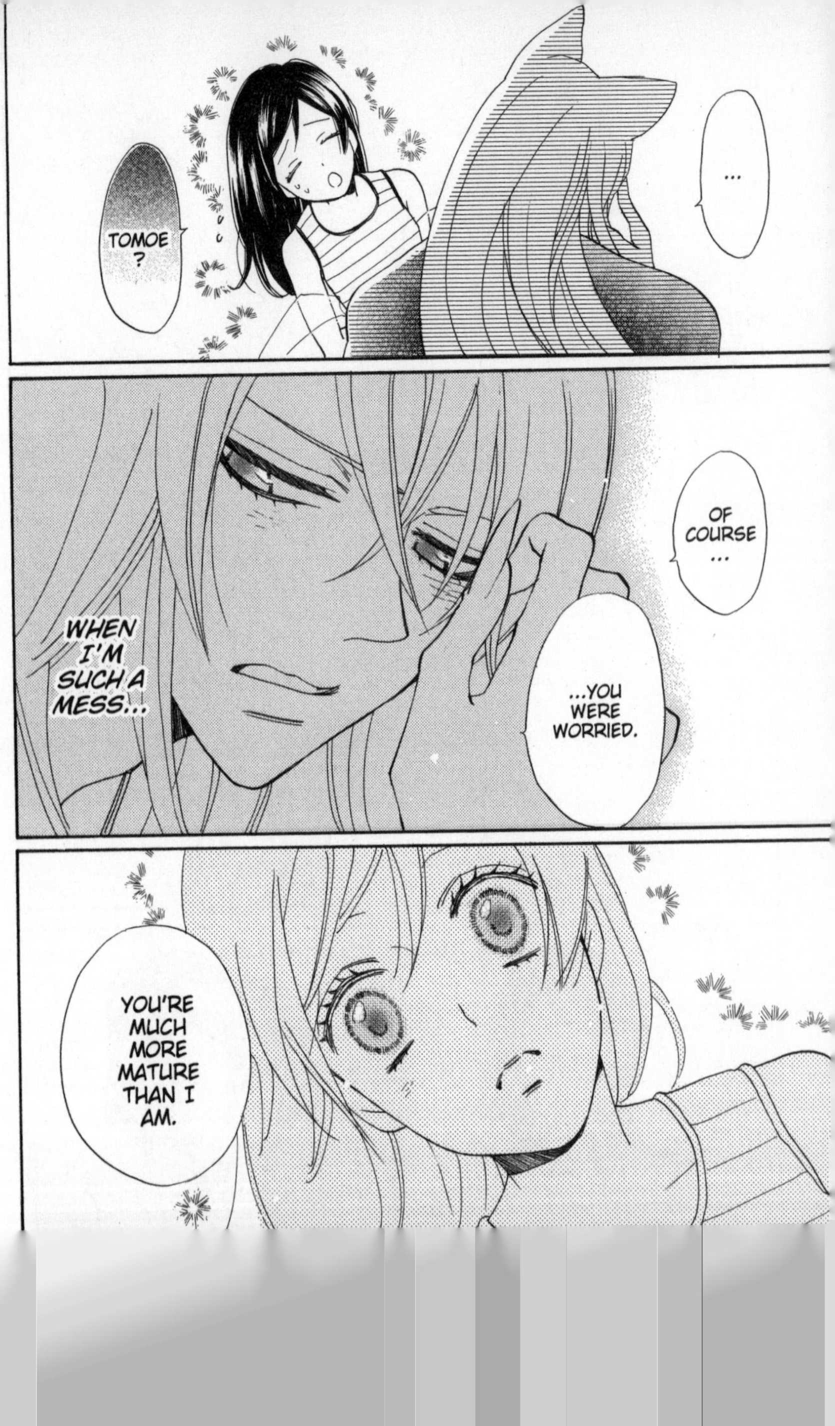
...
TOMOE?
OF COURSE...
...YOU WERE WORRIED.
WHEN I'M SUCH A MESS...
YOU'RE MUCH MORE MATURE THAN I AM.

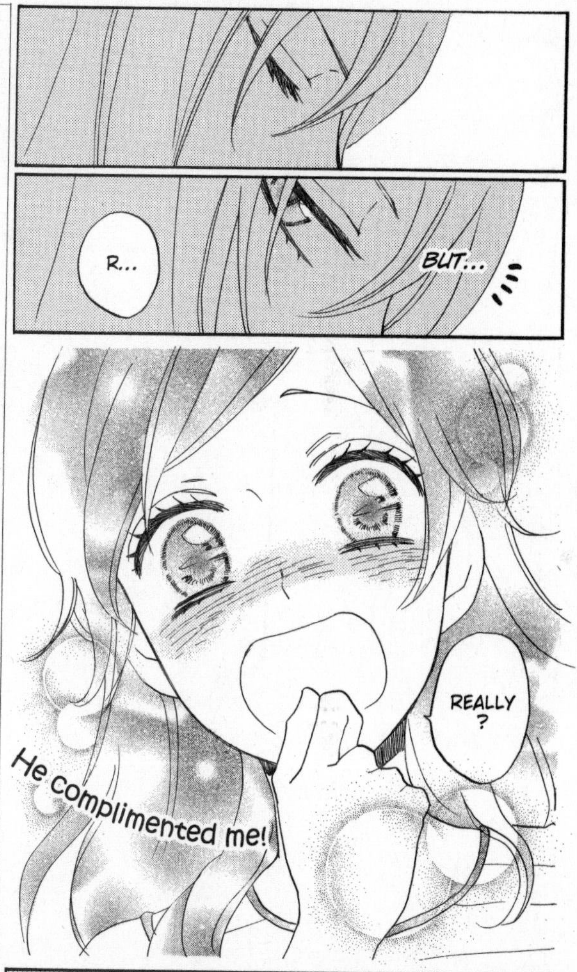
BUT...
R...
REALLY?
He complimented me!
I'LL GO LOOK FOR ÔKUNI-NUSHI!
I'll find him!
DASH
THINGS ARE GONNA BE TOUGH.

I sneaked out of Japan and went to France.

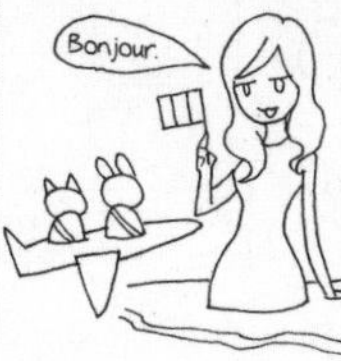
Bonjour.

The bakery in front of my hotel had delicious bread, so I bought bread there every morning...

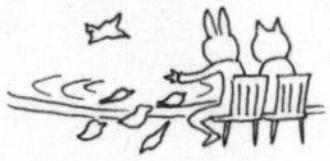

...and had breakfast on a bench at Tuileries Gardens while playing with birds. What peaceful days...

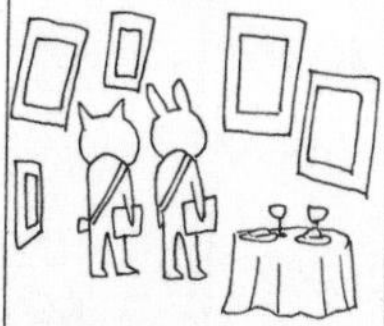

I visited all the museums I wanted. My days were so enriching. It was such a great journey...

But I had terrible jet lag when I returned, and it took a while to recover from it.

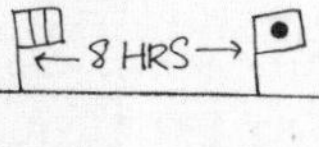
← 8 HRS →

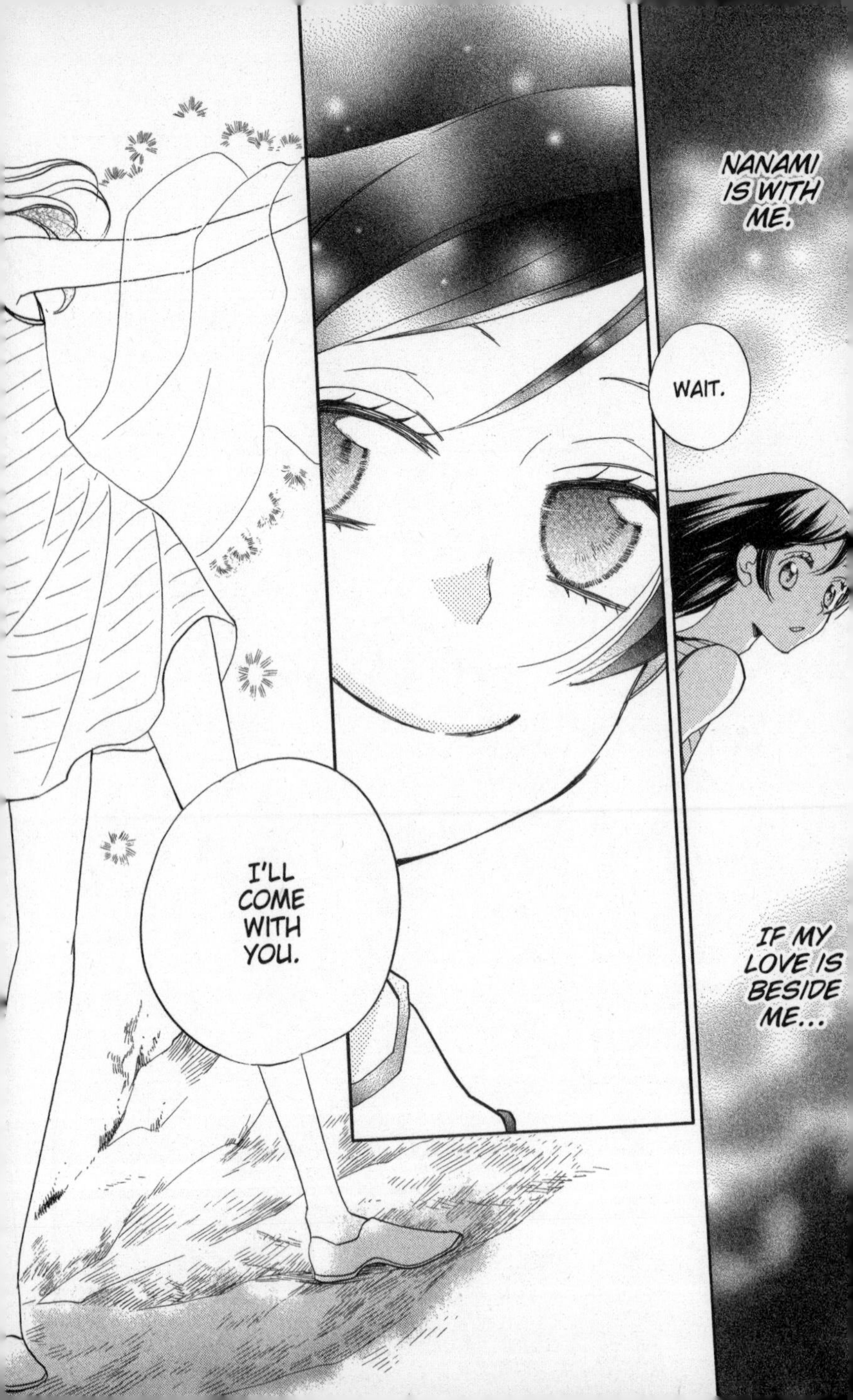
NANAMI IS WITH ME.
WAIT.
IF MY LOVE IS BESIDE ME...
I'LL COME WITH YOU.

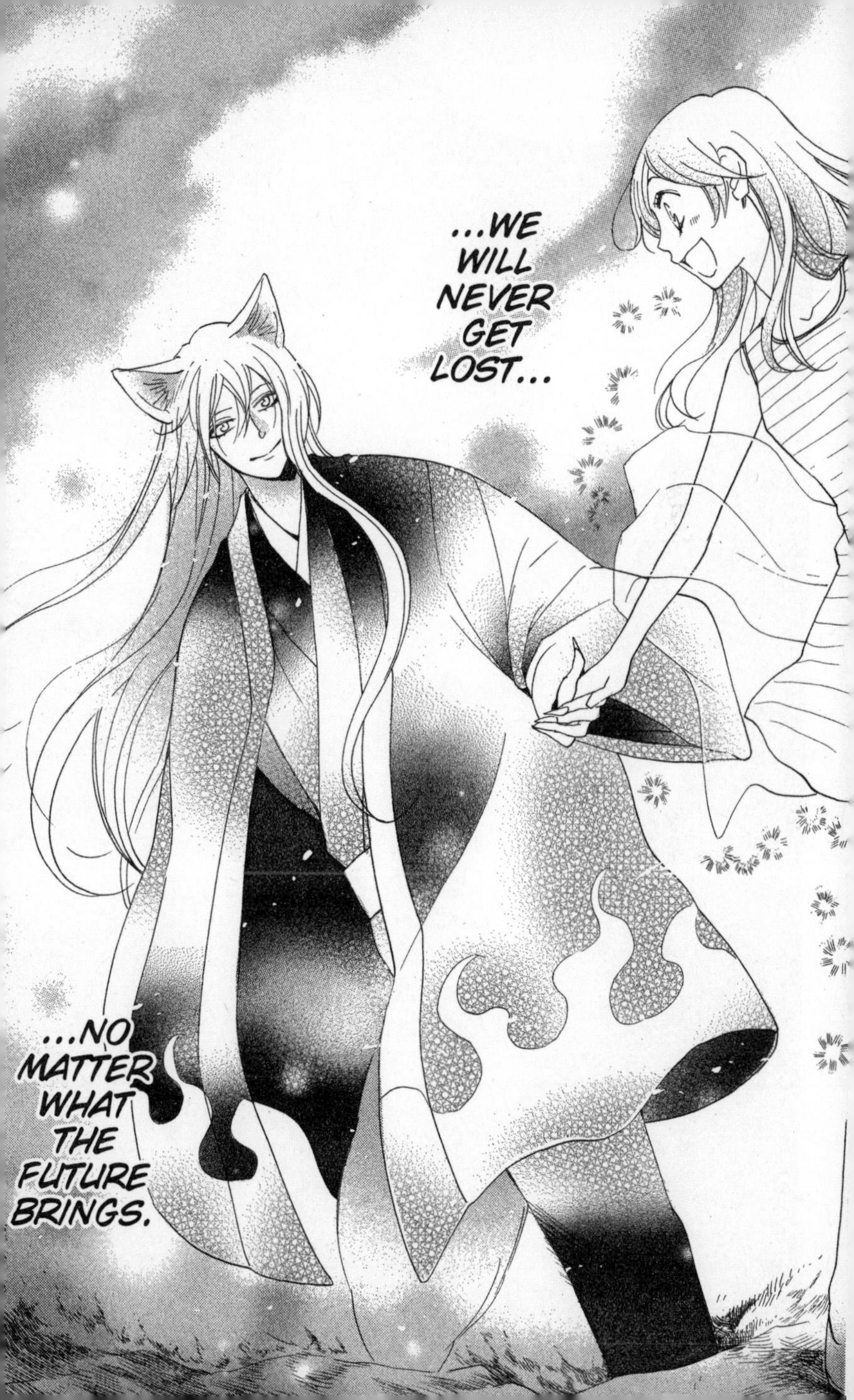
...WE WILL NEVER GET LOST...
...NO MATTER WHAT THE FUTURE BRINGS.

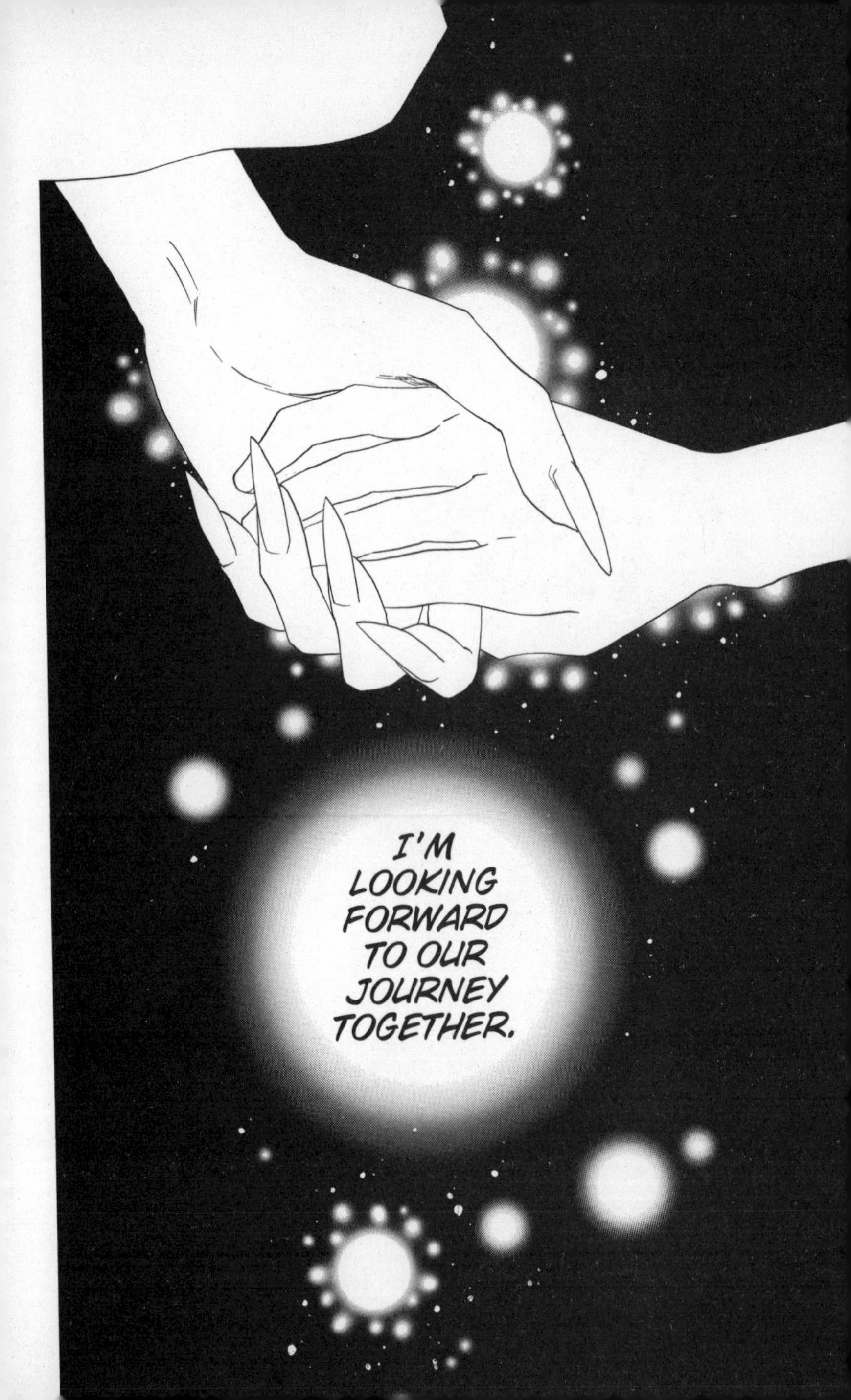
I'M LOOKING FORWARD TO OUR JOURNEY TOGETHER.

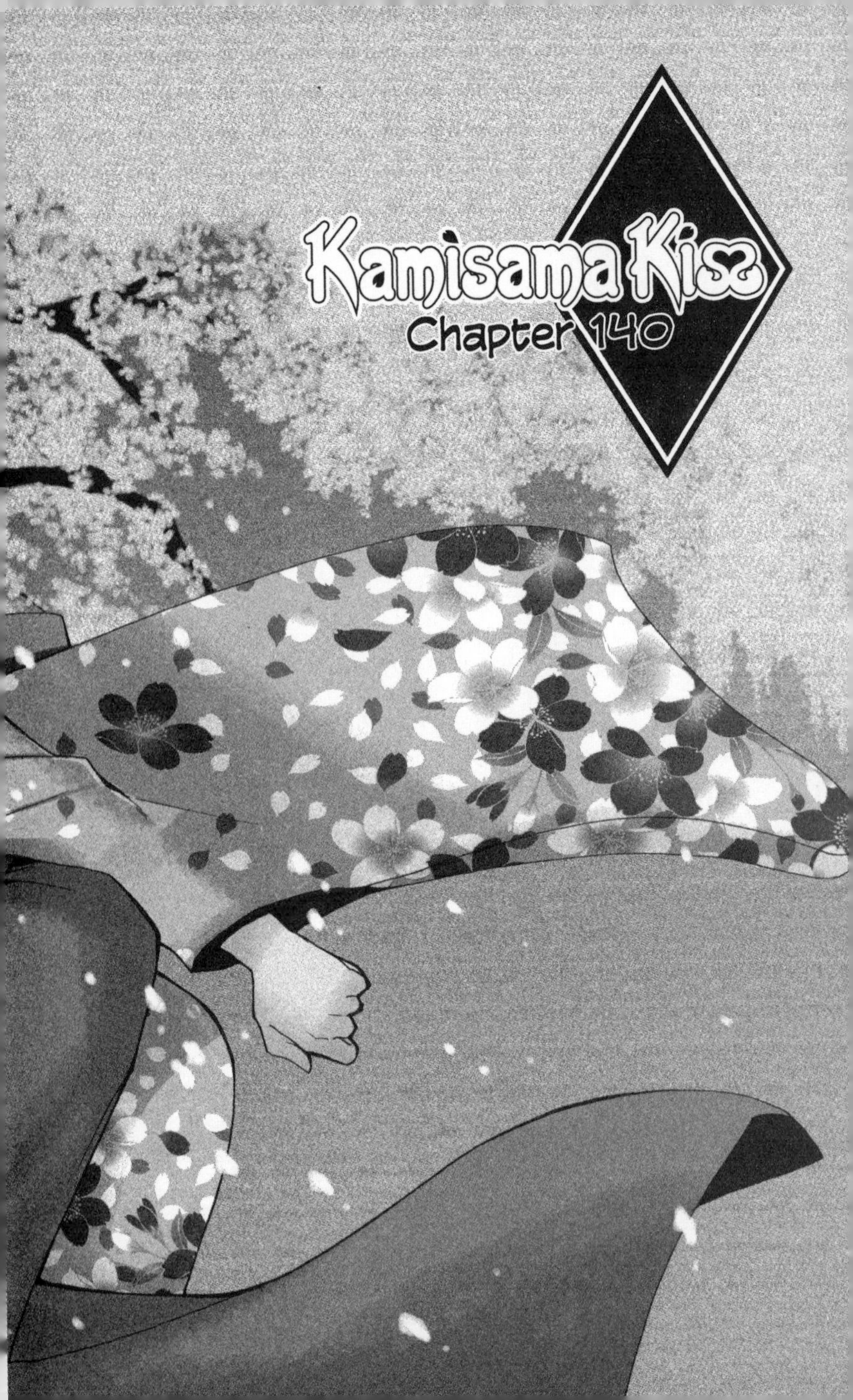
Kamisama Kiss
Chapter 140

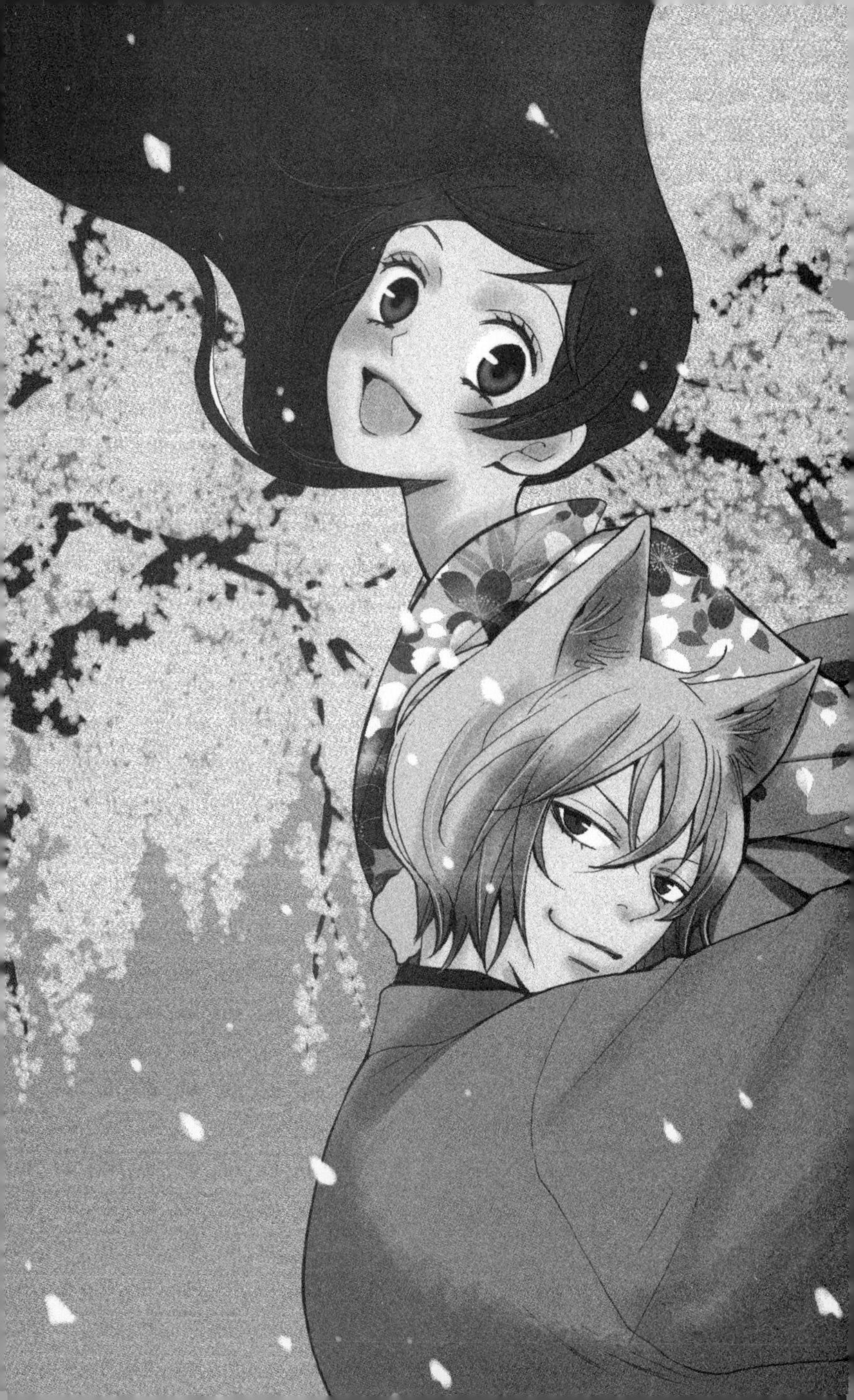

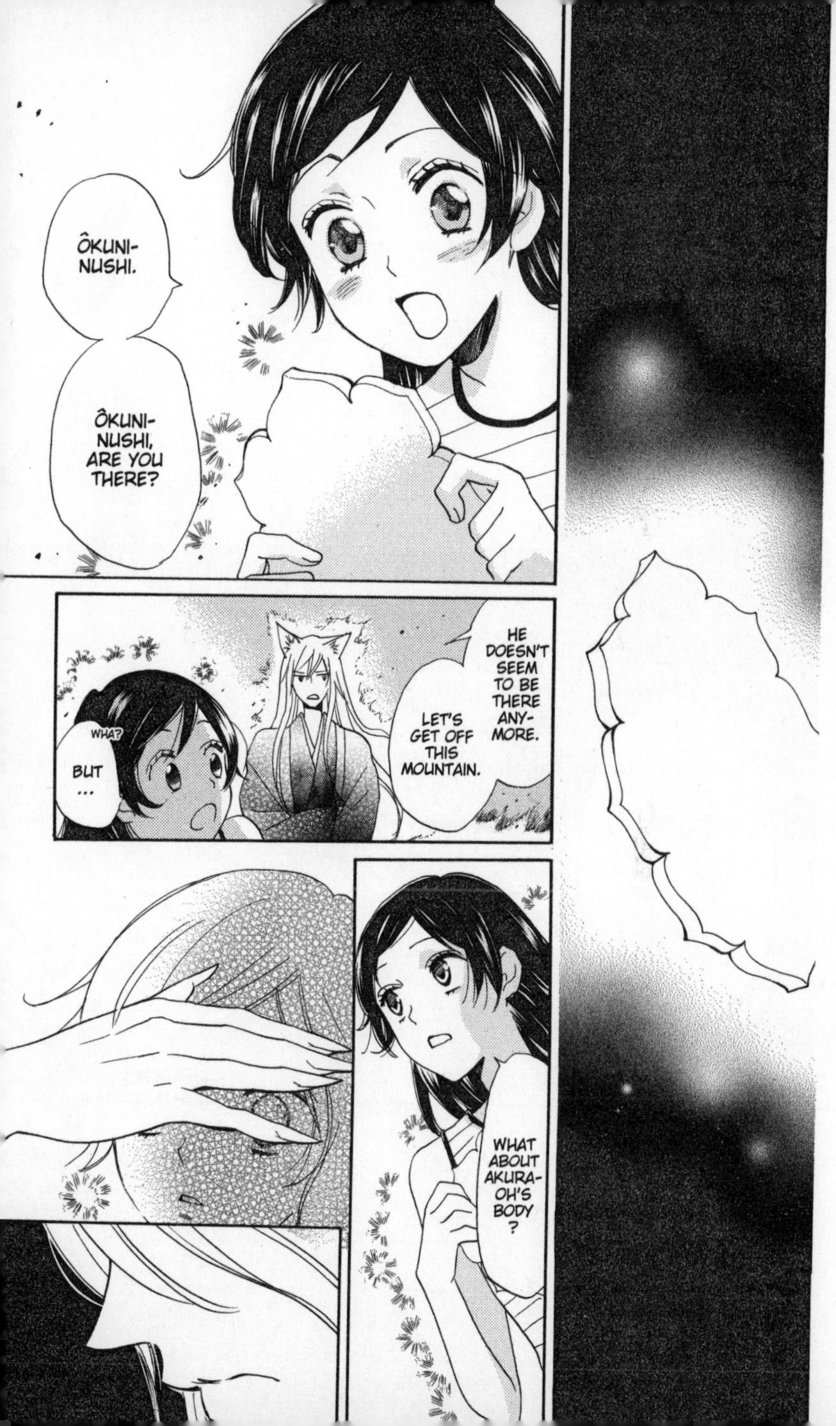
ÔKUNI-NUSHI.
ÔKUNI-NUSHI, ARE YOU THERE?
HE DOESN'T SEEM TO BE THERE ANY-MORE.
LET'S GET OFF THIS MOUNTAIN.
WHA?
BUT ...
WHAT ABOUT AKURA-OH'S BODY?

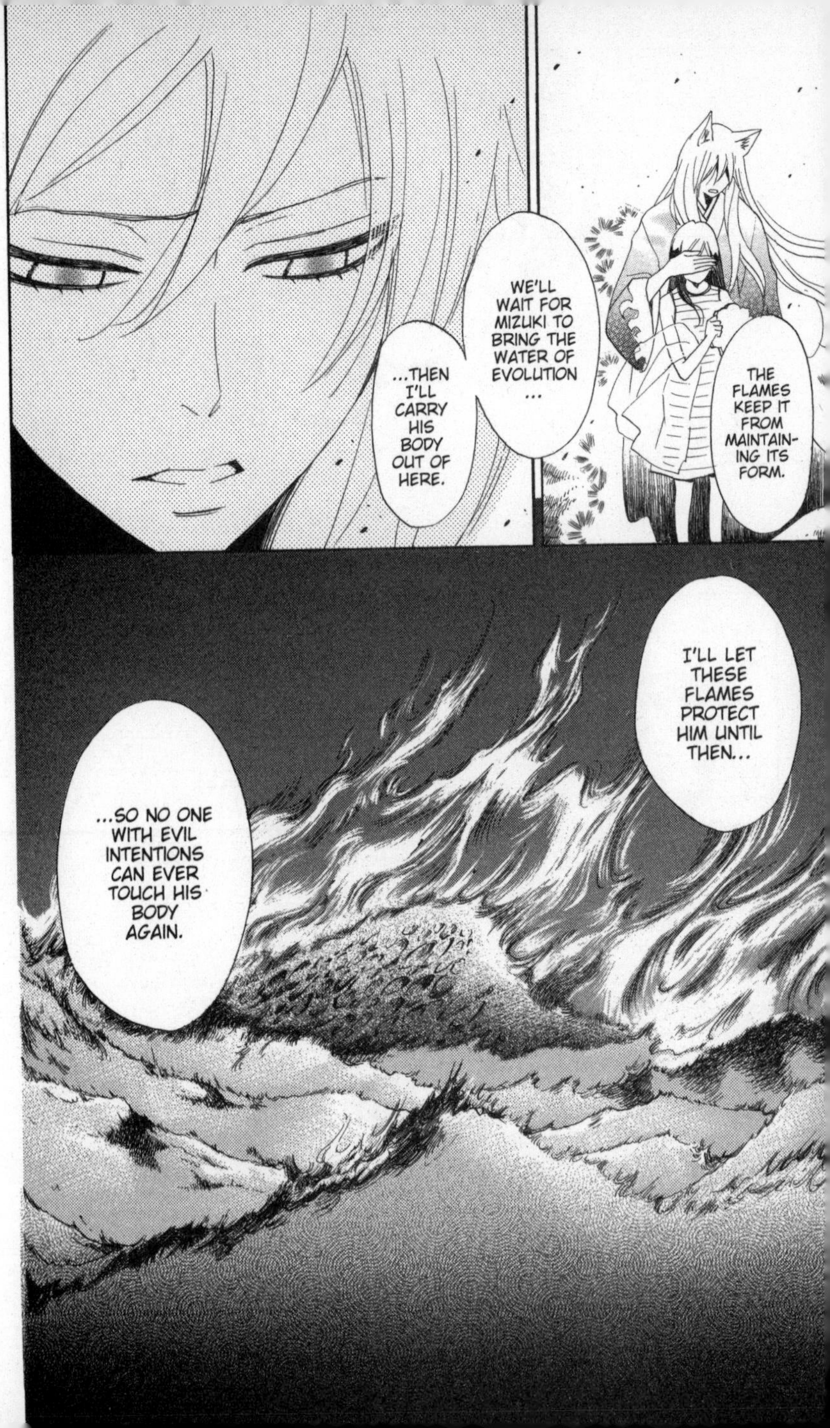
THE FLAMES KEEP IT FROM MAINTAINING ITS FORM.
WE'LL WAIT FOR MIZUKI TO BRING THE WATER OF EVOLUTION...
...THEN I'LL CARRY HIS BODY OUT OF HERE.
I'LL LET THESE FLAMES PROTECT HIM UNTIL THEN...
...SO NO ONE WITH EVIL INTENTIONS CAN EVER TOUCH HIS BODY AGAIN.

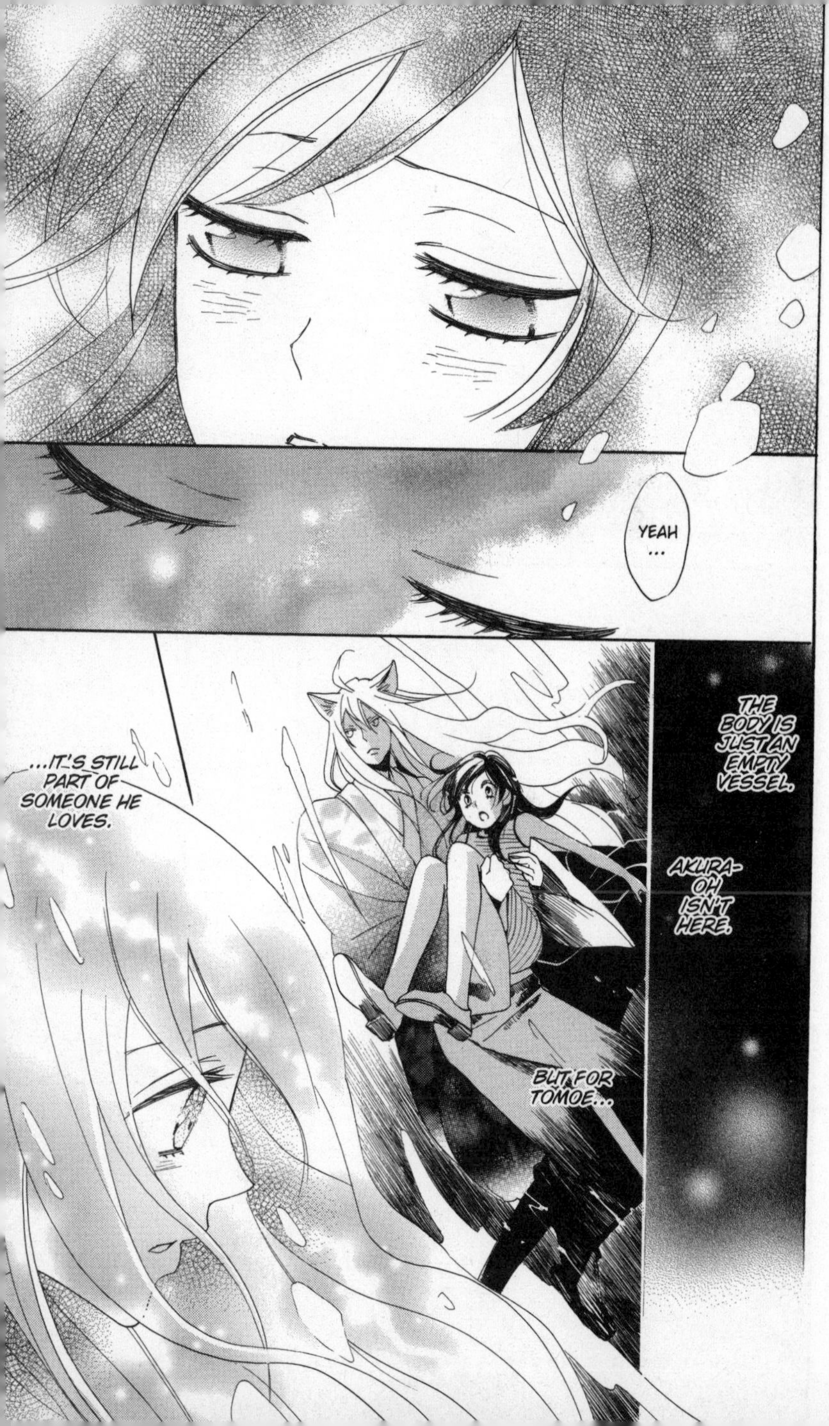
YEAH ...
THE BODY IS JUST AN EMPTY VESSEL.
AKURA-OH ISN'T HERE.
BUT FOR TOMOE...
...IT'S STILL PART OF SOMEONE HE LOVES.

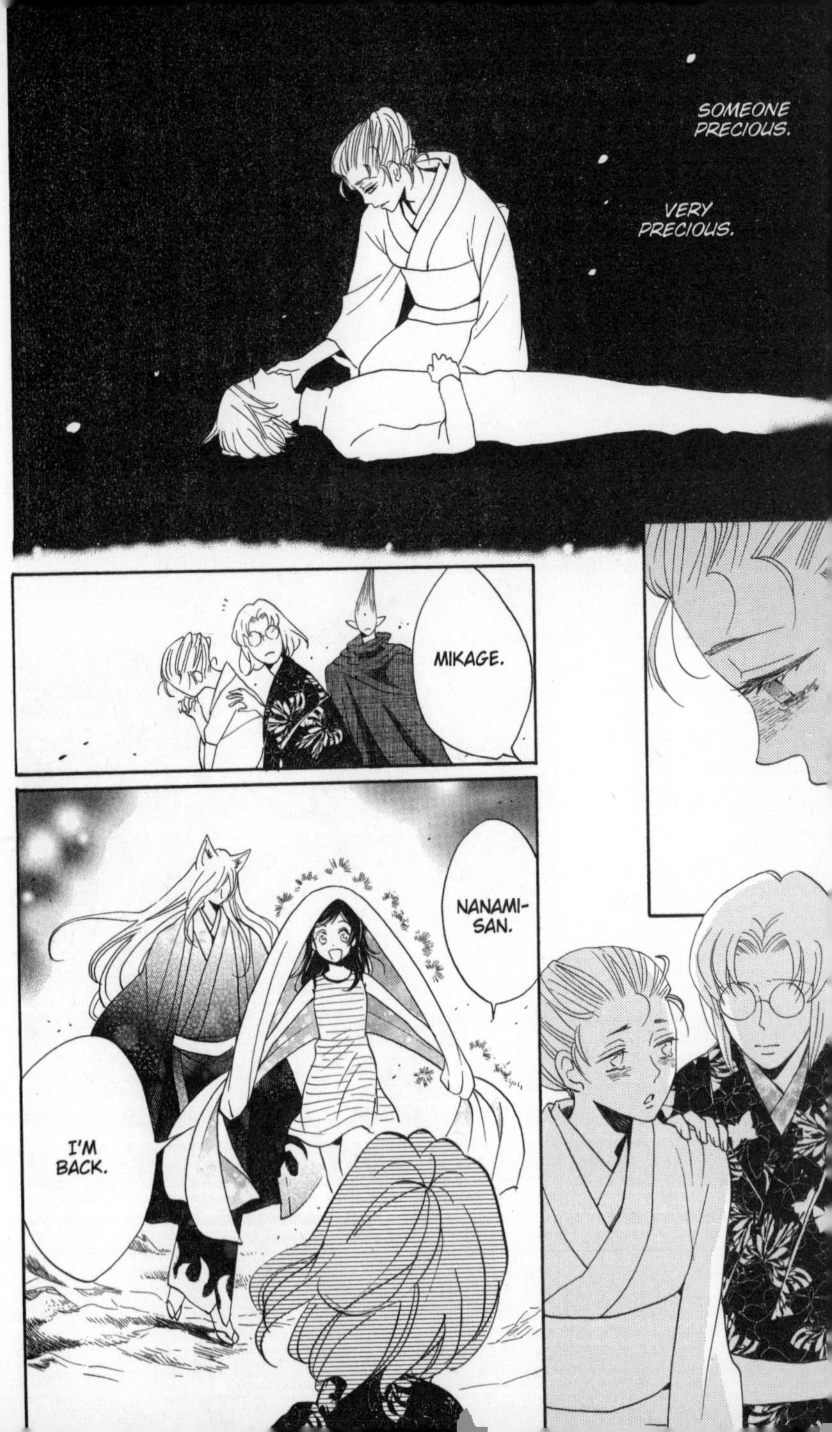
SOMEONE PRECIOUS.
VERY PRECIOUS.
MIKAGE.
NANAMI-SAN.
I'M BACK.

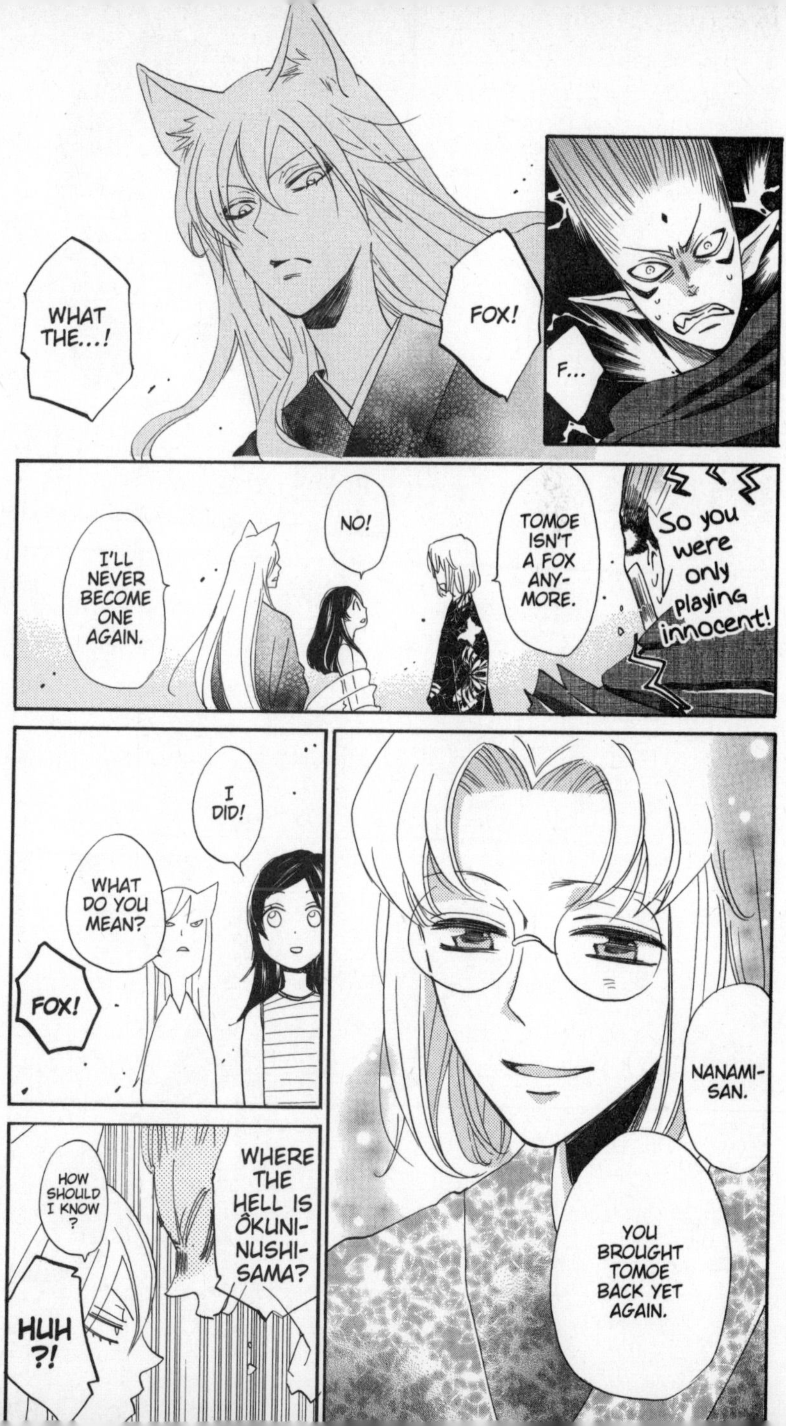
F...
FOX!
WHAT THE...!
So you were only playing innocent!
TOMOE ISN'T A FOX ANYMORE.
NO!
I'LL NEVER BECOME ONE AGAIN.
NANAMI-SAN.
YOU BROUGHT TOMOE BACK YET AGAIN.
I DID!
WHAT DO YOU MEAN?
FOX!
WHERE THE HELL IS ÔKUNINUSHI-SAMA?
HOW SHOULD I KNOW?
HUH?!

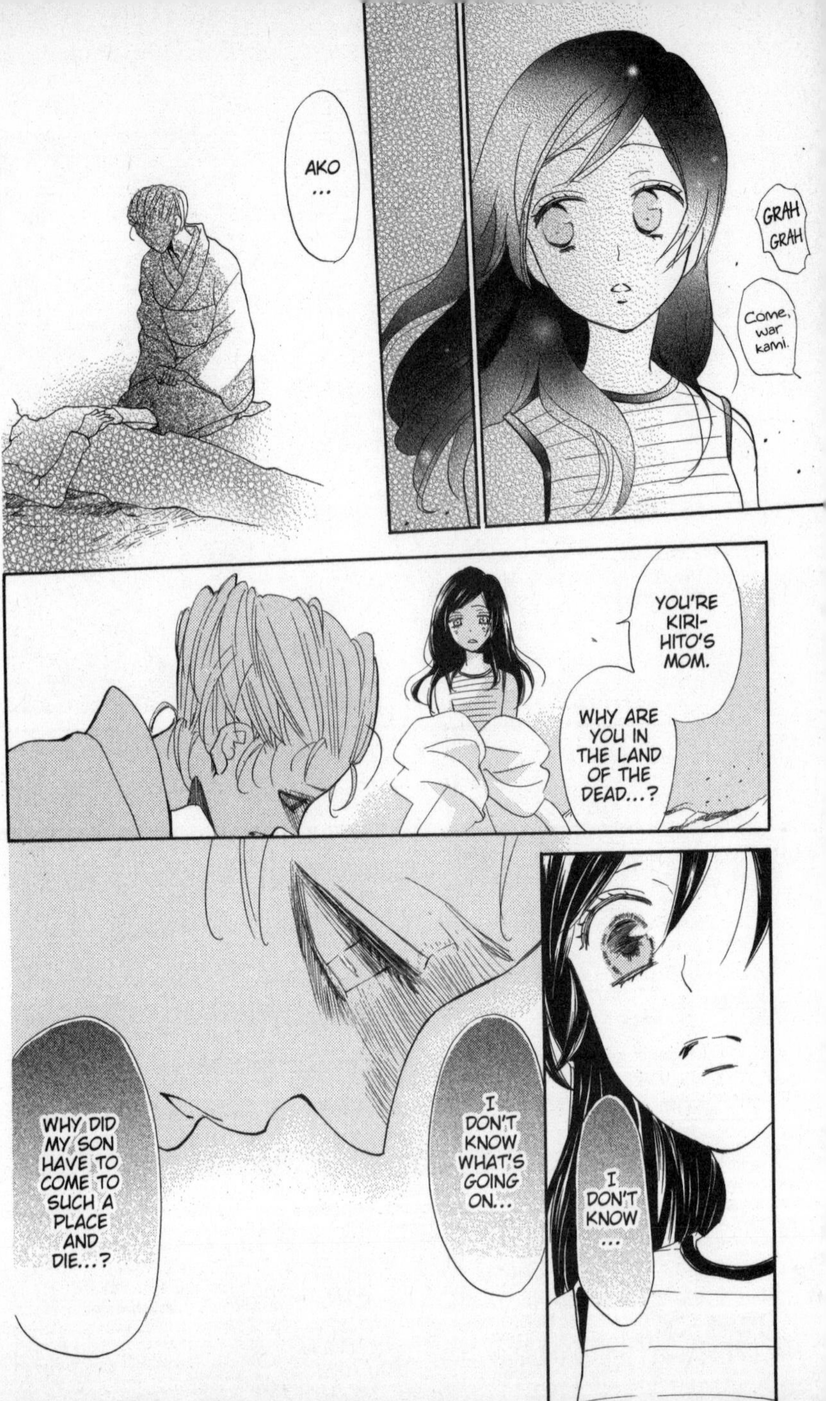
GRAH GRAH
Come, war kami.
AKO ...
YOU'RE KIRI-HITO'S MOM.
WHY ARE YOU IN THE LAND OF THE DEAD...?
I DON'T KNOW ...
I DON'T KNOW WHAT'S GOING ON...
WHY DID MY SON HAVE TO COME TO SUCH A PLACE AND DIE...?

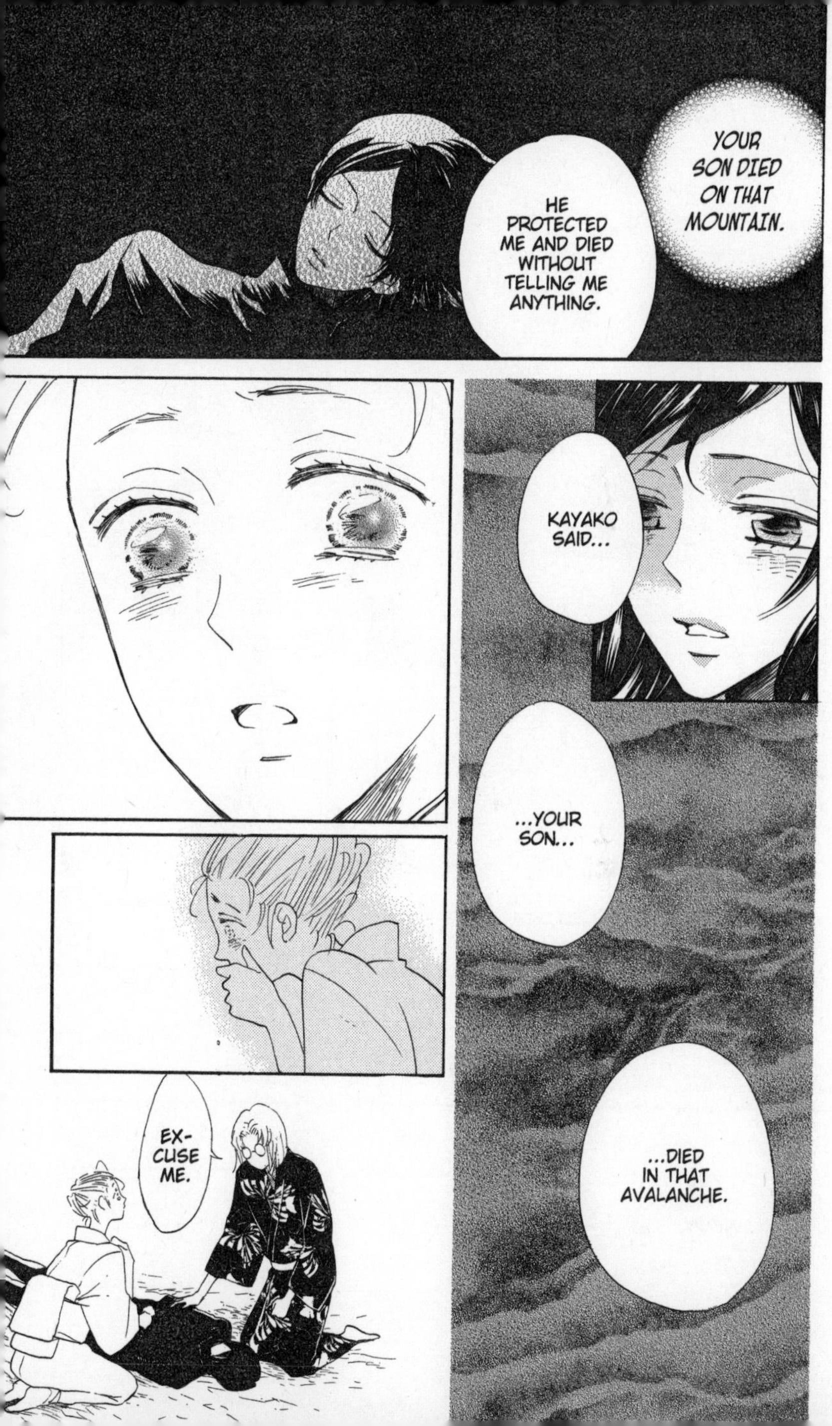
YOUR SON DIED ON THAT MOUNTAIN.
HE PROTECTED ME AND DIED WITHOUT TELLING ME ANYTHING.
KAYAKO SAID...
...YOUR SON...
...DIED IN THAT AVALANCHE.
EX-CUSE ME.

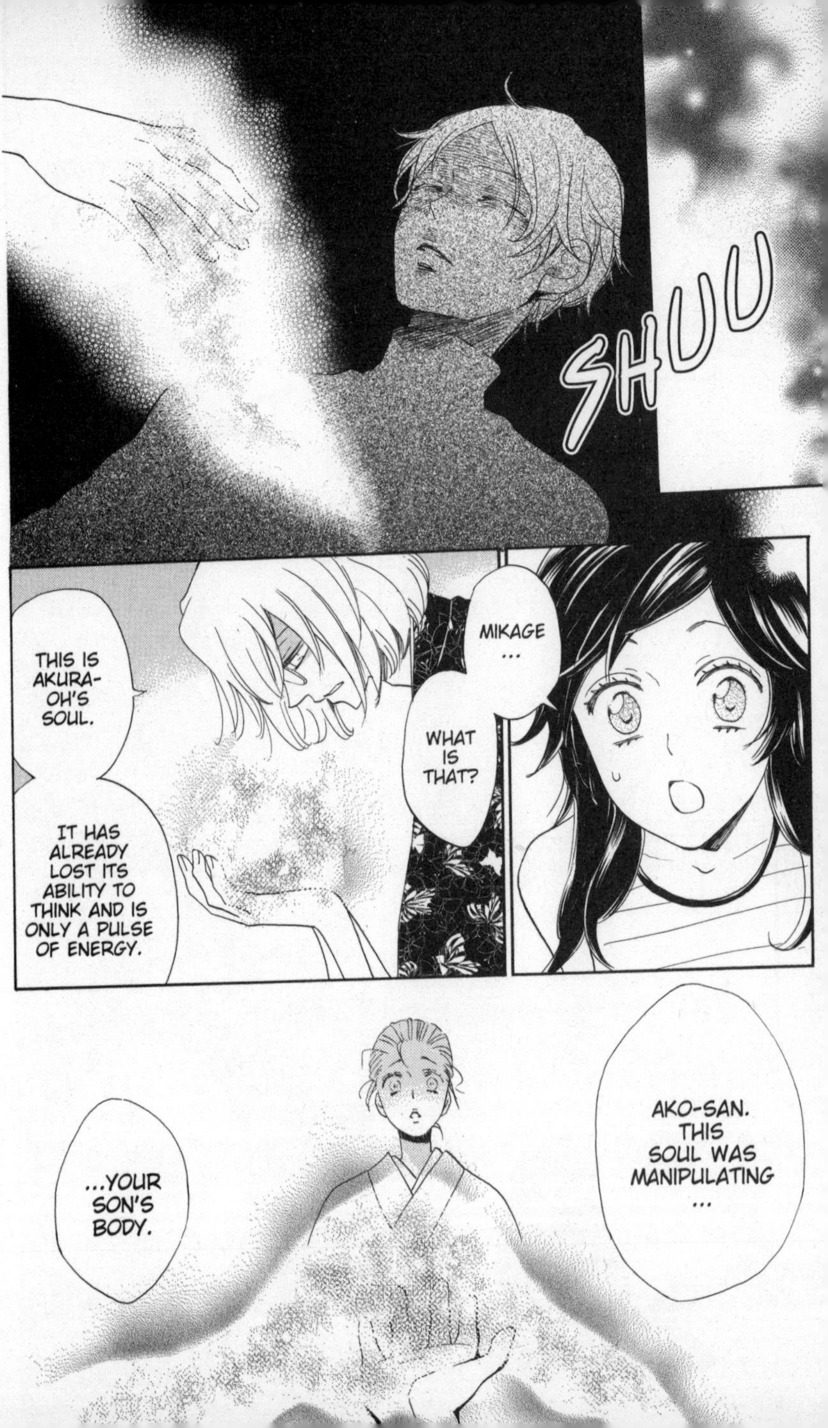
SHUU
MIKAGE ...
WHAT IS THAT?
THIS IS AKURA-OH'S SOUL.
IT HAS ALREADY LOST ITS ABILITY TO THINK AND IS ONLY A PULSE OF ENERGY.
AKO-SAN. THIS SOUL WAS MANIPULATING ...
...YOUR SON'S BODY.

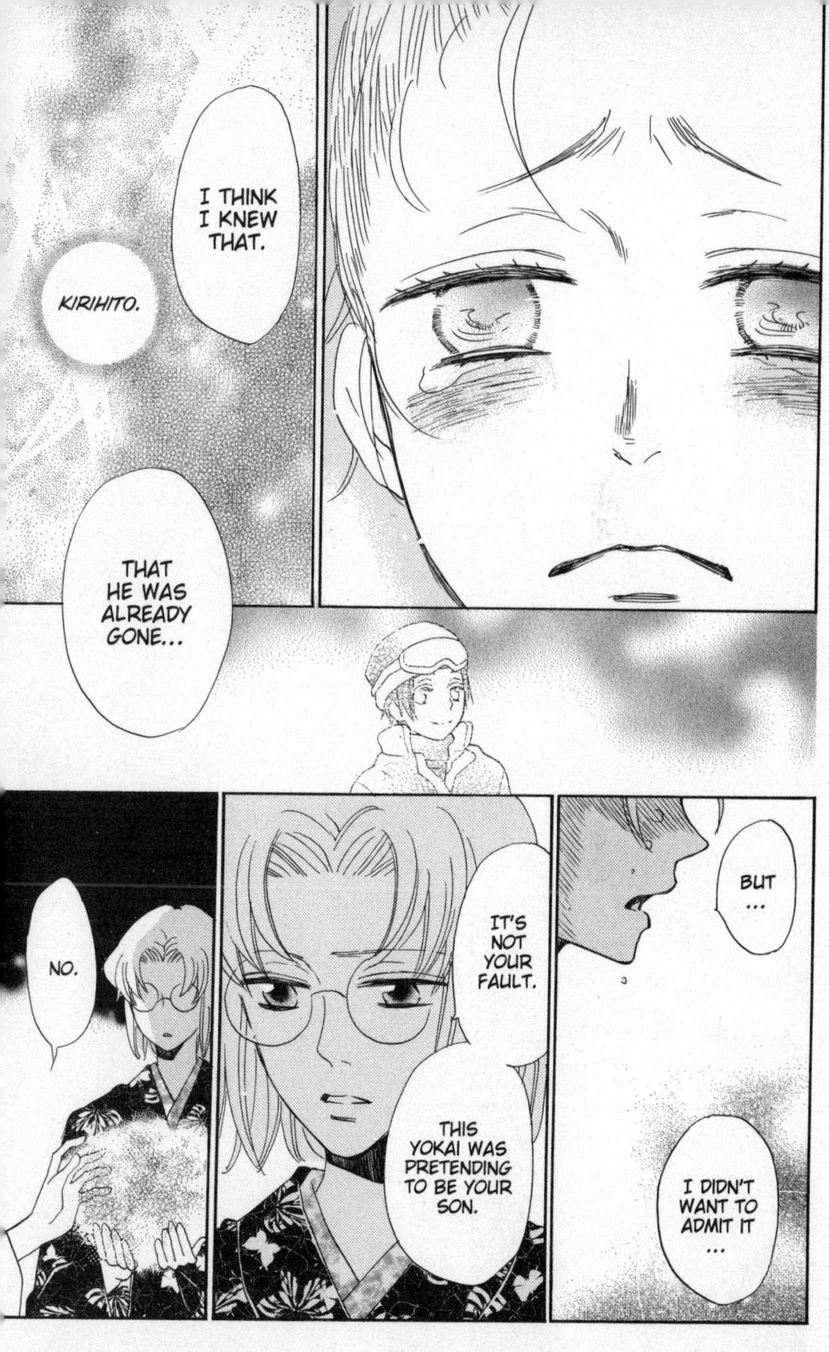
I THINK I KNEW THAT.
KIRIHITO.
THAT HE WAS ALREADY GONE...
BUT ...
I DIDN'T WANT TO ADMIT IT ...
IT'S NOT YOUR FAULT.
THIS YOKAI WAS PRETENDING TO BE YOUR SON.
NO.

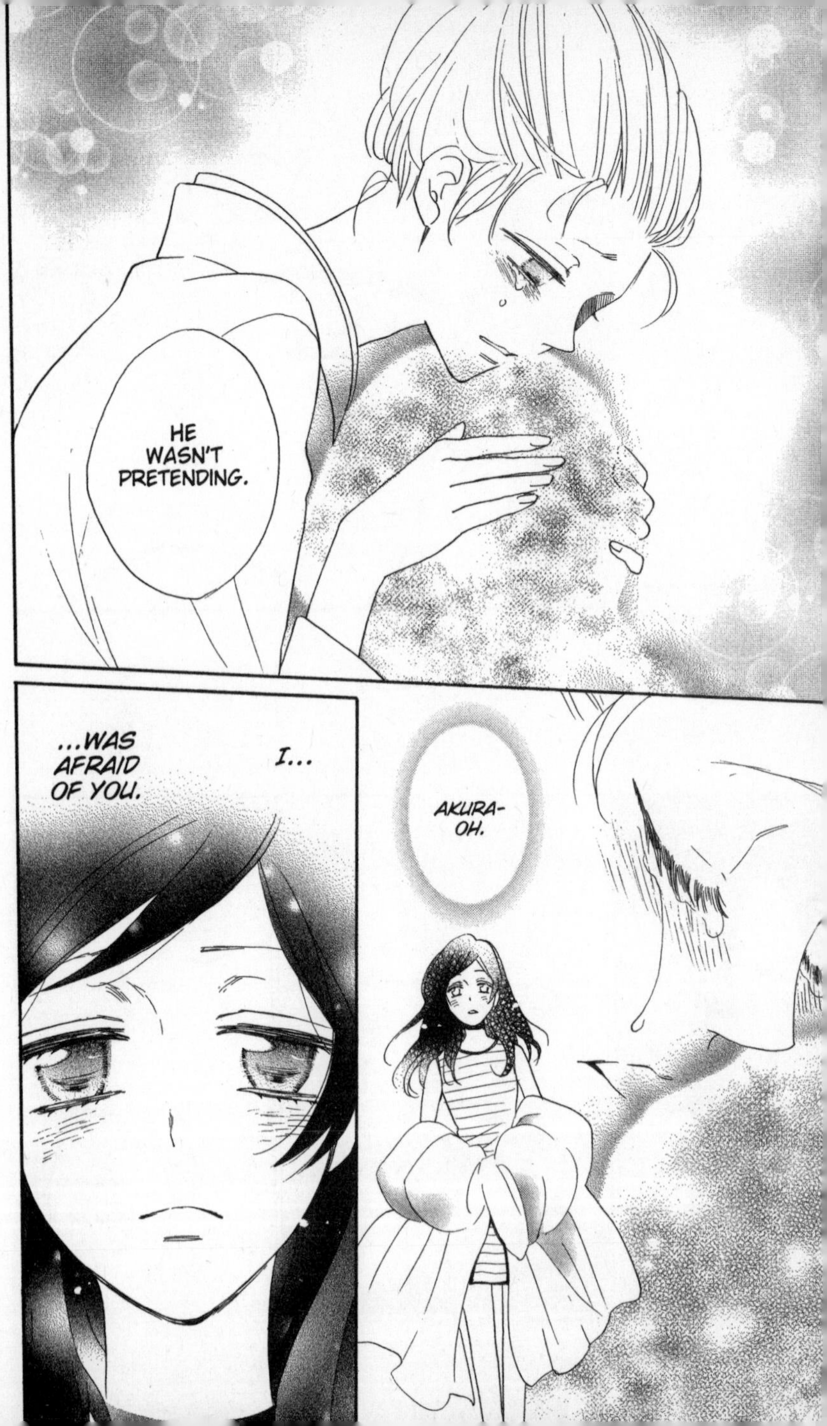
HE WASN'T PRETENDING.
AKURA-OH.
I...
...WAS AFRAID OF YOU.

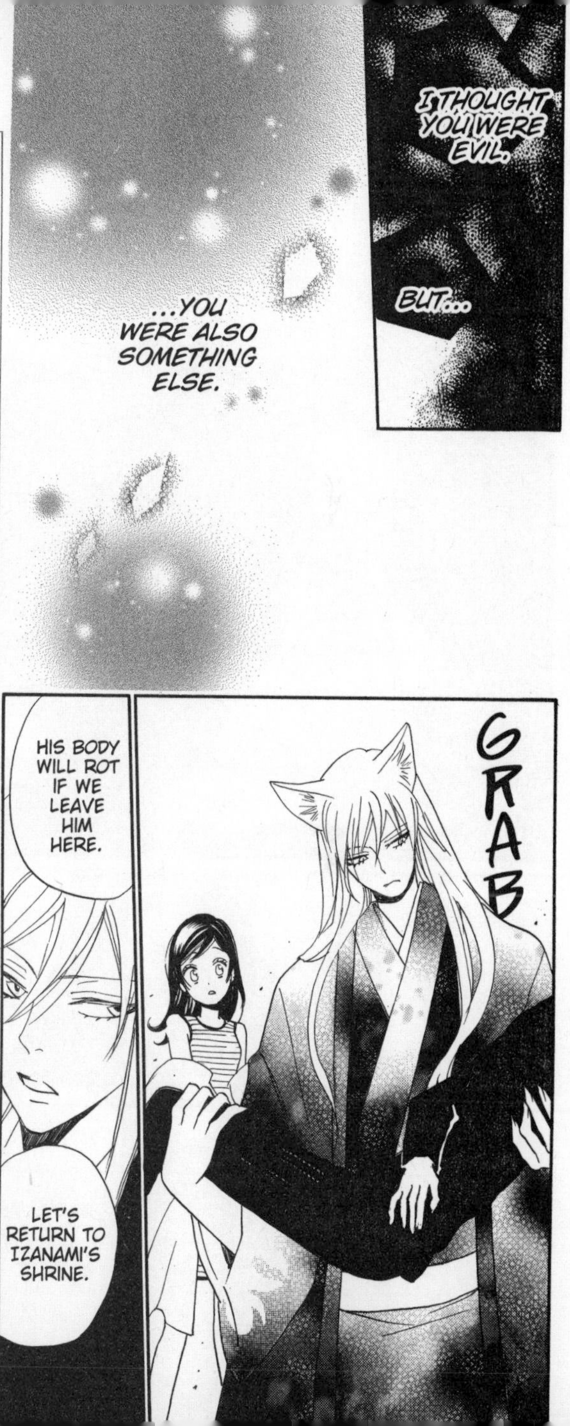
I THOUGHT YOU WERE EVIL.
BUT...
...YOU WERE ALSO SOMETHING ELSE.
GRAB
HIS BODY WILL ROT IF WE LEAVE HIM HERE.
LET'S RETURN TO IZANAMI'S SHRINE.

III

I visited the Catacombs of Paris.

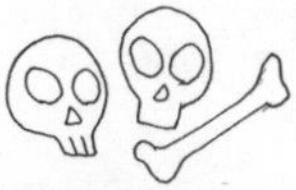

The catacombs are underground ossuaries with the remains of six million people.

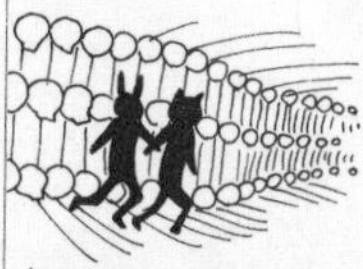

It was so huge I felt like I was going to get lost. There were so many bones piled up along the walls. When I finally reached the exit and went outside...

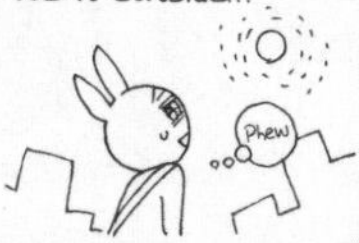
Phew

...I felt very relieved to have come back from a monochrome world to the colorful world aboveground. It was a very interesting experience! Do visit the catacombs when you visit Paris.

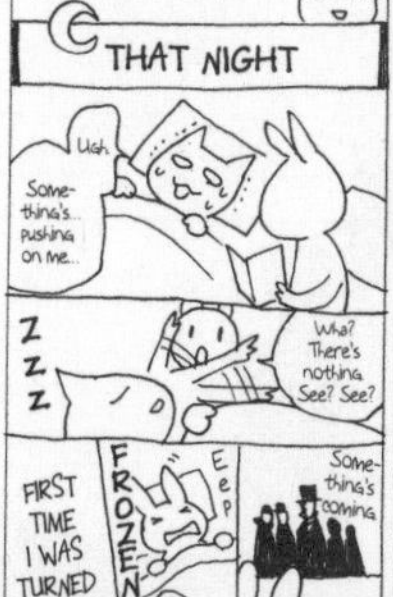
THAT NIGHT
Ugh.
Some-thing's pushing on me...
Z Z Z
Wha? There's nothing See? See?
Some-thing's coming
Eep
FROZEN
FIRST TIME I WAS TURNED TO STONE.
Z Z Z

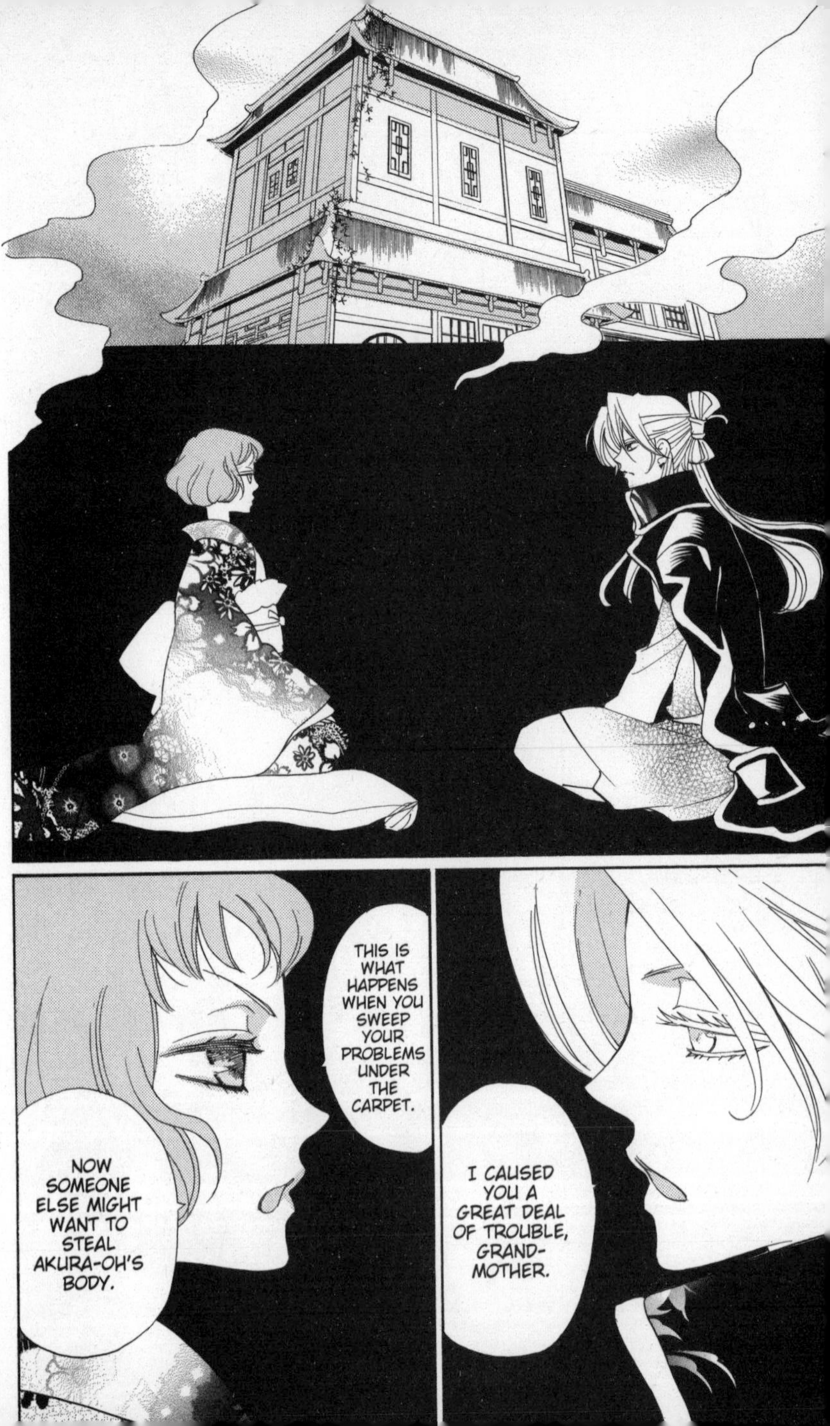
I CAUSED YOU A GREAT DEAL OF TROUBLE, GRAND-MOTHER.
THIS IS WHAT HAPPENS WHEN YOU SWEEP YOUR PROBLEMS UNDER THE CARPET.
NOW SOMEONE ELSE MIGHT WANT TO STEAL AKURA-OH'S BODY.

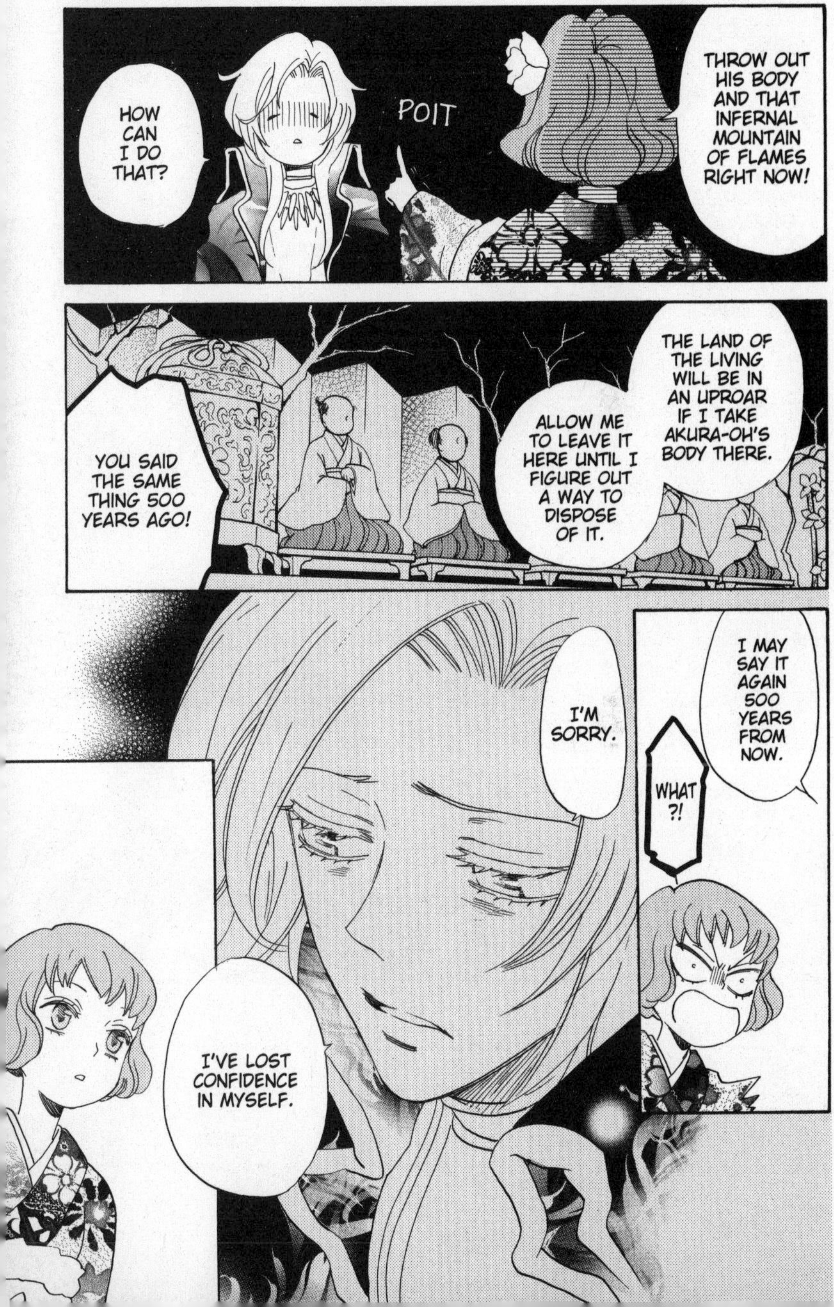
THROW OUT HIS BODY AND THAT INFERNAL MOUNTAIN OF FLAMES RIGHT NOW!
POIT
HOW CAN I DO THAT?
THE LAND OF THE LIVING WILL BE IN AN UPROAR IF I TAKE AKURA-OH'S BODY THERE.
ALLOW ME TO LEAVE IT HERE UNTIL I FIGURE OUT A WAY TO DISPOSE OF IT.
YOU SAID THE SAME THING 500 YEARS AGO!
I MAY SAY IT AGAIN 500 YEARS FROM NOW.
WHAT ?!
I'M SORRY.
I'VE LOST CONFIDENCE IN MYSELF.

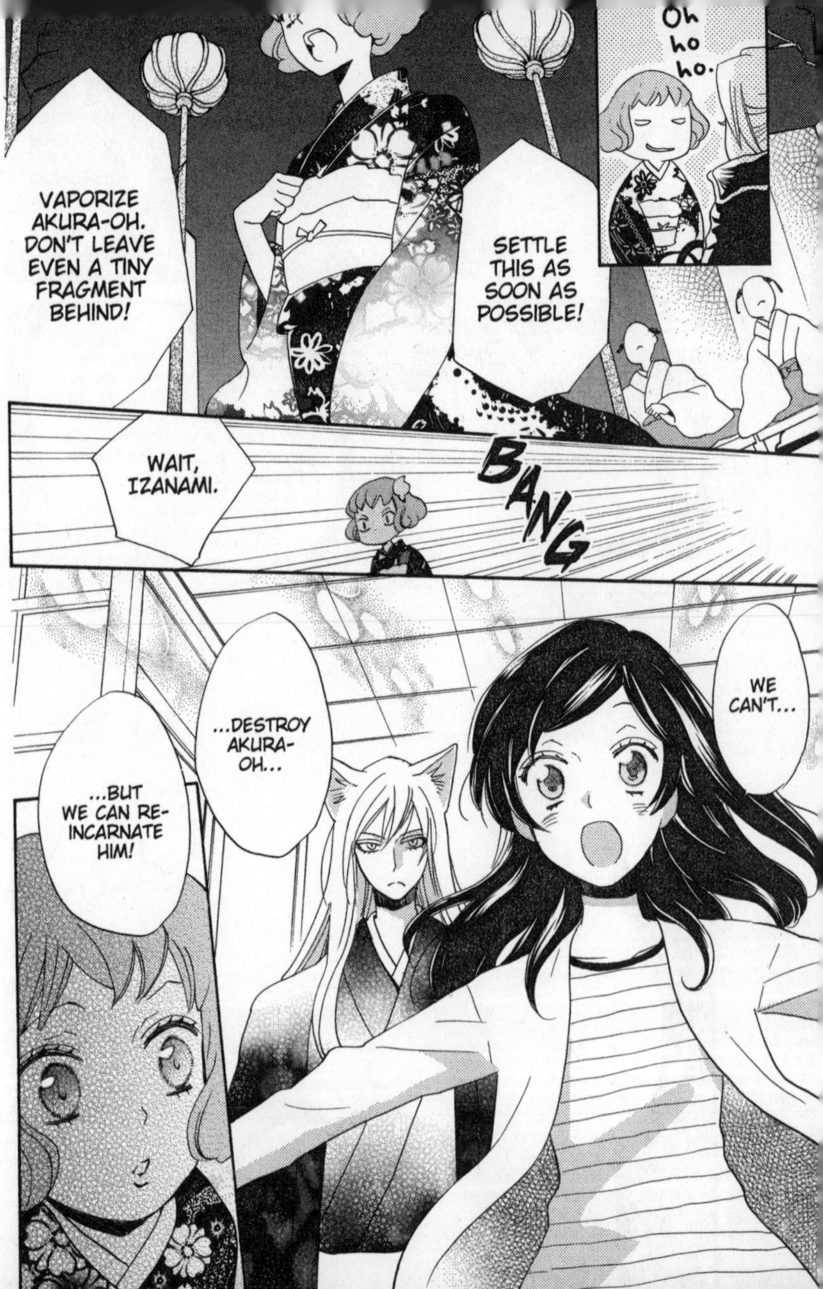
Oh ho ho.
SETTLE THIS AS SOON AS POSSIBLE!
VAPORIZE AKURA-OH. DON'T LEAVE EVEN A TINY FRAGMENT BEHIND!
BANG
WAIT, IZANAMI.
WE CAN'T...
...DESTROY AKURA-OH...
...BUT WE CAN RE-INCARNATE HIM!

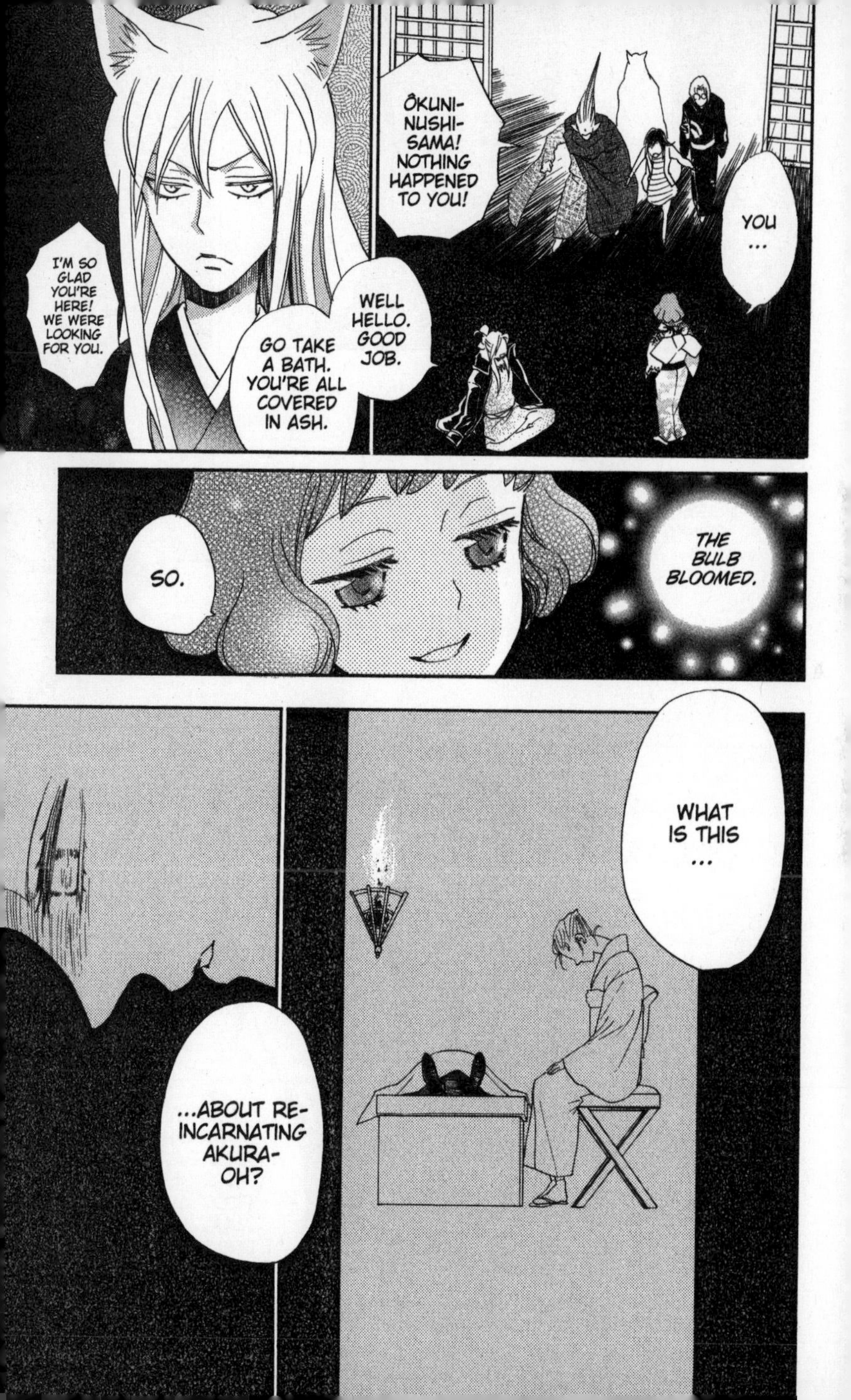

ÔKUNI-NUSHI-SAMA! NOTHING HAPPENED TO YOU!
YOU ...
WELL HELLO. GOOD JOB.
GO TAKE A BATH. YOU'RE ALL COVERED IN ASH.
I'M SO GLAD YOU'RE HERE! WE WERE LOOKING FOR YOU.
THE BULB BLOOMED.
SO.
WHAT IS THIS ...
...ABOUT RE-INCARNATING AKURA-OH?

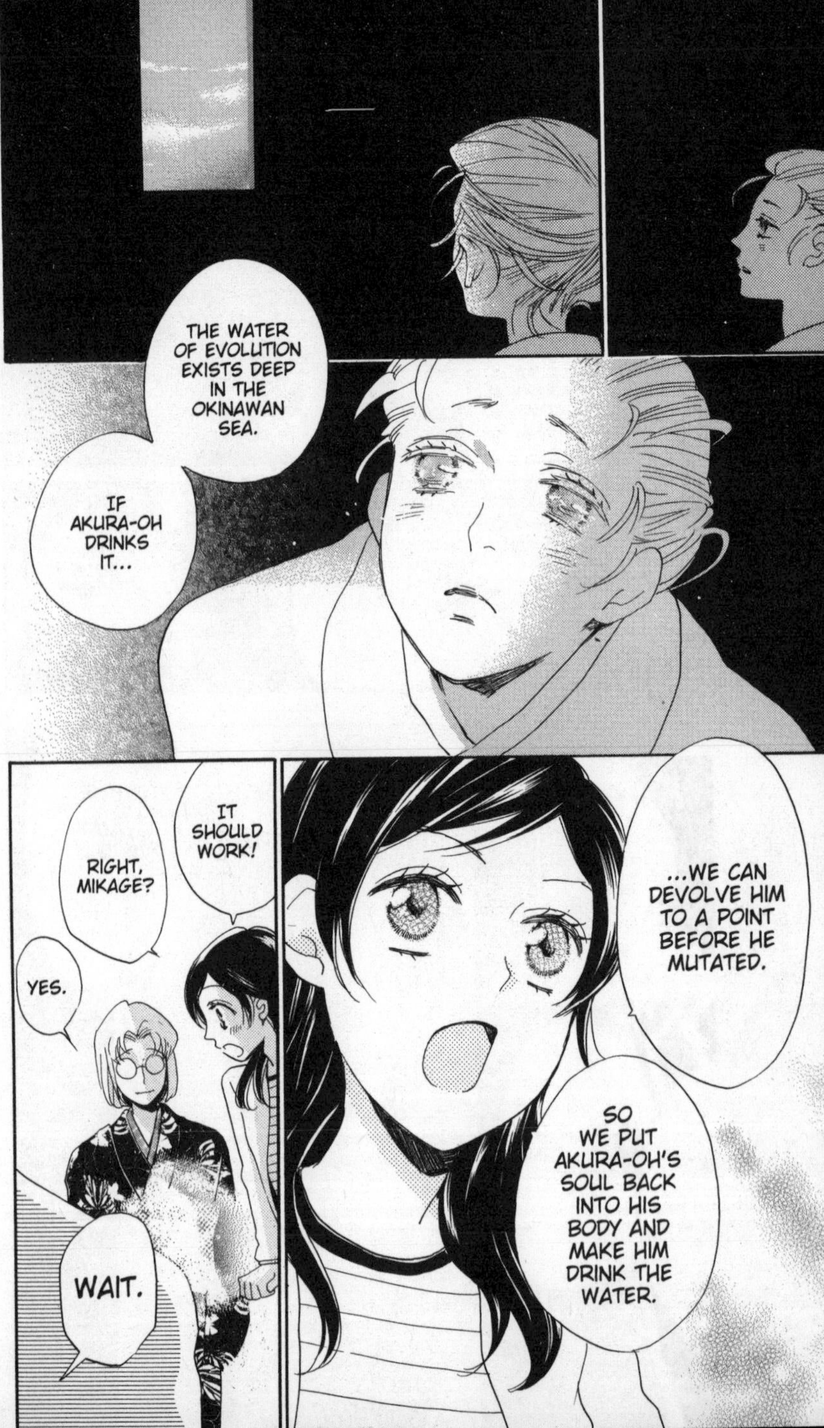
THE WATER OF EVOLUTION EXISTS DEEP IN THE OKINAWAN SEA.
IF AKURA-OH DRINKS IT...
...WE CAN DEVOLVE HIM TO A POINT BEFORE HE MUTATED.
SO WE PUT AKURA-OH'S SOUL BACK INTO HIS BODY AND MAKE HIM DRINK THE WATER.
IT SHOULD WORK!
RIGHT, MIKAGE?
YES.
WAIT.

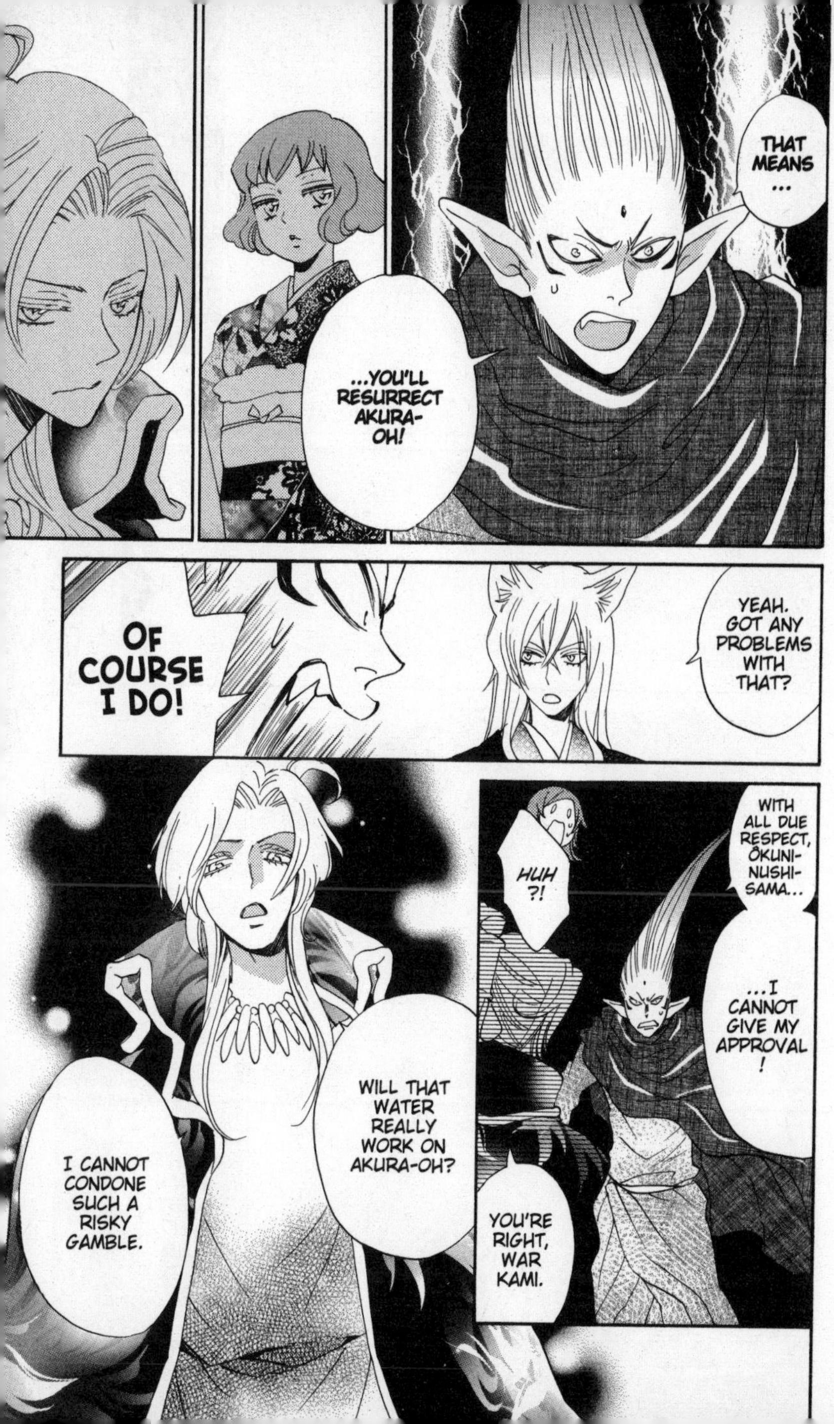
THAT MEANS...
...YOU'LL RESURRECT AKURA-OH!
YEAH. GOT ANY PROBLEMS WITH THAT?
OF COURSE I DO!
WITH ALL DUE RESPECT, ŌKUNI-NUSHI-SAMA...
HUH?!
...I CANNOT GIVE MY APPROVAL!
YOU'RE RIGHT, WAR KAMI.
WILL THAT WATER REALLY WORK ON AKURA-OH?
I CANNOT CONDONE SUCH A RISKY GAMBLE.

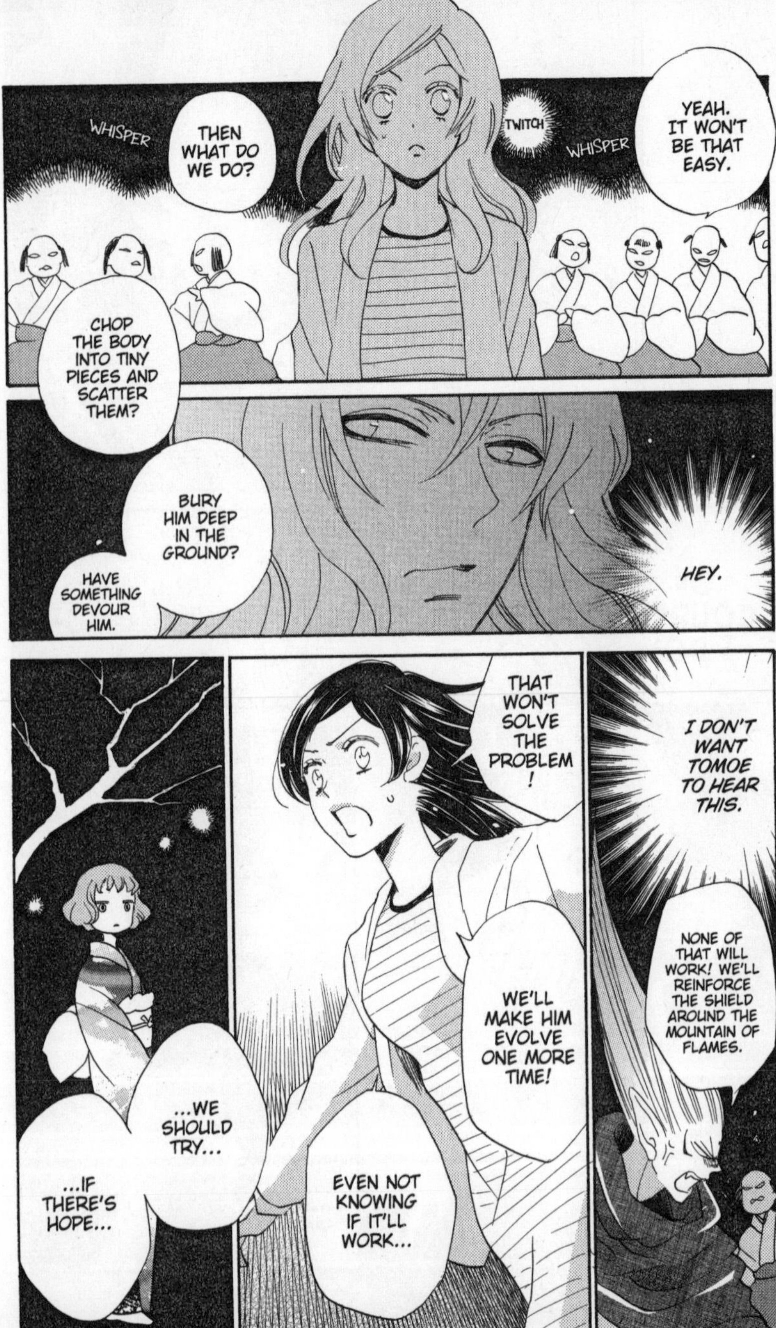
YEAH. IT WON'T BE THAT EASY.
WHISPER
TWITCH
THEN WHAT DO WE DO?
WHISPER
CHOP THE BODY INTO TINY PIECES AND SCATTER THEM?
HEY.
BURY HIM DEEP IN THE GROUND?
HAVE SOMETHING DEVOUR HIM.
I DON'T WANT TOMOE TO HEAR THIS.
NONE OF THAT WILL WORK! WE'LL REINFORCE THE SHIELD AROUND THE MOUNTAIN OF FLAMES.
THAT WON'T SOLVE THE PROBLEM!
WE'LL MAKE HIM EVOLVE ONE MORE TIME!
EVEN NOT KNOWING IF IT'LL WORK...
...WE SHOULD TRY...
...IF THERE'S HOPE...

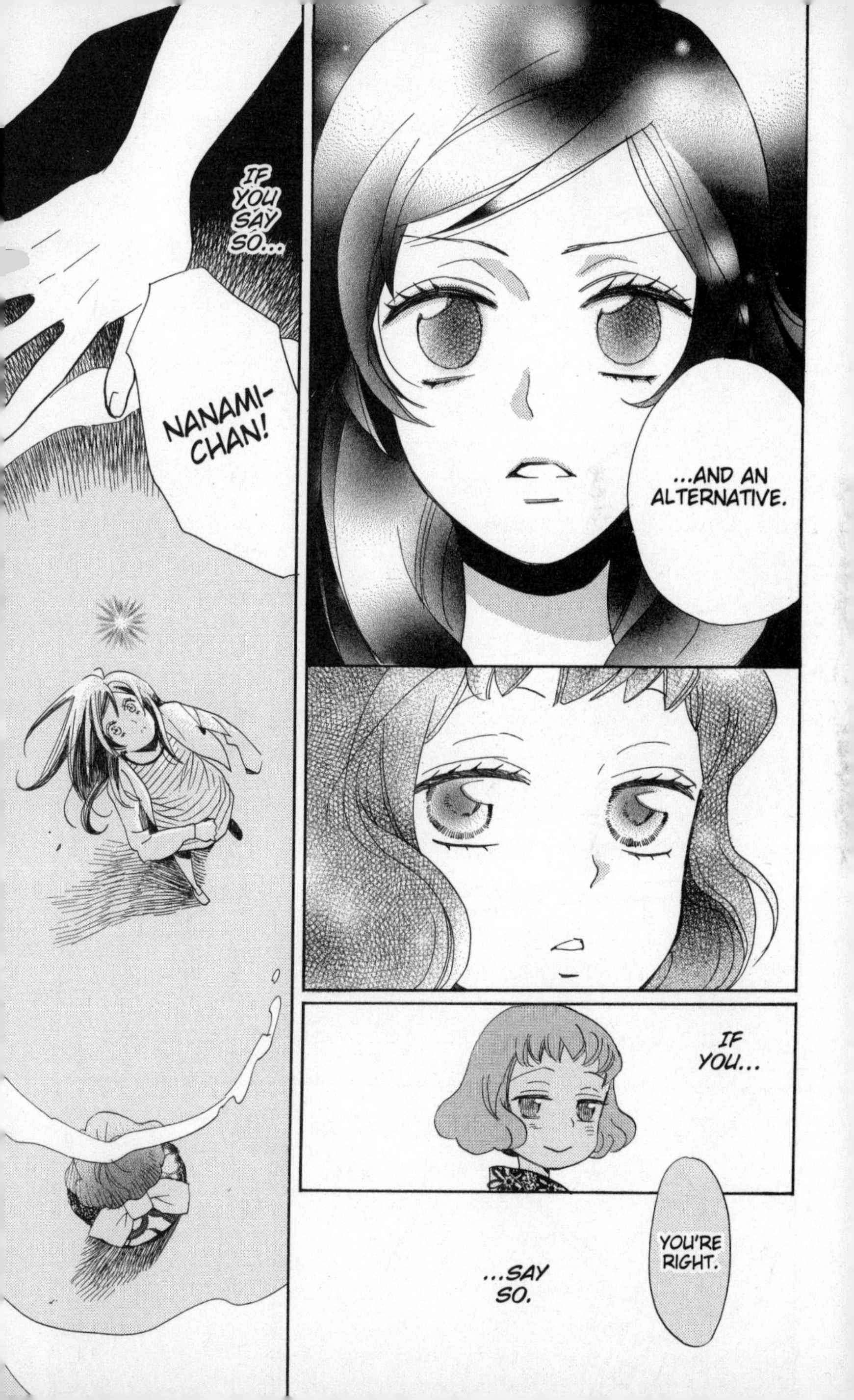
...AND AN ALTERNATIVE.
IF YOU...
YOU'RE RIGHT.
...SAY SO.
IF YOU SAY SO...
NANAMI-CHAN!

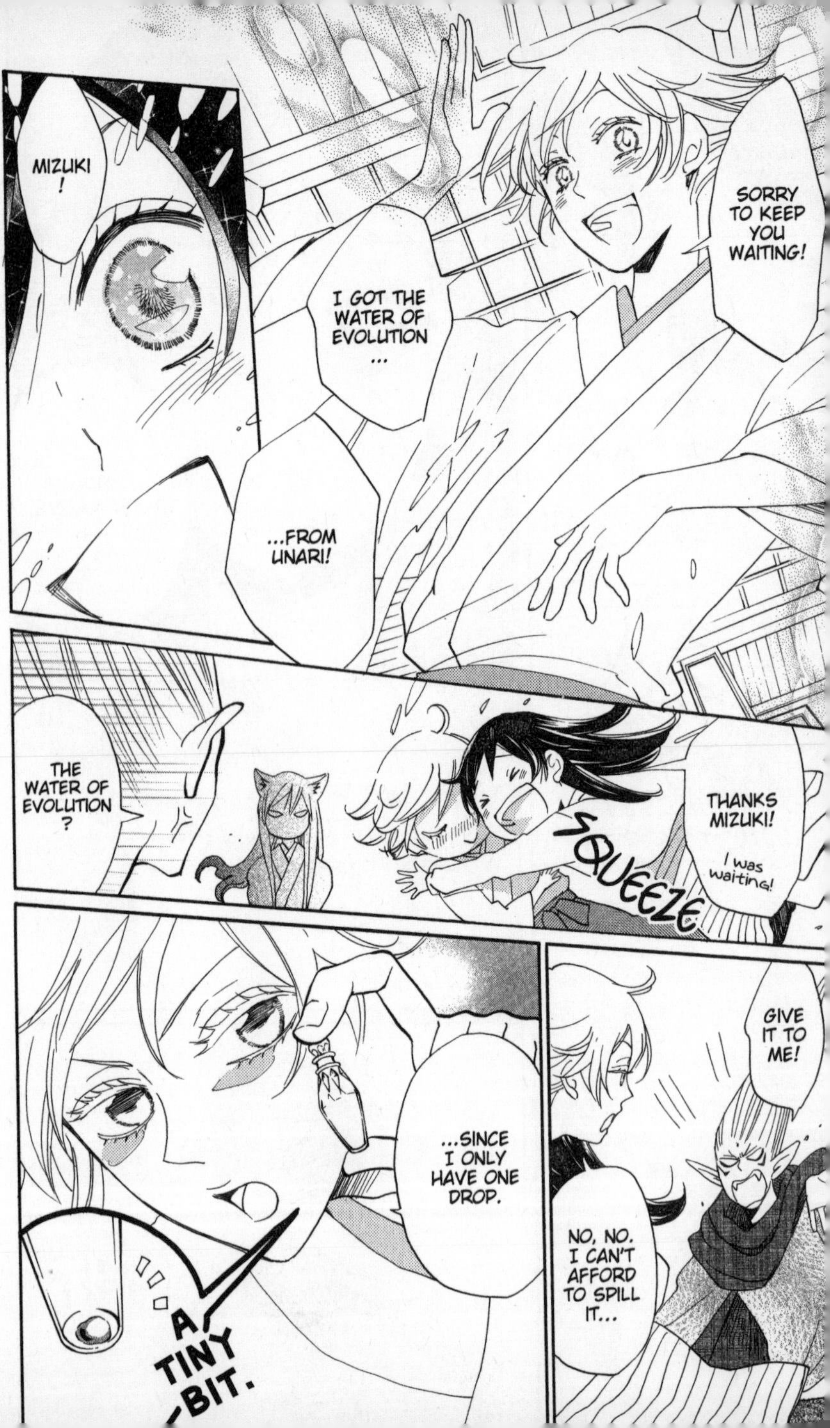
SORRY TO KEEP YOU WAITING!
I GOT THE WATER OF EVOLUTION...
...FROM UNARI!
MIZUKI!
THANKS MIZUKI!
I was waiting!
SQUEEZE
THE WATER OF EVOLUTION?
GIVE IT TO ME!
NO, NO. I CAN'T AFFORD TO SPILL IT...
...SINCE I ONLY HAVE ONE DROP.
A TINY BIT.

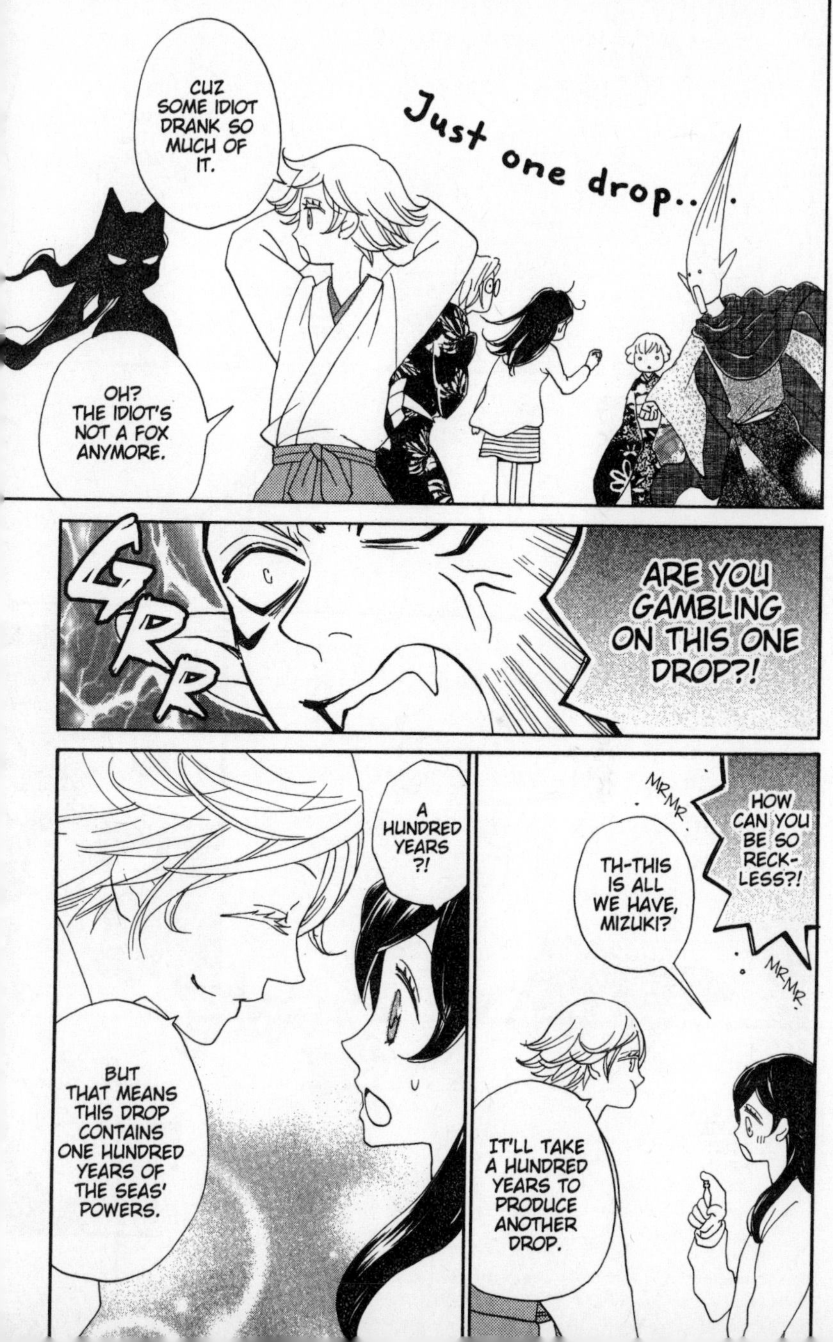
Just one drop...
CUZ SOME IDIOT DRANK SO MUCH OF IT.
OH? THE IDIOT'S NOT A FOX ANYMORE.
ARE YOU GAMBLING ON THIS ONE DROP?!
GRR
HOW CAN YOU BE SO RECK-LESS?!
MRMR
MRMR
TH-THIS IS ALL WE HAVE, MIZUKI?
IT'LL TAKE A HUNDRED YEARS TO PRODUCE ANOTHER DROP.
A HUNDRED YEARS ?!
BUT THAT MEANS THIS DROP CONTAINS ONE HUNDRED YEARS OF THE SEAS' POWERS.

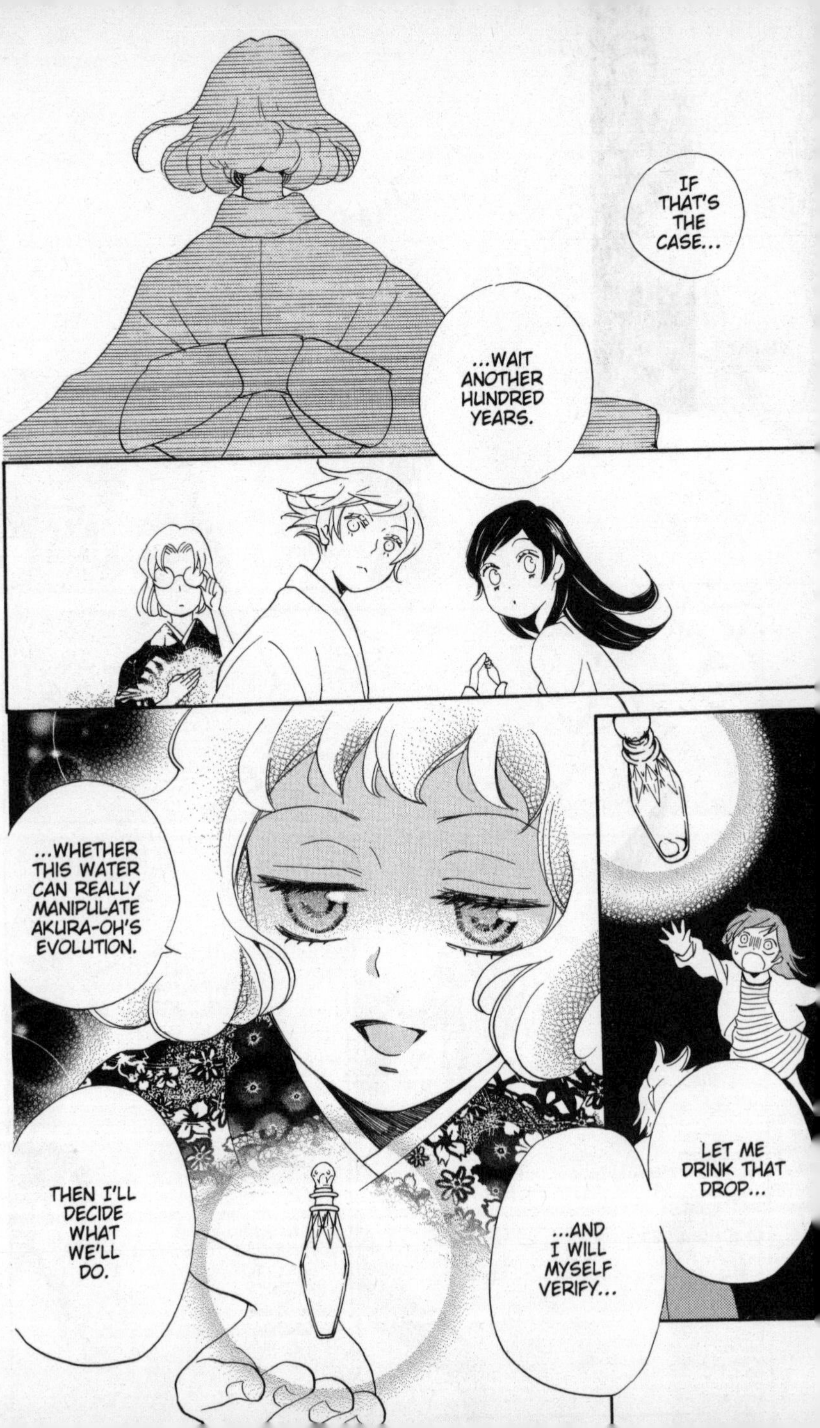
IF THAT'S THE CASE...
...WAIT ANOTHER HUNDRED YEARS.
LET ME DRINK THAT DROP...
...AND I WILL MYSELF VERIFY...
...WHETHER THIS WATER CAN REALLY MANIPULATE AKURA-OH'S EVOLUTION.
THEN I'LL DECIDE WHAT WE'LL DO.

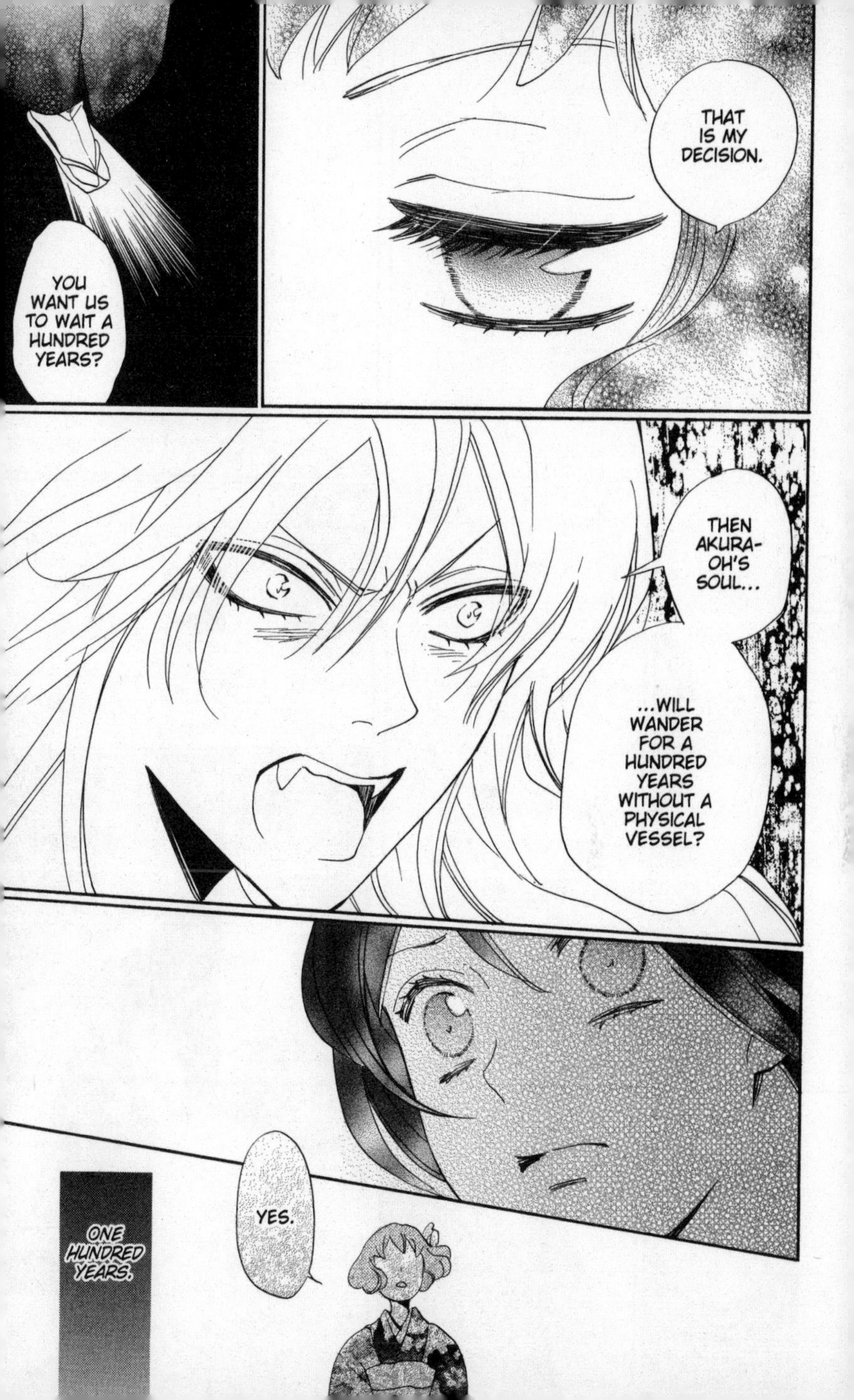
THAT IS MY DECISION.
YOU WANT US TO WAIT A HUNDRED YEARS?
THEN AKURA-OH'S SOUL...
...WILL WANDER FOR A HUNDRED YEARS WITHOUT A PHYSICAL VESSEL?
YES.
ONE HUNDRED YEARS.

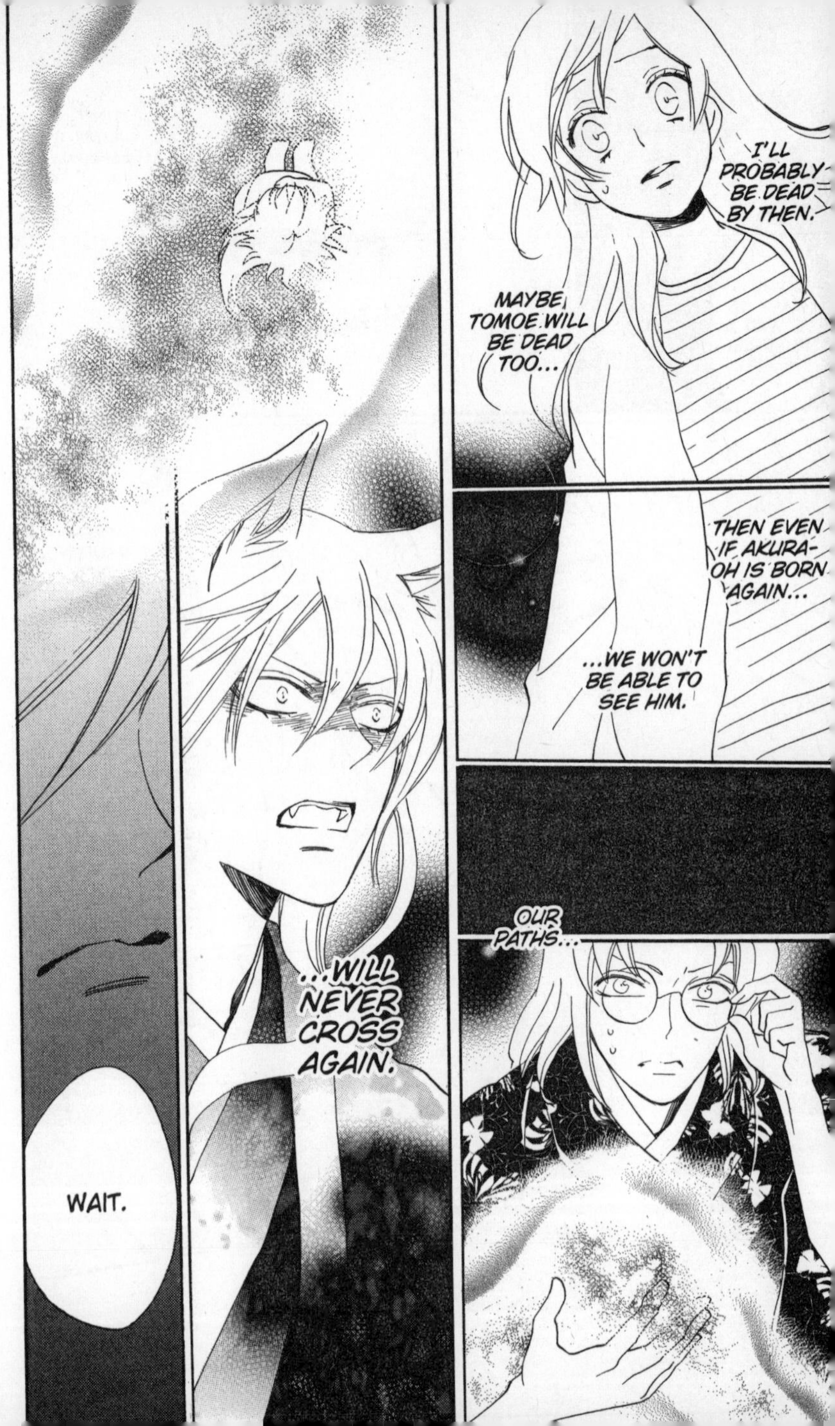
I'LL PROBABLY BE DEAD BY THEN.
MAYBE TOMOE WILL BE DEAD TOO...
THEN EVEN IF AKURA-OH IS BORN AGAIN...
...WE WON'T BE ABLE TO SEE HIM.
OUR PATHS...
...WILL NEVER CROSS AGAIN.
WAIT.

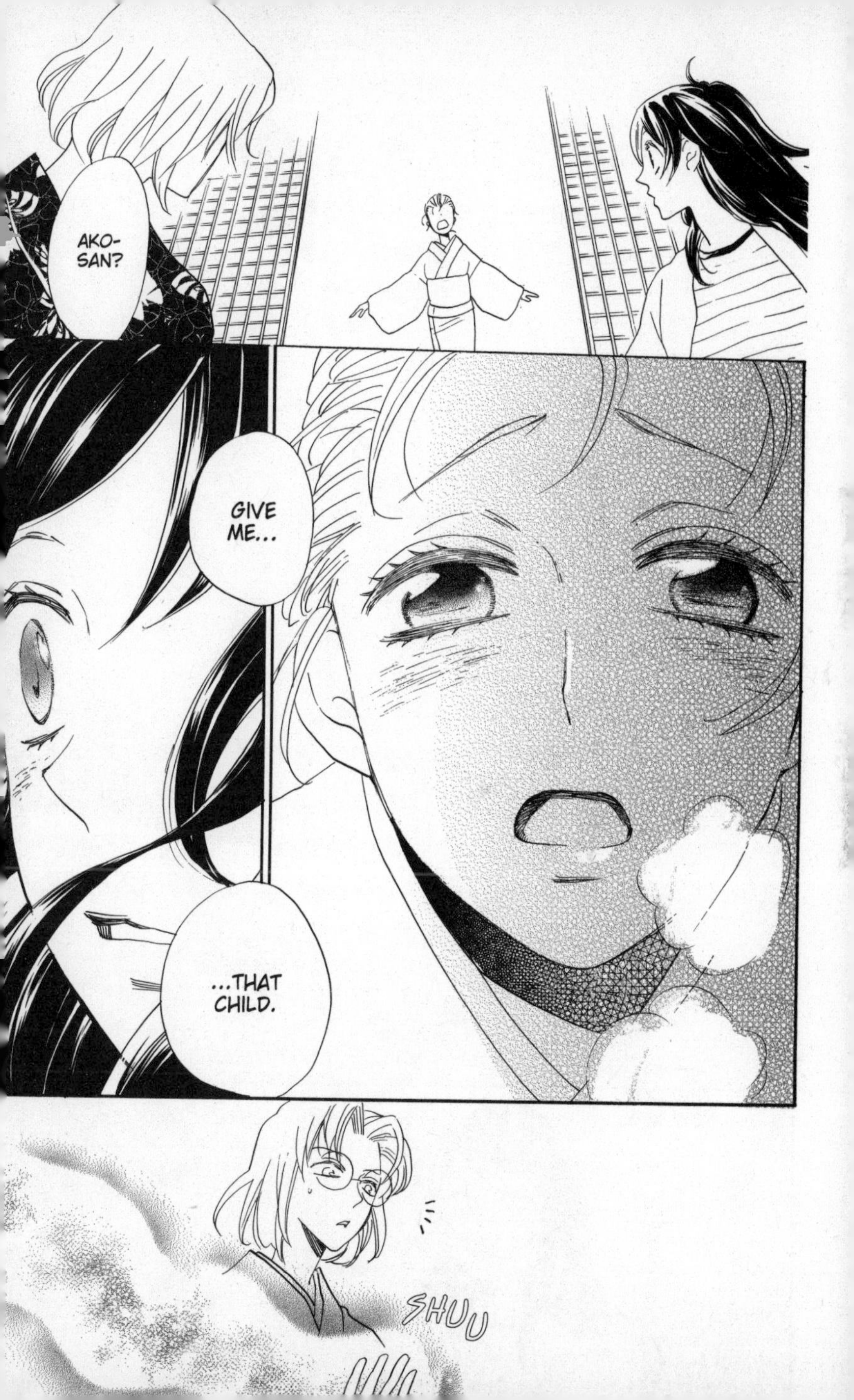
AKO-
SAN?
GIVE
ME...
...THAT
CHILD.
SHUU

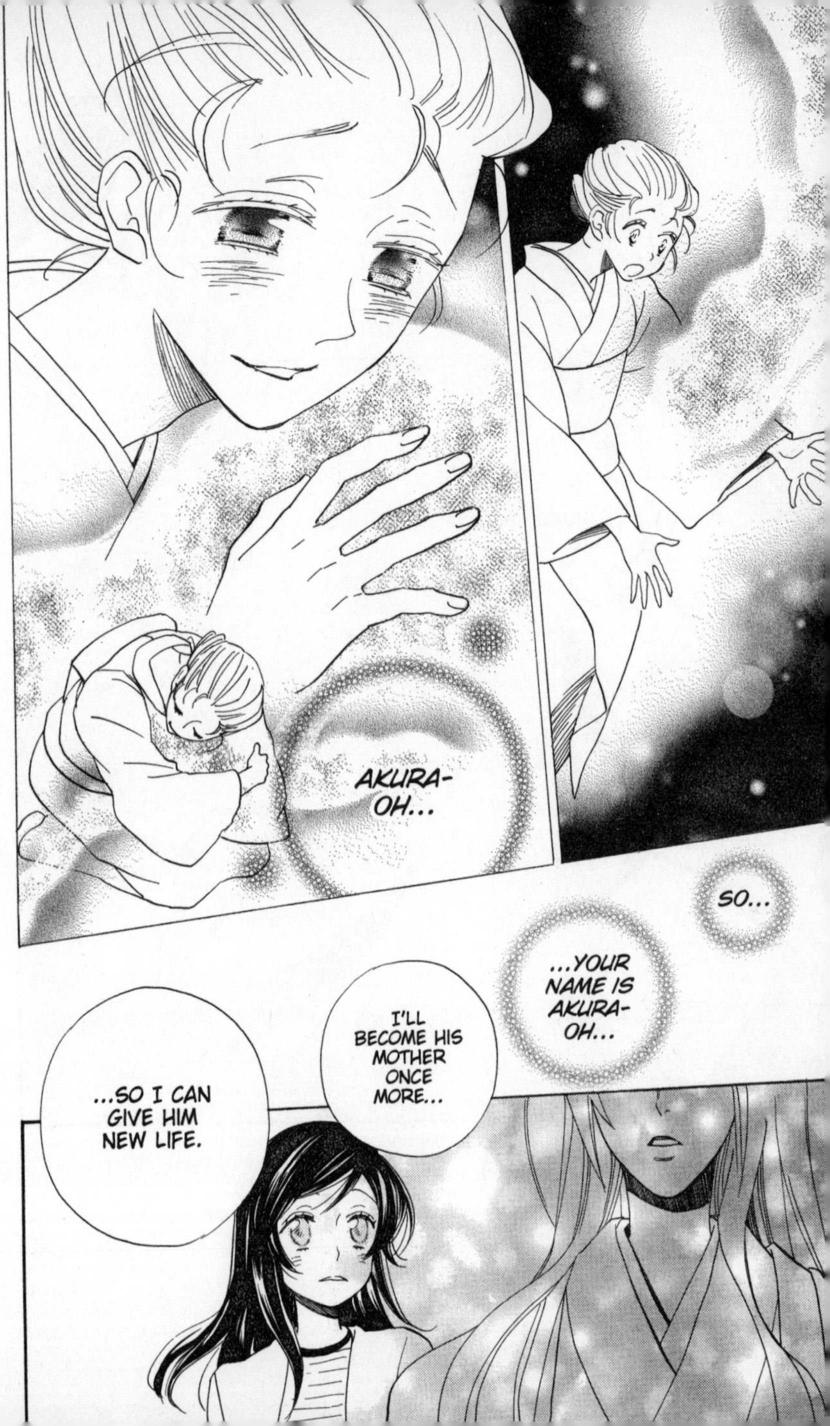
AKURA-OH...
SO...
...YOUR NAME IS AKURA-OH...
I'LL BECOME HIS MOTHER ONCE MORE...
...SO I CAN GIVE HIM NEW LIFE.

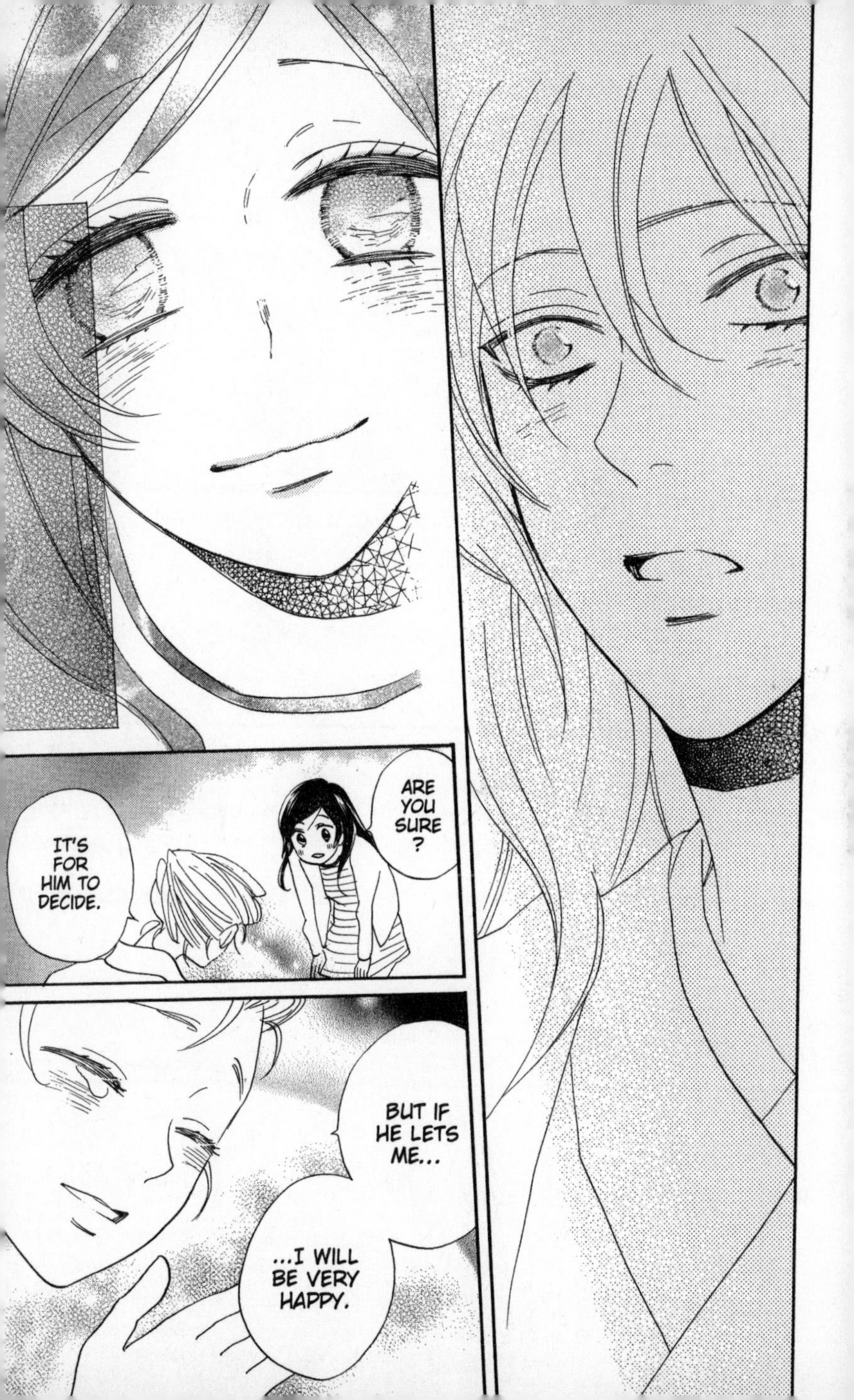
ARE YOU SURE?
IT'S FOR HIM TO DECIDE.
BUT IF HE LETS ME...
...I WILL BE VERY HAPPY.

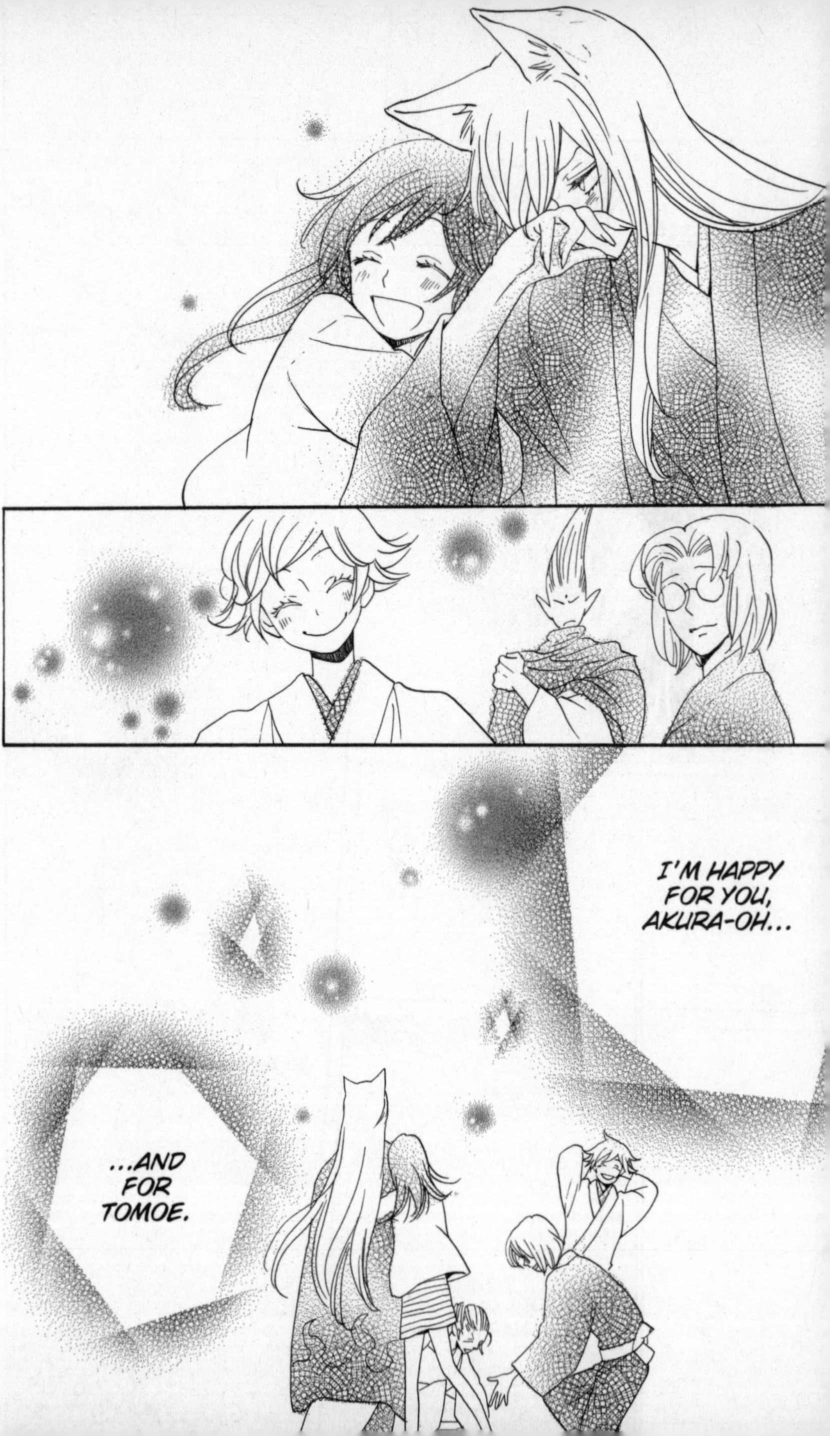
I'M HAPPY FOR YOU, AKURA-OH...
...AND FOR TOMOE.

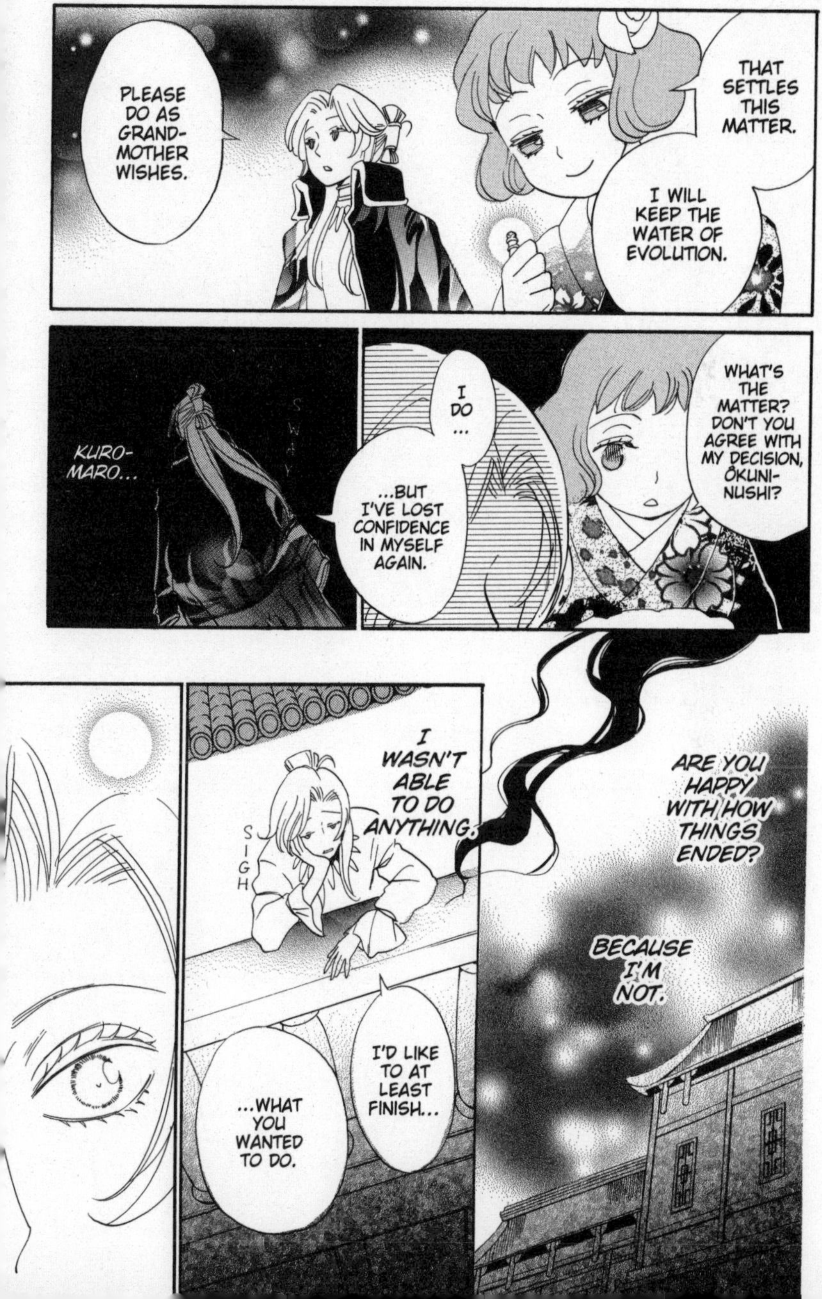
THAT SETTLES THIS MATTER.
I WILL KEEP THE WATER OF EVOLUTION.
PLEASE DO AS GRANDMOTHER WISHES.
WHAT'S THE MATTER? DON'T YOU AGREE WITH MY DECISION, ŌKUNINUSHI?
I DO...
...BUT I'VE LOST CONFIDENCE IN MYSELF AGAIN.
SWAY
KUROMARO...
ARE YOU HAPPY WITH HOW THINGS ENDED?
BECAUSE I'M NOT.
I WASN'T ABLE TO DO ANYTHING.
SIGH
I'D LIKE TO AT LEAST FINISH...
...WHAT YOU WANTED TO DO.

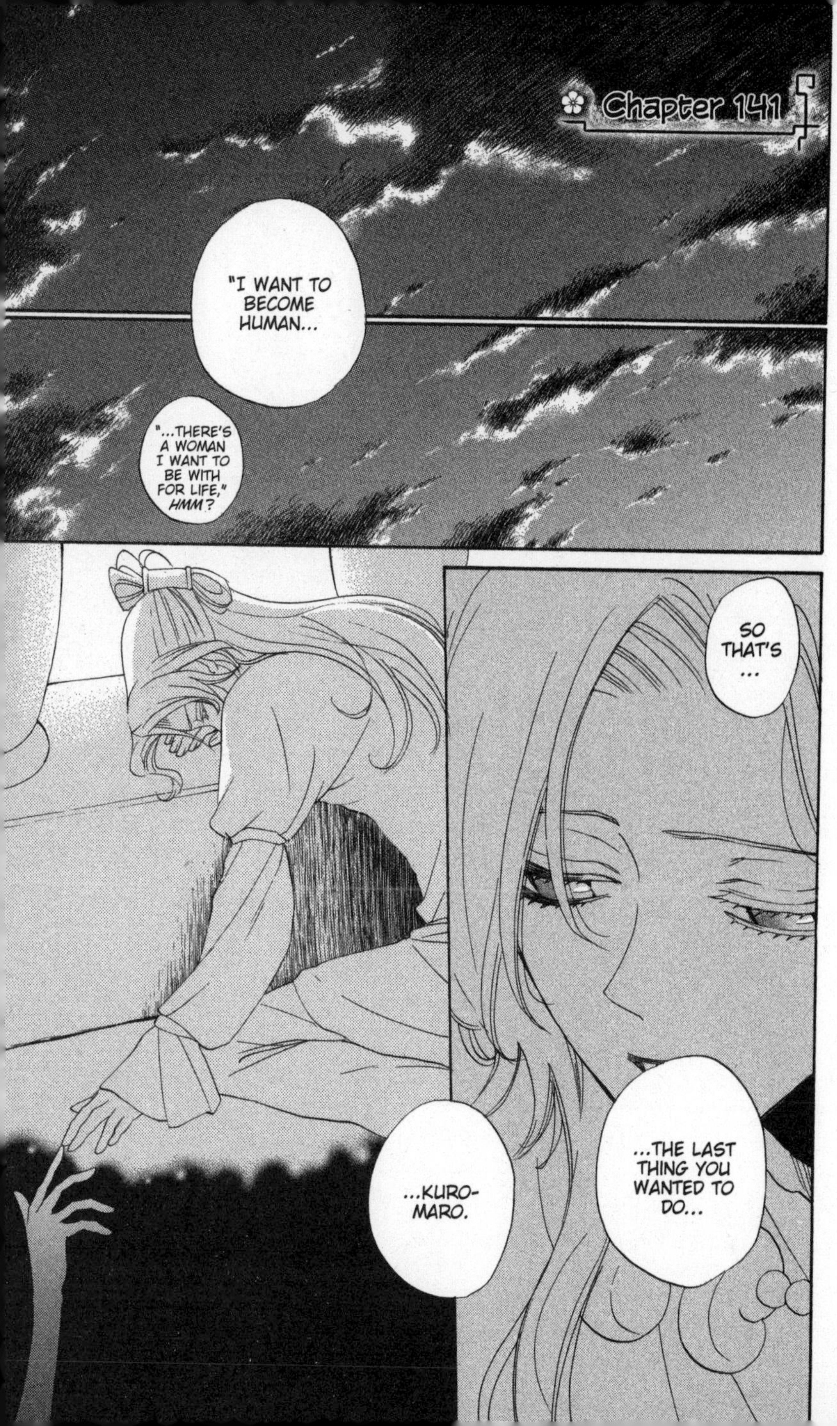
Chapter 141
"I WANT TO BECOME HUMAN...
"...THERE'S A WOMAN I WANT TO BE WITH FOR LIFE," HMM?
SO THAT'S...
...THE LAST THING YOU WANTED TO DO...
...KURO-MARO.

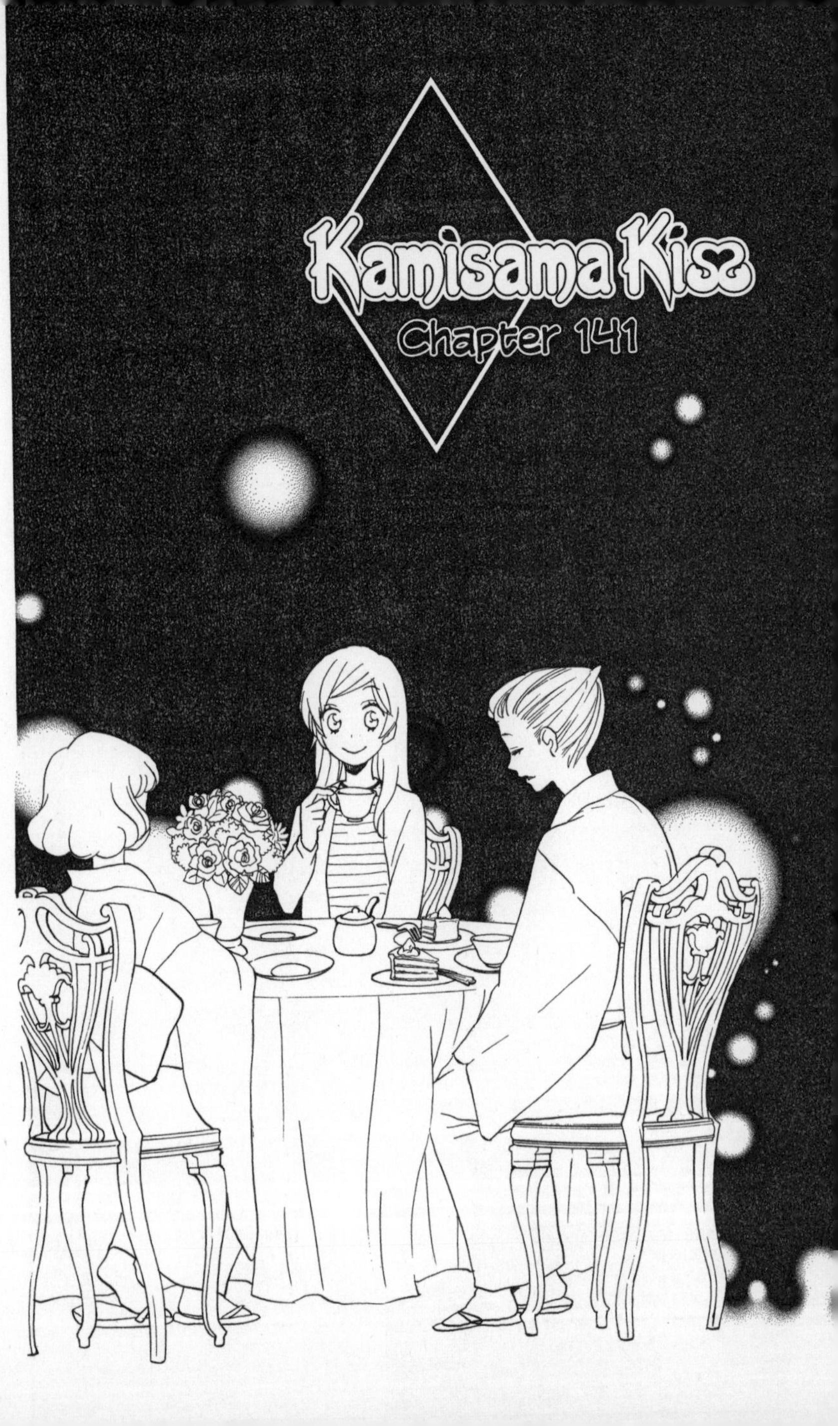
Kamisama Kiss
Chapter 141

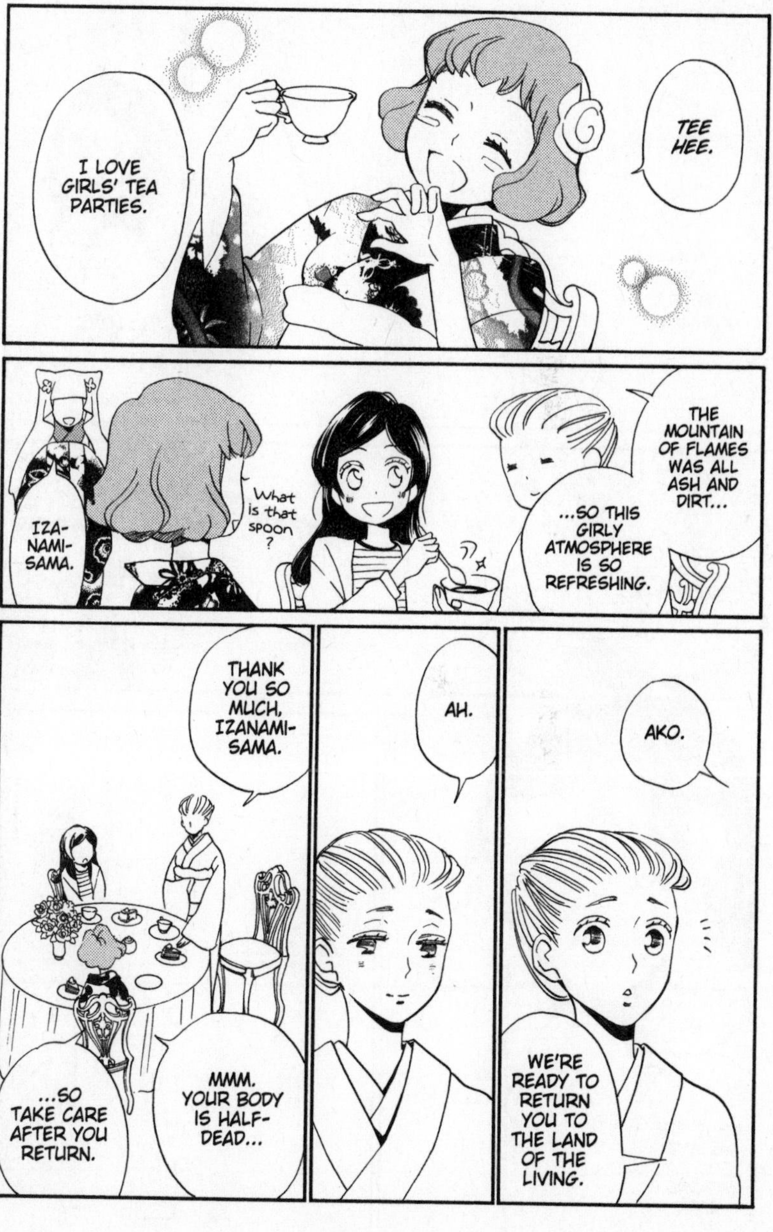
TEE HEE.
I LOVE GIRLS' TEA PARTIES.
THE MOUNTAIN OF FLAMES WAS ALL ASH AND DIRT...
...SO THIS GIRLY ATMOSPHERE IS SO REFRESHING.
What is that spoon?
IZANAMI-SAMA.
AKO.
WE'RE READY TO RETURN YOU TO THE LAND OF THE LIVING.
AH.
THANK YOU SO MUCH, IZANAMI-SAMA.
MMM. YOUR BODY IS HALF-DEAD...
...SO TAKE CARE AFTER YOU RETURN.

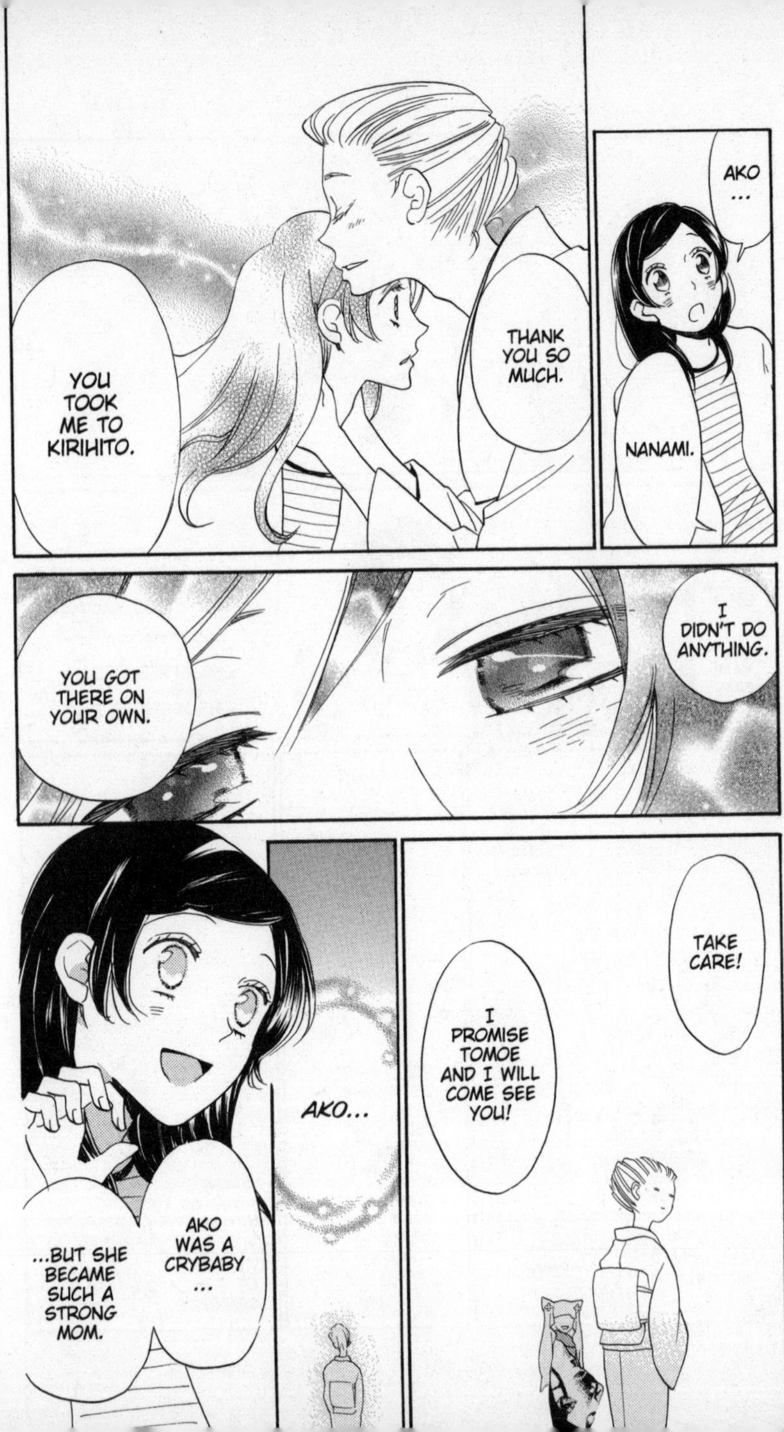
AKO ...
NANAMI.
THANK YOU SO MUCH.
YOU TOOK ME TO KIRIHITO.
I DIDN'T DO ANYTHING.
YOU GOT THERE ON YOUR OWN.
TAKE CARE!
I PROMISE TOMOE AND I WILL COME SEE YOU!
AKO...
AKO WAS A CRYBABY ...
...BUT SHE BECAME SUCH A STRONG MOM.

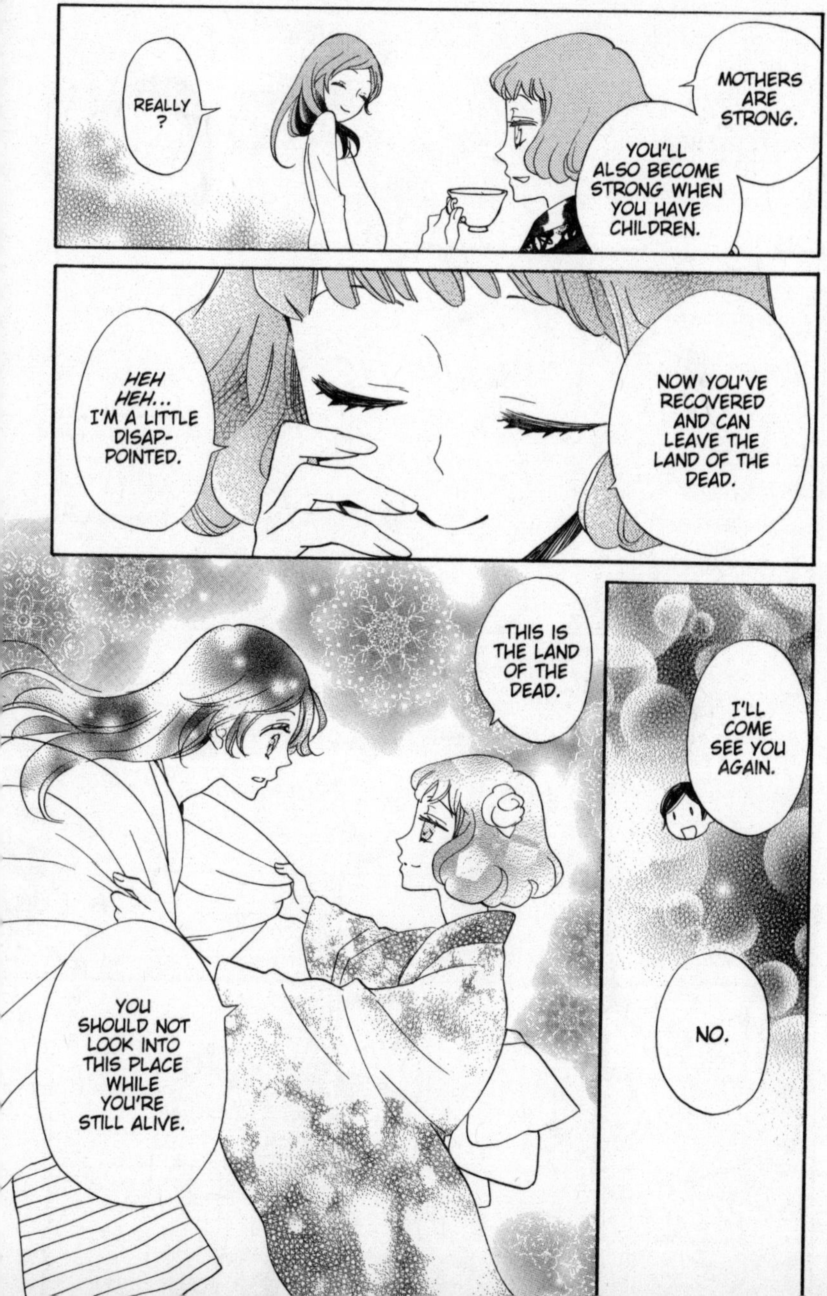
MOTHERS ARE STRONG.
YOU'LL ALSO BECOME STRONG WHEN YOU HAVE CHILDREN.
REALLY?
NOW YOU'VE RECOVERED AND CAN LEAVE THE LAND OF THE DEAD.
HEH HEH... I'M A LITTLE DISAPPOINTED.
I'LL COME SEE YOU AGAIN.
NO.
THIS IS THE LAND OF THE DEAD.
YOU SHOULD NOT LOOK INTO THIS PLACE WHILE YOU'RE STILL ALIVE.

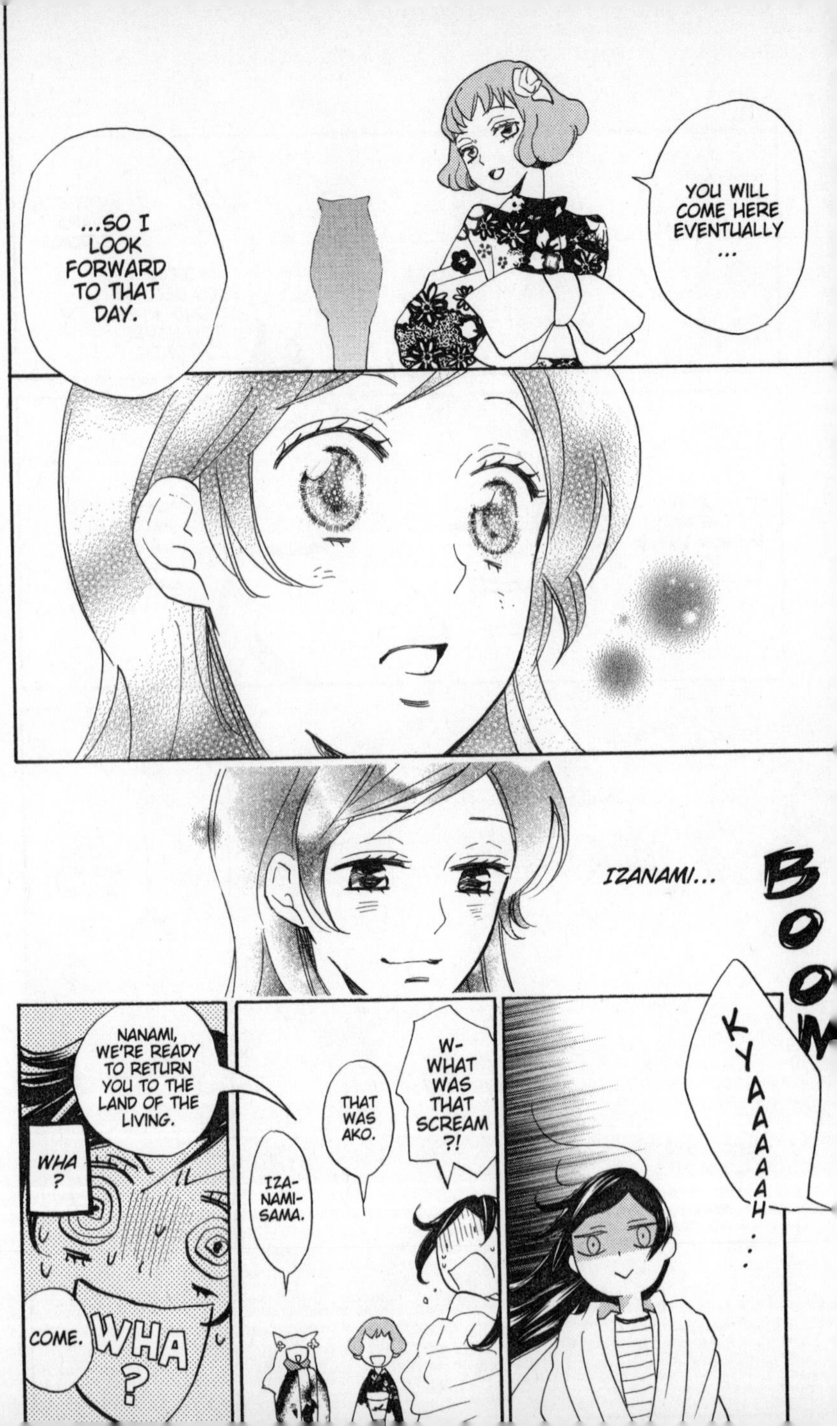
YOU WILL COME HERE EVENTUALLY ...
...SO I LOOK FORWARD TO THAT DAY.
IZANAMI...
BOOM
KYAAAAAAH...
W-WHAT WAS THAT SCREAM?!
THAT WAS AKO.
IZA-NAMI-SAMA.
NANAMI, WE'RE READY TO RETURN YOU TO THE LAND OF THE LIVING.
WHA?
COME.
WHA?

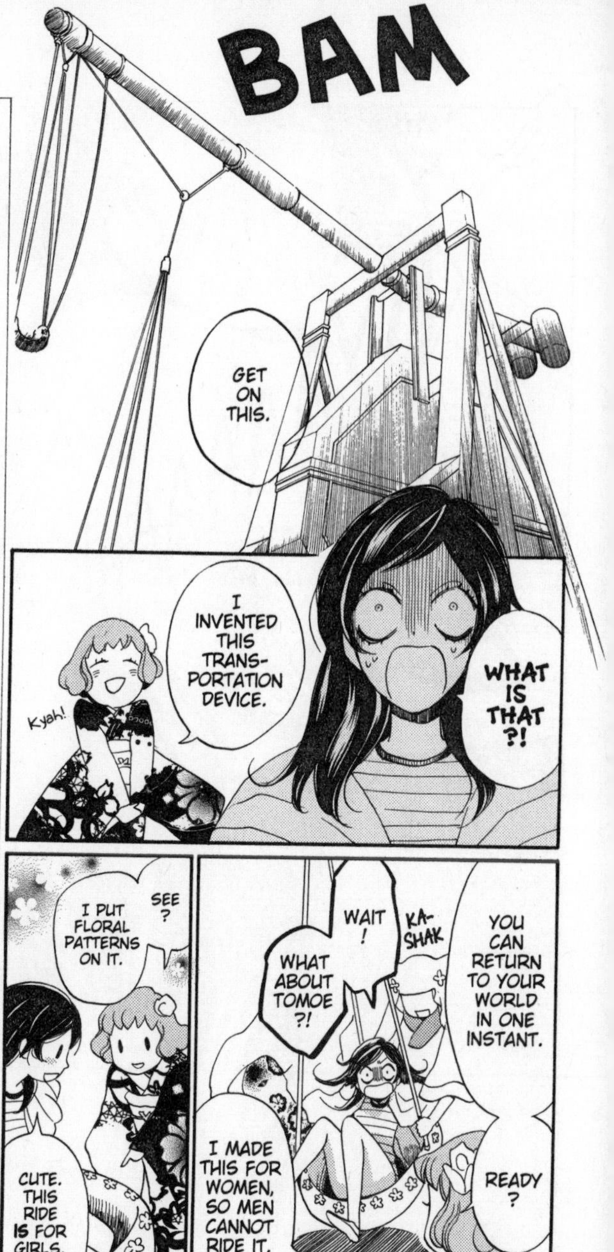
BAM
GET ON THIS.
WHAT IS THAT ?!
I INVENTED THIS TRANS-PORTATION DEVICE.
Kyah!
YOU CAN RETURN TO YOUR WORLD IN ONE INSTANT.
KA-SHAK
WAIT!
WHAT ABOUT TOMOE ?!
READY ?
I MADE THIS FOR WOMEN, SO MEN CANNOT RIDE IT.
SEE ?
I PUT FLORAL PATTERNS ON IT.
CUTE. THIS RIDE IS FOR GIRLS.

ABOUT MY PILLOWS

I've been having problems with my pillows for a couple of years now. When I wake up in the morning, my neck and shoulders hurt.

So I got a thin pillow. After I used it for a while...

...my face puffed up! And my glasses became tight. This wasn't good.

I then found out pillows that are too thin aren't good for you...

...so I made my pillow a little thicker. But then my neck started to hurt more day by day.

So I tried two pillows, slanted them...

...and tried a fluffy one.

I'm still wandering the night, looking for the right pillow.

Good night

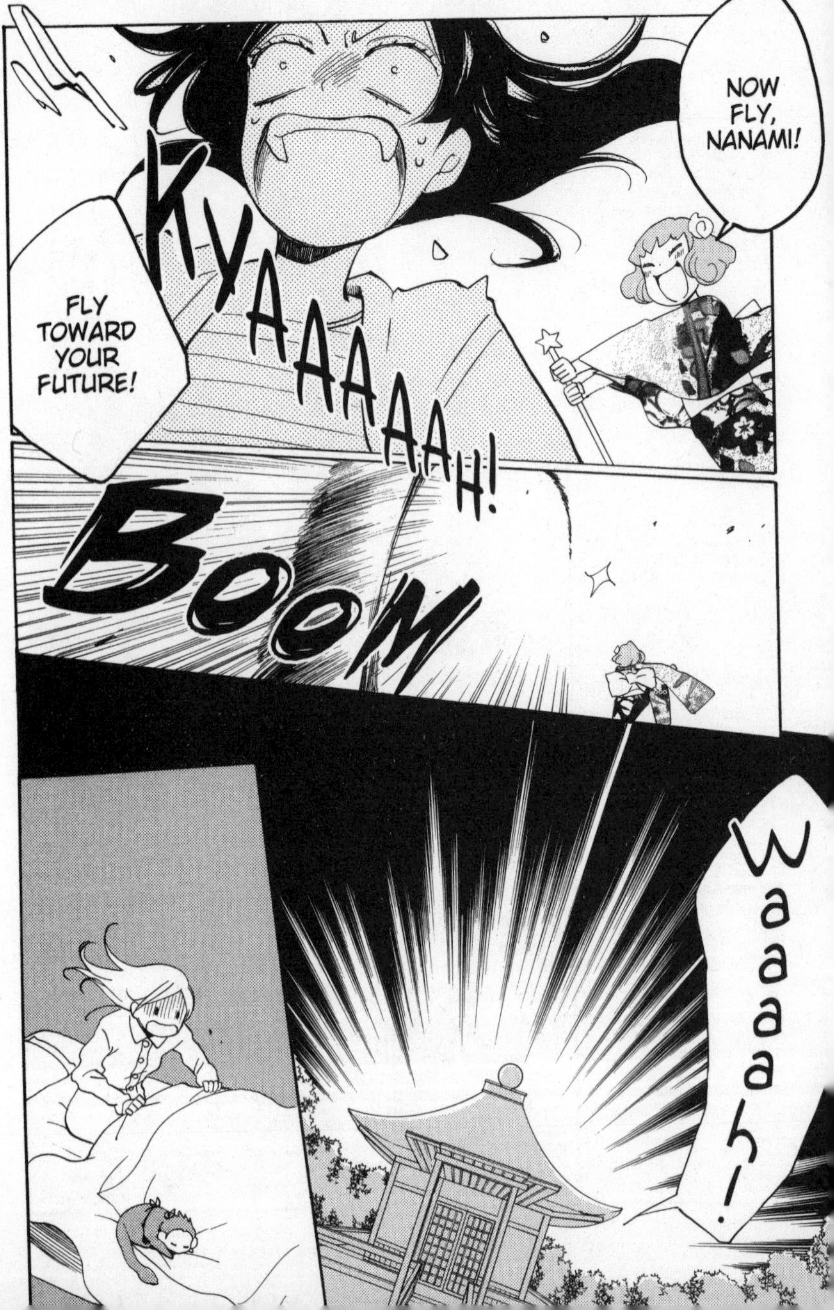
NOW FLY, NANAMI!
KYAAAAAH!
FLY TOWARD YOUR FUTURE!
BOOM
Waaaaah!

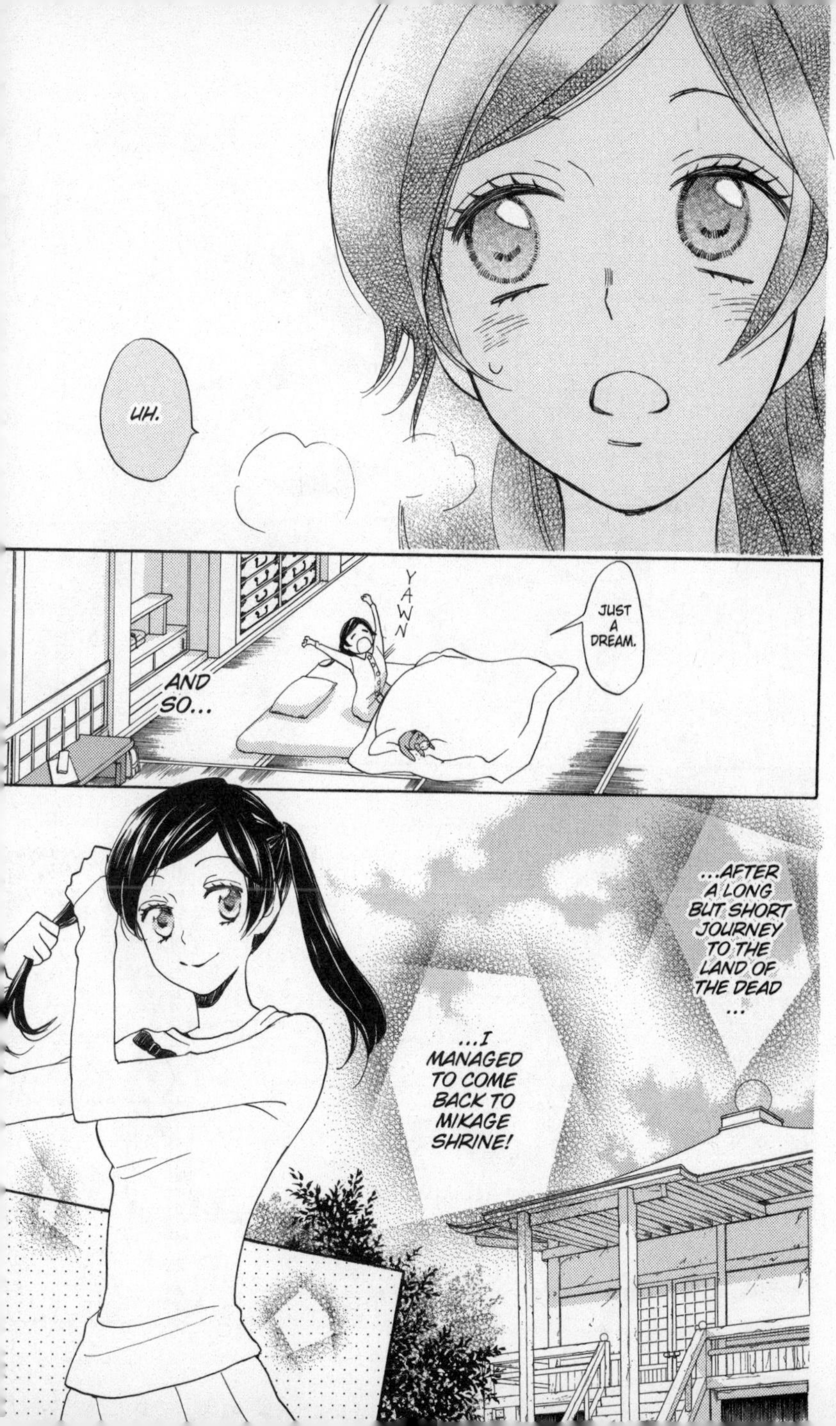
UH.
JUST A DREAM.
YAWN
AND SO...
...AFTER A LONG BUT SHORT JOURNEY TO THE LAND OF THE DEAD...
...I MANAGED TO COME BACK TO MIKAGE SHRINE!

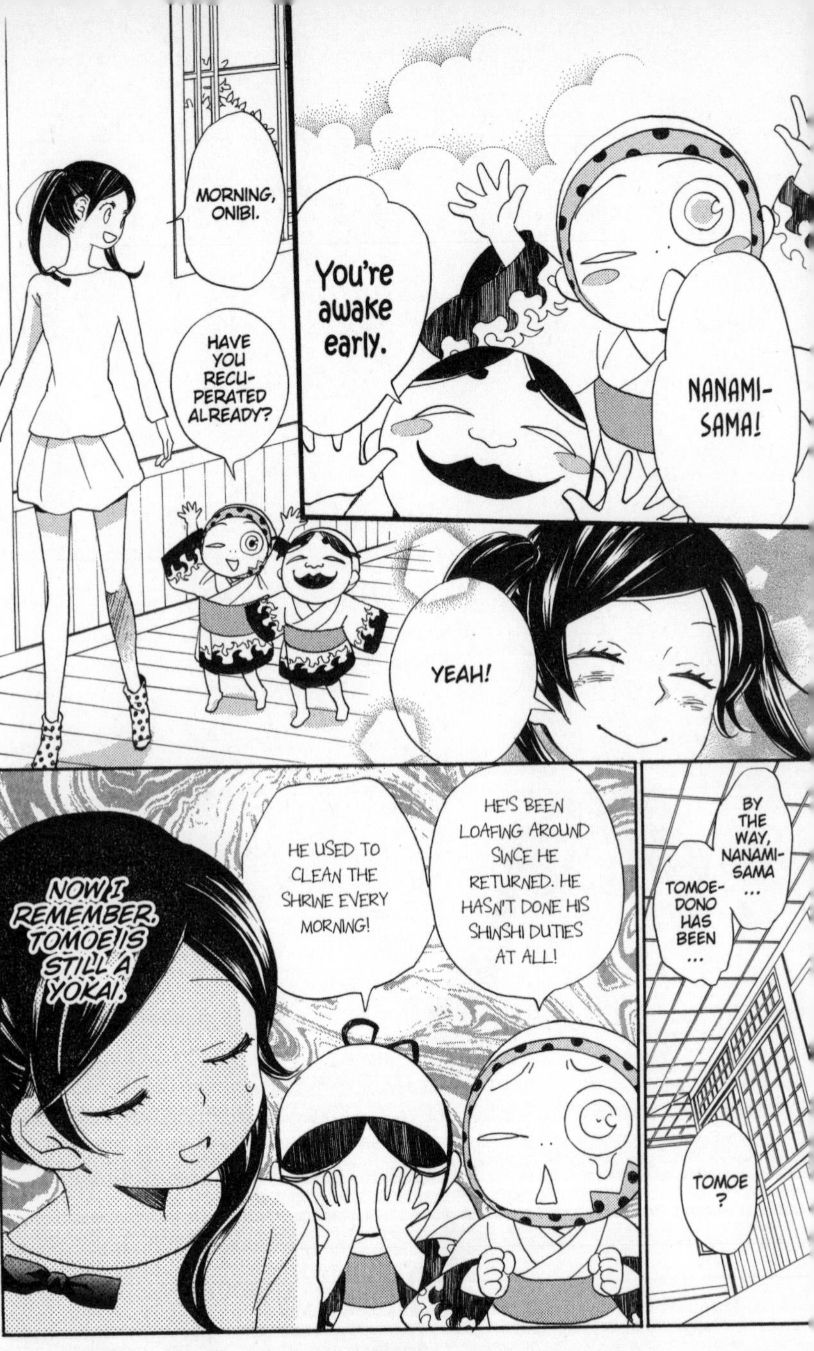
NANAMI-SAMA!
You're awake early.
YEAH!
MORNING, ONIBI.
HAVE YOU RECUPERATED ALREADY?
BY THE WAY, NANAMI-SAMA ...
TOMOE-DONO HAS BEEN ...
TOMOE ?
HE'S BEEN LOAFING AROUND SINCE HE RETURNED. HE HASN'T DONE HIS SHINSHI DUTIES AT ALL!
HE USED TO CLEAN THE SHRINE EVERY MORNING!
NOW I REMEMBER. TOMOE IS STILL A YOKAI.

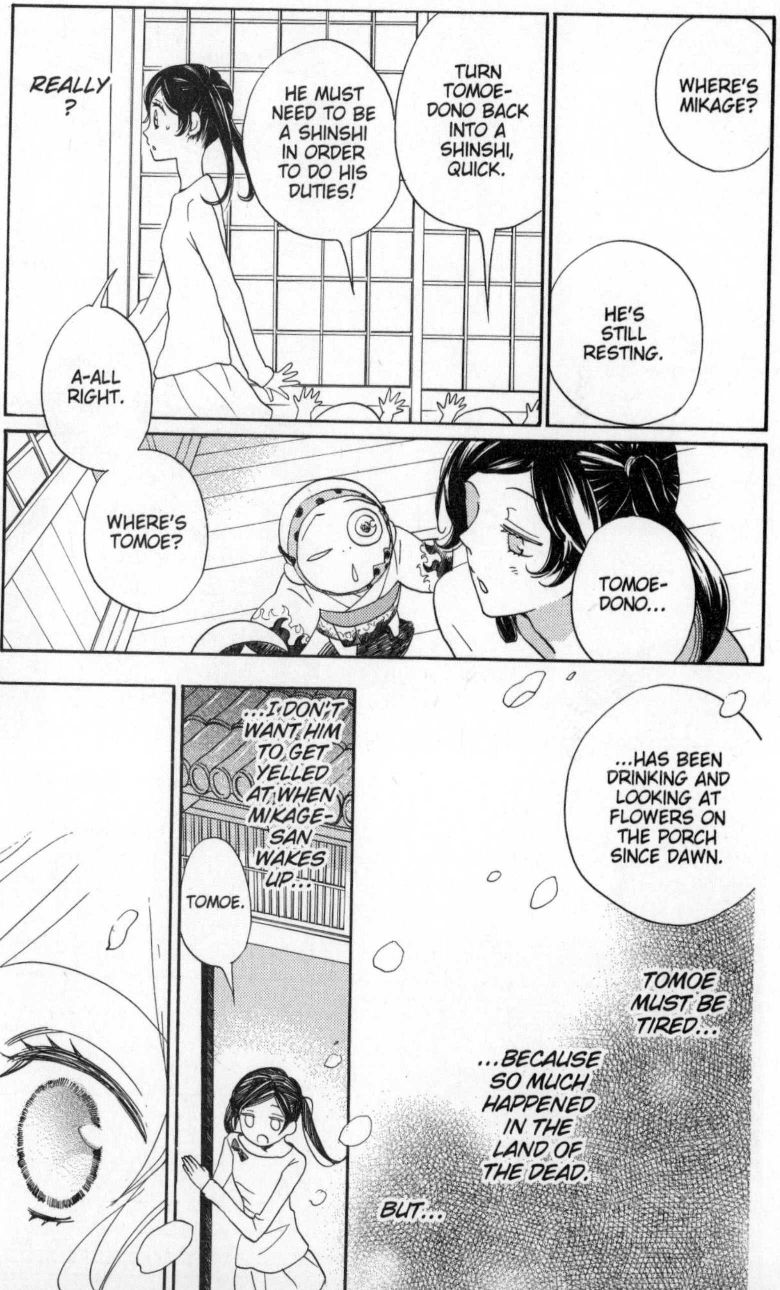
WHERE'S MIKAGE?
HE'S STILL RESTING.
TURN TOMOE-DONO BACK INTO A SHINSHI, QUICK.
HE MUST NEED TO BE A SHINSHI IN ORDER TO DO HIS DUTIES!
REALLY?
A-ALL RIGHT.
WHERE'S TOMOE?
TOMOE-DONO...
...HAS BEEN DRINKING AND LOOKING AT FLOWERS ON THE PORCH SINCE DAWN.
TOMOE MUST BE TIRED...
...BECAUSE SO MUCH HAPPENED IN THE LAND OF THE DEAD.
BUT...
...I DON'T WANT HIM TO GET YELLED AT WHEN MIKAGE-SAN WAKES UP...
TOMOE.

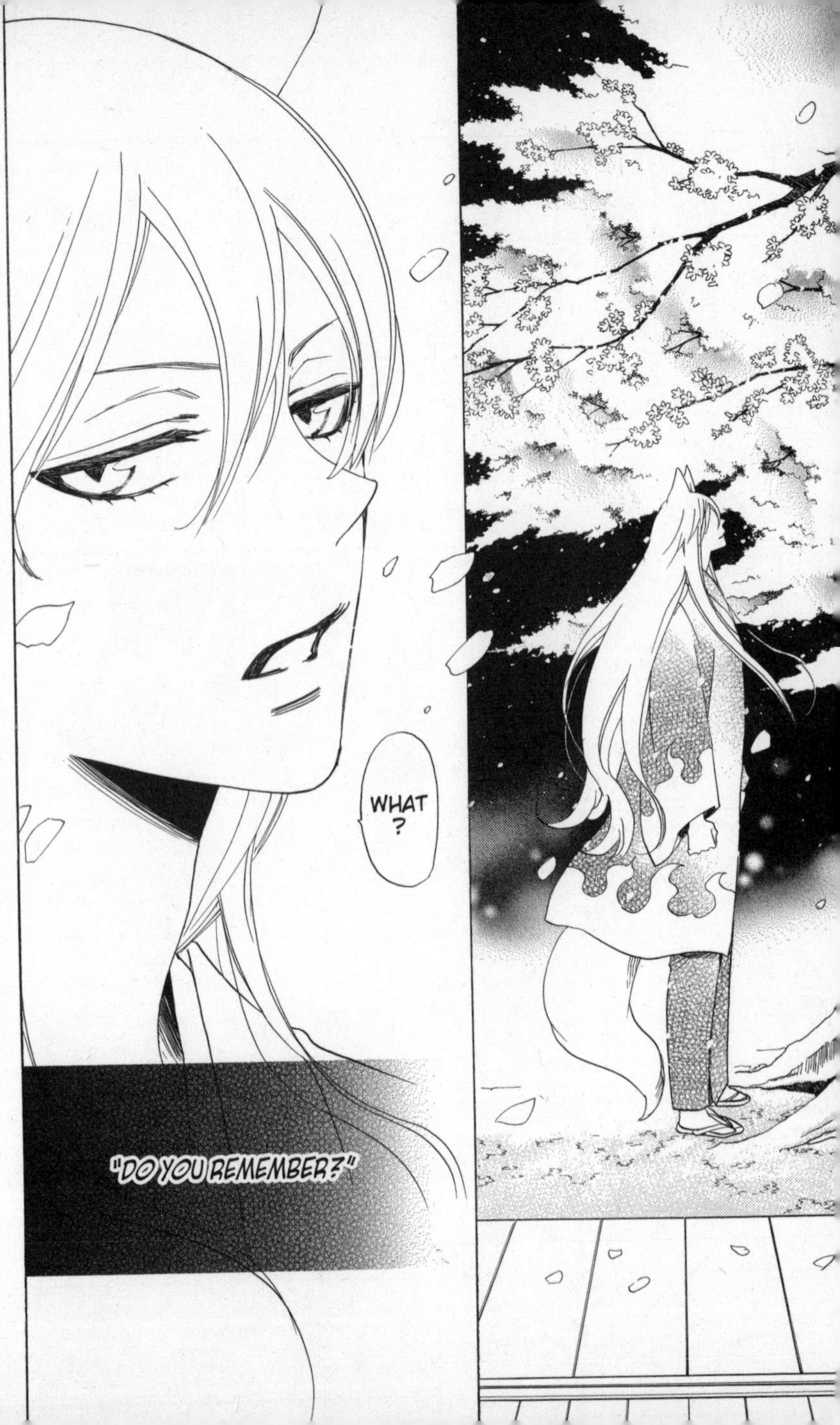
WHAT?
"DO YOU REMEMBER?"

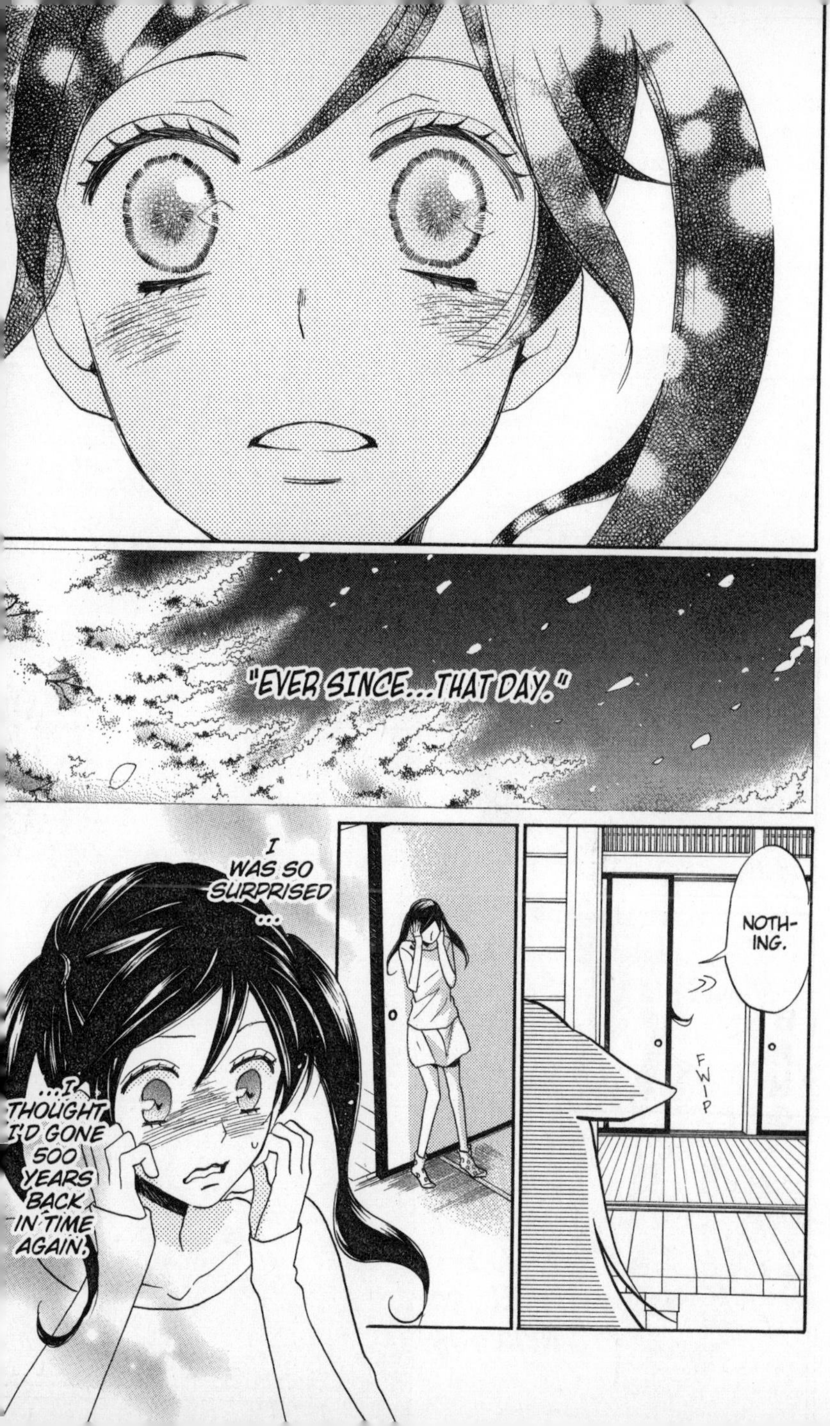
"EVER SINCE...THAT DAY."
NOTH-ING.
FWIP
I WAS SO SURPRISED...
...I THOUGHT I'D GONE 500 YEARS BACK IN TIME AGAIN.

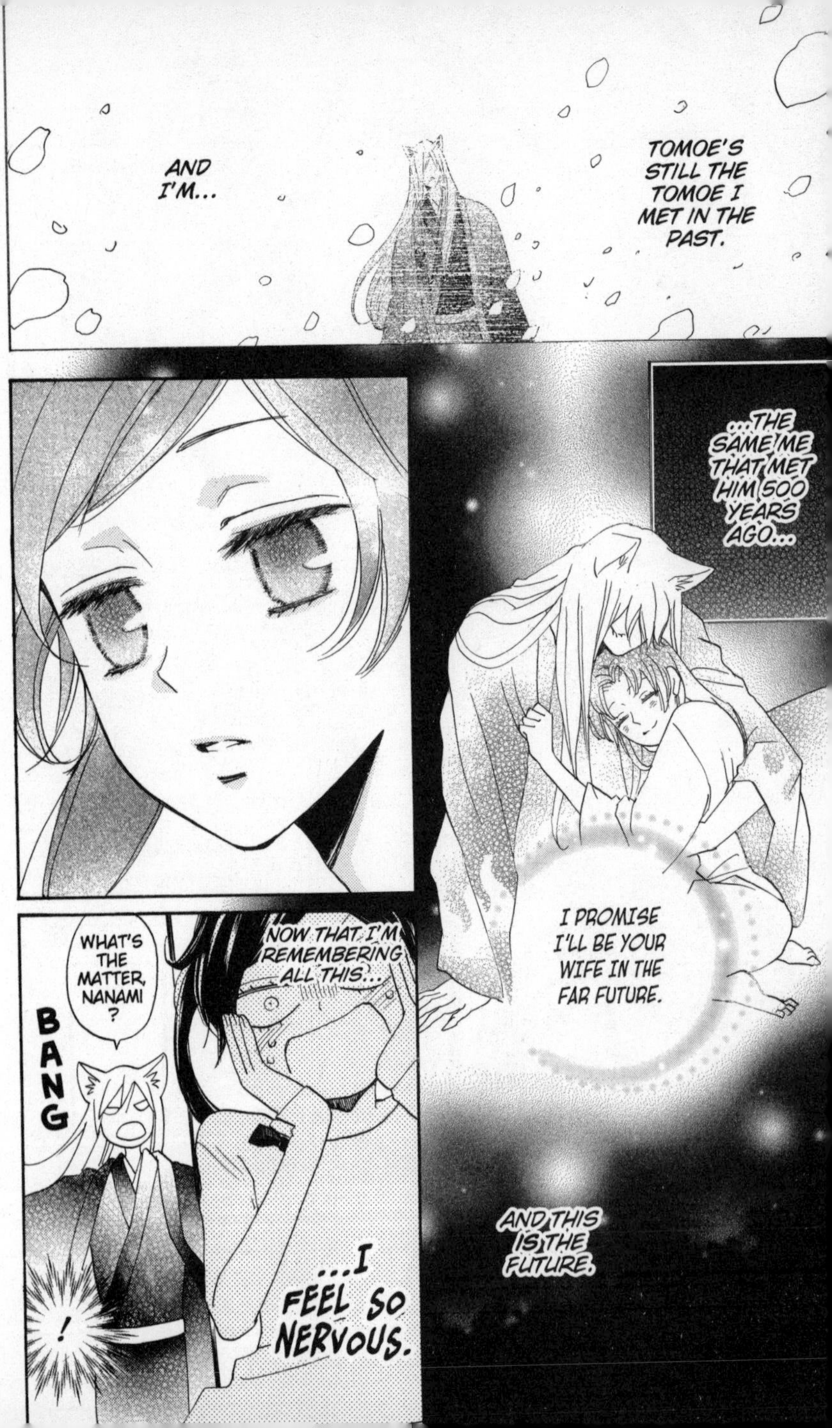
TOMOE'S STILL THE TOMOE I MET IN THE PAST.
AND I'M...
...THE SAME ME THAT MET HIM 500 YEARS AGO...
I PROMISE I'LL BE YOUR WIFE IN THE FAR FUTURE.
AND THIS IS THE FUTURE.
NOW THAT I'M REMEMBERING ALL THIS...
...I FEEL SO NERVOUS.
WHAT'S THE MATTER, NANAMI?
BANG
!

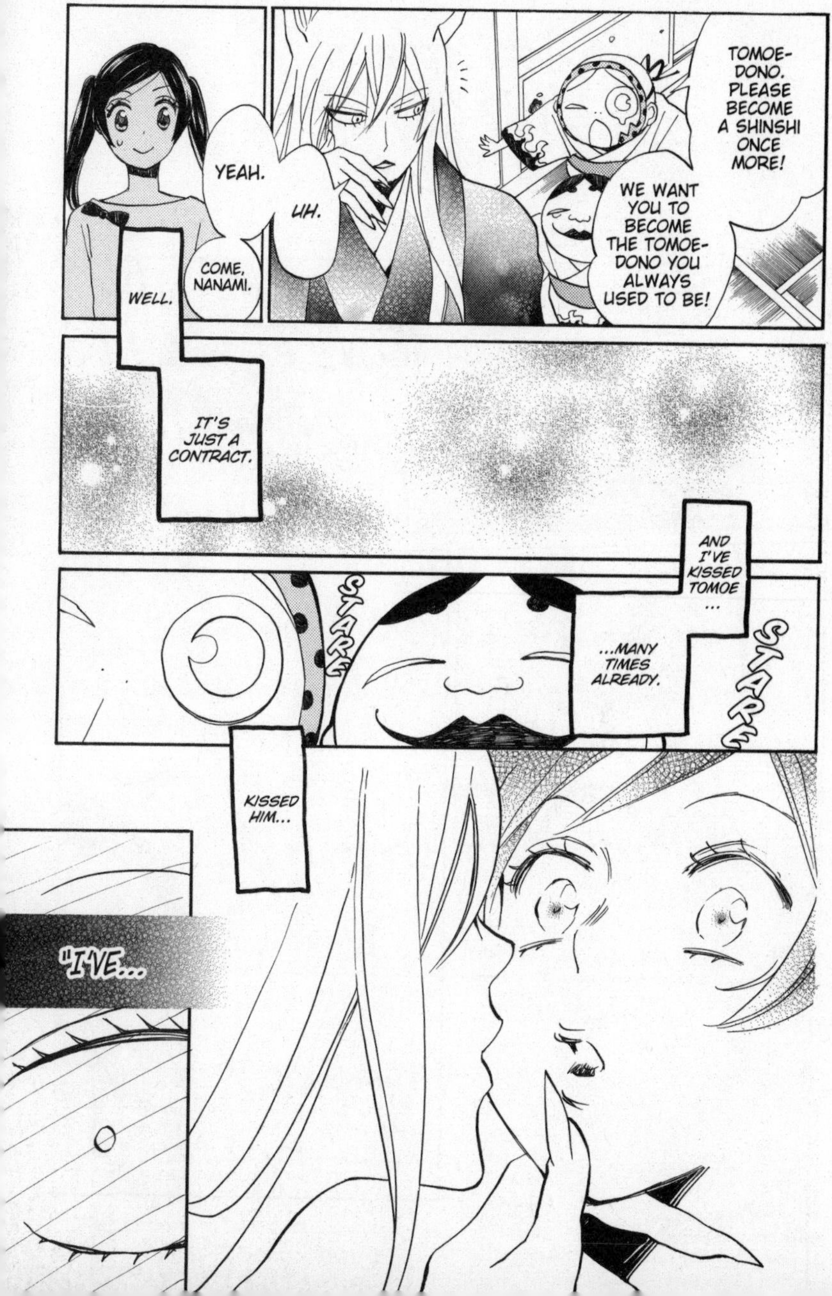
TOMOE-DONO. PLEASE BECOME A SHINSHI ONCE MORE!
WE WANT YOU TO BECOME THE TOMOE-DONO YOU ALWAYS USED TO BE!
UH.
YEAH.
COME, NANAMI.
WELL.
IT'S JUST A CONTRACT.
AND I'VE KISSED TOMOE ...
...MANY TIMES ALREADY.
STARE
STARE
KISSED HIM...
"I'VE...

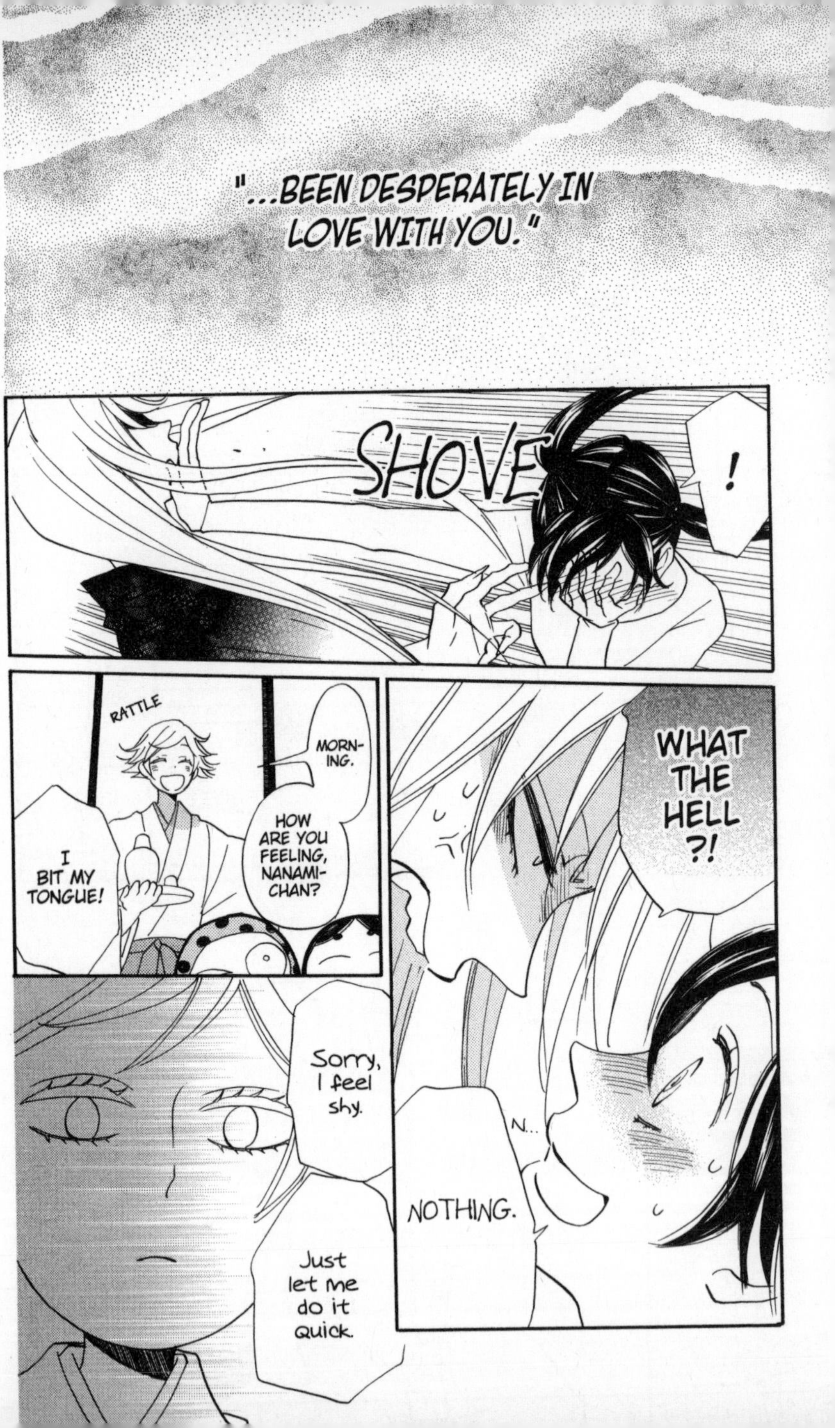
"...BEEN DESPERATELY IN LOVE WITH YOU."
!
SHOVE
WHAT THE HELL?!
N...
NOTHING.
MORNING.
RATTLE
HOW ARE YOU FEELING, NANAMI-CHAN?
I BIT MY TONGUE!
Sorry, I feel shy.
Just let me do it quick.

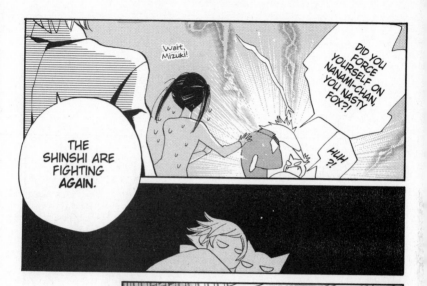

Wait, Mizuki!

DID YOU FORCE YOURSELF ON NANAMI-CHAN, YOU NASTY FOX?!

HUH?!

THE SHINSHI ARE FIGHTING AGAIN.

LONG TIME NO SEE, NANAMI.

WOW!

MOUNT KURAMA SENT ME WITH A GIFT TO CELEBRATE YOUR RECOVERY.

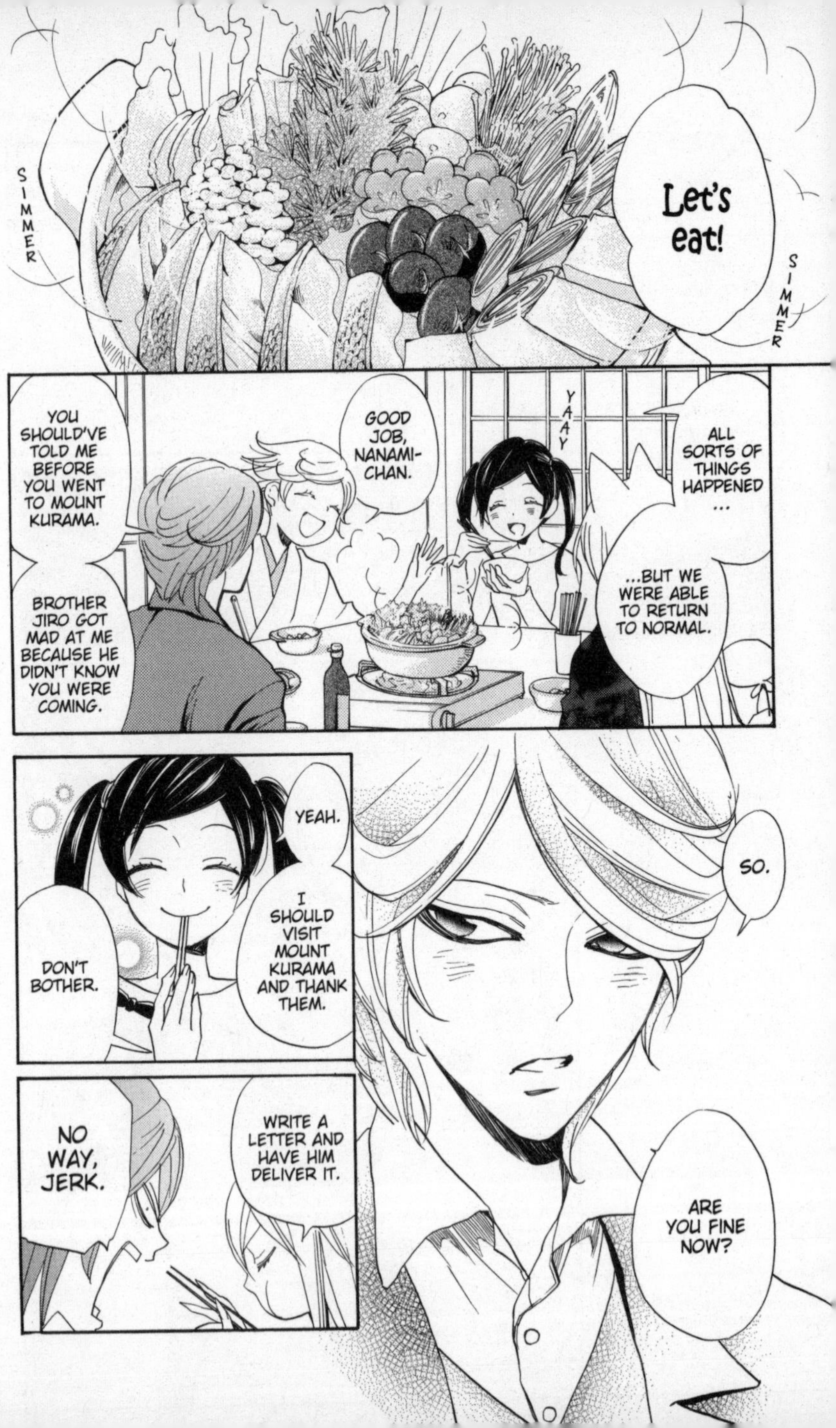
Let's eat!
SIMMER
SIMMER
ALL SORTS OF THINGS HAPPENED ...
...BUT WE WERE ABLE TO RETURN TO NORMAL.
YAAY
GOOD JOB, NANAMI-CHAN.
YOU SHOULD'VE TOLD ME BEFORE YOU WENT TO MOUNT KURAMA.
BROTHER JIRO GOT MAD AT ME BECAUSE HE DIDN'T KNOW YOU WERE COMING.
SO.
ARE YOU FINE NOW?
YEAH.
I SHOULD VISIT MOUNT KURAMA AND THANK THEM.
DON'T BOTHER.
WRITE A LETTER AND HAVE HIM DELIVER IT.
NO WAY, JERK.

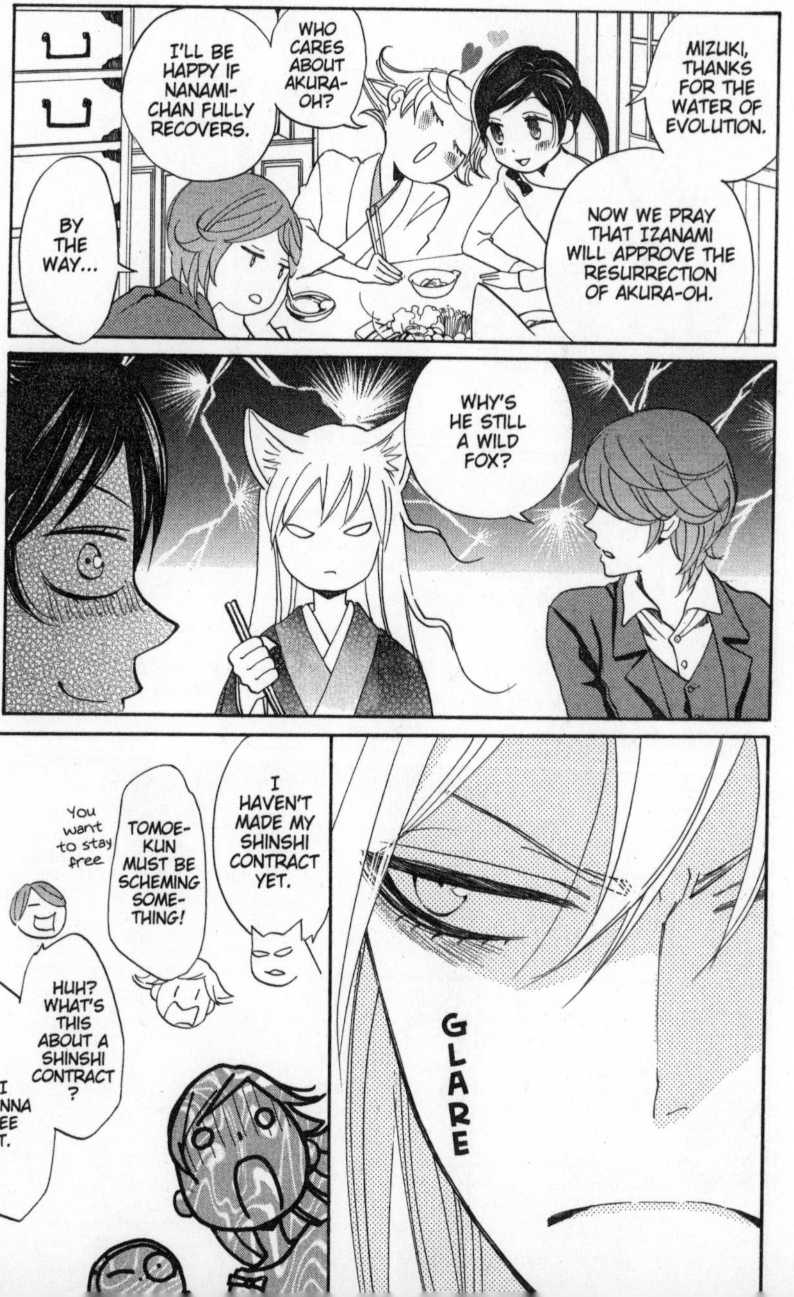
MIZUKI, THANKS FOR THE WATER OF EVOLUTION.
NOW WE PRAY THAT IZANAMI WILL APPROVE THE RESURRECTION OF AKURA-OH.
WHO CARES ABOUT AKURA-OH?
I'LL BE HAPPY IF NANAMI-CHAN FULLY RECOVERS.
BY THE WAY...
WHY'S HE STILL A WILD FOX?
GLARE
I HAVEN'T MADE MY SHINSHI CONTRACT YET.
TOMOE-KUN MUST BE SCHEMING SOMETHING!
You want to stay free
HUH? WHAT'S THIS ABOUT A SHINSHI CONTRACT?
I WANNA SEE IT.

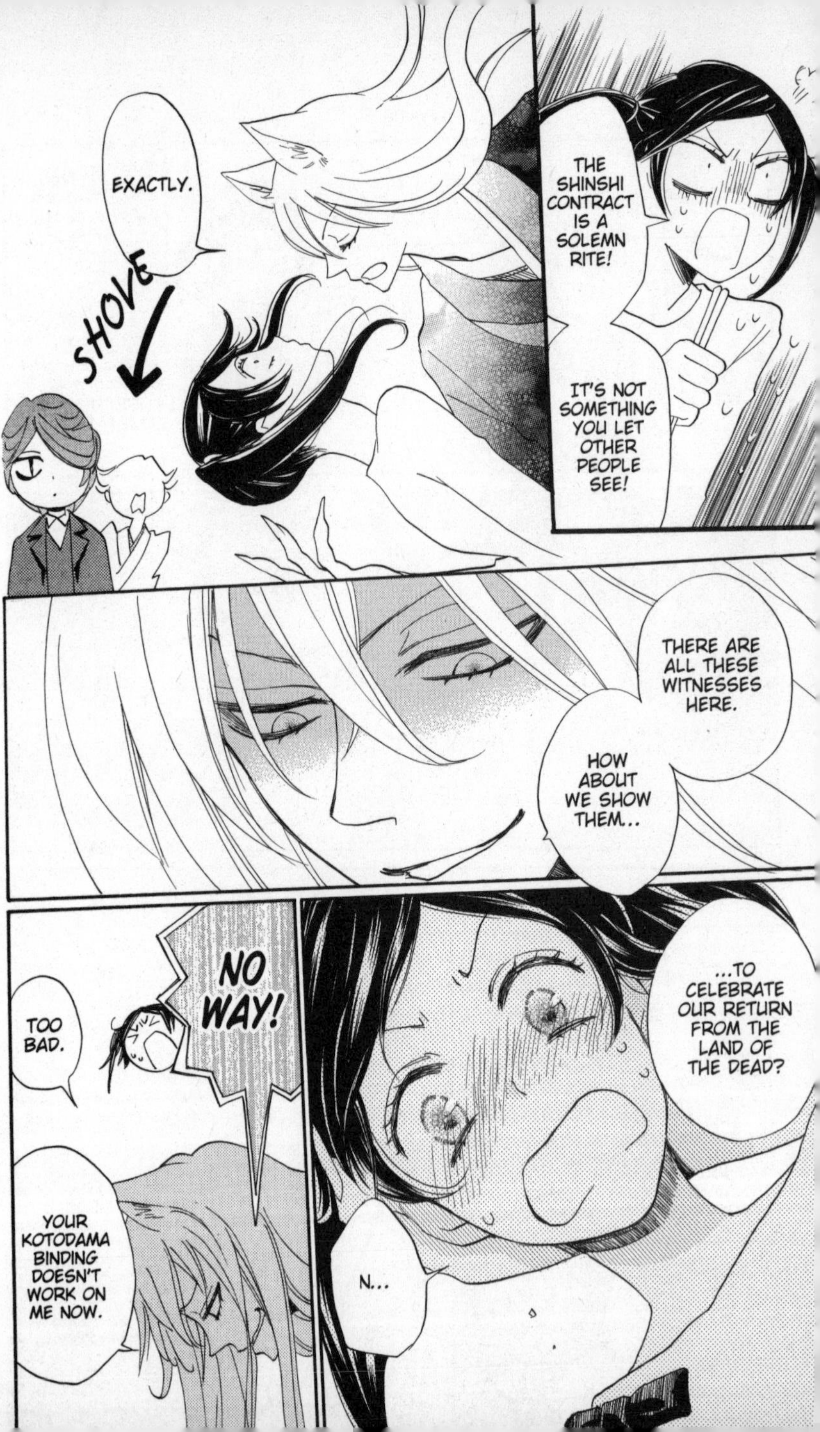
THE SHINSHI CONTRACT IS A SOLEMN RITE!
IT'S NOT SOMETHING YOU LET OTHER PEOPLE SEE!
EXACTLY.
SHOVE
THERE ARE ALL THESE WITNESSES HERE.
HOW ABOUT WE SHOW THEM...
...TO CELEBRATE OUR RETURN FROM THE LAND OF THE DEAD?
N...
NO WAY!
TOO BAD.
YOUR KOTODAMA BINDING DOESN'T WORK ON ME NOW.

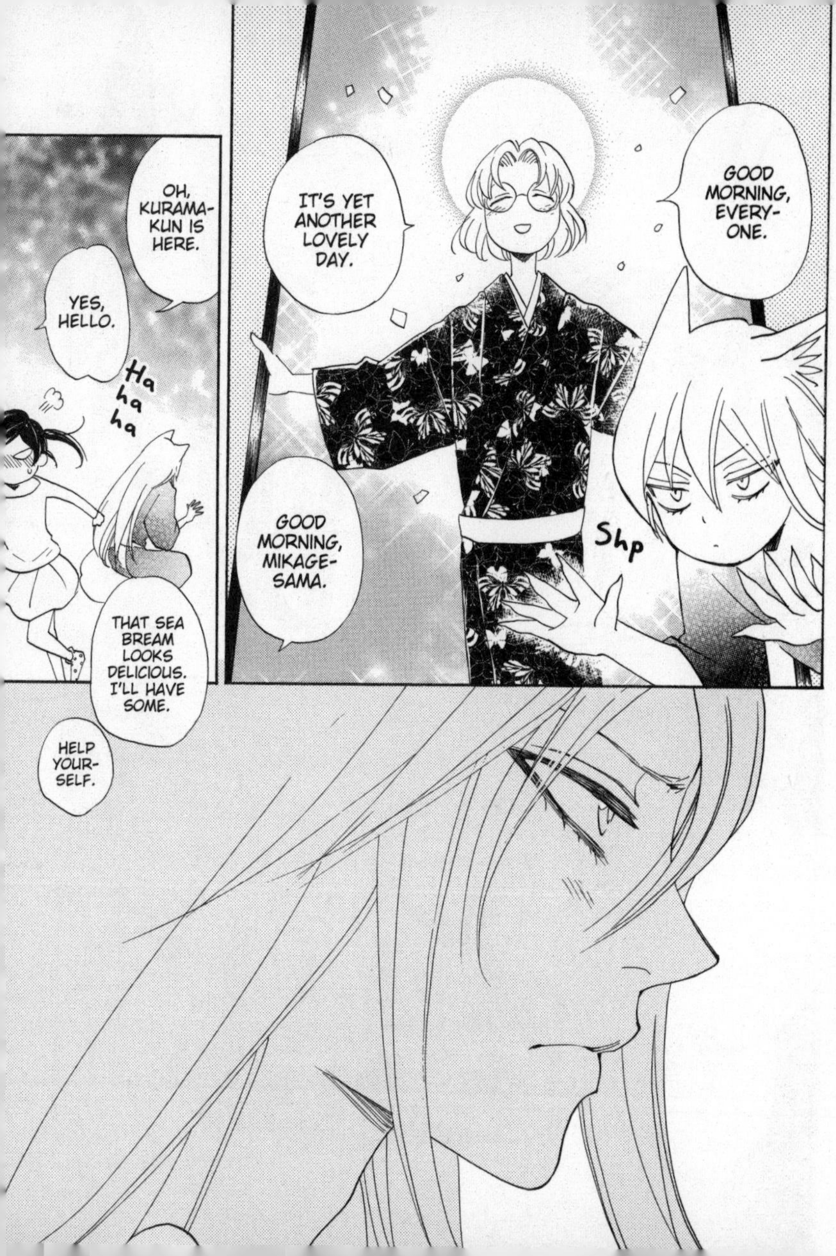
GOOD MORNING, EVERY-ONE.
IT'S YET ANOTHER LOVELY DAY.
GOOD MORNING, MIKAGE-SAMA.
Shp
OH, KURAMA-KUN IS HERE.
YES, HELLO.
Ha ha ha
THAT SEA BREAM LOOKS DELICIOUS. I'LL HAVE SOME.
HELP YOUR-SELF.

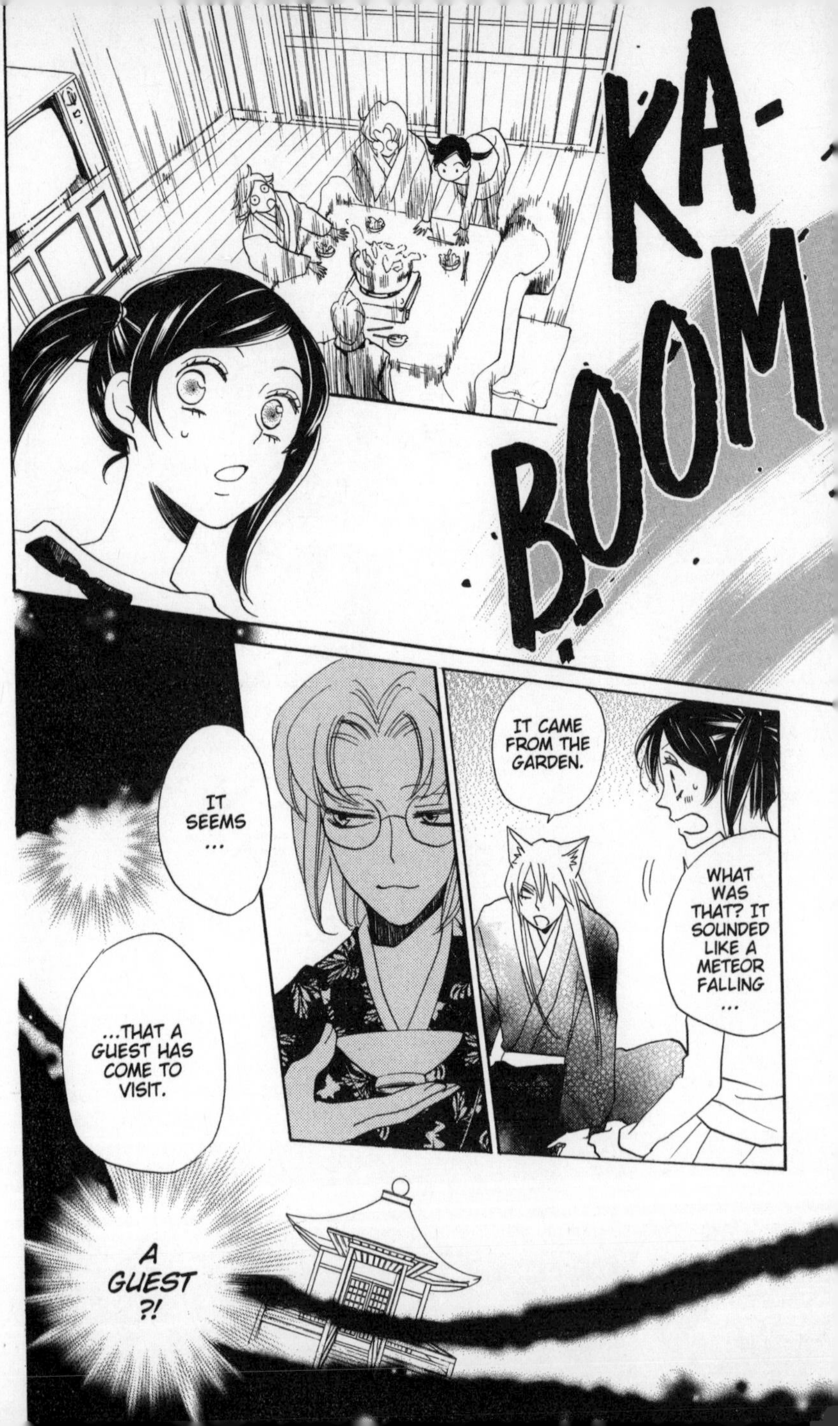
KA-BOOM
IT CAME FROM THE GARDEN.
WHAT WAS THAT? IT SOUNDED LIKE A METEOR FALLING...
IT SEEMS...
...THAT A GUEST HAS COME TO VISIT.
A GUEST?!

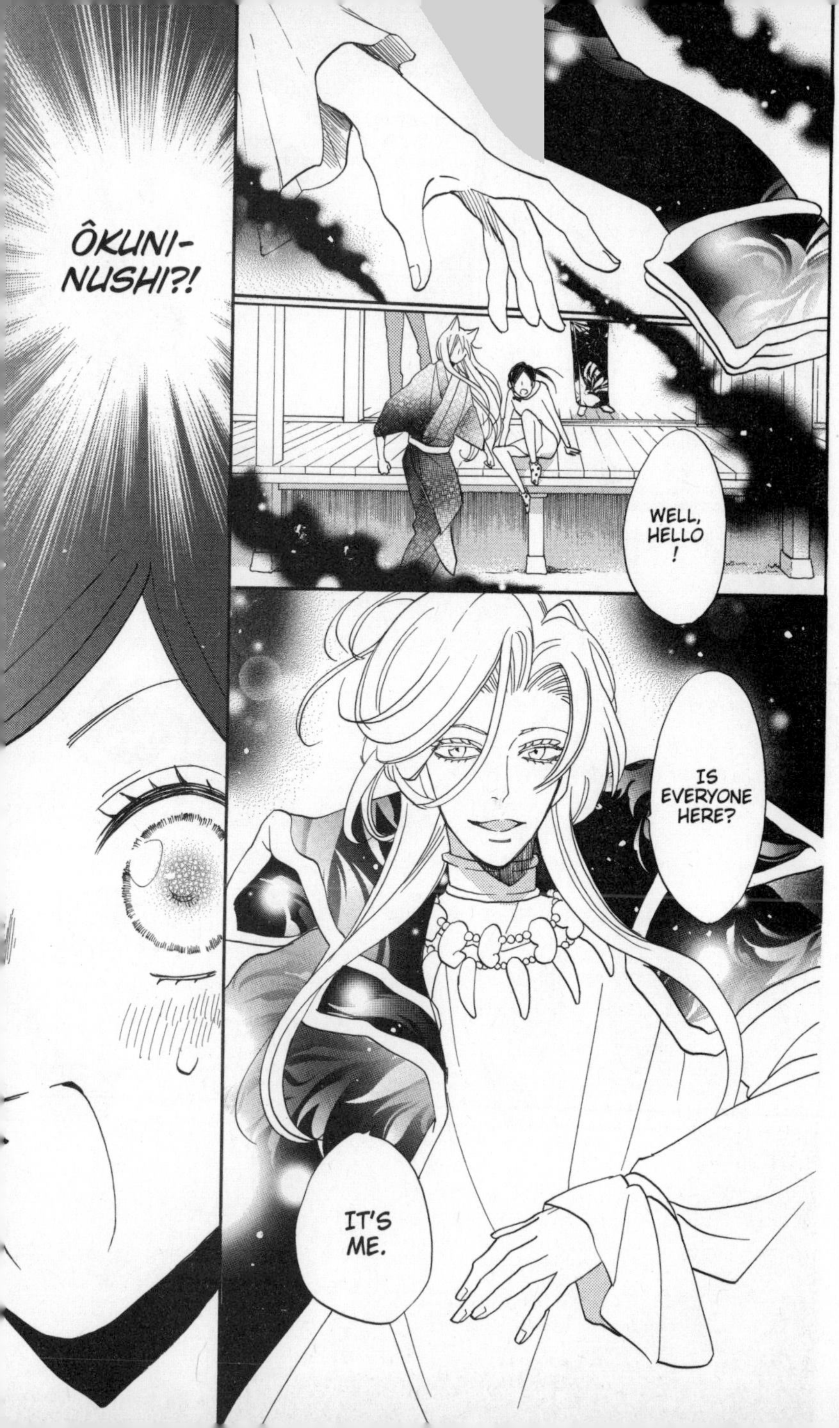
WELL, HELLO!
IS EVERYONE HERE?
IT'S ME.
ÔKUNI-NUSHI?!

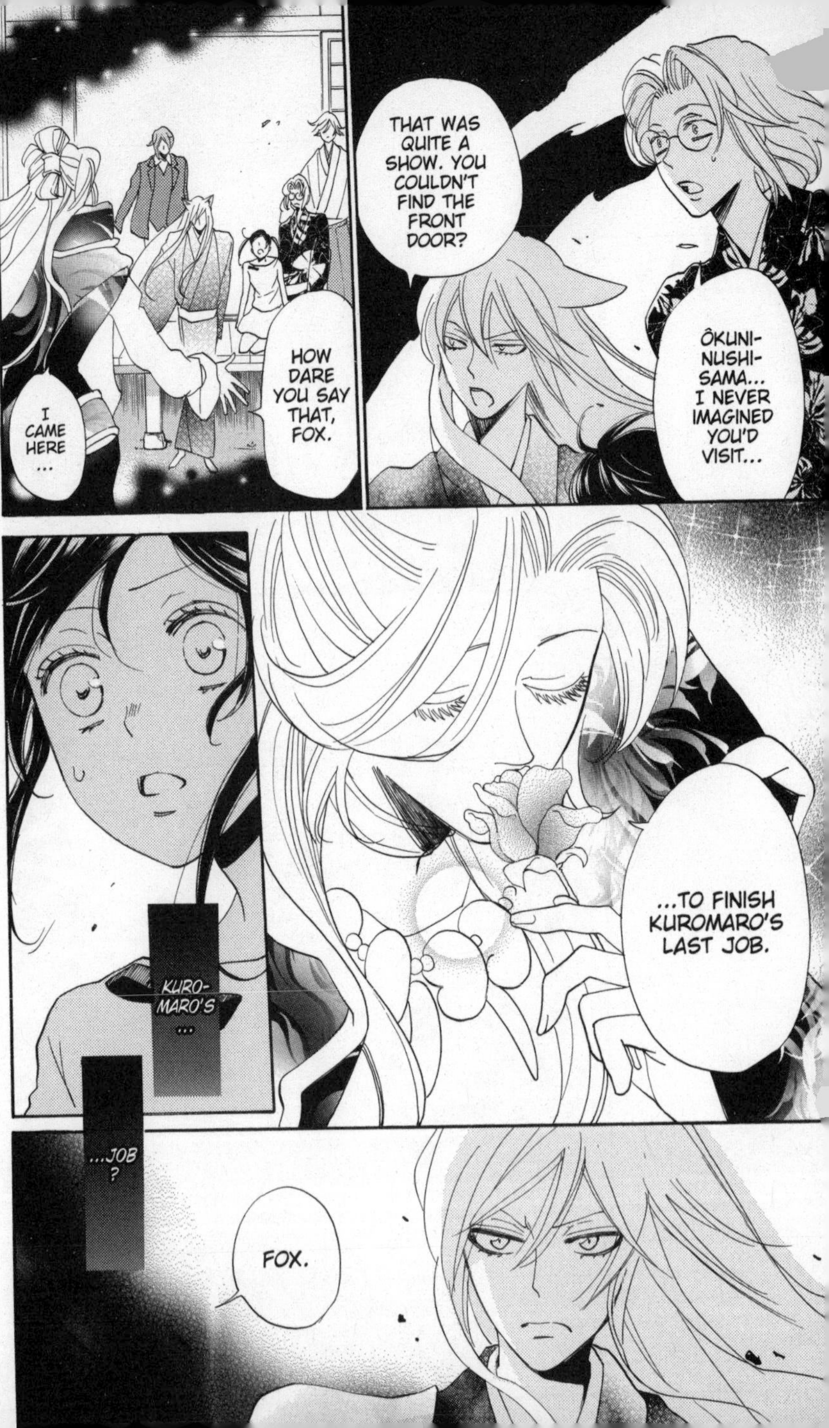
ÔKUNI-NUSHI-SAMA... I NEVER IMAGINED YOU'D VISIT...
THAT WAS QUITE A SHOW. YOU COULDN'T FIND THE FRONT DOOR?
HOW DARE YOU SAY THAT, FOX.
I CAME HERE ...
...TO FINISH KUROMARO'S LAST JOB.
KURO-MARO'S ...
...JOB ?
FOX.

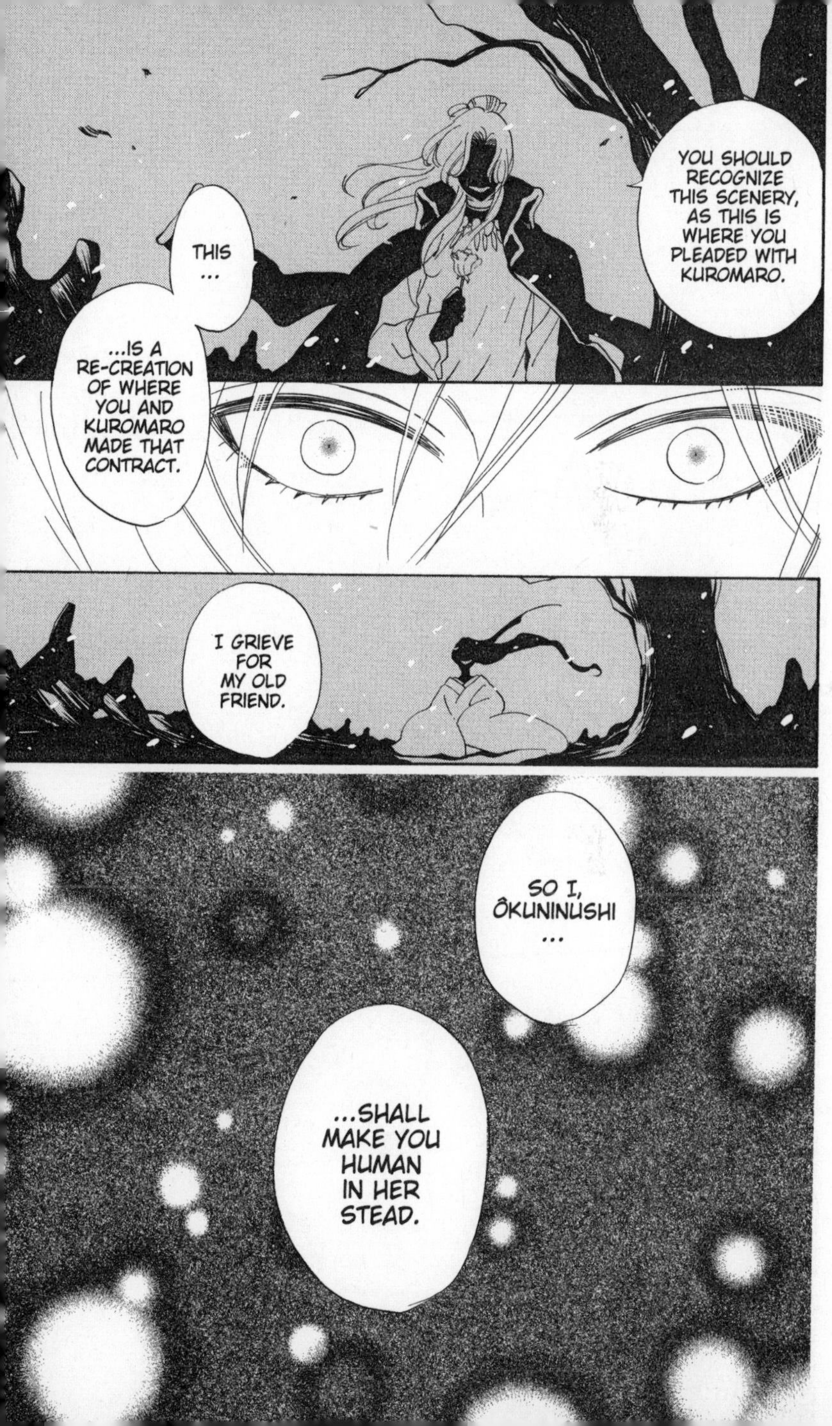
YOU SHOULD RECOGNIZE THIS SCENERY, AS THIS IS WHERE YOU PLEADED WITH KUROMARO.
THIS ...
...IS A RE-CREATION OF WHERE YOU AND KUROMARO MADE THAT CONTRACT.
I GRIEVE FOR MY OLD FRIEND.
SO I, ÔKUNINUSHI ...
...SHALL MAKE YOU HUMAN IN HER STEAD.

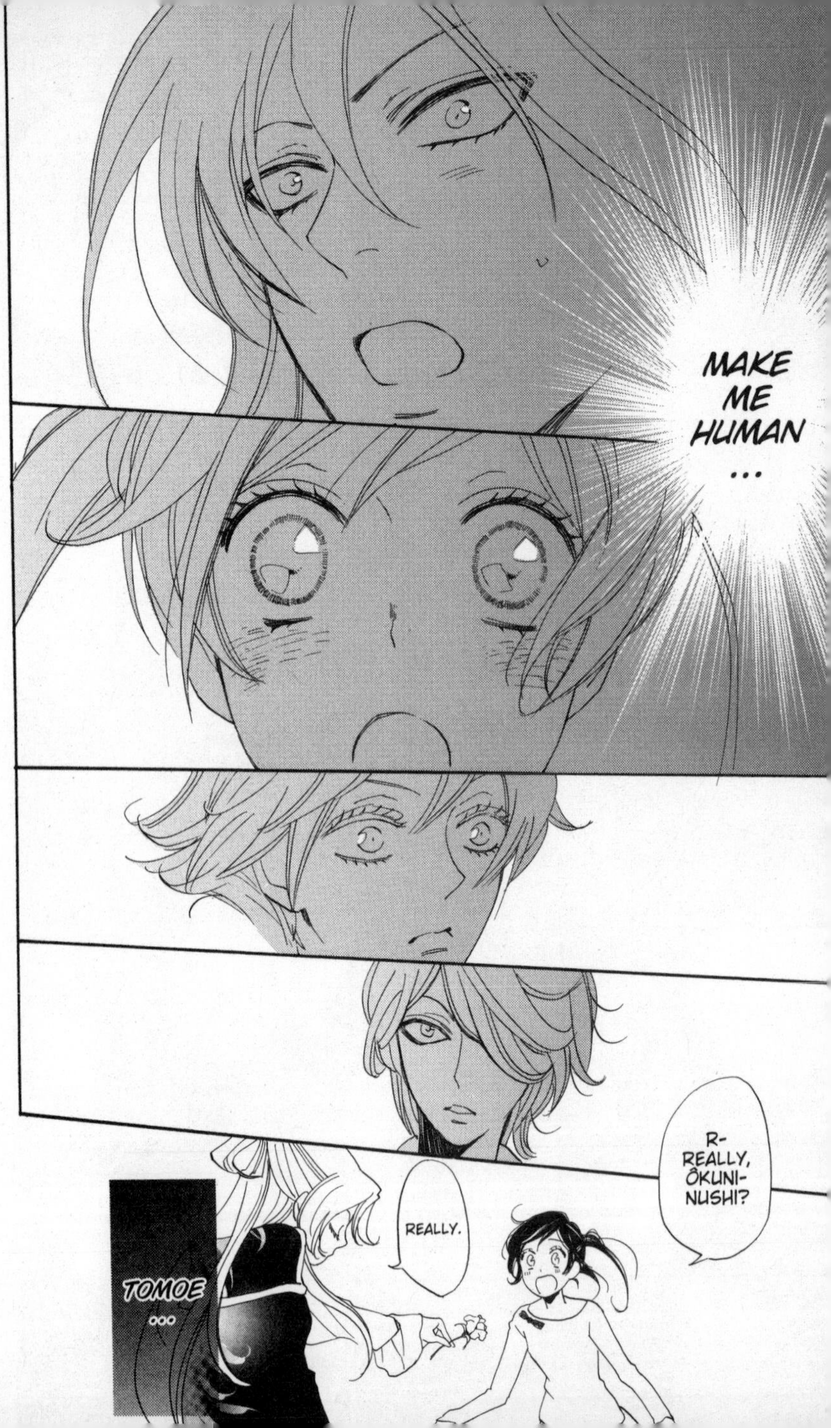
MAKE ME HUMAN ...
R-REALLY, ŌKUNI-NUSHI?
REALLY.
TOMOE ...

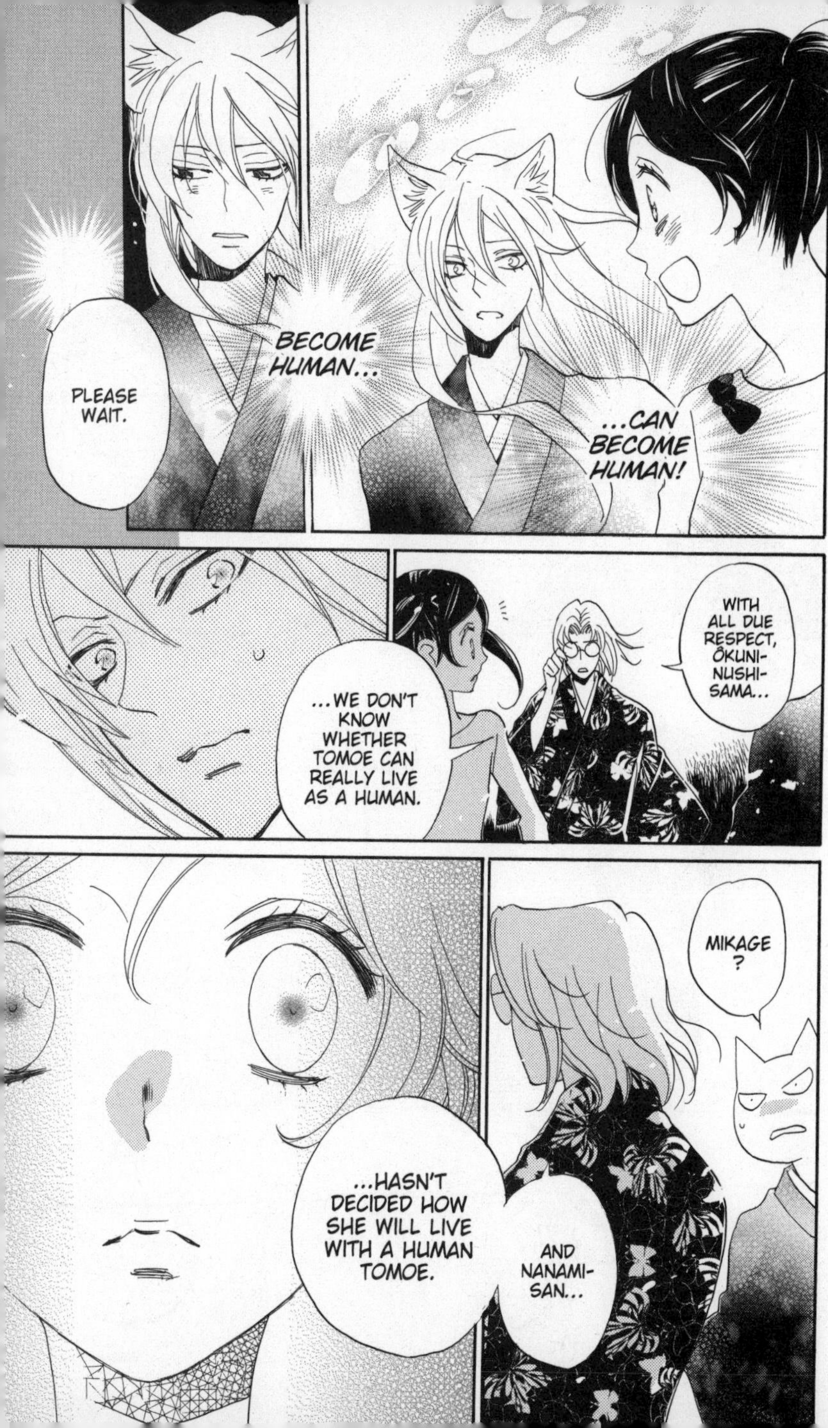
...CAN BECOME HUMAN!
BECOME HUMAN...
PLEASE WAIT.
WITH ALL DUE RESPECT, ŌKUNI-NUSHI-SAMA...
...WE DON'T KNOW WHETHER TOMOE CAN REALLY LIVE AS A HUMAN.
MIKAGE?
AND NANAMI-SAN...
...HASN'T DECIDED HOW SHE WILL LIVE WITH A HUMAN TOMOE.

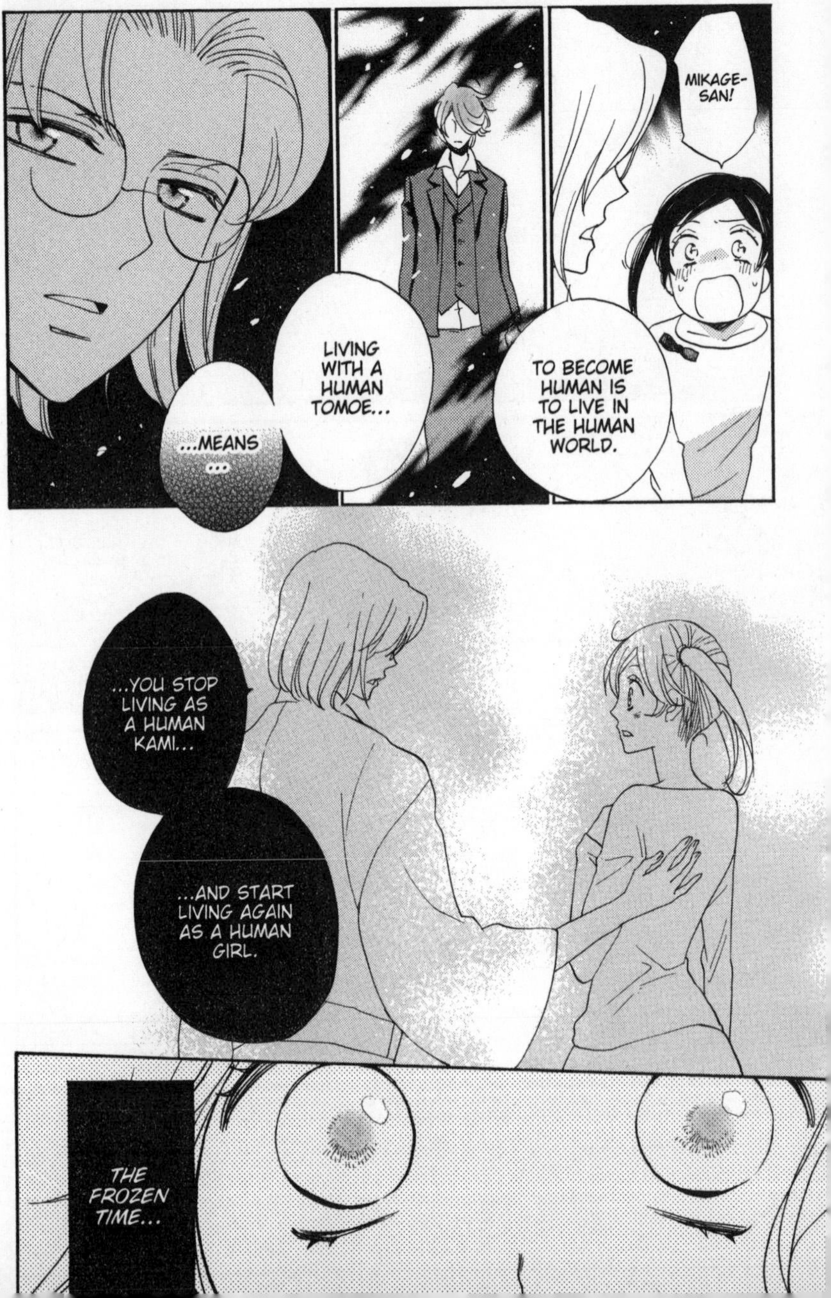
MIKAGE-SAN!
TO BECOME HUMAN IS TO LIVE IN THE HUMAN WORLD.
LIVING WITH A HUMAN TOMOE...
...MEANS ...
...YOU STOP LIVING AS A HUMAN KAMI...
...AND START LIVING AGAIN AS A HUMAN GIRL.
THE FROZEN TIME...

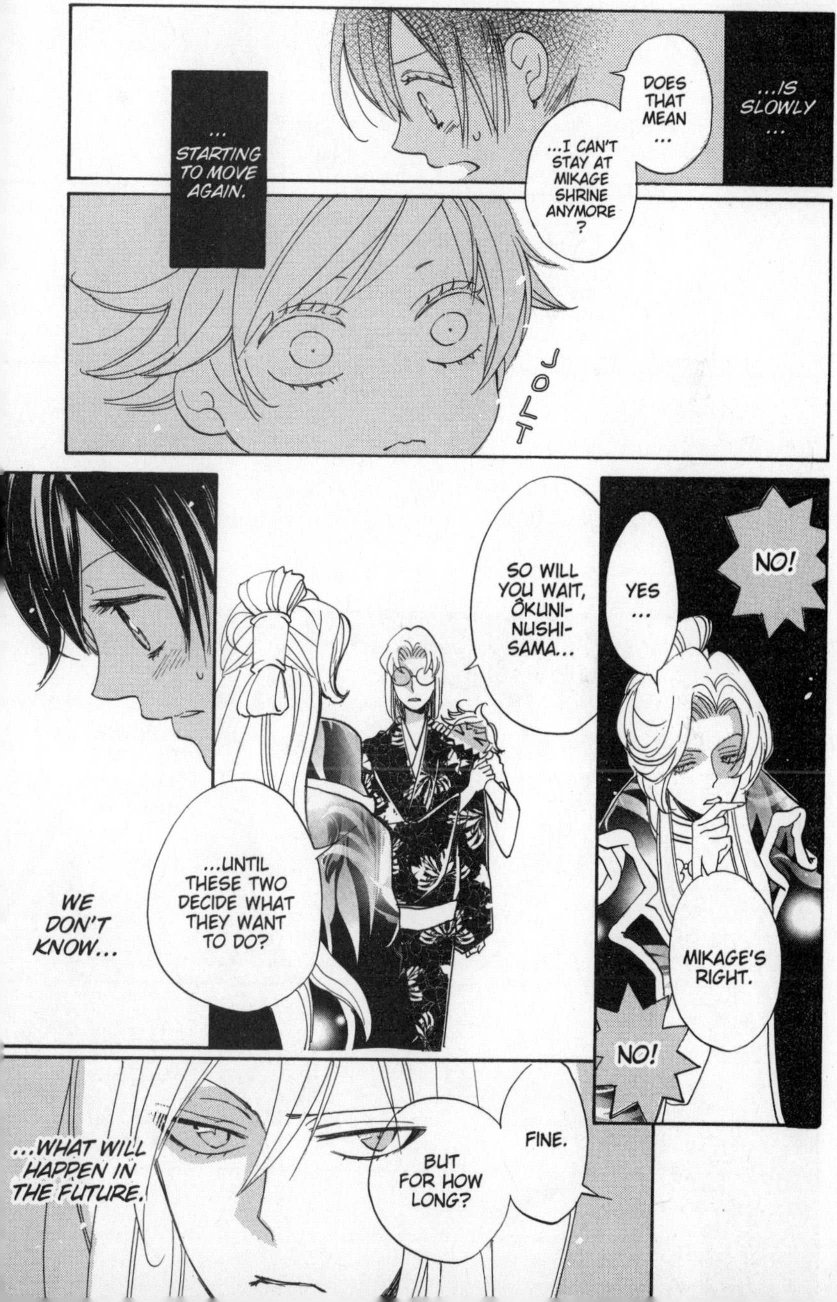
...IS SLOWLY...
DOES THAT MEAN...
...I CAN'T STAY AT MIKAGE SHRINE ANYMORE?
...STARTING TO MOVE AGAIN.
JOLT
SO WILL YOU WAIT, ŌKUNI-NUSHI-SAMA...
...UNTIL THESE TWO DECIDE WHAT THEY WANT TO DO?
YES...
NO!
MIKAGE'S RIGHT.
NO!
WE DON'T KNOW...
FINE.
BUT FOR HOW LONG?
...WHAT WILL HAPPEN IN THE FUTURE.

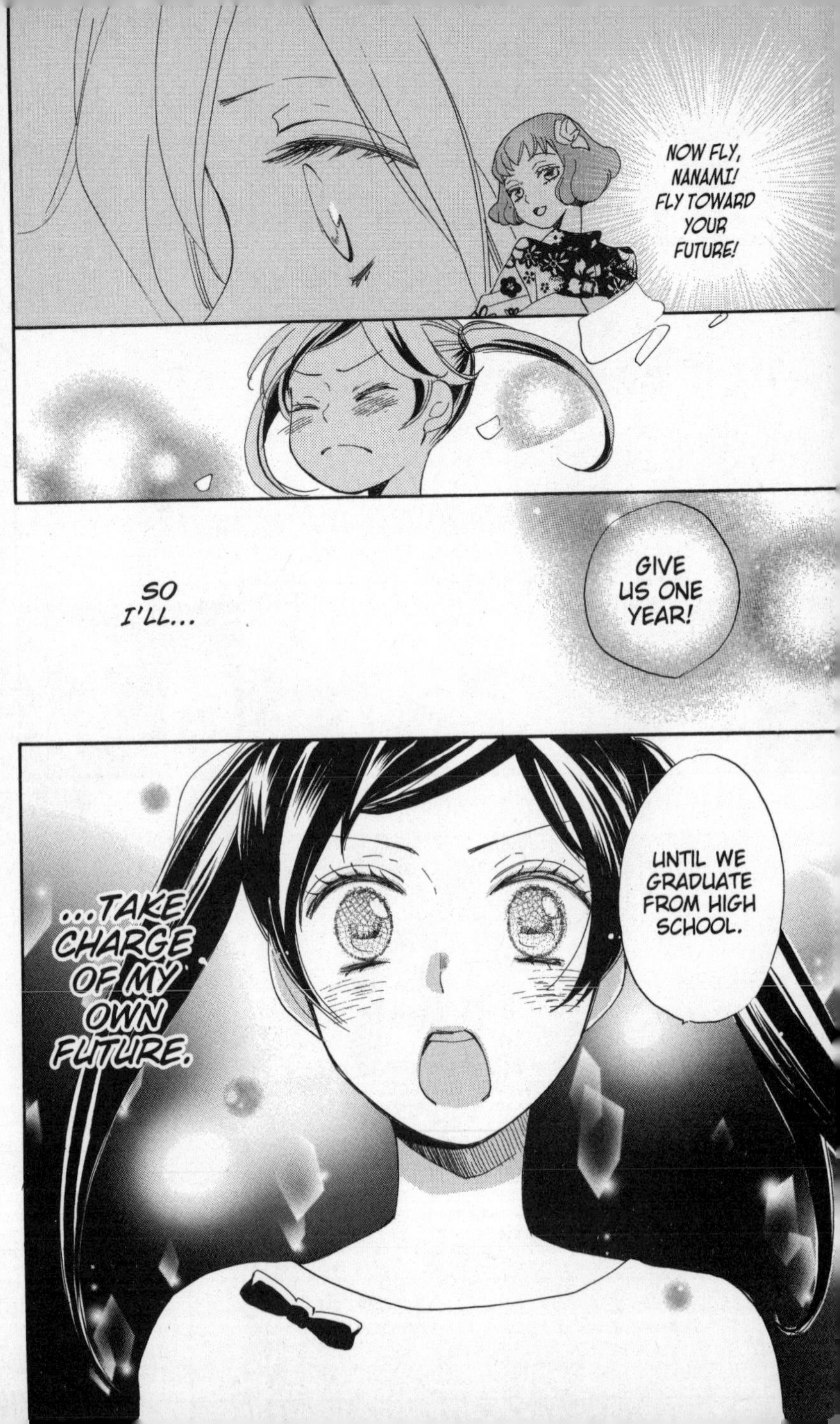
NOW FLY, NANAMI! FLY TOWARD YOUR FUTURE!
GIVE US ONE YEAR!
SO I'LL...
UNTIL WE GRADUATE FROM HIGH SCHOOL.
...TAKE CHARGE OF MY OWN FUTURE.

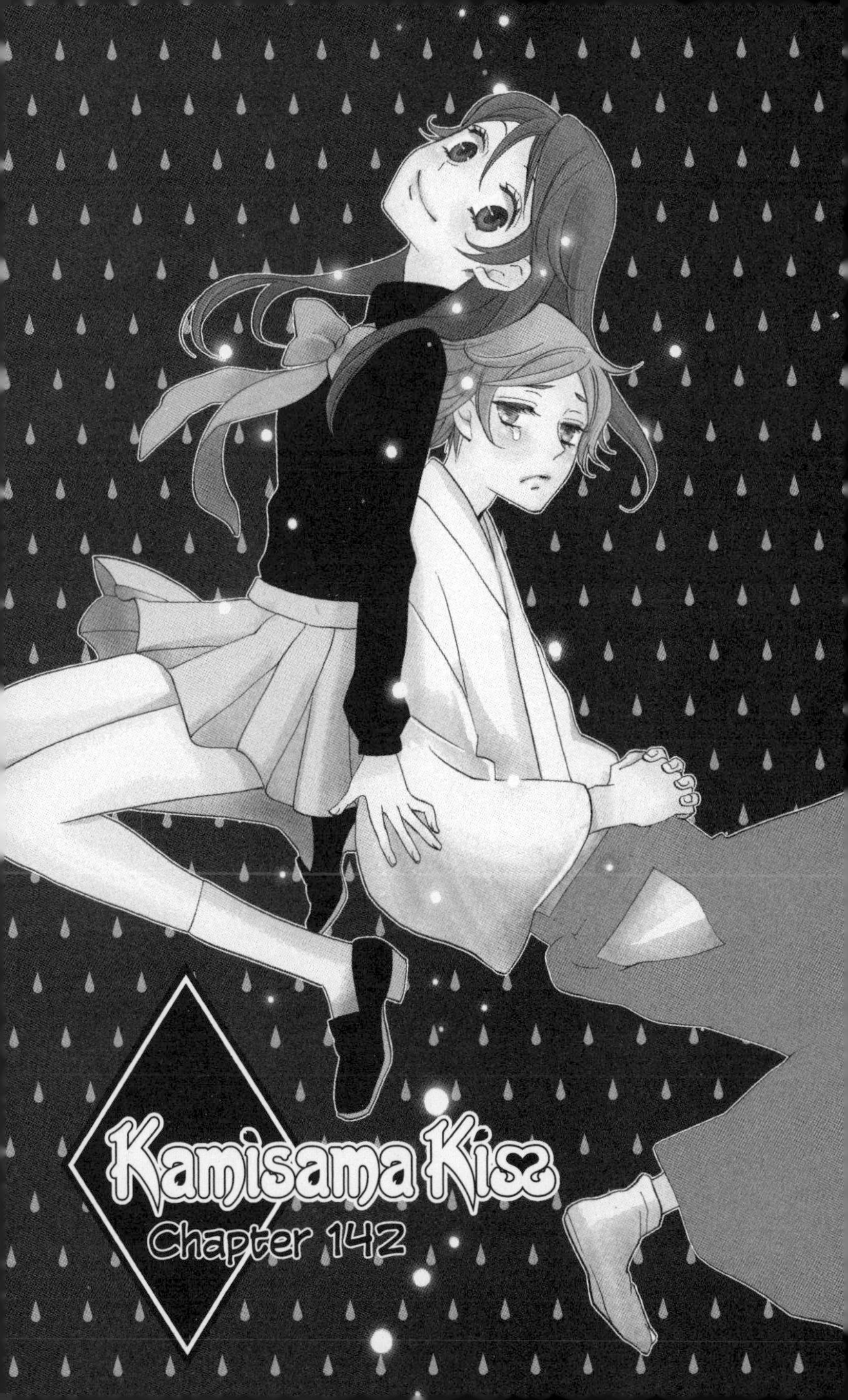
Kamisama Kiss
Chapter 142

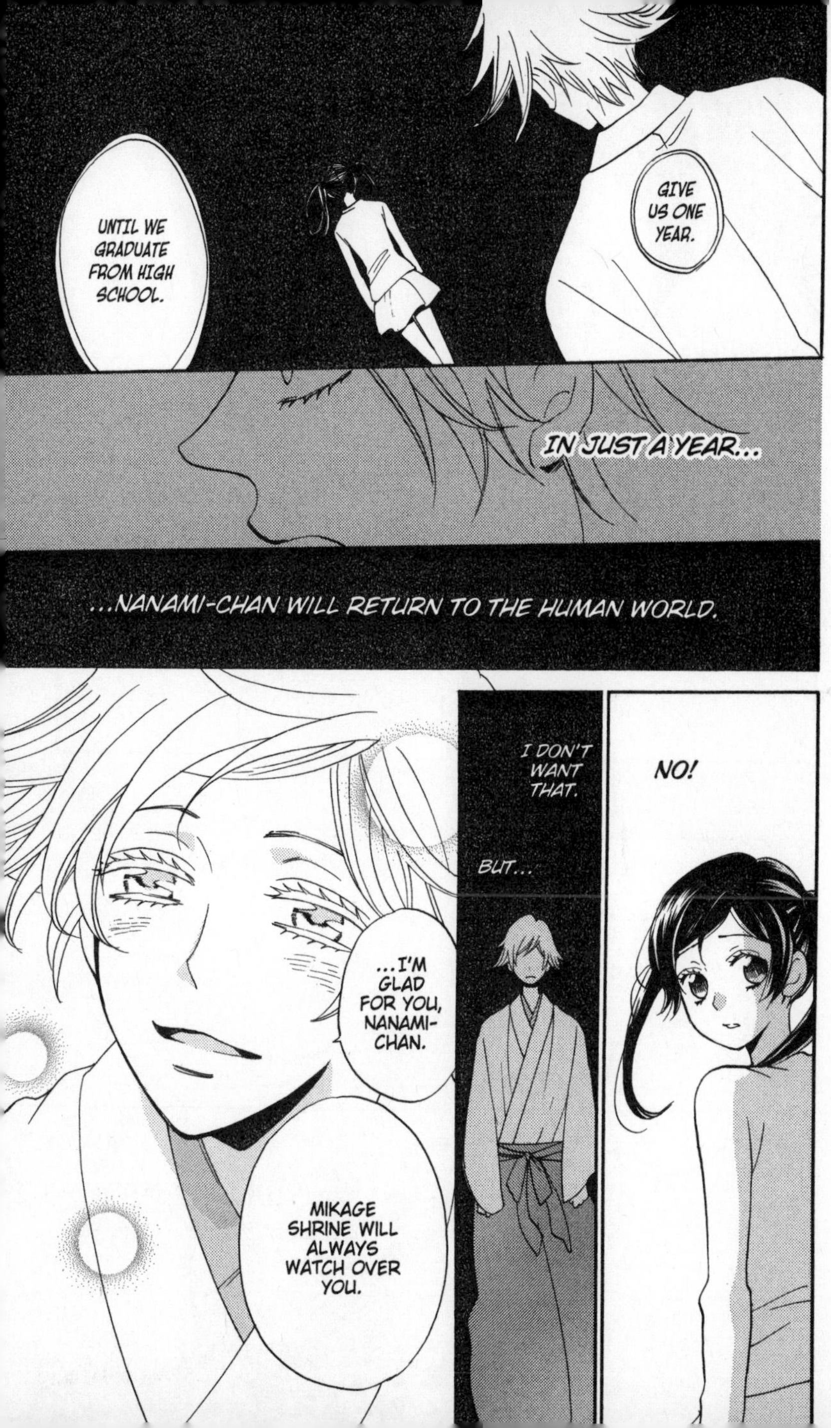
GIVE US ONE YEAR.
UNTIL WE GRADUATE FROM HIGH SCHOOL.
IN JUST A YEAR...
...NANAMI-CHAN WILL RETURN TO THE HUMAN WORLD.
NO!
I DON'T WANT THAT.
BUT...
...I'M GLAD FOR YOU, NANAMI-CHAN.
MIKAGE SHRINE WILL ALWAYS WATCH OVER YOU.

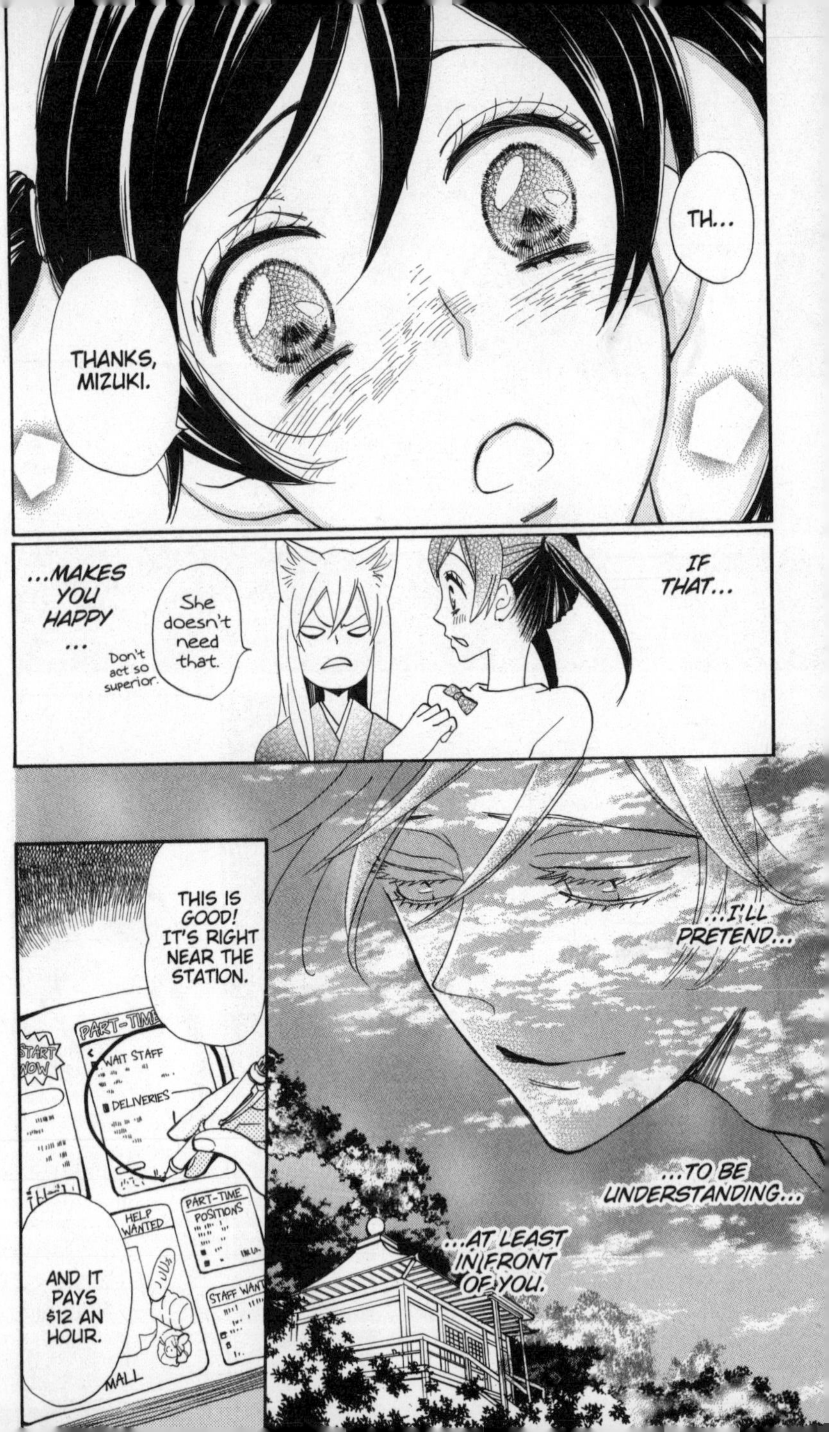
TH...
THANKS, MIZUKI.
IF THAT...
She doesn't need that.
Don't act so superior.
...MAKES YOU HAPPY ...
...I'LL PRETEND...
...TO BE UNDERSTANDING...
...AT LEAST IN FRONT OF YOU.
THIS IS GOOD! IT'S RIGHT NEAR THE STATION.
START NOW
WAIT STAFF
DELIVERIES
PART-TIME POSITIONS
HELP WANTED
AND IT PAYS $12 AN HOUR.
MALL

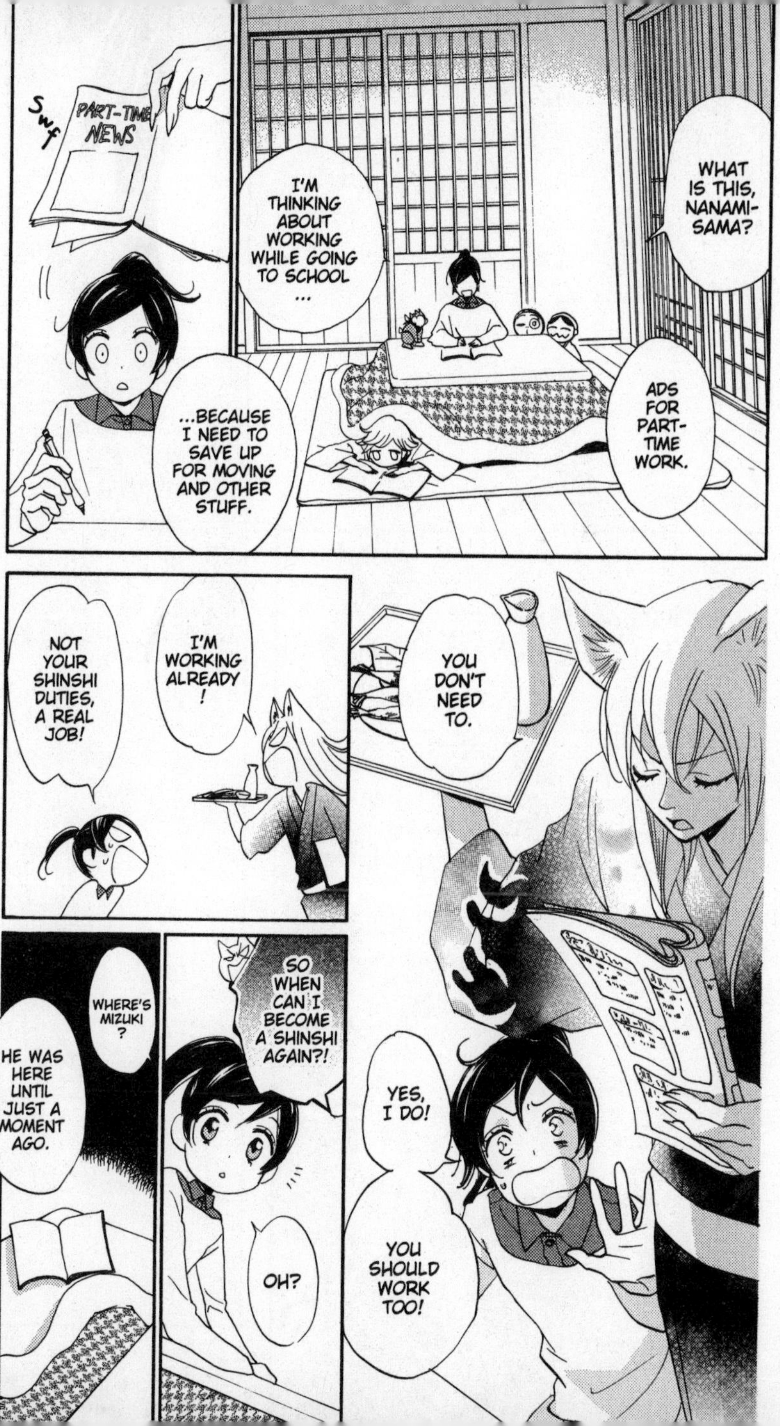
WHAT IS THIS, NANAMI-SAMA?
ADS FOR PART-TIME WORK.
I'M THINKING ABOUT WORKING WHILE GOING TO SCHOOL...
Swf
PART-TIME NEWS
...BECAUSE I NEED TO SAVE UP FOR MOVING AND OTHER STUFF.
YOU DON'T NEED TO.
YES, I DO!
YOU SHOULD WORK TOO!
I'M WORKING ALREADY!
NOT YOUR SHINSHI DUTIES, A REAL JOB!
SO WHEN CAN I BECOME A SHINSHI AGAIN?!
OH?
WHERE'S MIZUKI?
HE WAS HERE UNTIL JUST A MOMENT AGO.

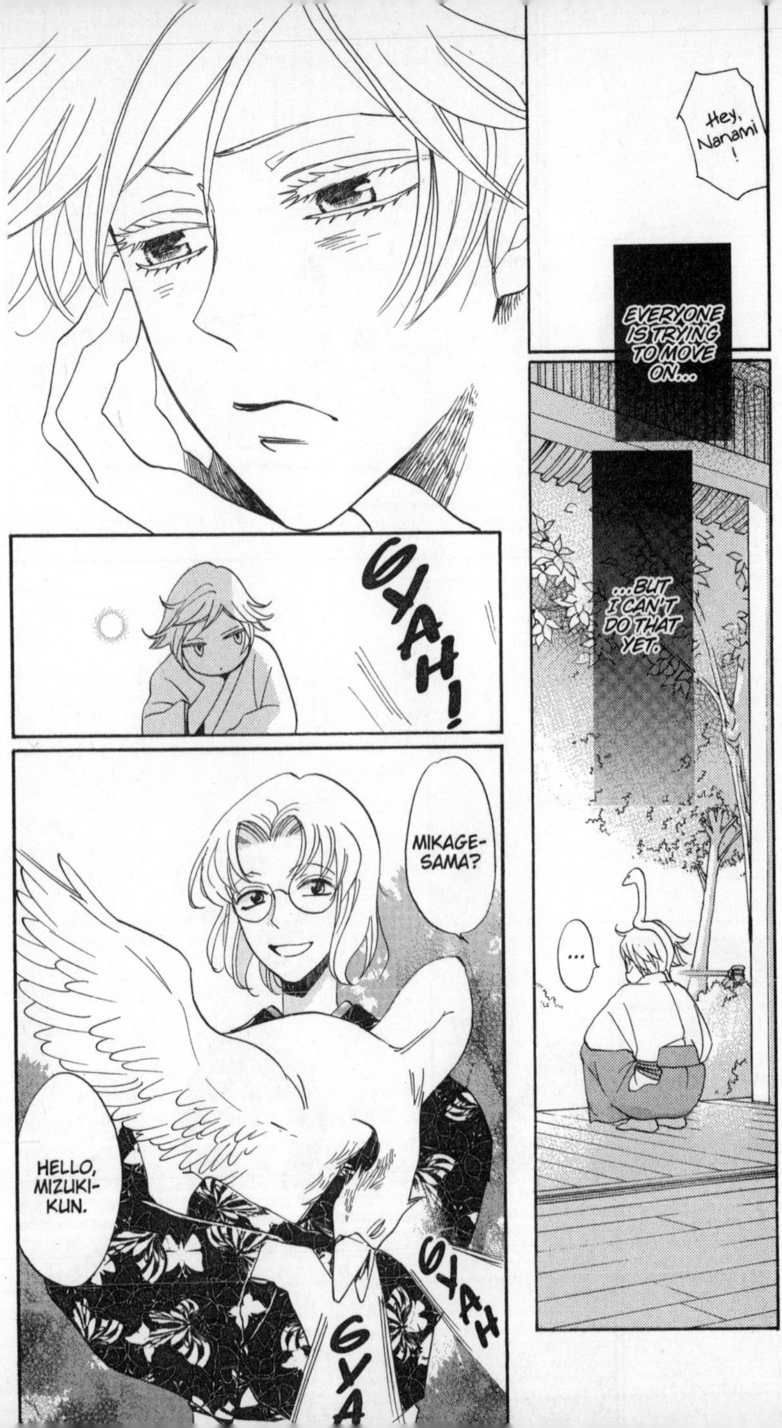
Hey, Nanami!
EVERYONE IS TRYING TO MOVE ON...
...BUT I CAN'T DO THAT YET.
...
SYAH!
MIKAGE-SAMA?
HELLO, MIZUKI-KUN.
SYAH
SYAH

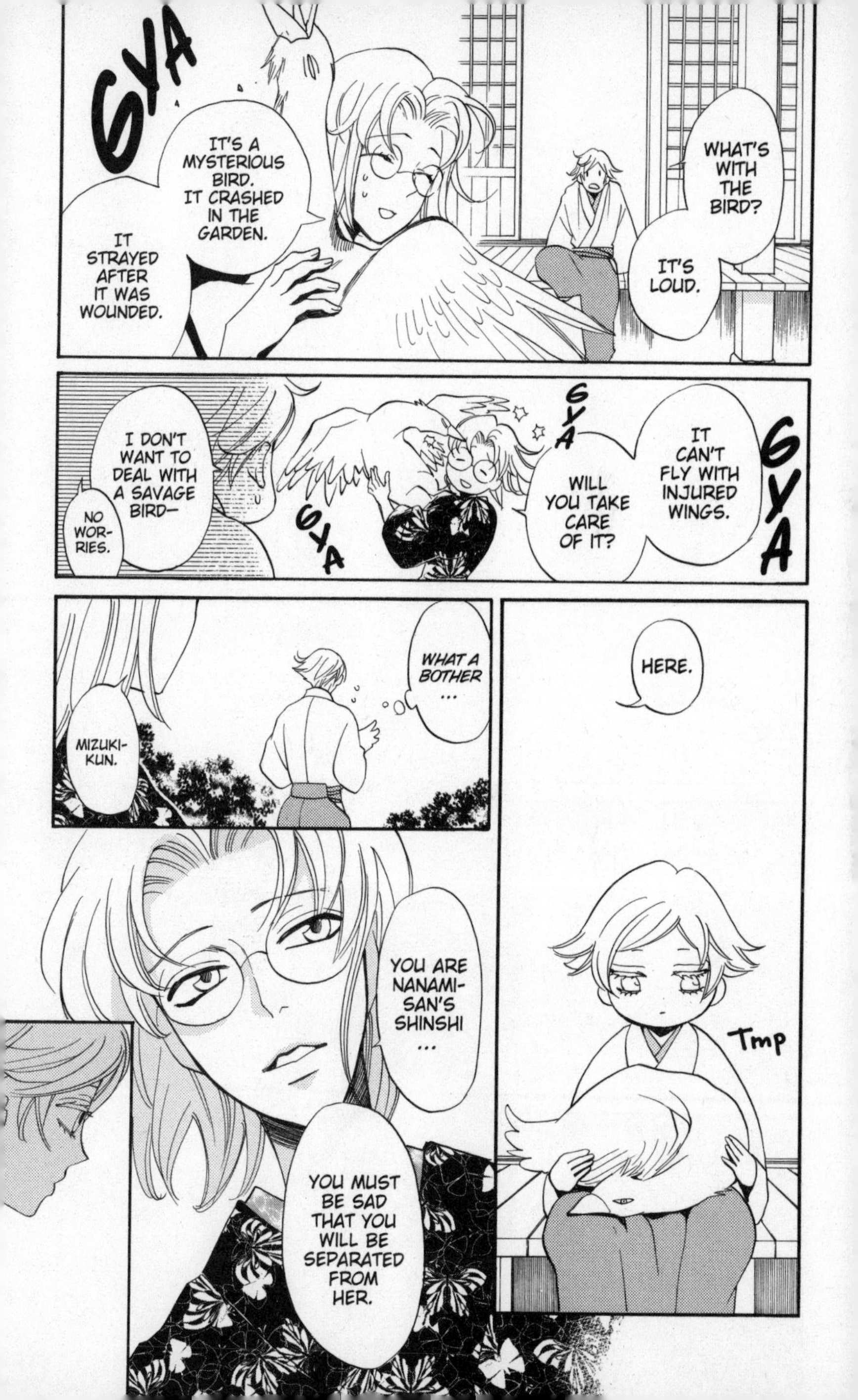
WHAT'S WITH THE BIRD?
IT'S LOUD.
GYA
IT'S A MYSTERIOUS BIRD. IT CRASHED IN THE GARDEN.
IT STRAYED AFTER IT WAS WOUNDED.
GYA
IT CAN'T FLY WITH INJURED WINGS.
GYA
WILL YOU TAKE CARE OF IT?
GYA
I DON'T WANT TO DEAL WITH A SAVAGE BIRD—
NO WOR-RIES.
HERE.
Tmp
WHAT A BOTHER...
MIZUKI-KUN.
YOU ARE NANAMI-SAN'S SHINSHI...
YOU MUST BE SAD THAT YOU WILL BE SEPARATED FROM HER.

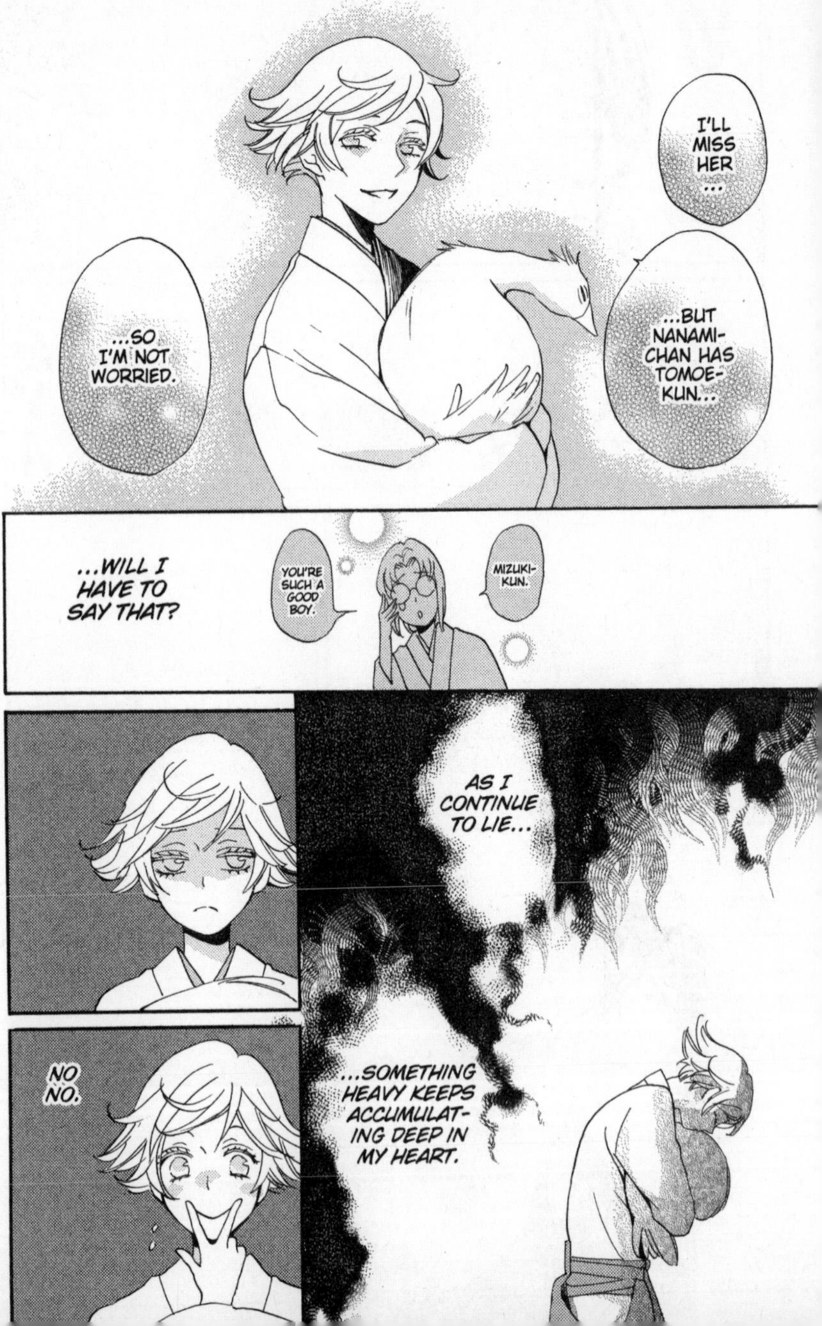
I'LL MISS HER...
...BUT NANAMI-CHAN HAS TOMOE-KUN...
...SO I'M NOT WORRIED.
MIZUKI-KUN.
YOU'RE SUCH A GOOD BOY.
...WILL I HAVE TO SAY THAT?
AS I CONTINUE TO LIE...
...SOMETHING HEAVY KEEPS ACCUMULATING DEEP IN MY HEART.
NO NO.

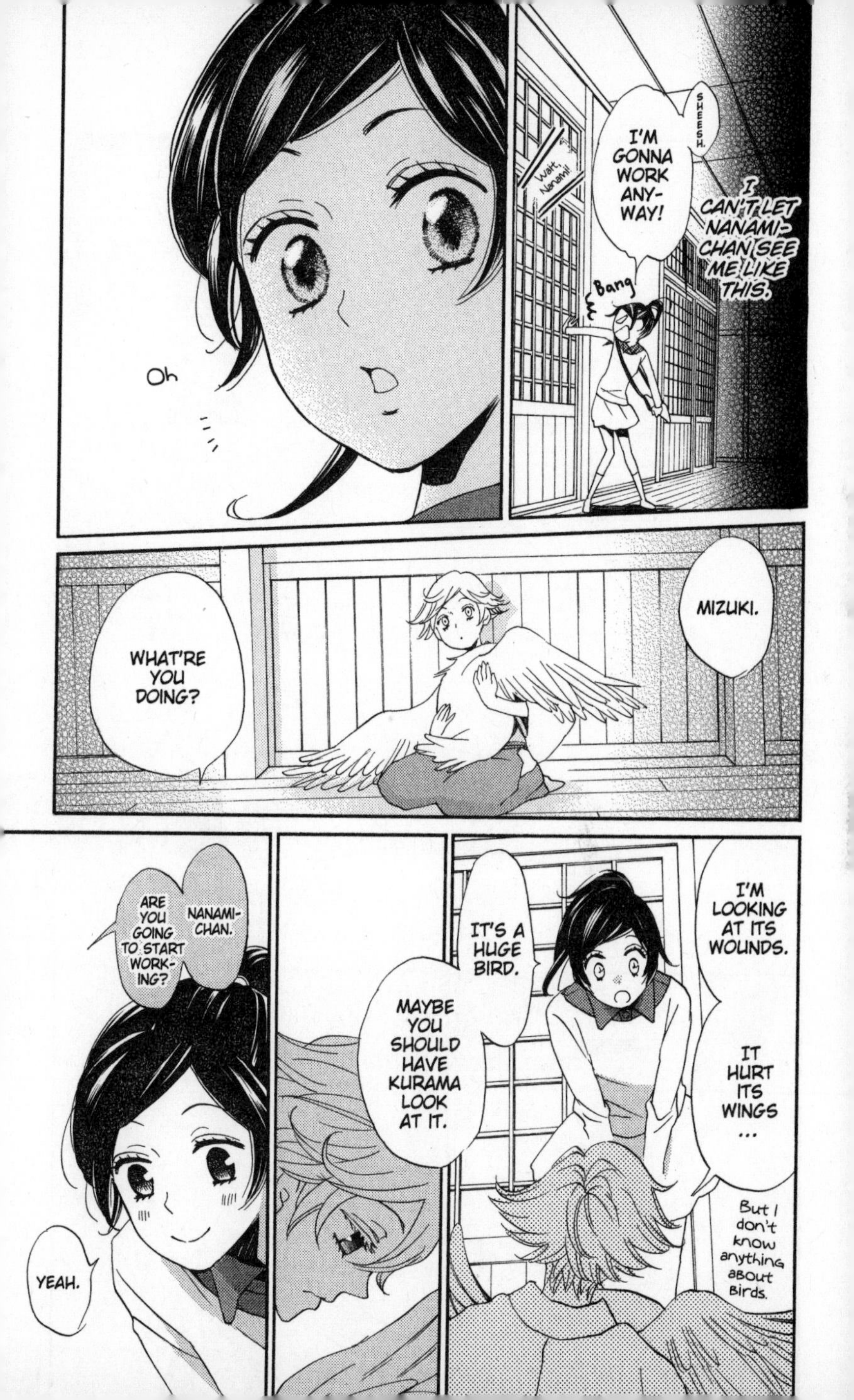
SHEESH.
I'M GONNA WORK ANYWAY!
Wait, Nanami!
Bang
I CAN'T LET NANAMI-CHAN SEE ME LIKE THIS.
Oh
MIZUKI.
WHAT'RE YOU DOING?
I'M LOOKING AT ITS WOUNDS.
IT HURT ITS WINGS...
IT'S A HUGE BIRD.
MAYBE YOU SHOULD HAVE KURAMA LOOK AT IT.
But I don't know anything about Birds.
NANAMI-CHAN.
ARE YOU GOING TO START WORKING?
YEAH.

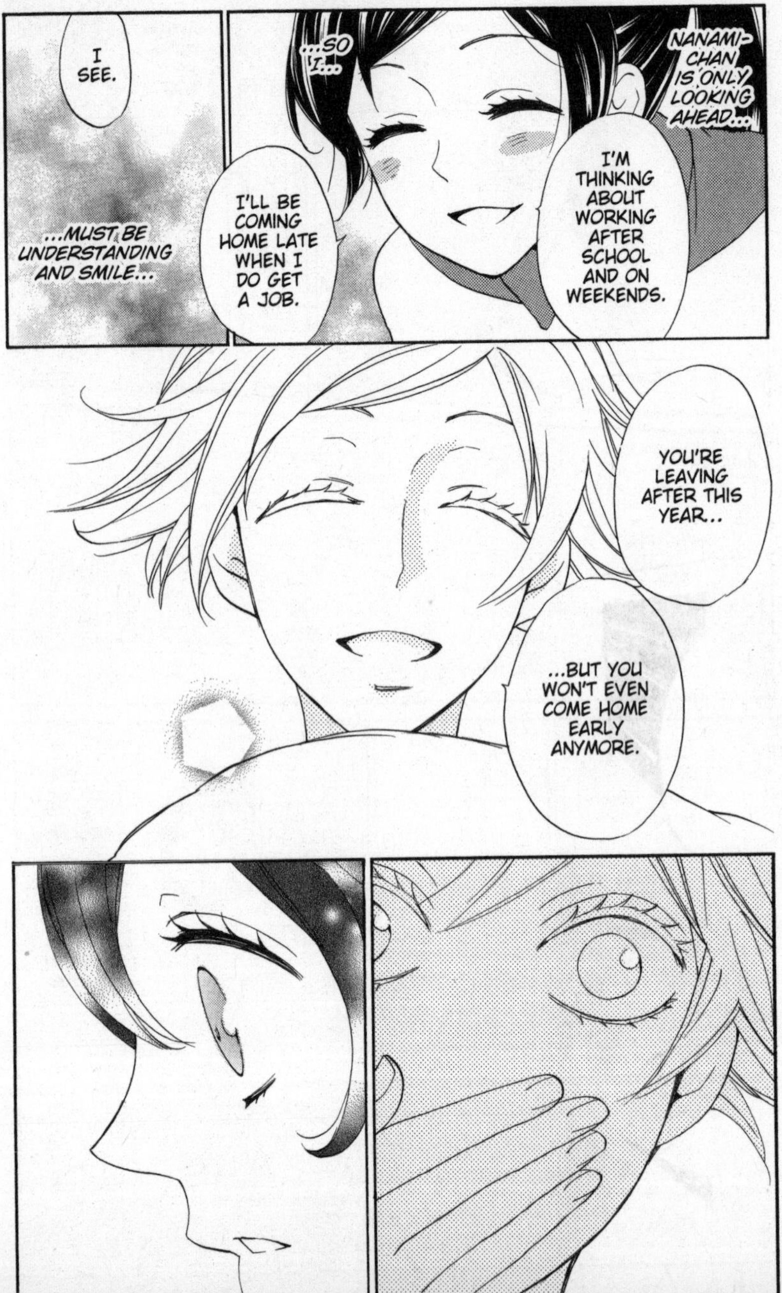
NANAMI-CHAN IS ONLY LOOKING AHEAD...
...SO I...
I'M THINKING ABOUT WORKING AFTER SCHOOL AND ON WEEKENDS.
I'LL BE COMING HOME LATE WHEN I DO GET A JOB.
I SEE.
...MUST BE UNDERSTANDING AND SMILE...
YOU'RE LEAVING AFTER THIS YEAR...
...BUT YOU WON'T EVEN COME HOME EARLY ANYMORE.

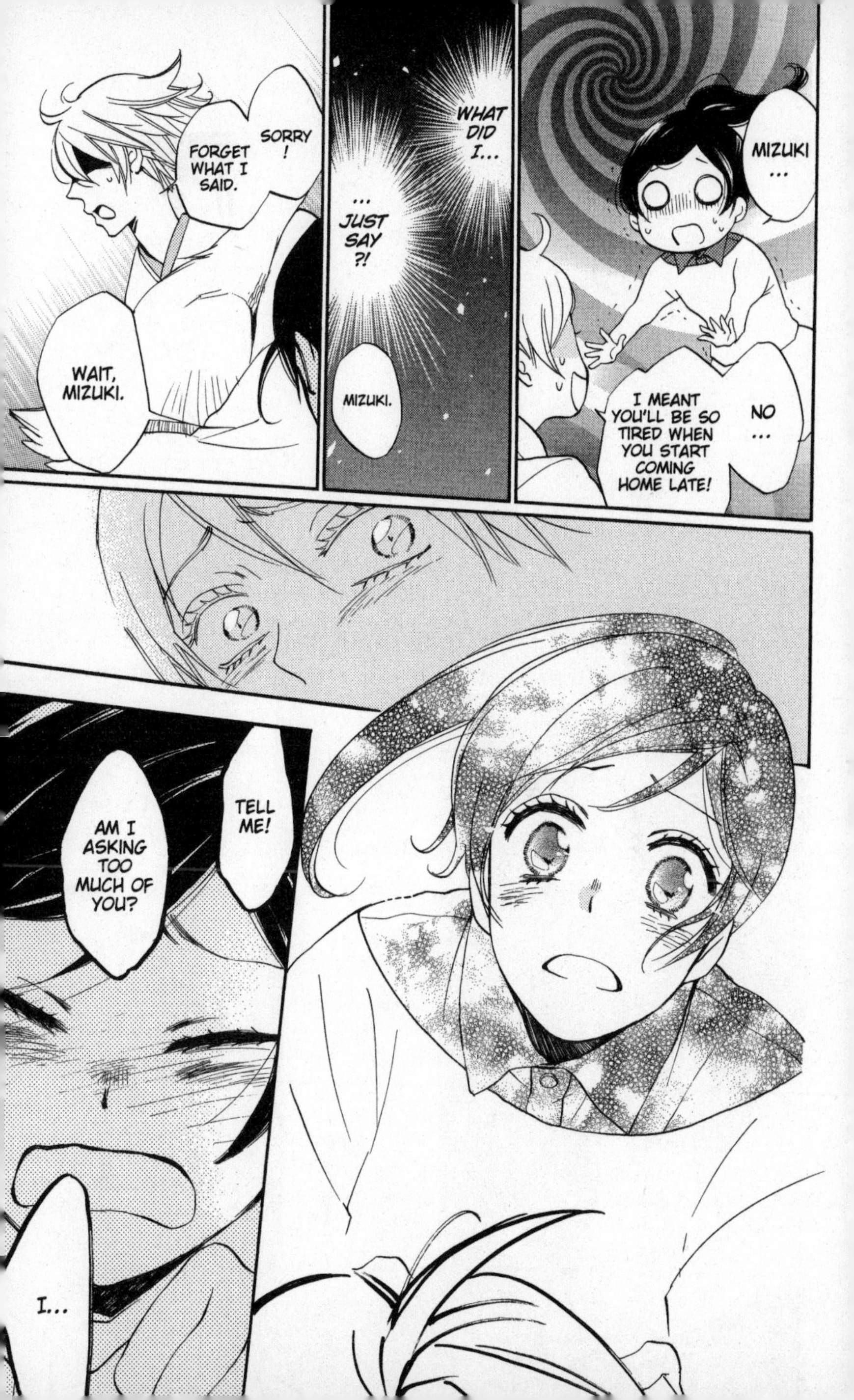
MIZUKI ...
NO ...
I MEANT YOU'LL BE SO TIRED WHEN YOU START COMING HOME LATE!
WHAT DID I...
... JUST SAY ?!
MIZUKI.
SORRY!
FORGET WHAT I SAID.
WAIT, MIZUKI.
TELL ME!
AM I ASKING TOO MUCH OF YOU?
I...

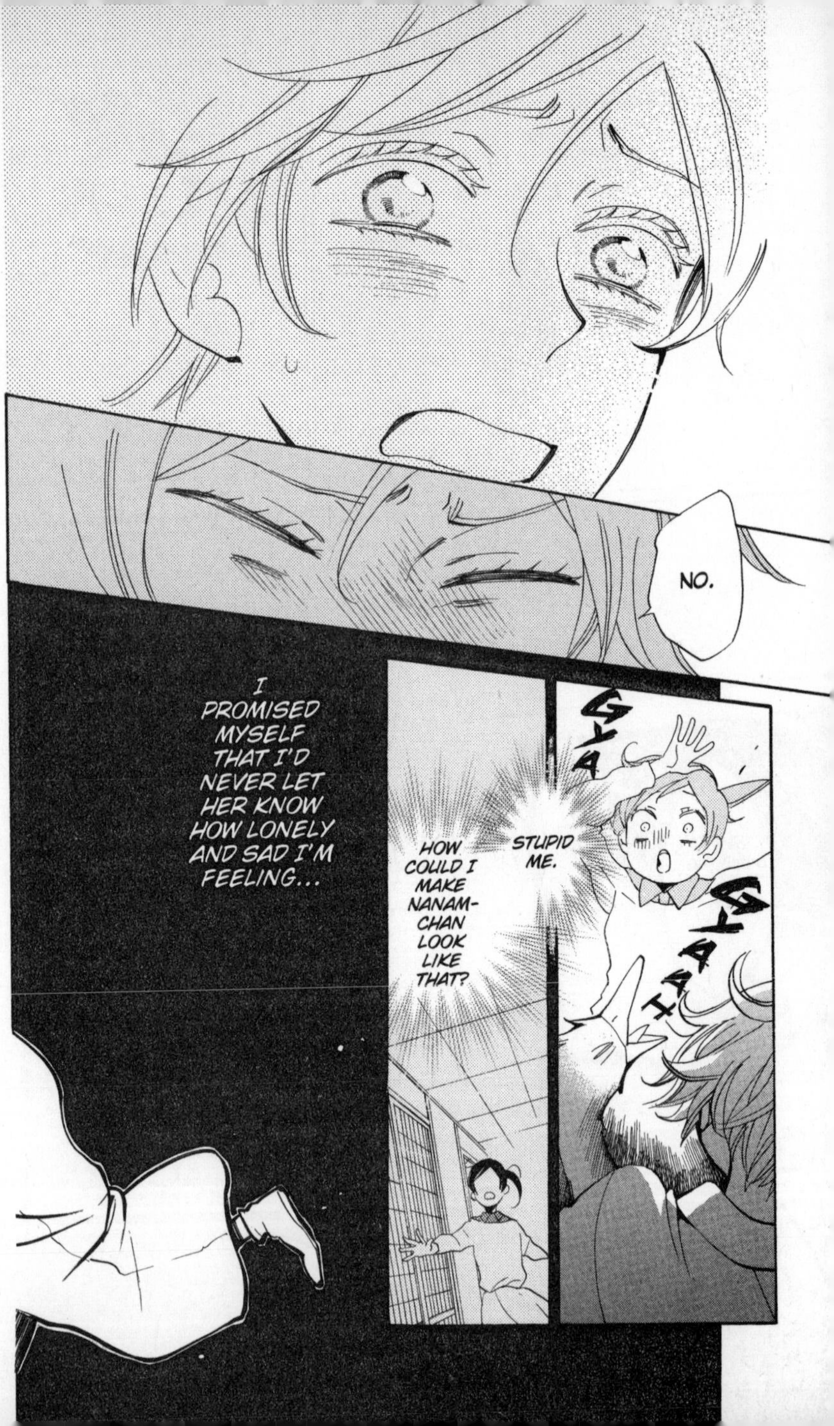
NO.
GYA
GYAAH
STUPID ME.
HOW COULD I MAKE NANAM-CHAN LOOK LIKE THAT?
I PROMISED MYSELF THAT I'D NEVER LET HER KNOW HOW LONELY AND SAD I'M FEELING...

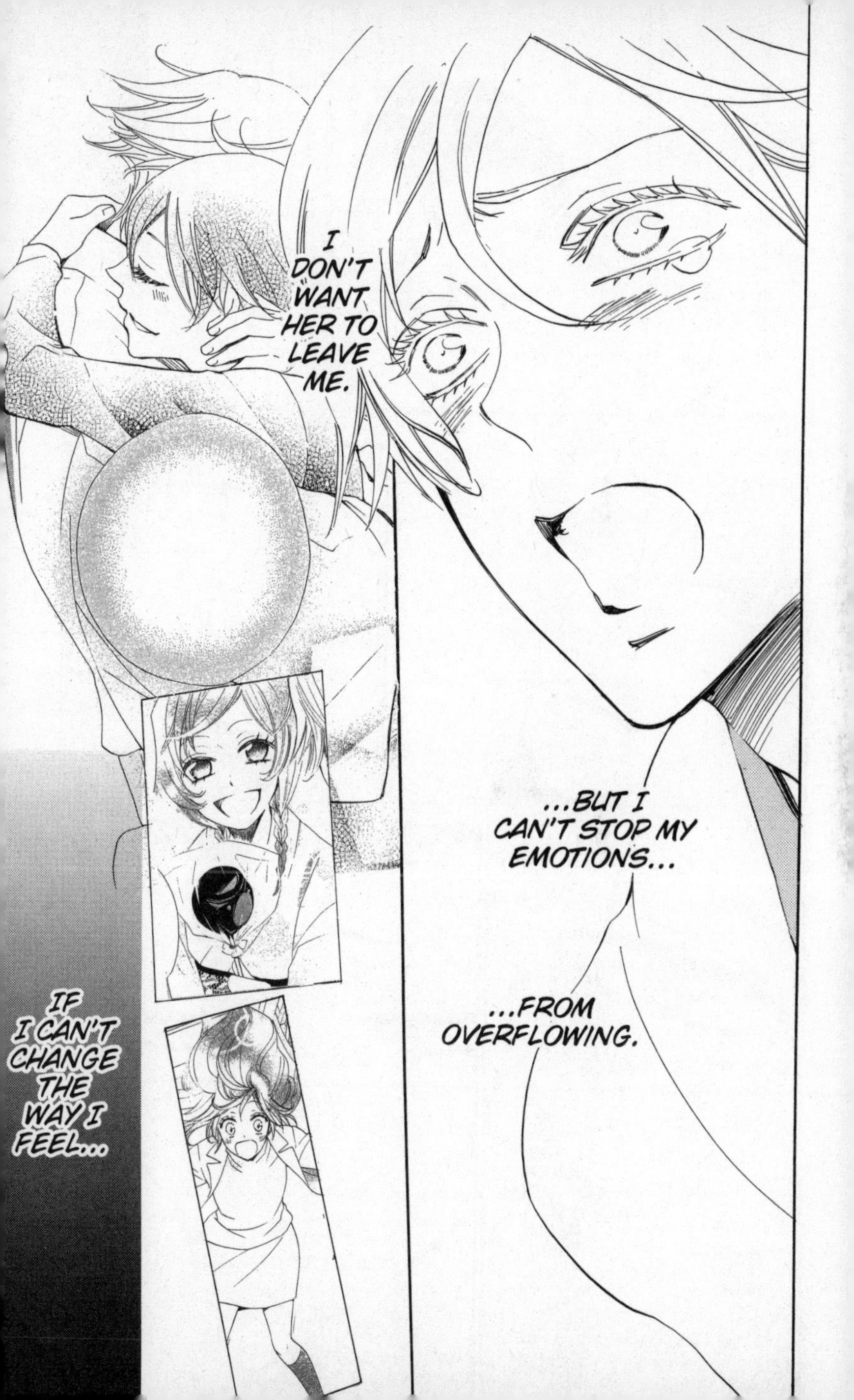
I DON'T WANT HER TO LEAVE ME.
...BUT I CAN'T STOP MY EMOTIONS...
...FROM OVERFLOWING.
IF I CAN'T CHANGE THE WAY I FEEL...

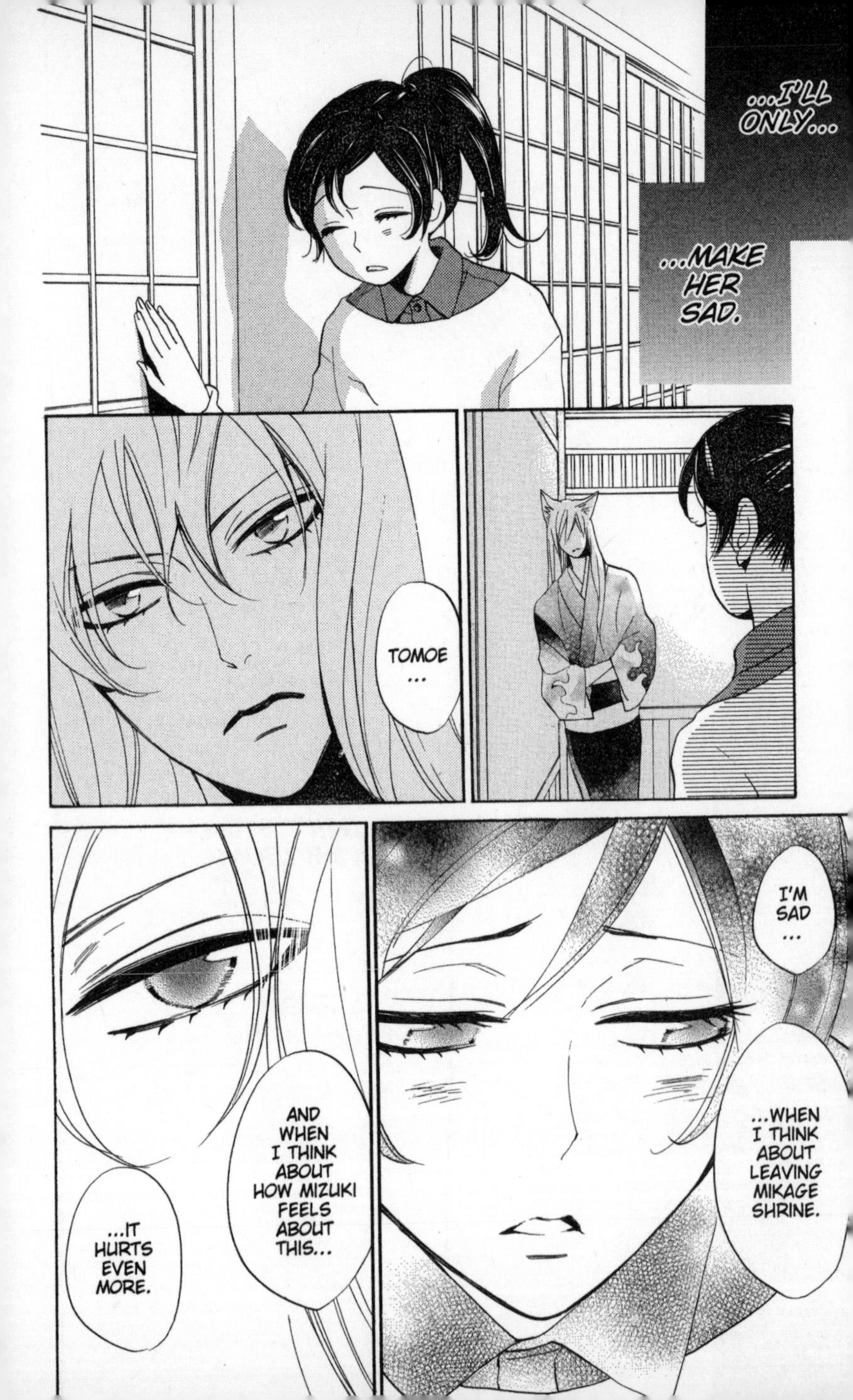
...I'LL ONLY...
...MAKE HER SAD.
TOMOE...
I'M SAD...
...WHEN I THINK ABOUT LEAVING MIKAGE SHRINE.
AND WHEN I THINK ABOUT HOW MIZUKI FEELS ABOUT THIS...
...IT HURTS EVEN MORE.

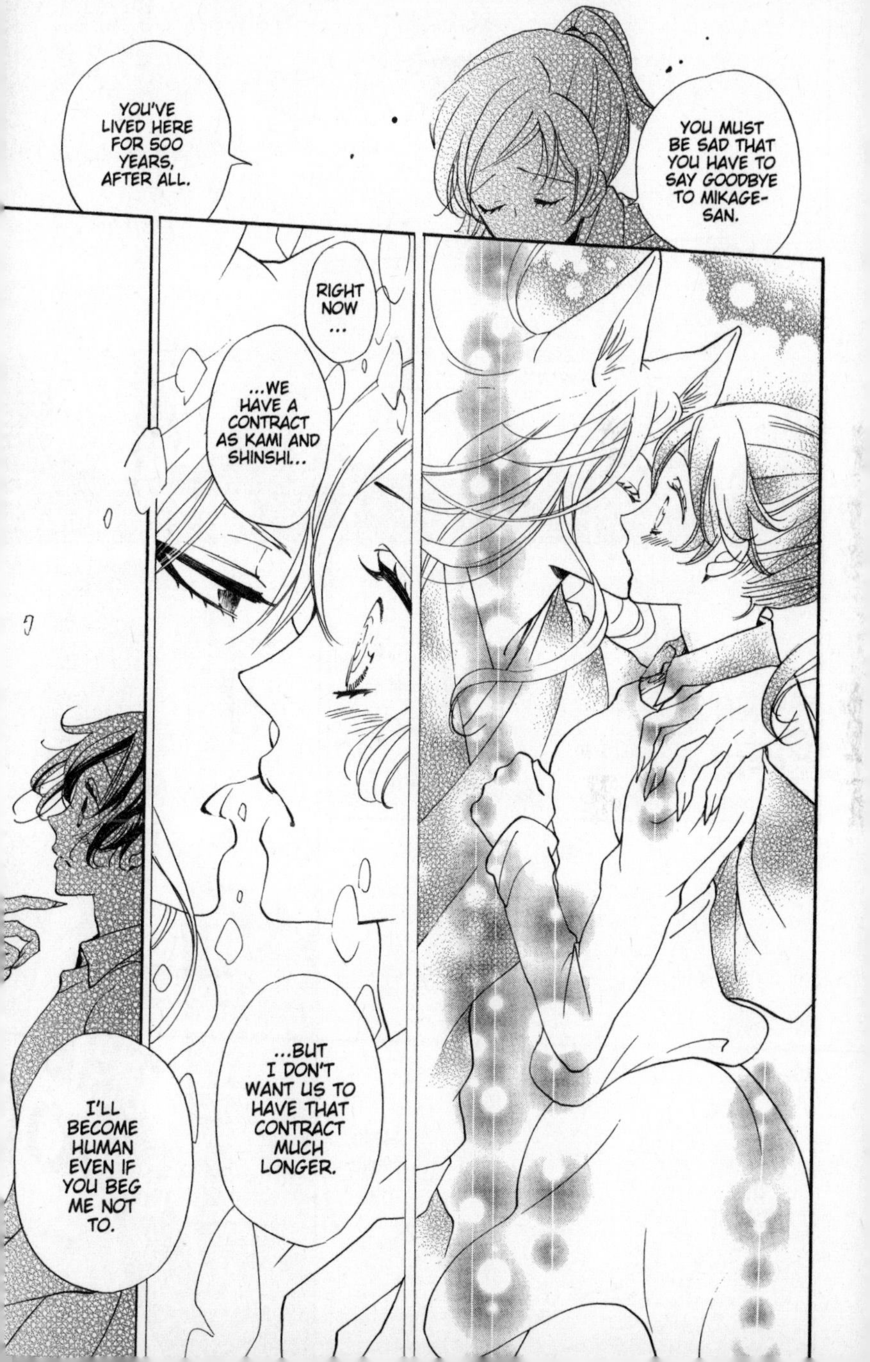
YOU MUST BE SAD THAT YOU HAVE TO SAY GOODBYE TO MIKAGE-SAN.
YOU'VE LIVED HERE FOR 500 YEARS, AFTER ALL.
RIGHT NOW...
...WE HAVE A CONTRACT AS KAMI AND SHINSHI...
...BUT I DON'T WANT US TO HAVE THAT CONTRACT MUCH LONGER.
I'LL BECOME HUMAN EVEN IF YOU BEG ME NOT TO.

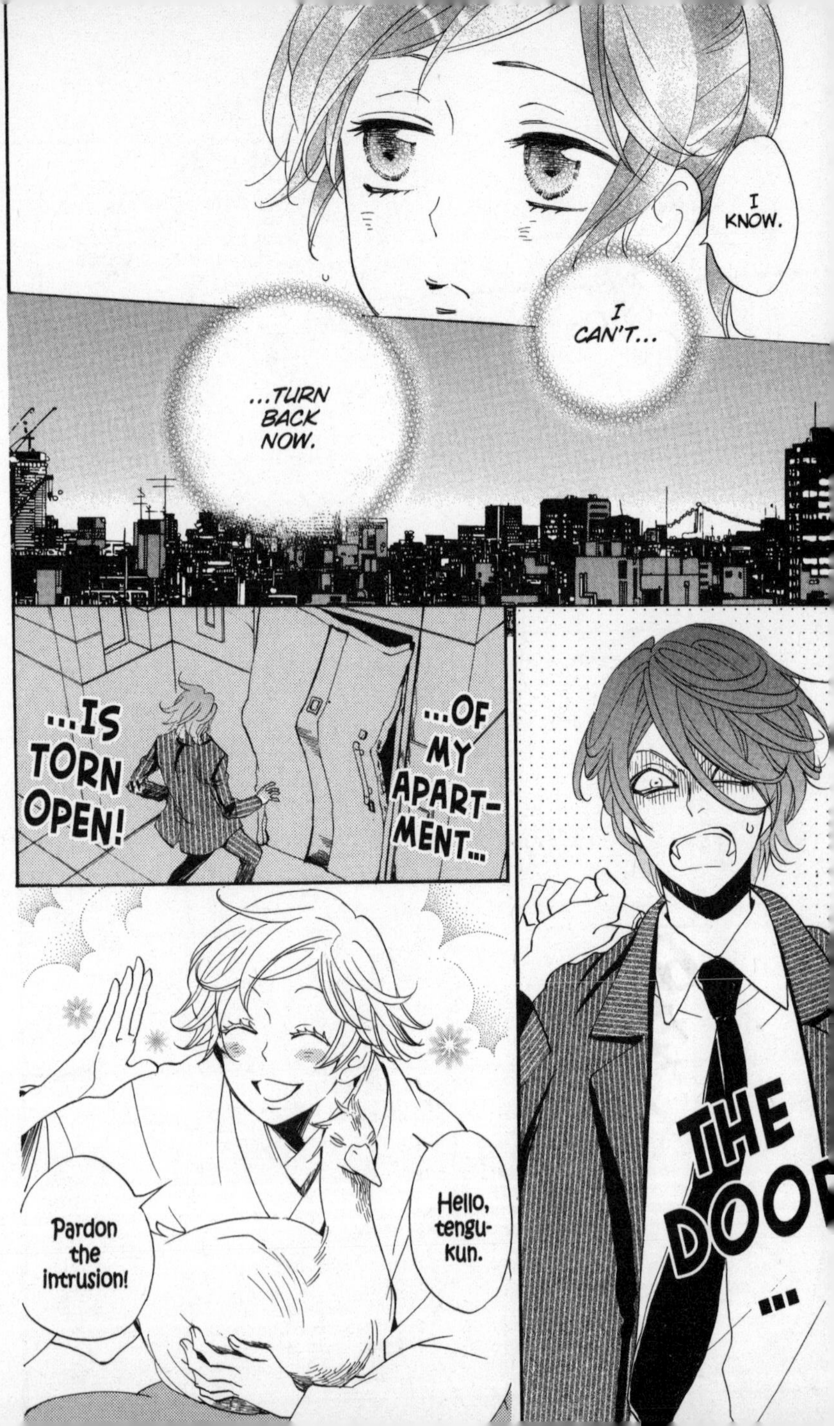
I KNOW.
I CAN'T...
...TURN BACK NOW.
THE DOO
...
...OF MY APARTMENT...
...IS TORN OPEN!
Hello, tengu-kun.
Pardon the intrusion!

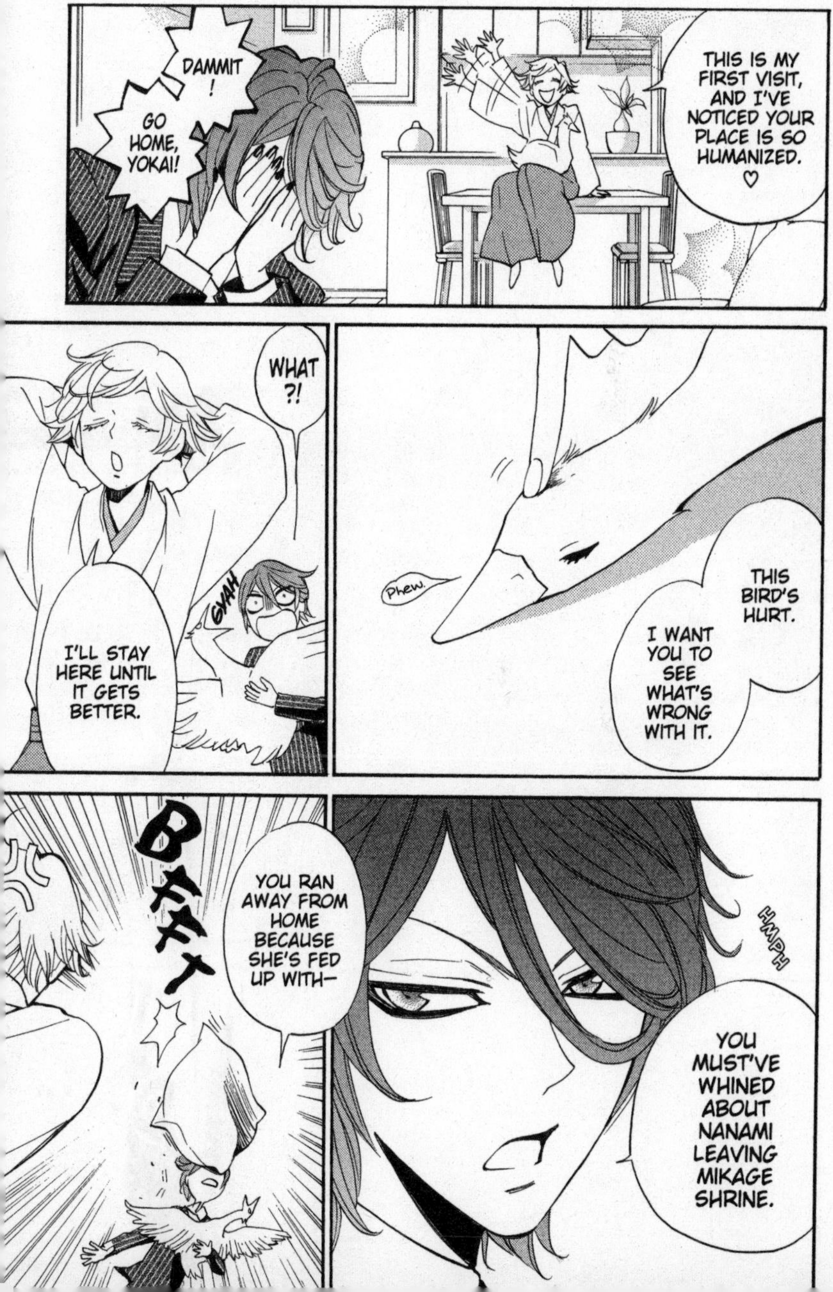
THIS IS MY FIRST VISIT, AND I'VE NOTICED YOUR PLACE IS SO HUMANIZED. ♡
DAMMIT!
GO HOME, YOKAI!
THIS BIRD'S HURT.
I WANT YOU TO SEE WHAT'S WRONG WITH IT.
Phew.
WHAT?!
GYAH
I'LL STAY HERE UNTIL IT GETS BETTER.
HMPH
YOU MUST'VE WHINED ABOUT NANAMI LEAVING MIKAGE SHRINE.
YOU RAN AWAY FROM HOME BECAUSE SHE'S FED UP WITH–

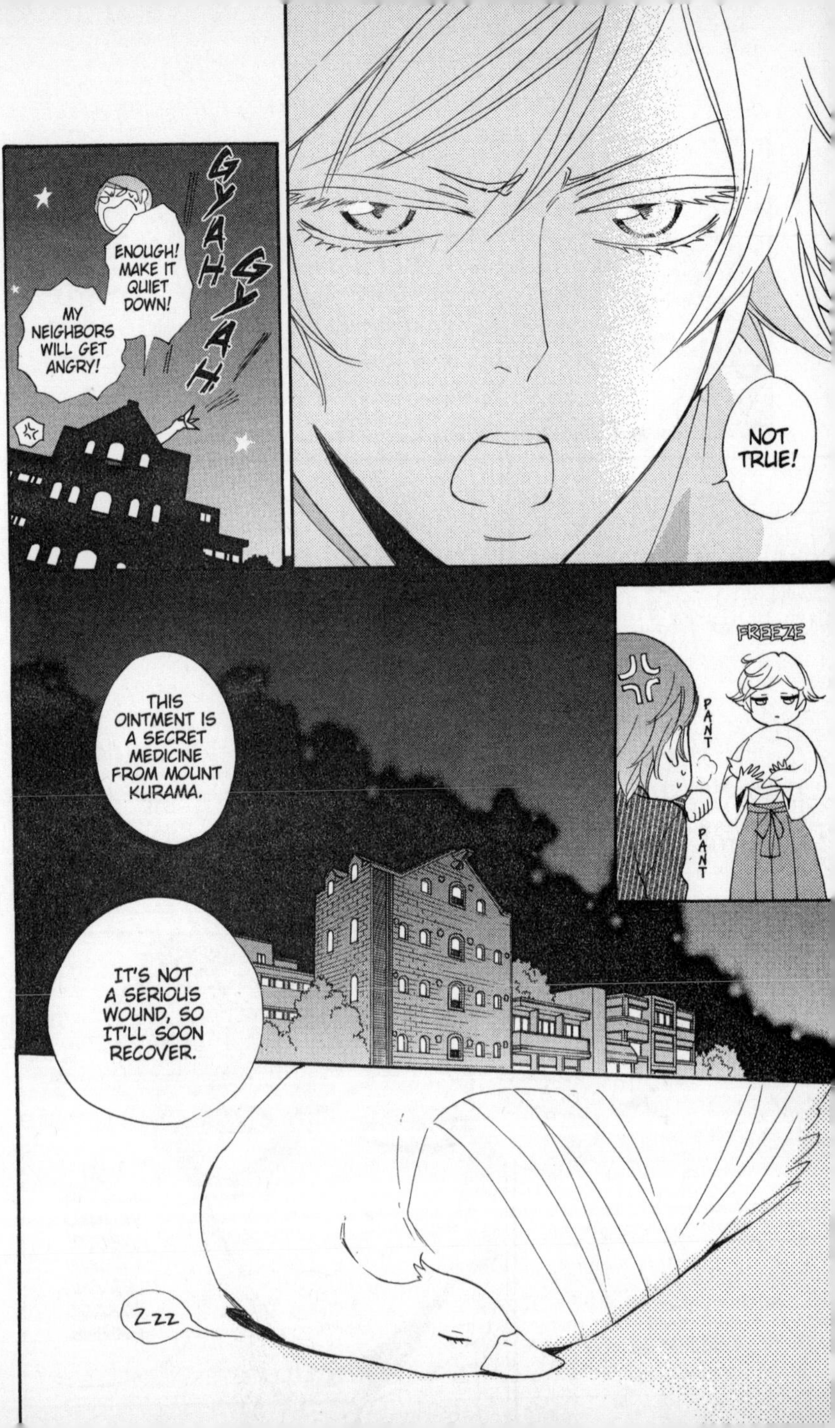
NOT TRUE!
GYAH GYAH
ENOUGH! MAKE IT QUIET DOWN!
MY NEIGHBORS WILL GET ANGRY!
FREEZE
PANT PANT
THIS OINTMENT IS A SECRET MEDICINE FROM MOUNT KURAMA.
IT'S NOT A SERIOUS WOUND, SO IT'LL SOON RECOVER.
Zzz

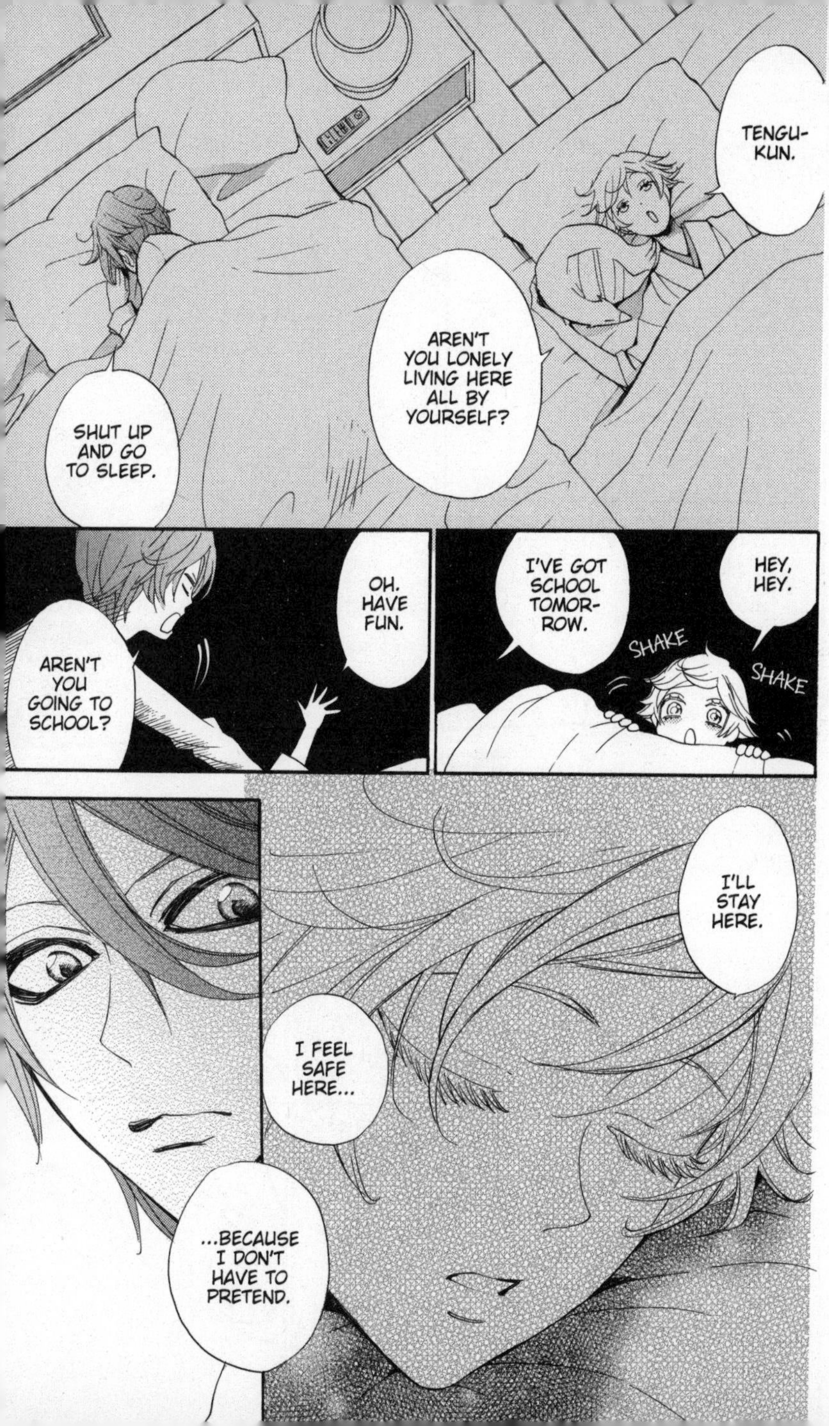
TENGU-KUN.
AREN'T YOU LONELY LIVING HERE ALL BY YOURSELF?
SHUT UP AND GO TO SLEEP.
HEY, HEY.
I'VE GOT SCHOOL TOMOR-ROW.
SHAKE
SHAKE
OH. HAVE FUN.
AREN'T YOU GOING TO SCHOOL?
I'LL STAY HERE.
I FEEL SAFE HERE...
...BECAUSE I DON'T HAVE TO PRETEND.

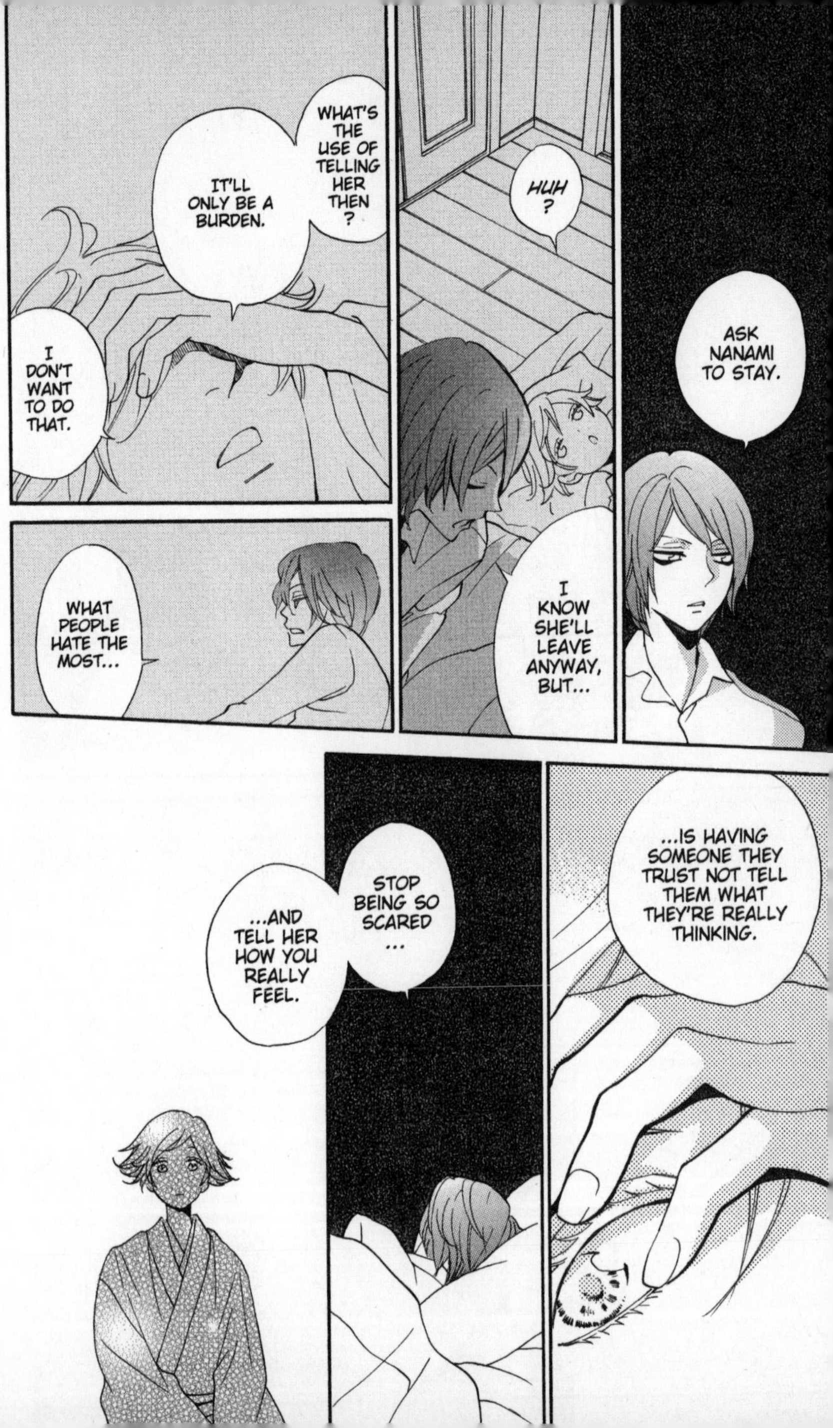
ASK NANAMI TO STAY.
HUH?
I KNOW SHE'LL LEAVE ANYWAY, BUT...
WHAT'S THE USE OF TELLING HER THEN?
IT'LL ONLY BE A BURDEN.
I DON'T WANT TO DO THAT.
WHAT PEOPLE HATE THE MOST...
...IS HAVING SOMEONE THEY TRUST NOT TELL THEM WHAT THEY'RE REALLY THINKING.
STOP BEING SO SCARED...
...AND TELL HER HOW YOU REALLY FEEL.

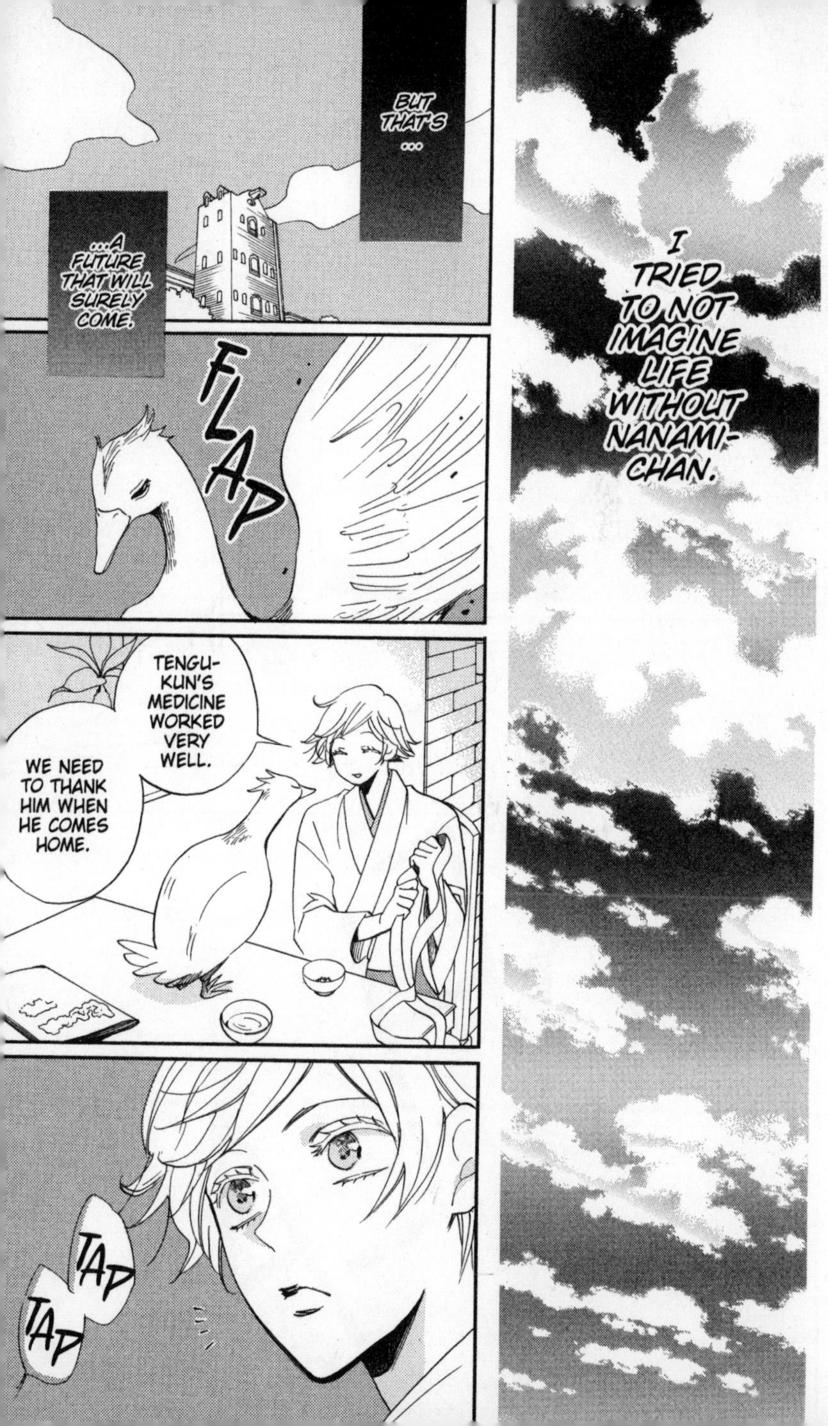
I TRIED TO NOT IMAGINE LIFE WITHOUT NANAMI-CHAN.
BUT THAT'S...
...A FUTURE THAT WILL SURELY COME.
FLAP
TENGU-KUN'S MEDICINE WORKED VERY WELL.
WE NEED TO THANK HIM WHEN HE COMES HOME.
TAP
TAP

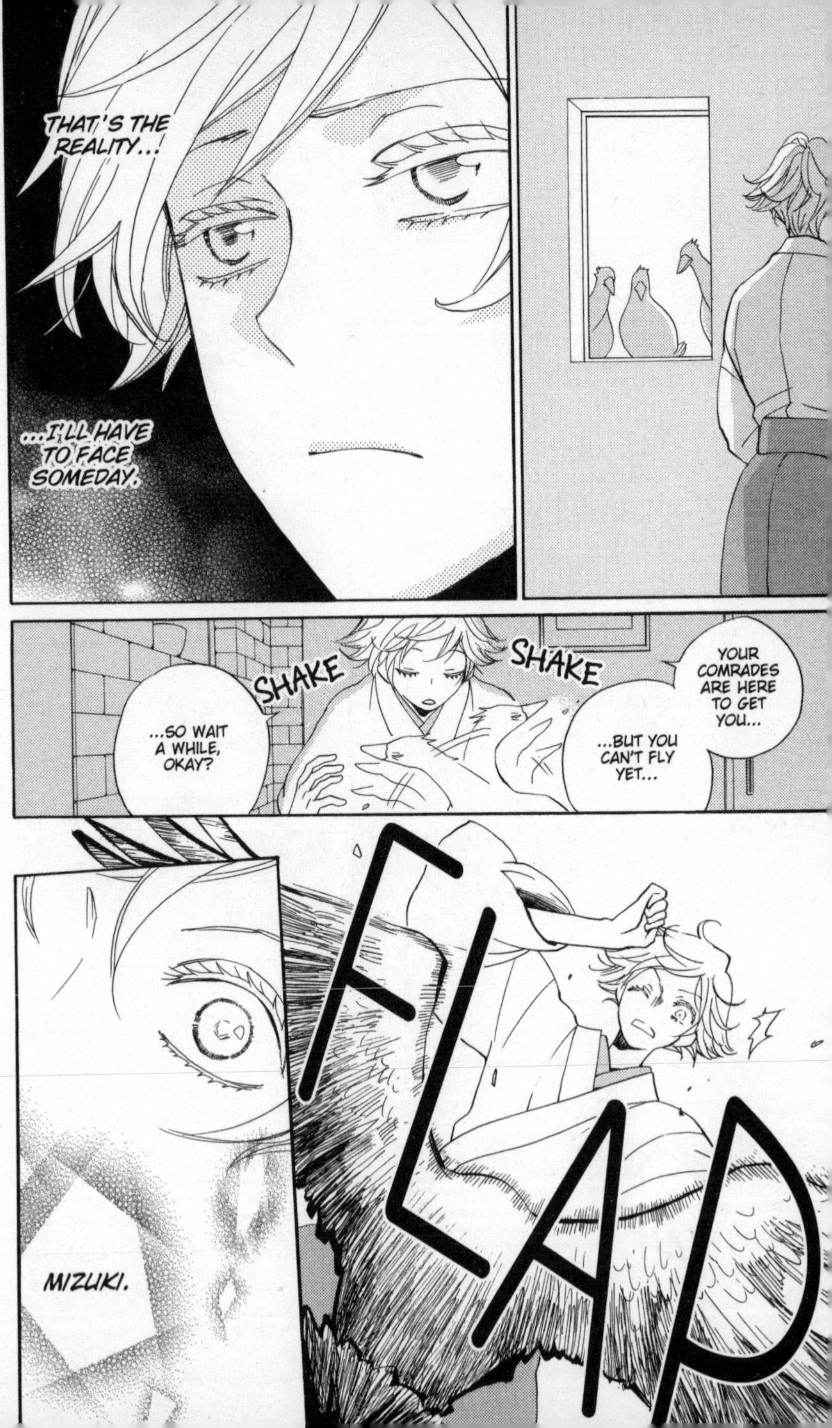
THAT'S THE REALITY...
...I'LL HAVE TO FACE SOMEDAY.
YOUR COMRADES ARE HERE TO GET YOU...
SHAKE
...BUT YOU CAN'T FLY YET...
SHAKE
...SO WAIT A WHILE, OKAY?
FLAP
MIZUKI.

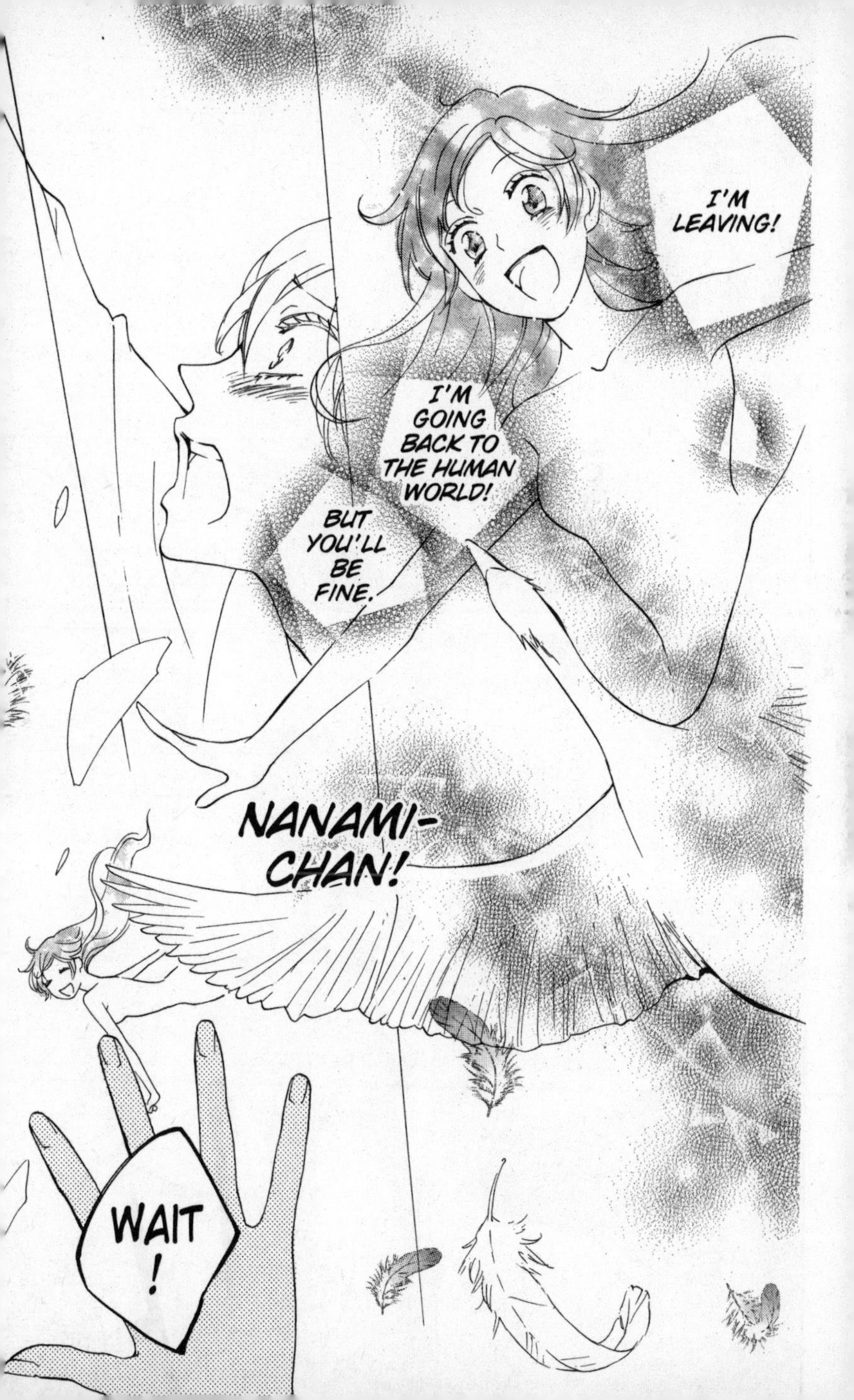
I'M LEAVING!
I'M GOING BACK TO THE HUMAN WORLD!
BUT YOU'LL BE FINE.
NANAMI-CHAN!
WAIT!

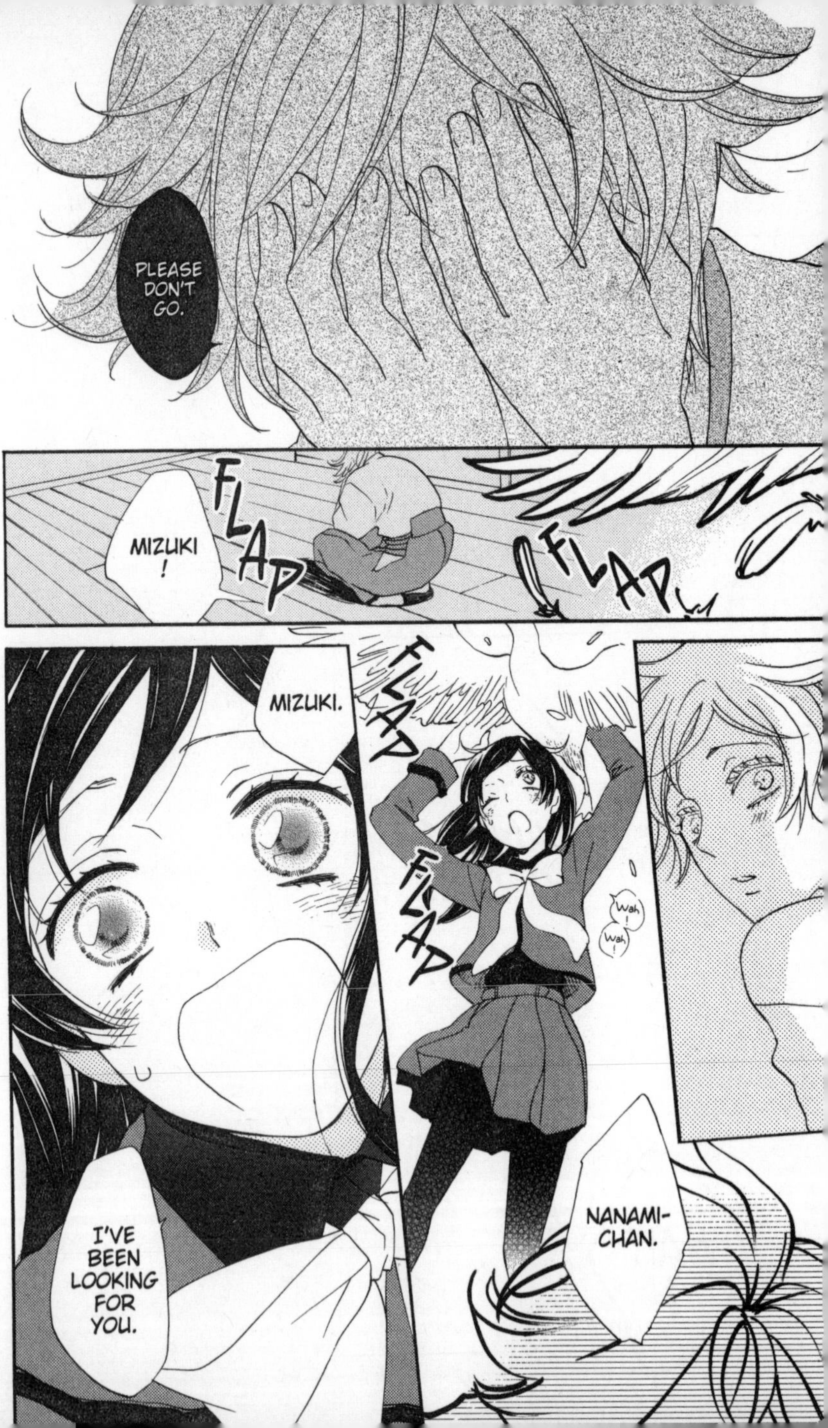
PLEASE DON'T GO.
FLAP
FLAP
MIZUKI!
FLAP
FLAP
Wah! Wah!
MIZUKI.
NANAMI-CHAN.
I'VE BEEN LOOKING FOR YOU.

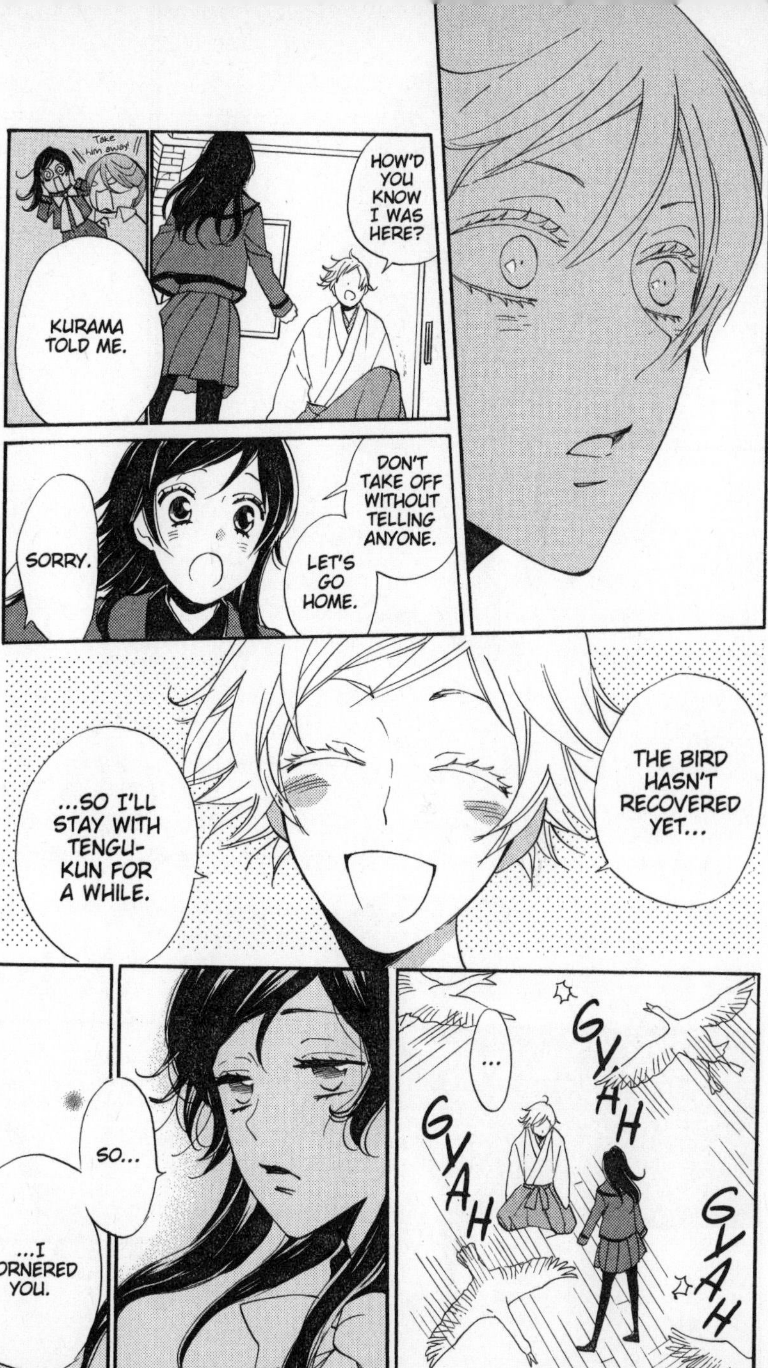
HOW'D YOU KNOW I WAS HERE?
Take him away!
KURAMA TOLD ME.
DON'T TAKE OFF WITHOUT TELLING ANYONE.
LET'S GO HOME.
SORRY.
THE BIRD HASN'T RECOVERED YET...
...SO I'LL STAY WITH TENGU-KUN FOR A WHILE.
GYAH
...
GYAH
GYAH
SO...
...I CORNERED YOU.

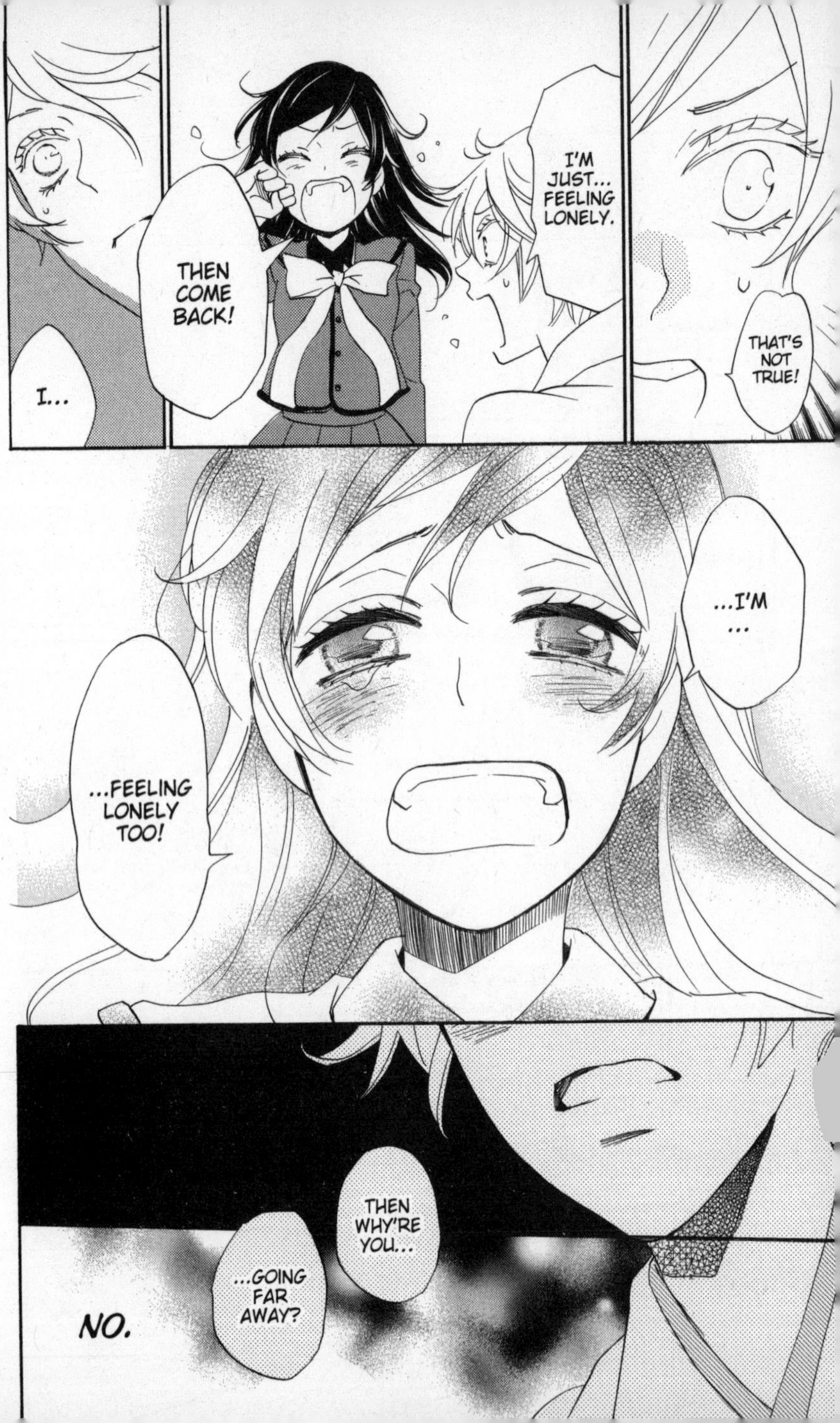
THAT'S NOT TRUE!
I'M JUST... FEELING LONELY.
THEN COME BACK!
I...
...I'M ...
...FEELING LONELY TOO!
THEN WHY'RE YOU...
...GOING FAR AWAY?
NO.

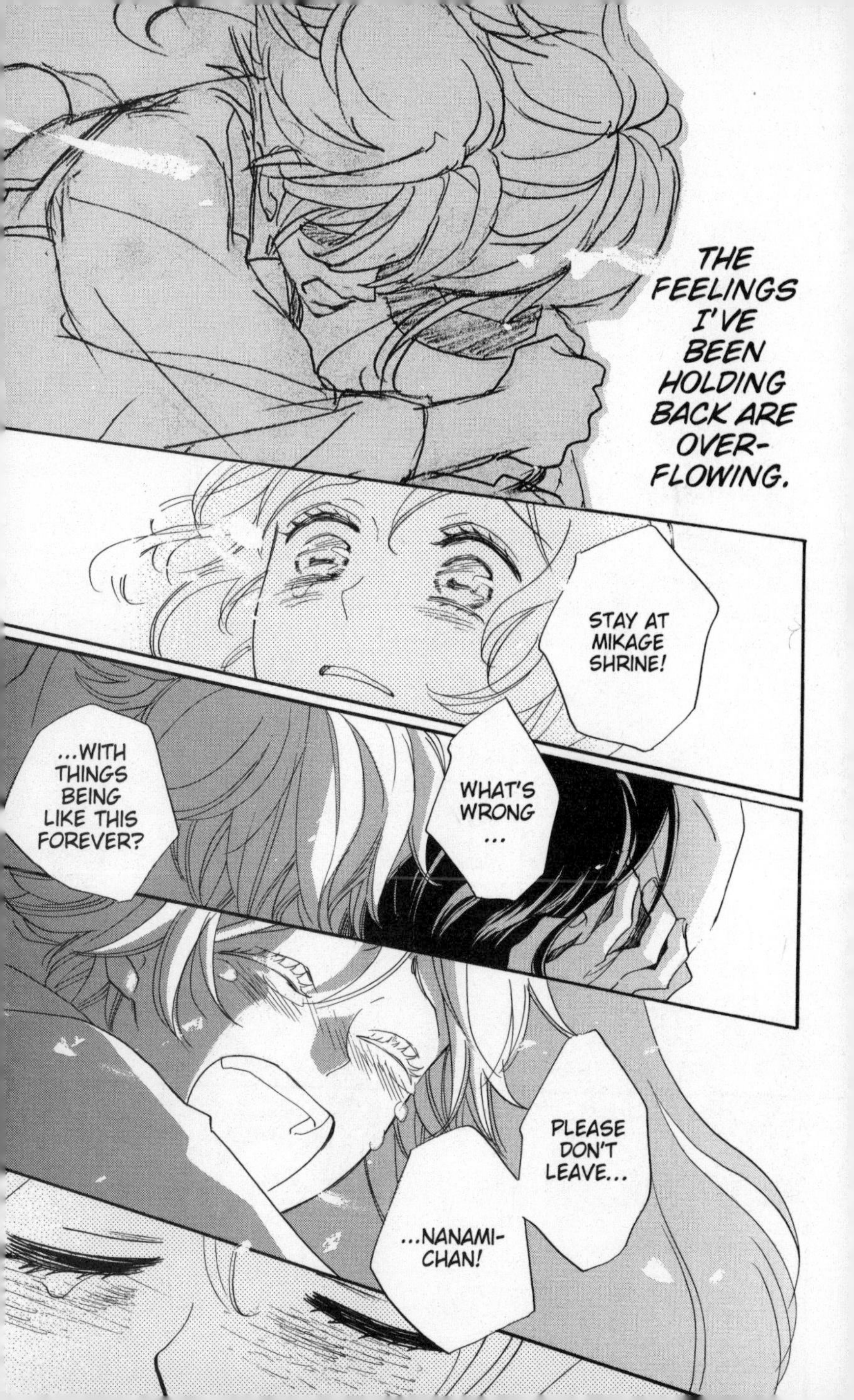
THE FEELINGS I'VE BEEN HOLDING BACK ARE OVER-FLOWING.
STAY AT MIKAGE SHRINE!
WHAT'S WRONG ...
...WITH THINGS BEING LIKE THIS FOREVER?
PLEASE DON'T LEAVE...
...NANAMI-CHAN!

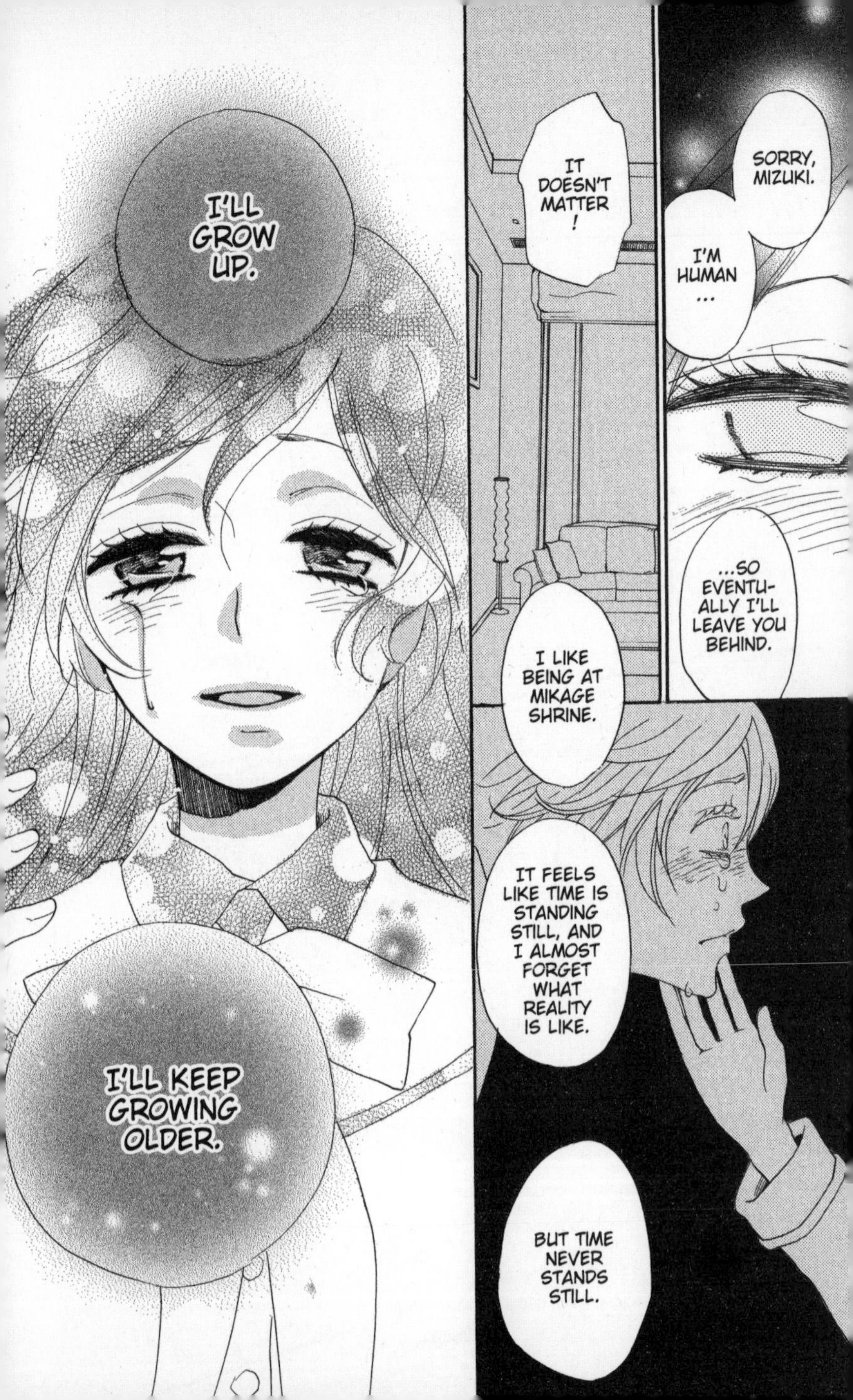
SORRY, MIZUKI.
I'M HUMAN...
...SO EVENTUALLY I'LL LEAVE YOU BEHIND.
IT DOESN'T MATTER!
I LIKE BEING AT MIKAGE SHRINE.
IT FEELS LIKE TIME IS STANDING STILL, AND I ALMOST FORGET WHAT REALITY IS LIKE.
BUT TIME NEVER STANDS STILL.
I'LL GROW UP.
I'LL KEEP GROWING OLDER.

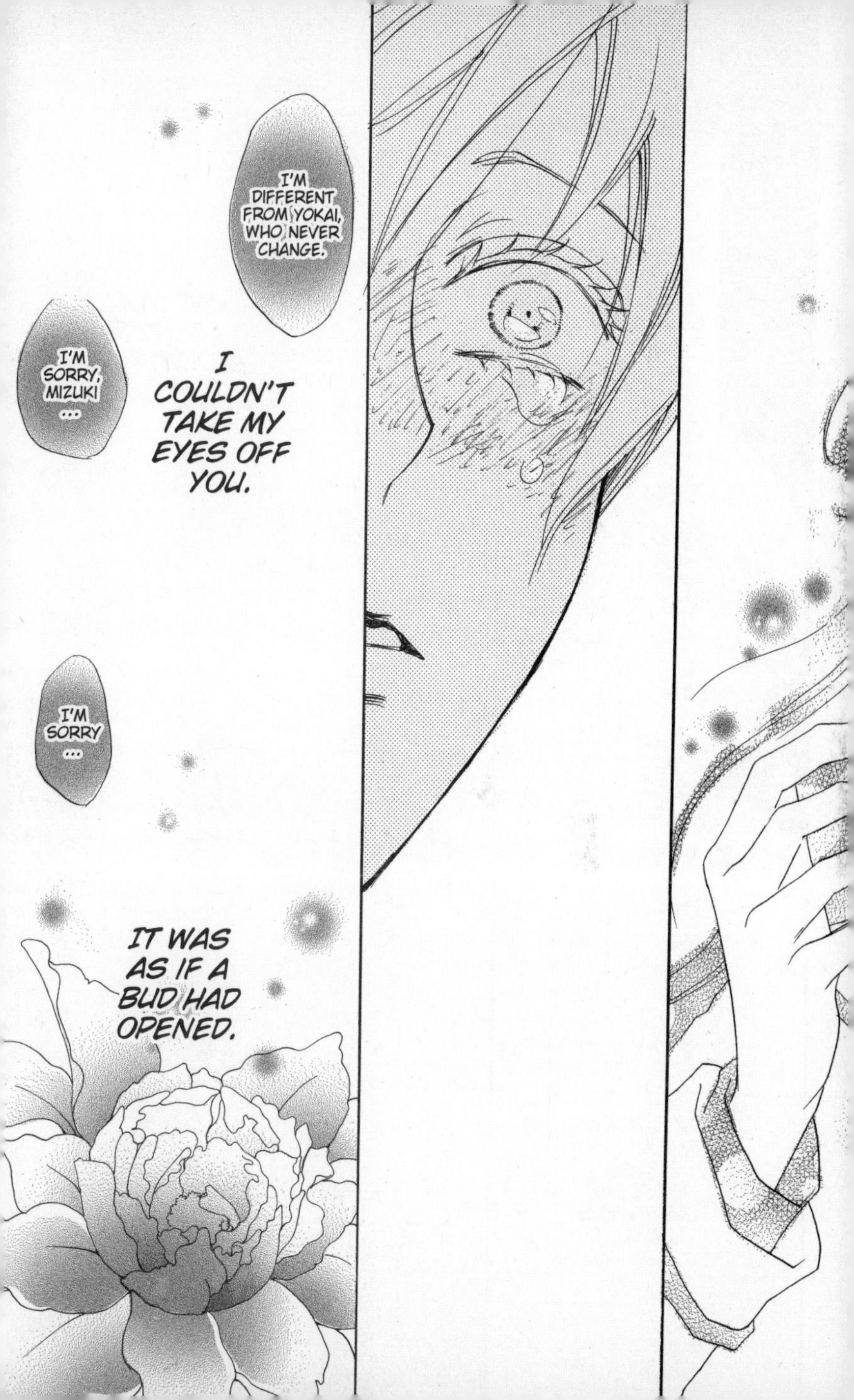
I'M DIFFERENT FROM YOKAI, WHO NEVER CHANGE.
I COULDN'T TAKE MY EYES OFF YOU.
I'M SORRY, MIZUKI...
I'M SORRY...
IT WAS AS IF A BUD HAD OPENED.

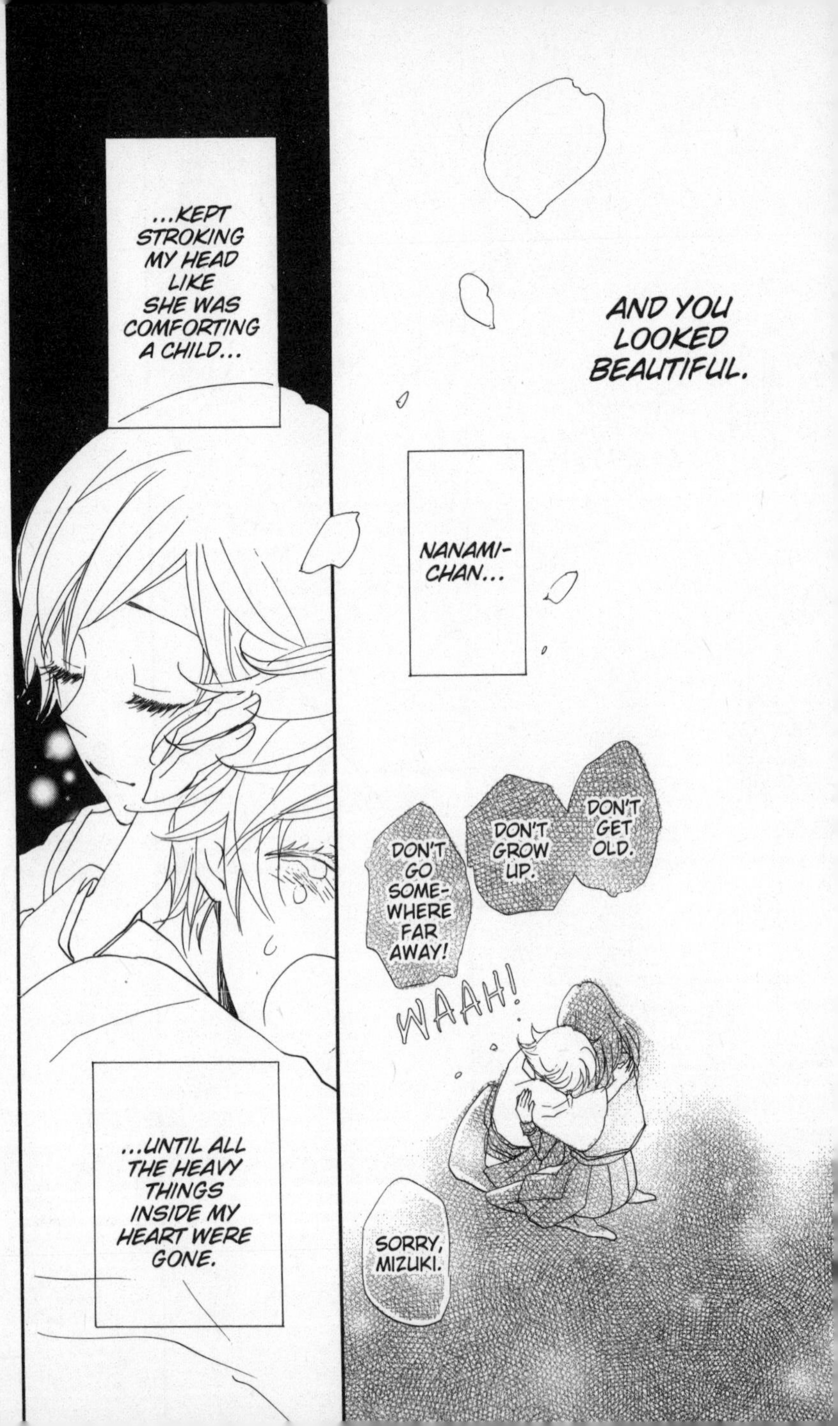
AND YOU LOOKED BEAUTIFUL.
NANAMI-CHAN...
DON'T GET OLD.
DON'T GROW UP.
DON'T GO SOMEWHERE FAR AWAY!
WAAH!
SORRY, MIZUKI.
...KEPT STROKING MY HEAD LIKE SHE WAS COMFORTING A CHILD...
...UNTIL ALL THE HEAVY THINGS INSIDE MY HEART WERE GONE.

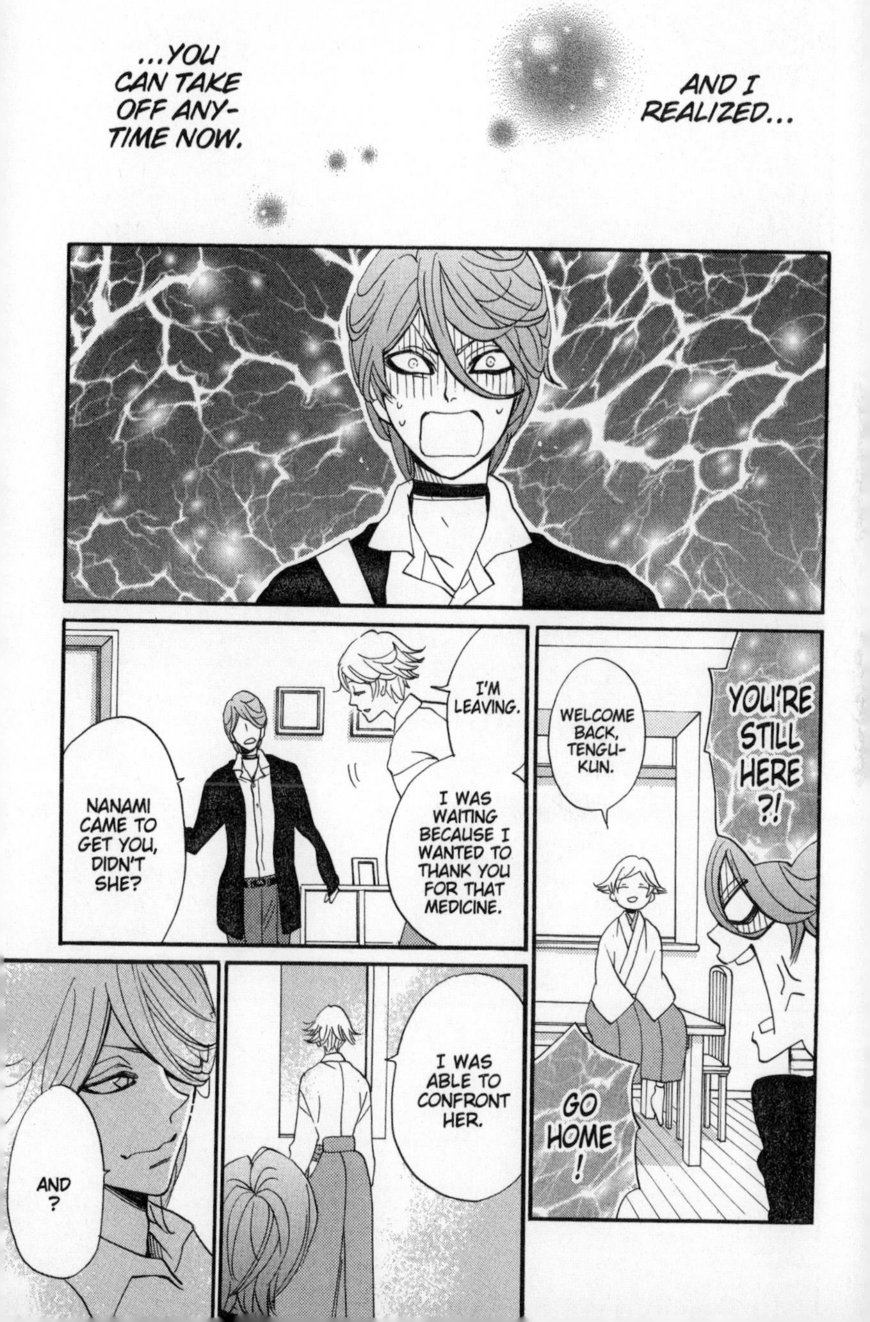
AND I REALIZED...
...YOU CAN TAKE OFF ANY-TIME NOW.
WELCOME BACK, TENGU-KUN.
YOU'RE STILL HERE?!
GO HOME!
I'M LEAVING.
NANAMI CAME TO GET YOU, DIDN'T SHE?
I WAS WAITING BECAUSE I WANTED TO THANK YOU FOR THAT MEDICINE.
I WAS ABLE TO CONFRONT HER.
AND?

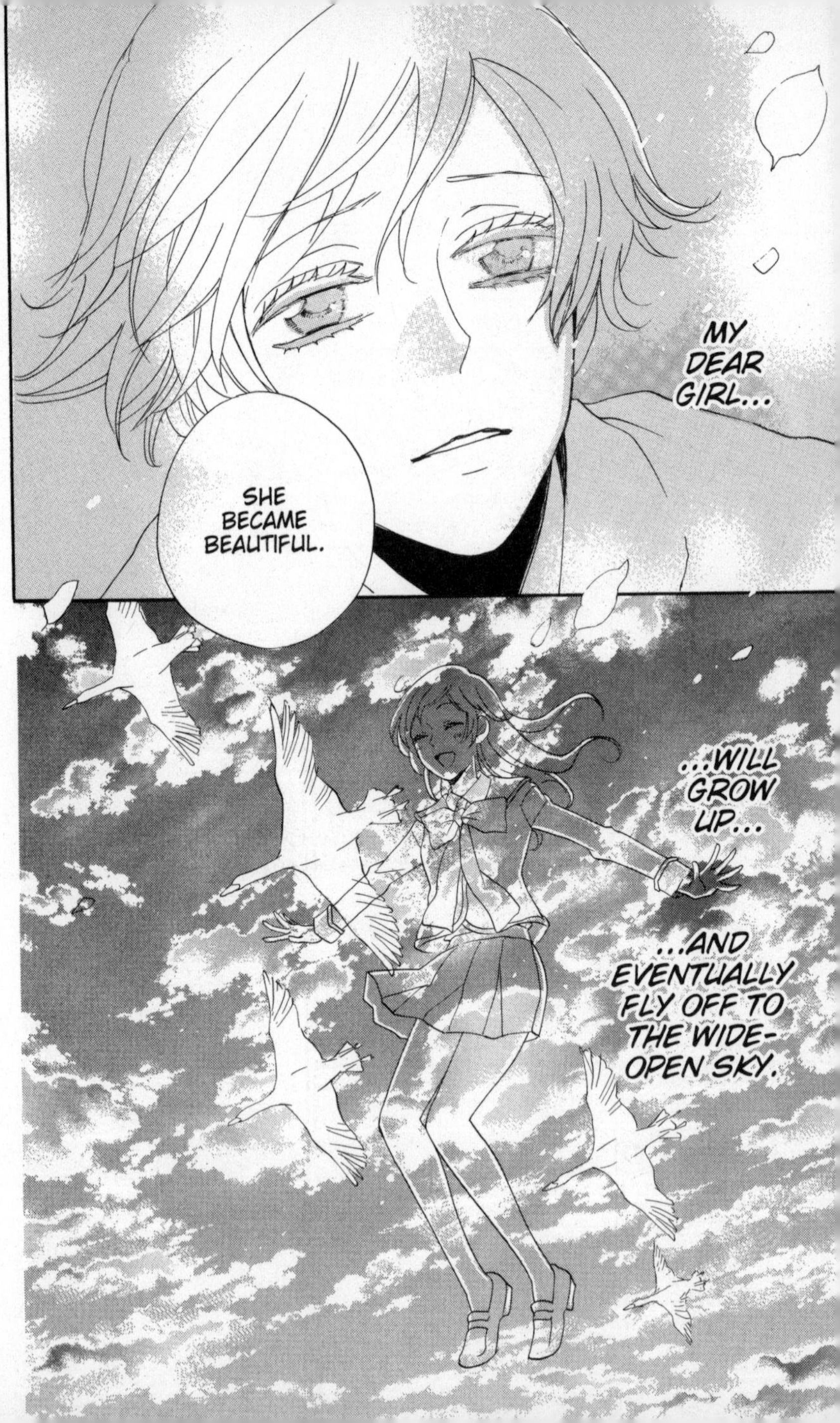
MY DEAR GIRL...
SHE BECAME BEAUTIFUL.
...WILL GROW UP...
...AND EVENTUALLY FLY OFF TO THE WIDE-OPEN SKY.

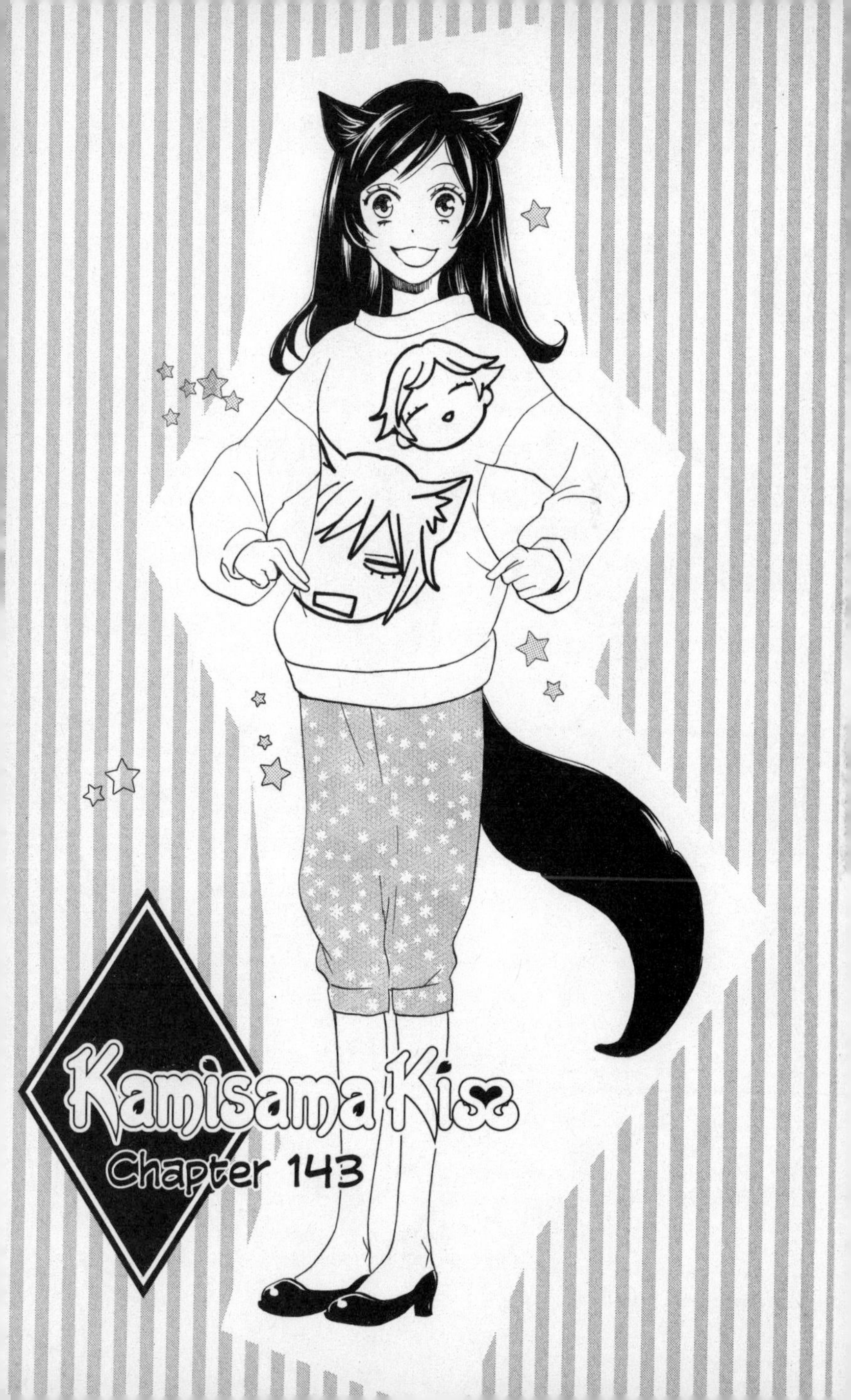
Kamisama Kiss
Chapter 143

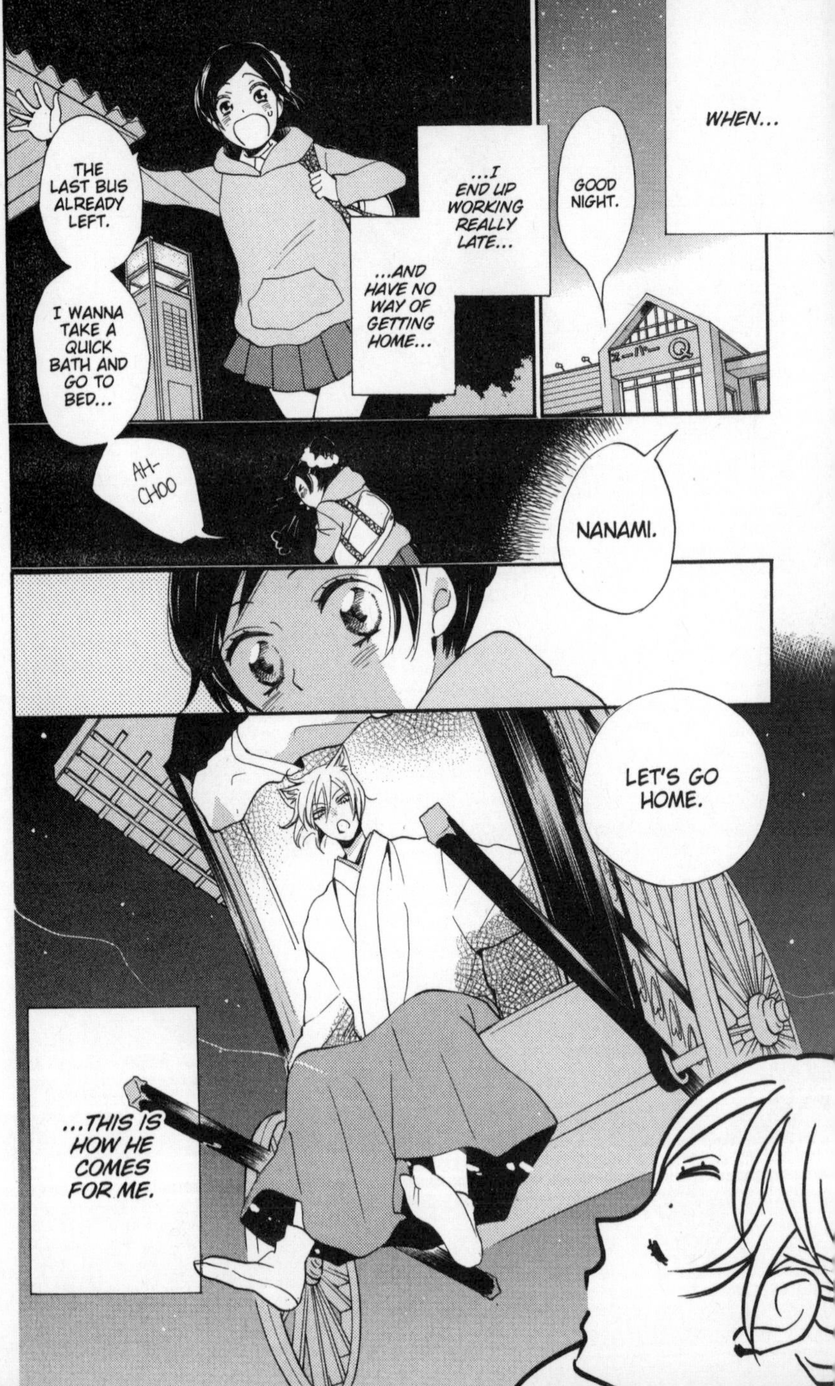
WHEN...
GOOD NIGHT.
...I END UP WORKING REALLY LATE...
...AND HAVE NO WAY OF GETTING HOME...
THE LAST BUS ALREADY LEFT.
I WANNA TAKE A QUICK BATH AND GO TO BED...
NANAMI.
AH-CHOO
LET'S GO HOME.
...THIS IS HOW HE COMES FOR ME.

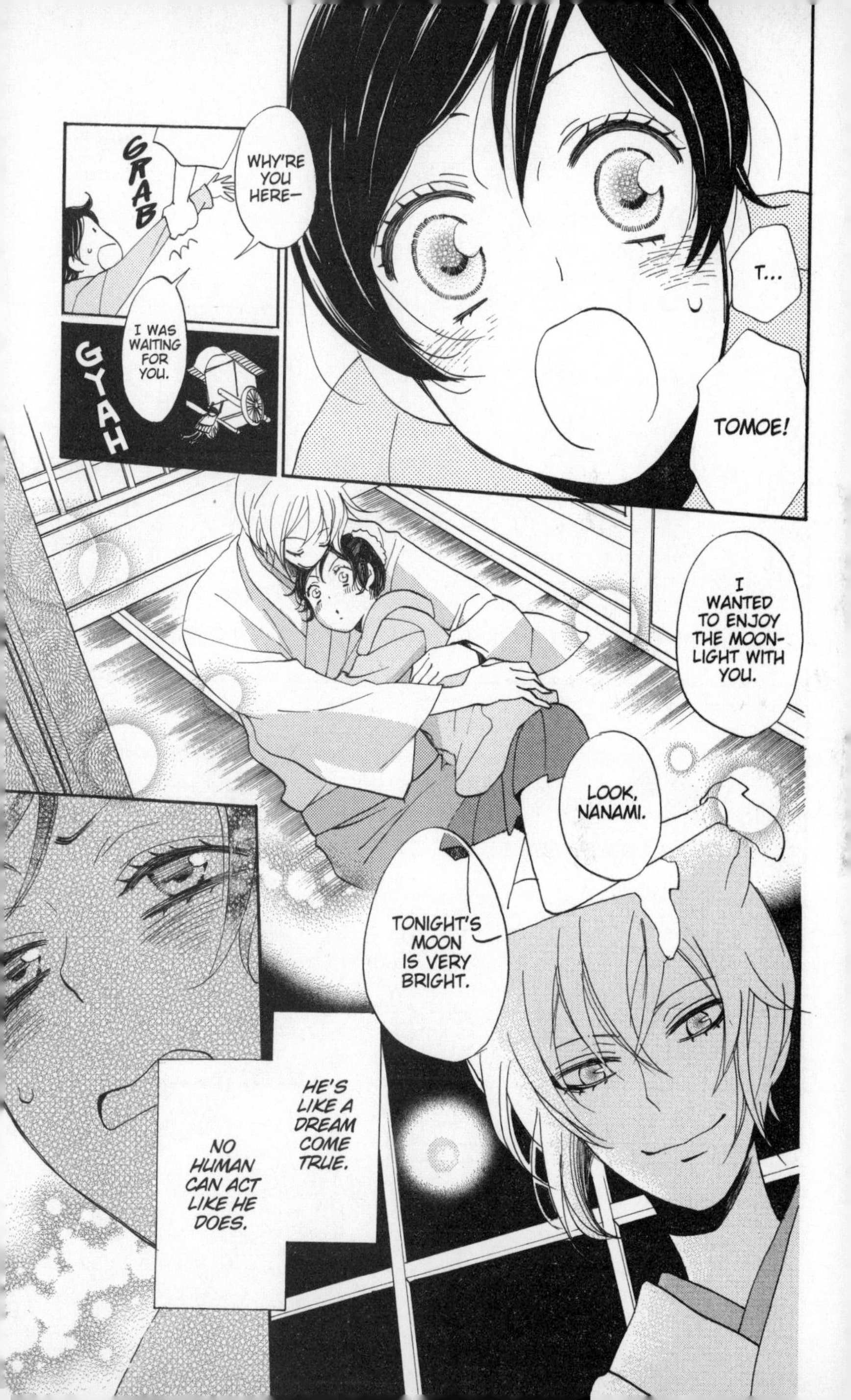
T...
TOMOE!
GRAB
WHY'RE YOU HERE—
GYAH
I WAS WAITING FOR YOU.
I WANTED TO ENJOY THE MOON-LIGHT WITH YOU.
LOOK, NANAMI.
TONIGHT'S MOON IS VERY BRIGHT.
HE'S LIKE A DREAM COME TRUE.
NO HUMAN CAN ACT LIKE HE DOES.

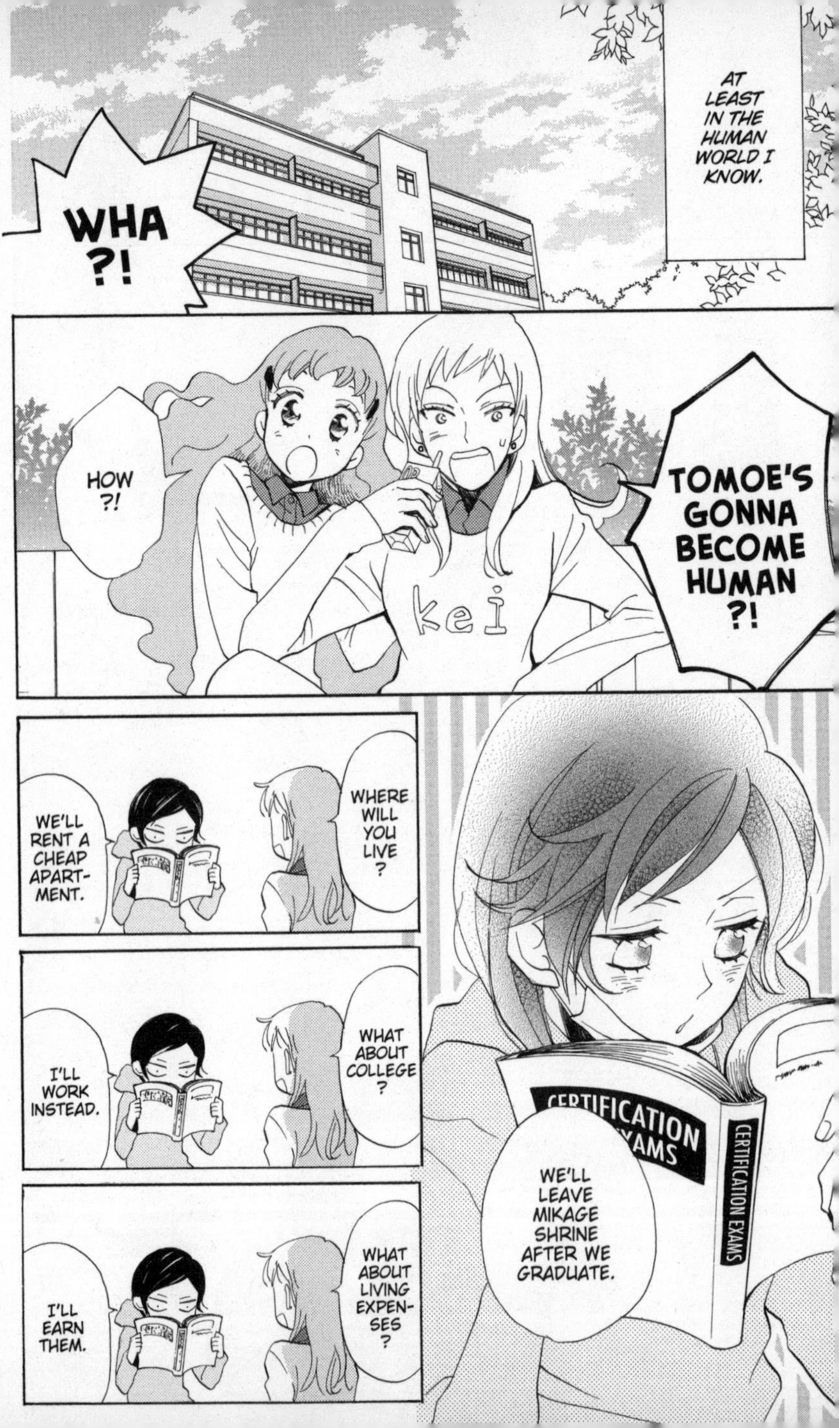

AT LEAST IN THE HUMAN WORLD I KNOW.
WHA?!
TOMOE'S GONNA BECOME HUMAN?!
kei
HOW?!
CERTIFICATION EXAMS
CERTIFICATION EXAMS
WE'LL LEAVE MIKAGE SHRINE AFTER WE GRADUATE.
WHERE WILL YOU LIVE?
WE'LL RENT A CHEAP APARTMENT.
WHAT ABOUT COLLEGE?
I'LL WORK INSTEAD.
WHAT ABOUT LIVING EXPENSES?
I'LL EARN THEM.

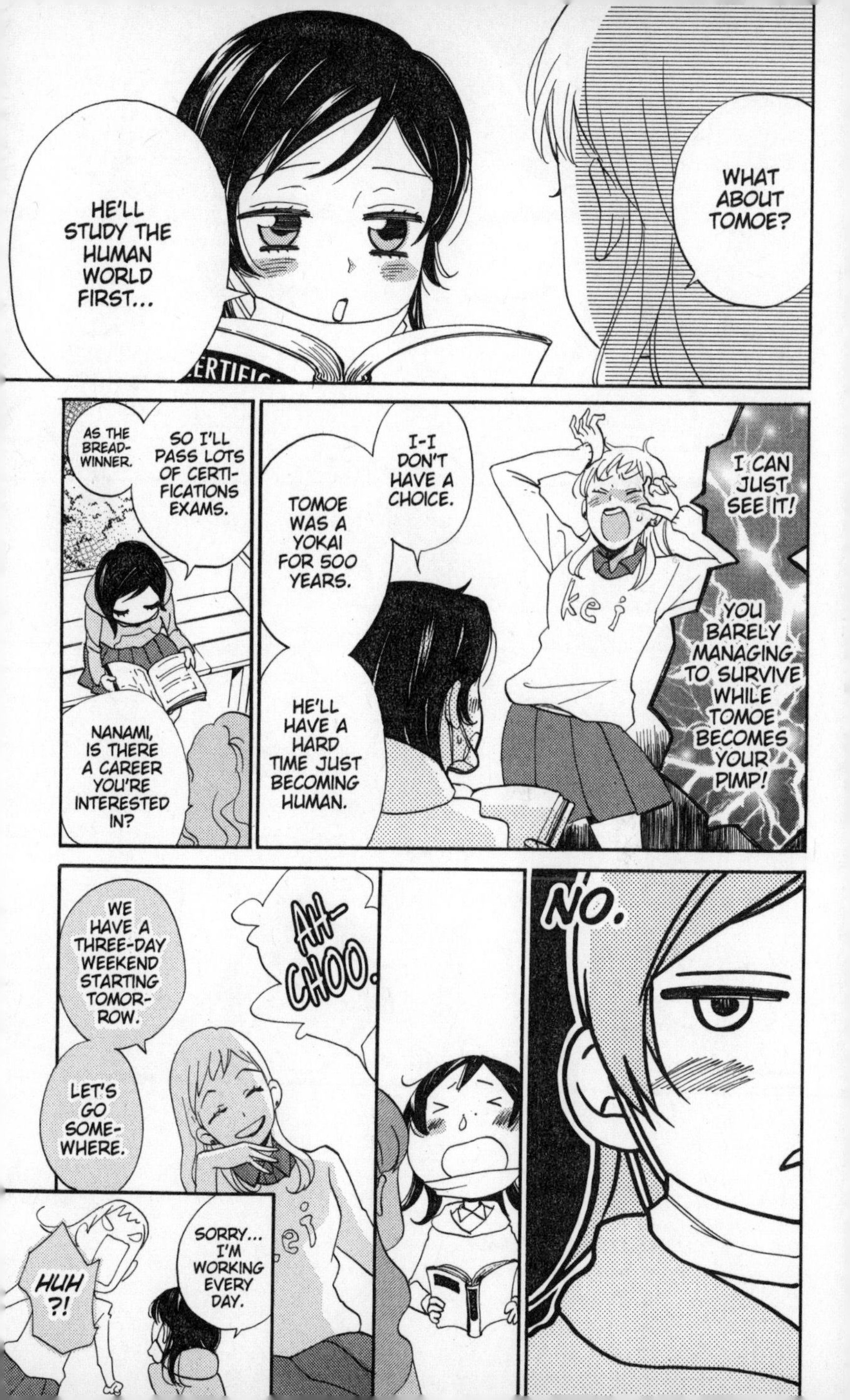

WHAT ABOUT TOMOE?
HE'LL STUDY THE HUMAN WORLD FIRST...
CERTIFIC
I CAN JUST SEE IT!
YOU BARELY MANAGING TO SURVIVE WHILE TOMOE BECOMES YOUR PIMP!
I-I DON'T HAVE A CHOICE.
TOMOE WAS A YOKAI FOR 500 YEARS.
HE'LL HAVE A HARD TIME JUST BECOMING HUMAN.
kei
SO I'LL PASS LOTS OF CERTI-FICATIONS EXAMS.
AS THE BREAD-WINNER.
NANAMI, IS THERE A CAREER YOU'RE INTERESTED IN?
NO.
AH-CHOO.
WE HAVE A THREE-DAY WEEKEND STARTING TOMOR-ROW.
LET'S GO SOME-WHERE.
SORRY... I'M WORKING EVERY DAY.
HUH?!

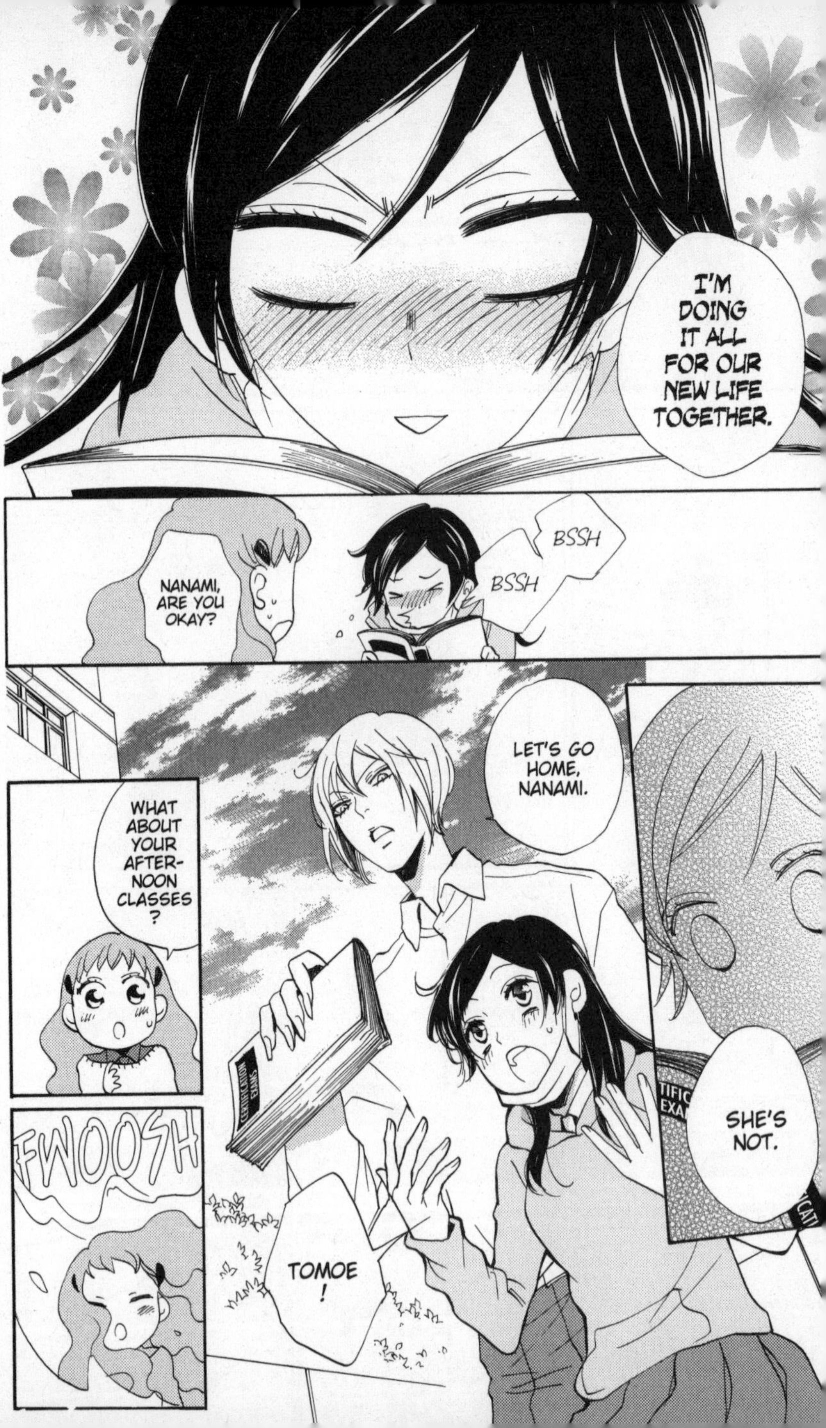
I'M DOING IT ALL FOR OUR NEW LIFE TOGETHER.
BSSH
BSSH
NANAMI, ARE YOU OKAY?
SHE'S NOT.
LET'S GO HOME, NANAMI.
TOMOE!
WHAT ABOUT YOUR AFTERNOON CLASSES?
FWOOSH

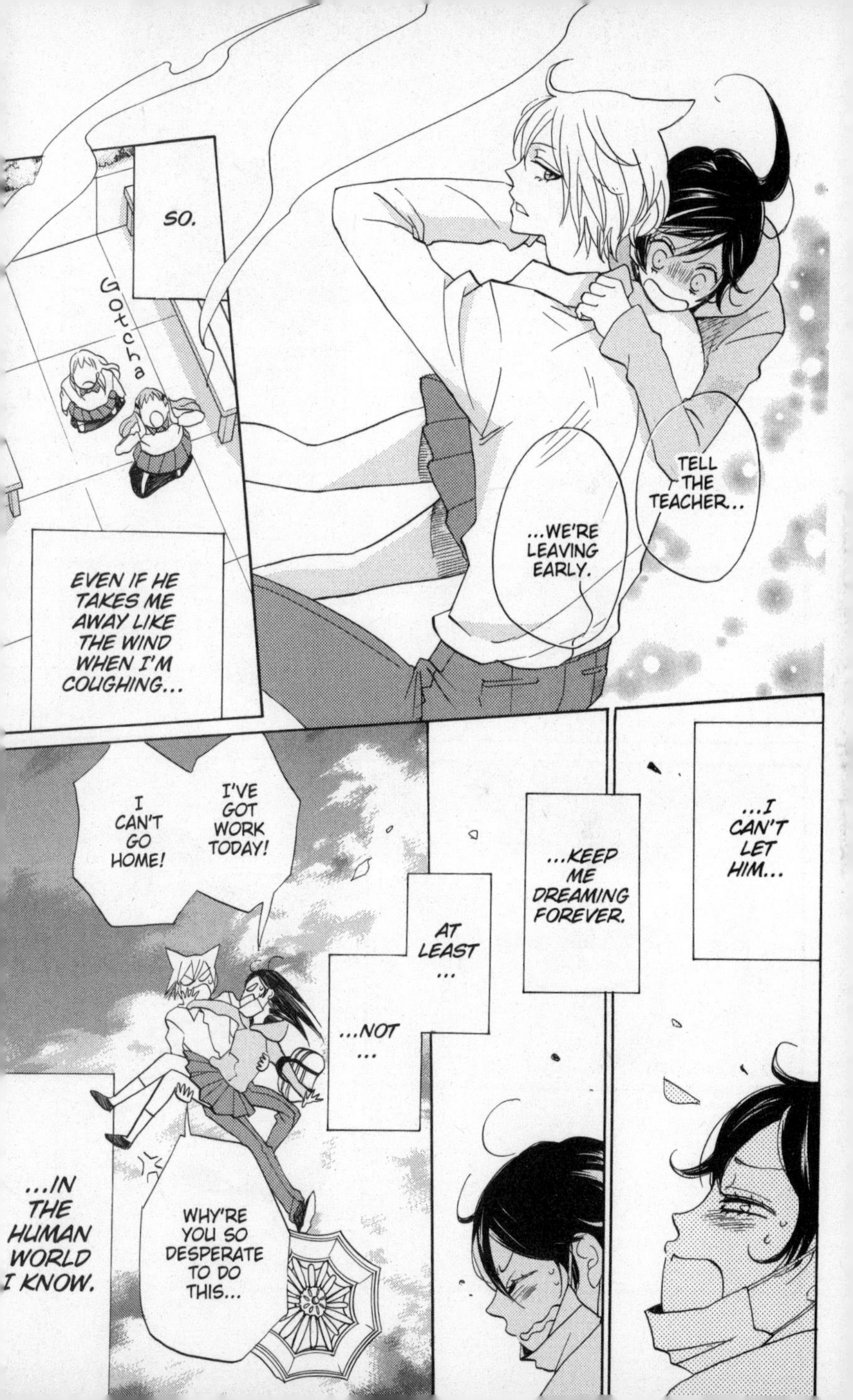
TELL THE TEACHER...
...WE'RE LEAVING EARLY.
SO.
Gotcha
EVEN IF HE TAKES ME AWAY LIKE THE WIND WHEN I'M COUGHING...
...I CAN'T LET HIM...
...KEEP ME DREAMING FOREVER.
AT LEAST...
...NOT...
I'VE GOT WORK TODAY!
I CAN'T GO HOME!
WHY'RE YOU SO DESPERATE TO DO THIS...
...IN THE HUMAN WORLD I KNOW.

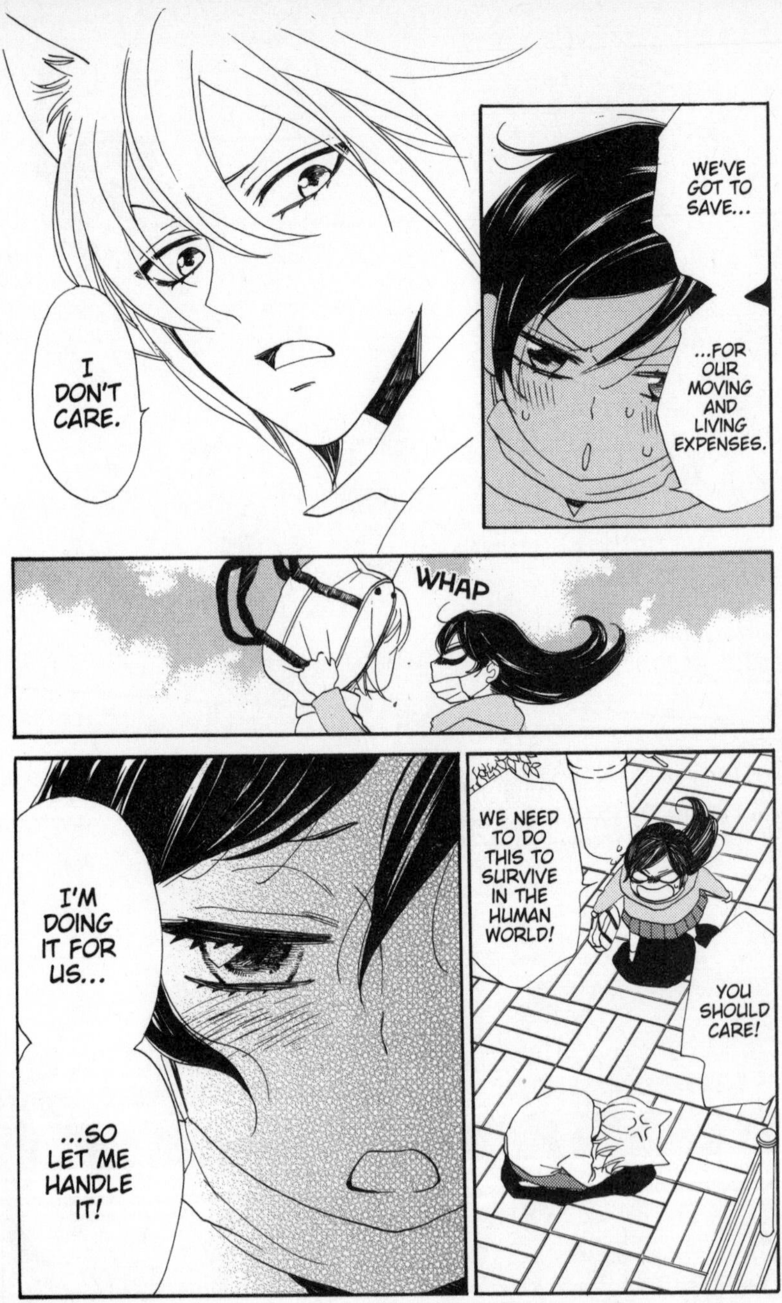
WE'VE GOT TO SAVE...
...FOR OUR MOVING AND LIVING EXPENSES.
I DON'T CARE.
WHAP
WE NEED TO DO THIS TO SURVIVE IN THE HUMAN WORLD!
YOU SHOULD CARE!
I'M DOING IT FOR US...
...SO LET ME HANDLE IT!

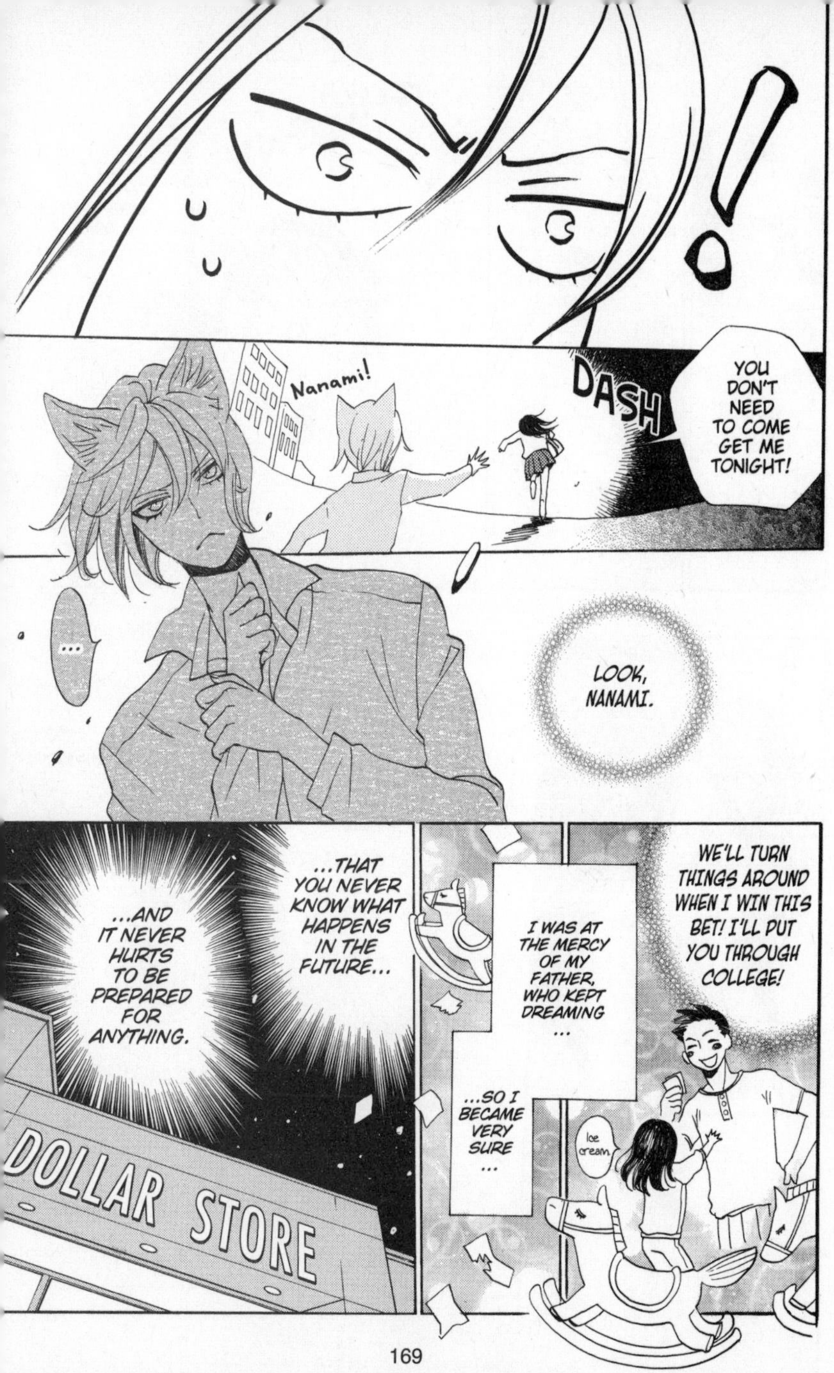
!
YOU DON'T NEED TO COME GET ME TONIGHT!
DASH
Nanami!
LOOK, NANAMI.
...
WE'LL TURN THINGS AROUND WHEN I WIN THIS BET! I'LL PUT YOU THROUGH COLLEGE!
Ice cream
I WAS AT THE MERCY OF MY FATHER, WHO KEPT DREAMING...
...SO I BECAME VERY SURE...
...THAT YOU NEVER KNOW WHAT HAPPENS IN THE FUTURE...
...AND IT NEVER HURTS TO BE PREPARED FOR ANYTHING.
DOLLAR STORE

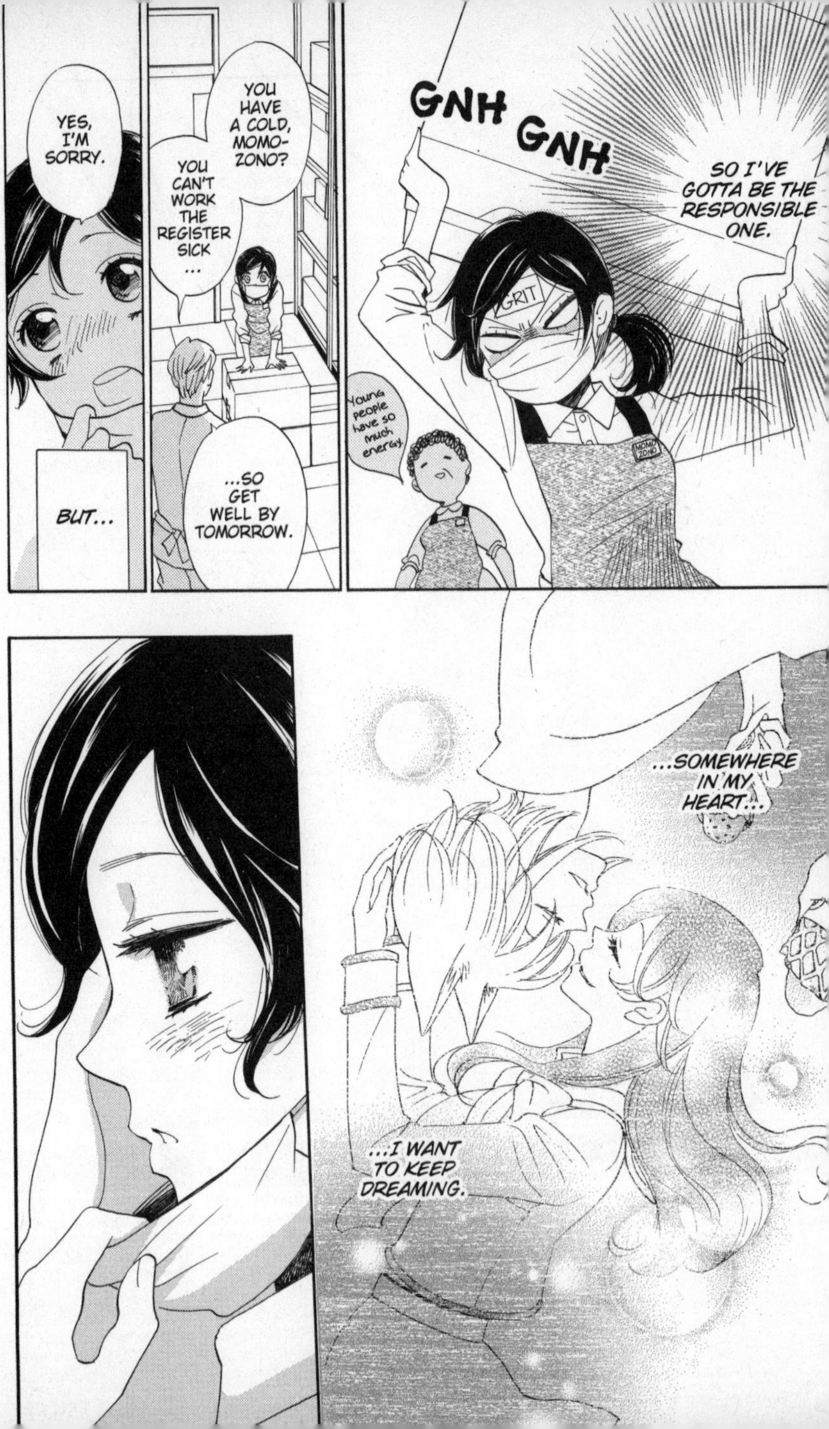
SO I'VE GOTTA BE THE RESPONSIBLE ONE.
GNH GNH
GRIT
MOMO ZONO
Young people have so much energy.
YOU HAVE A COLD, MOMO-ZONO?
YOU CAN'T WORK THE REGISTER SICK...
...SO GET WELL BY TOMORROW.
YES, I'M SORRY.
BUT...
...SOMEWHERE IN MY HEART...
...I WANT TO KEEP DREAMING.

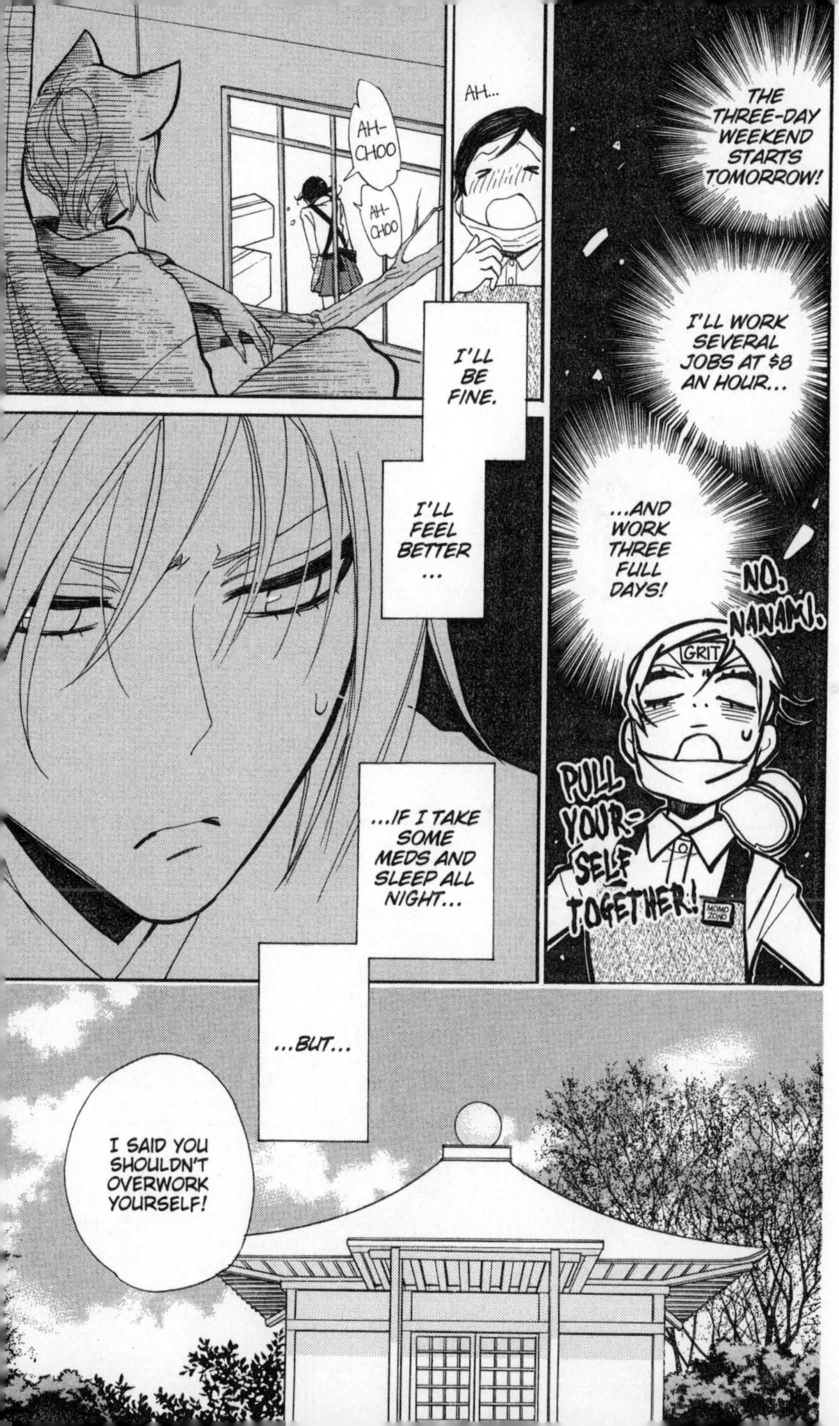
THE THREE-DAY WEEKEND STARTS TOMORROW!
I'LL WORK SEVERAL JOBS AT $8 AN HOUR...
...AND WORK THREE FULL DAYS!
NO, NANAMI.
GRIT
PULL YOURSELF TOGETHER!
MOMO ZONO
AH...
AH-CHOO
AH-CHOO
I'LL BE FINE.
I'LL FEEL BETTER...
...IF I TAKE SOME MEDS AND SLEEP ALL NIGHT...
...BUT...
I SAID YOU SHOULDN'T OVERWORK YOURSELF!

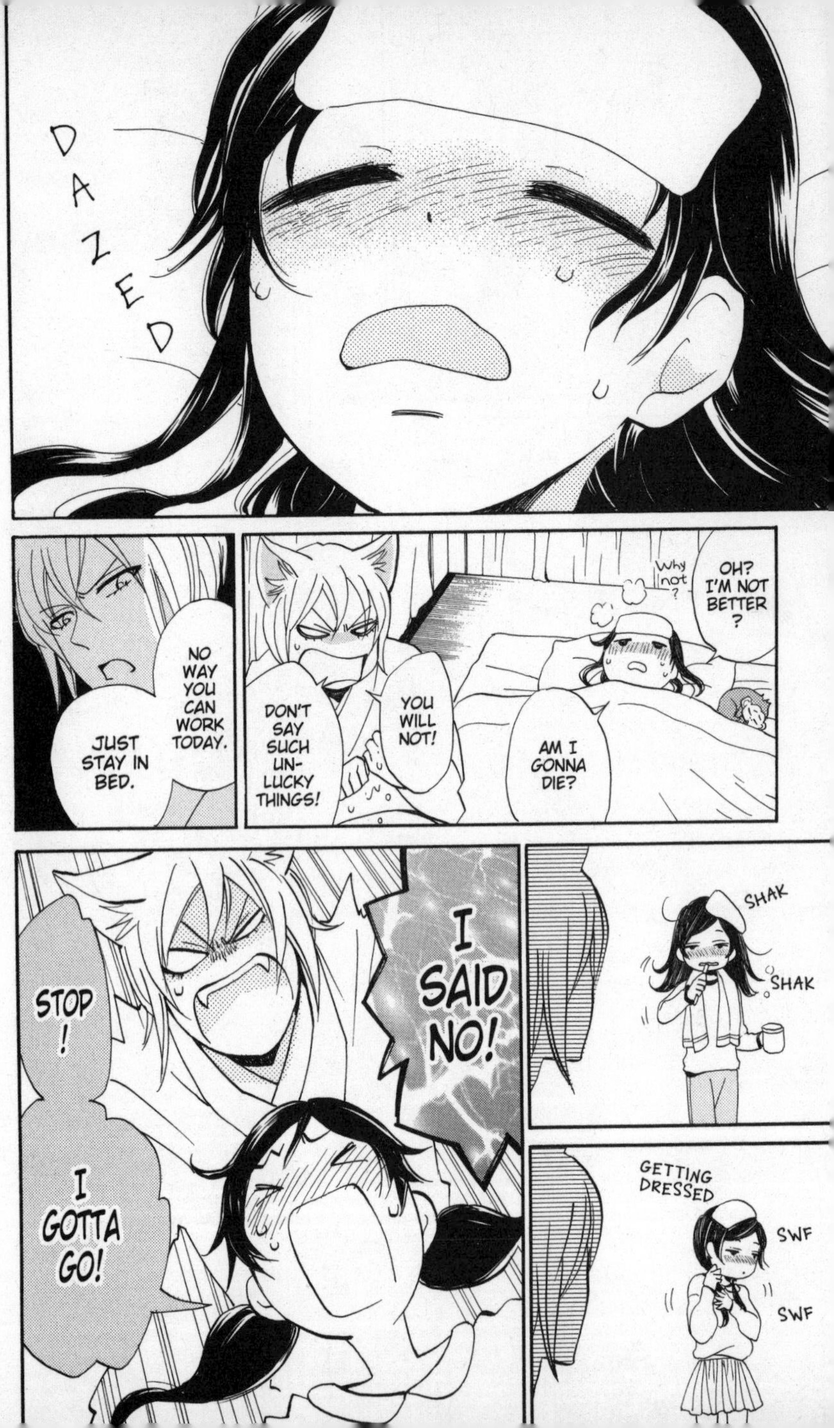
DAZED
OH? I'M NOT BETTER?
Why not?
AM I GONNA DIE?
YOU WILL NOT!
DON'T SAY SUCH UN-LUCKY THINGS!
NO WAY YOU CAN WORK TODAY.
JUST STAY IN BED.
SHAK
SHAK
GETTING DRESSED
SWF
SWF
I SAID NO!
STOP!
I GOTTA GO!

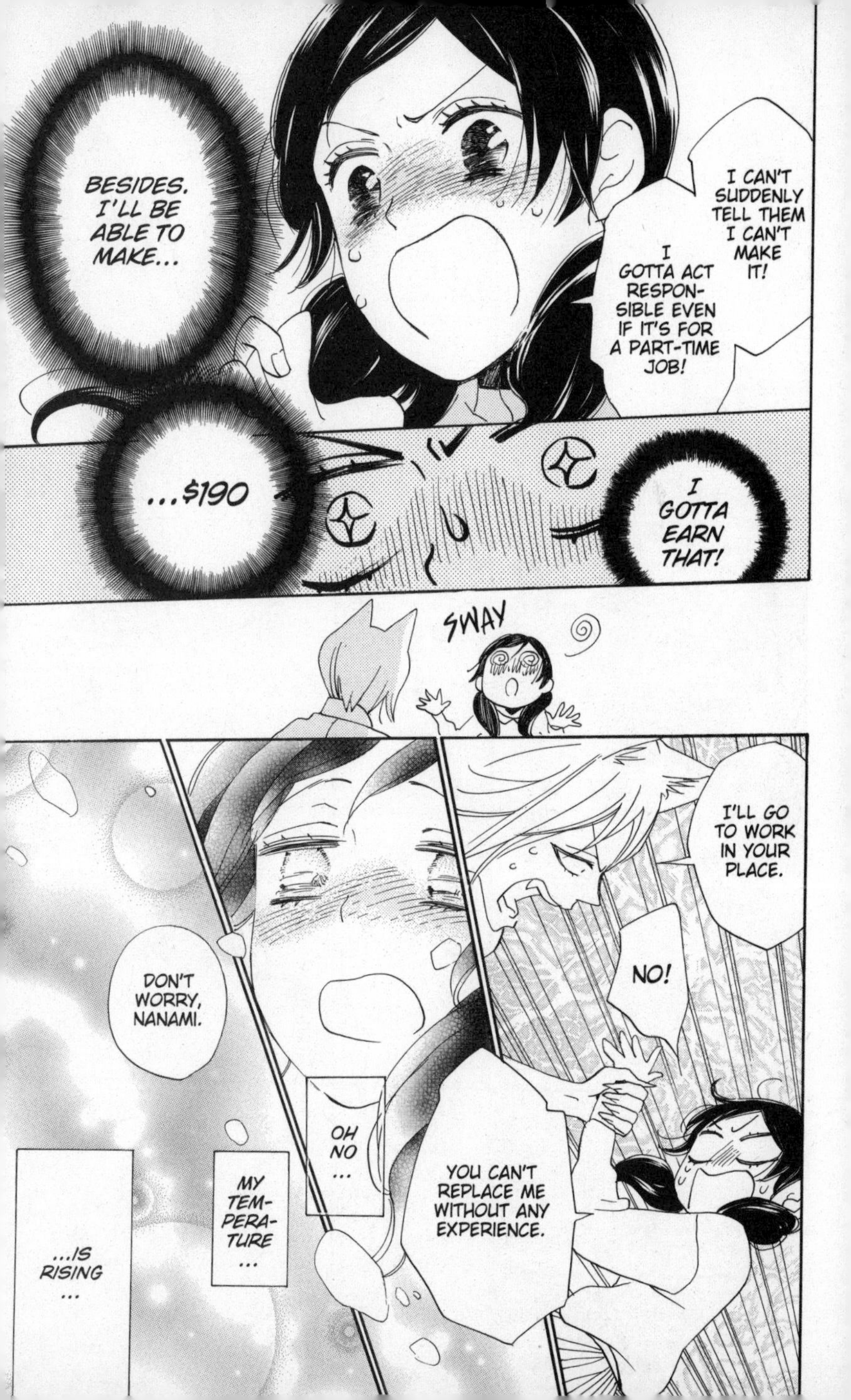
I CAN'T SUDDENLY TELL THEM I CAN'T MAKE IT!
I GOTTA ACT RESPONSIBLE EVEN IF IT'S FOR A PART-TIME JOB!
BESIDES. I'LL BE ABLE TO MAKE...
...$190
I GOTTA EARN THAT!
SWAY
I'LL GO TO WORK IN YOUR PLACE.
NO!
YOU CAN'T REPLACE ME WITHOUT ANY EXPERIENCE.
DON'T WORRY, NANAMI.
OH NO...
MY TEMPERATURE...
...IS RISING...

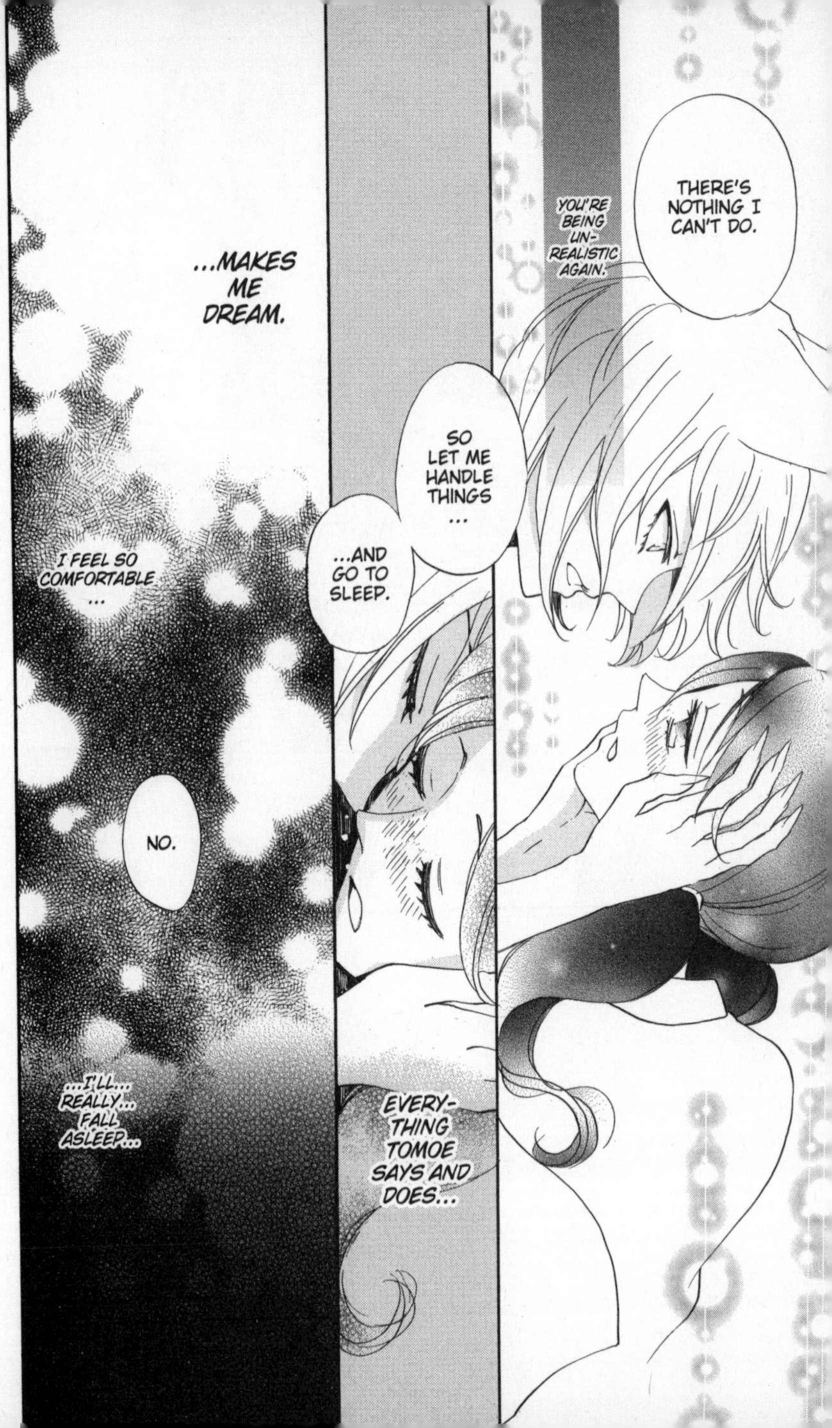
THERE'S NOTHING I CAN'T DO.
YOU'RE BEING UN-REALISTIC AGAIN.
SO LET ME HANDLE THINGS...
...AND GO TO SLEEP.
EVERY-THING TOMOE SAYS AND DOES...
...MAKES ME DREAM.
I FEEL SO COMFORTABLE...
NO.
...I'LL... REALLY... FALL ASLEEP...

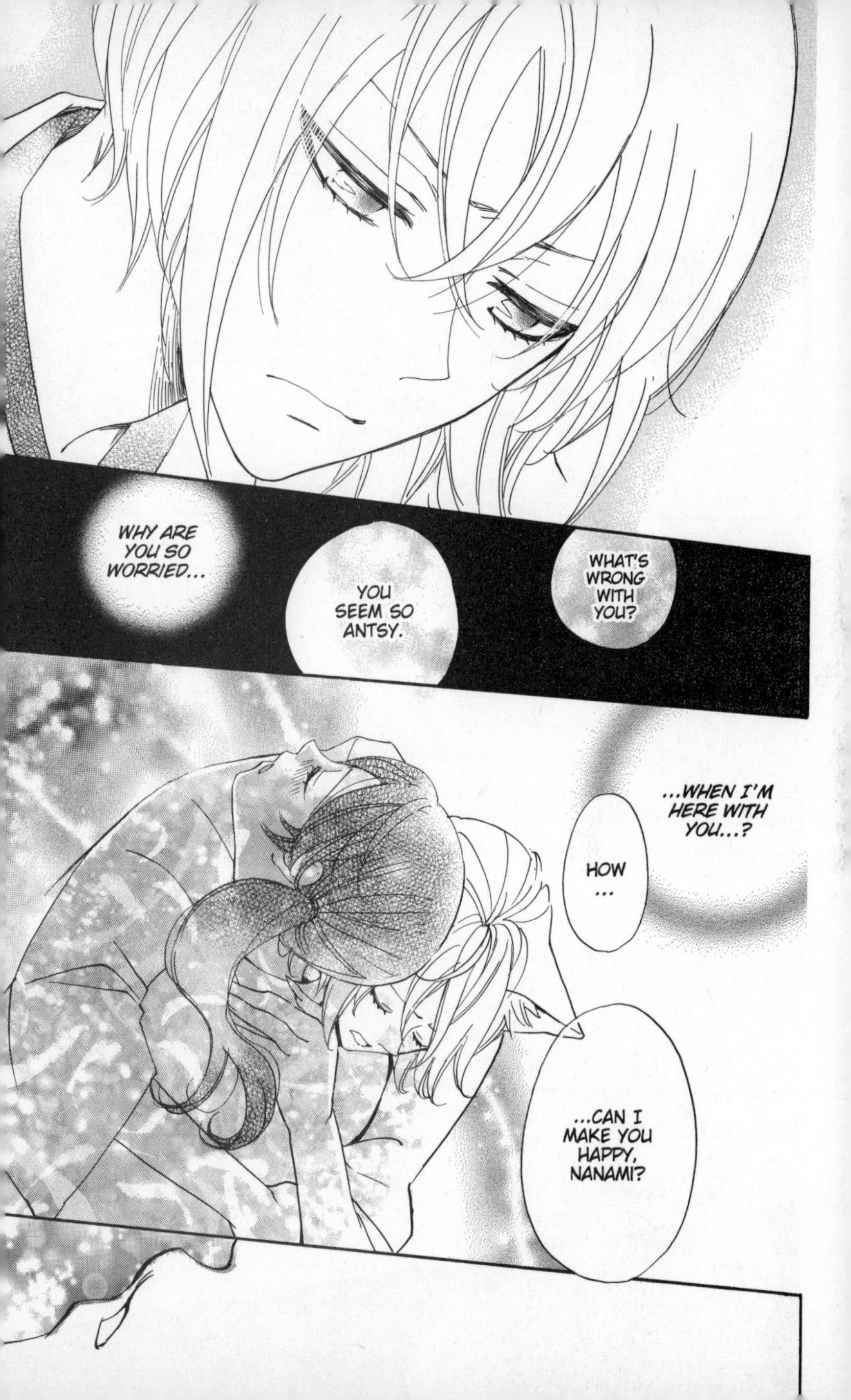
WHAT'S WRONG WITH YOU?
YOU SEEM SO ANTSY.
WHY ARE YOU SO WORRIED...
...WHEN I'M HERE WITH YOU...?
HOW ...
...CAN I MAKE YOU HAPPY, NANAMI?

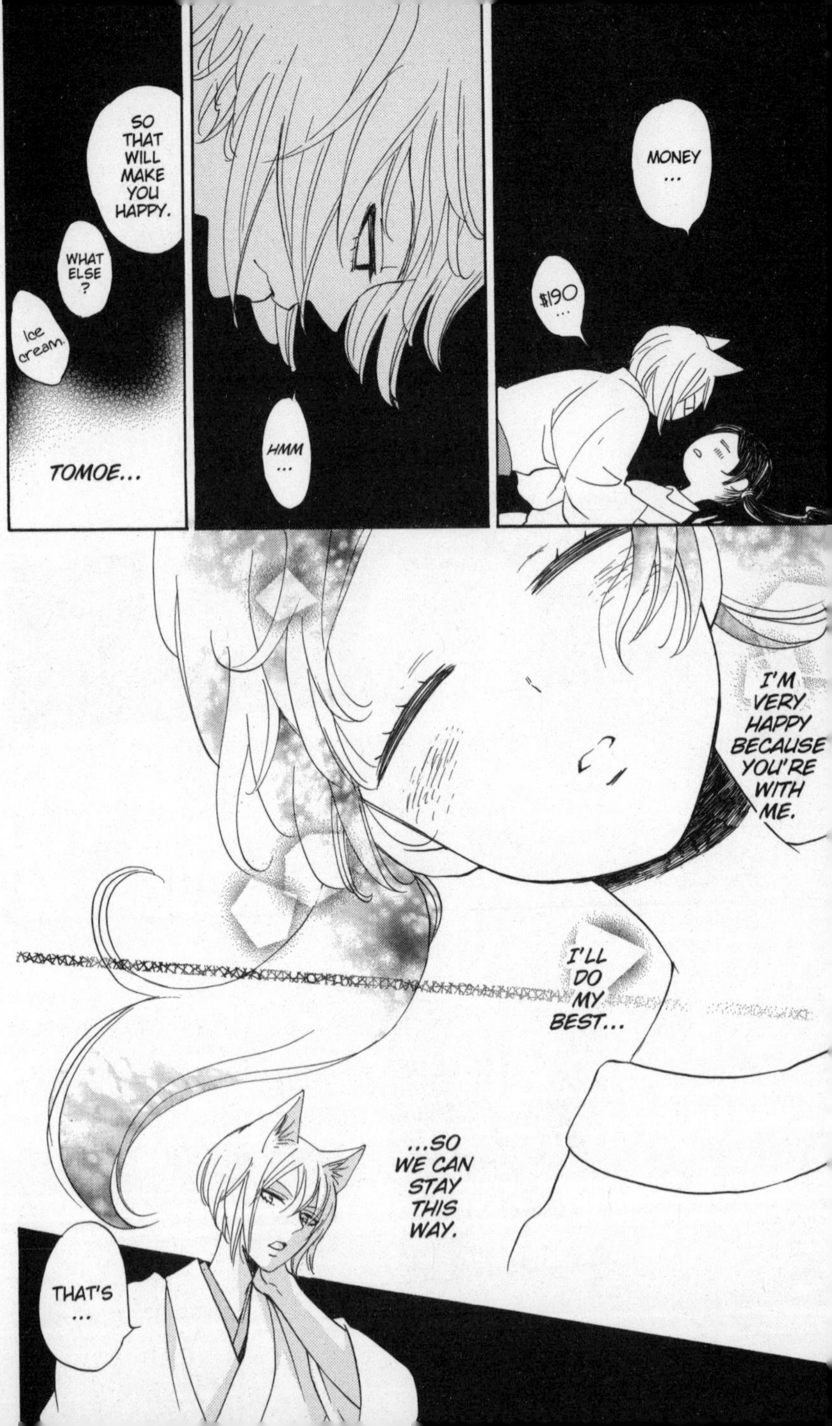
MONEY...
$190...
HMM...
SO THAT WILL MAKE YOU HAPPY.
WHAT ELSE?
Ice cream.
TOMOE...
I'M VERY HAPPY BECAUSE YOU'RE WITH ME.
I'LL DO MY BEST...
...SO WE CAN STAY THIS WAY.
THAT'S...

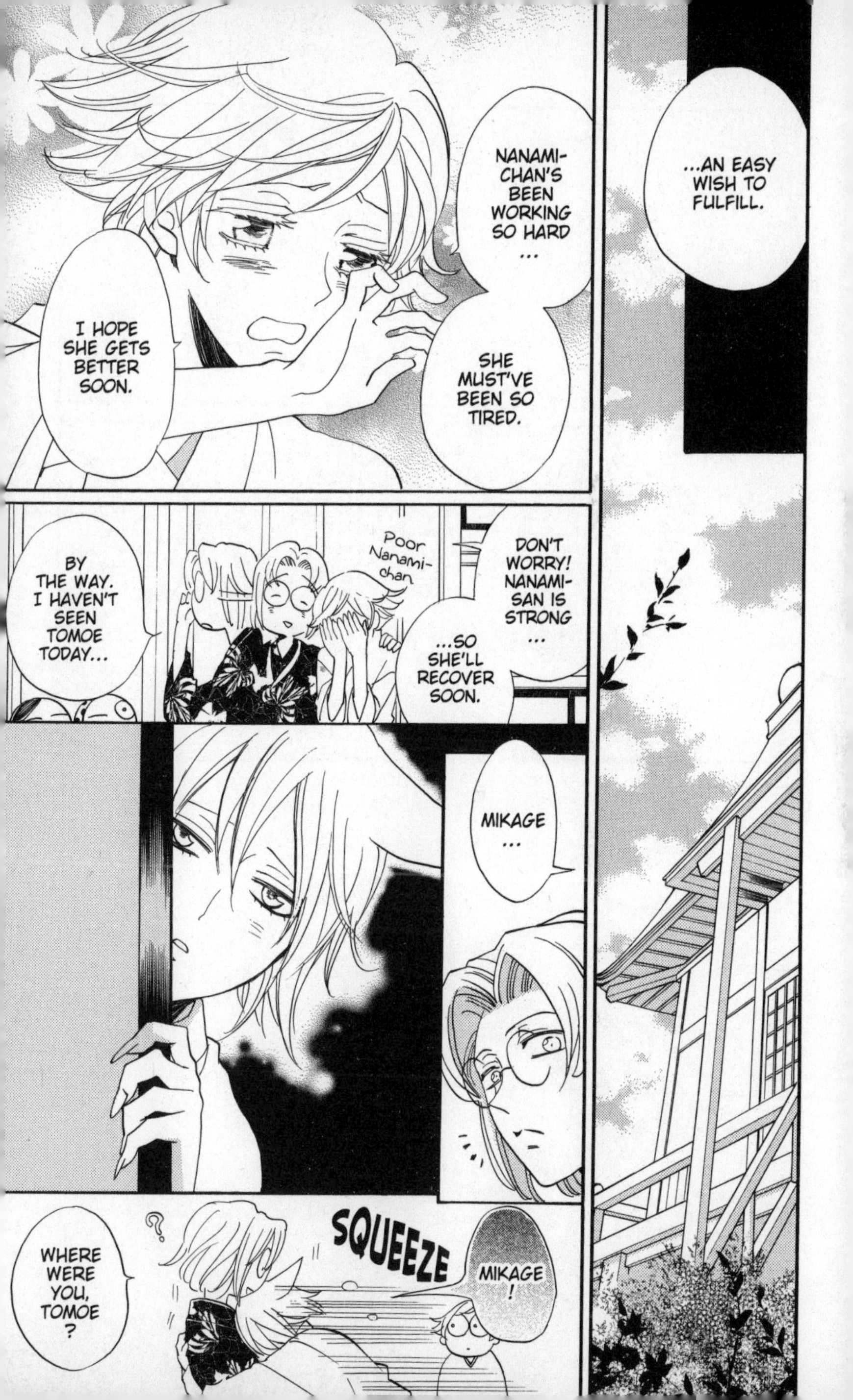
...AN EASY WISH TO FULFILL.
NANAMI-CHAN'S BEEN WORKING SO HARD ...
SHE MUST'VE BEEN SO TIRED.
I HOPE SHE GETS BETTER SOON.
DON'T WORRY! NANAMI-SAN IS STRONG ...
...SO SHE'LL RECOVER SOON.
Poor Nanami-chan.
BY THE WAY. I HAVEN'T SEEN TOMOE TODAY...
MIKAGE ...
MIKAGE !
SQUEEZE
?
WHERE WERE YOU, TOMOE ?

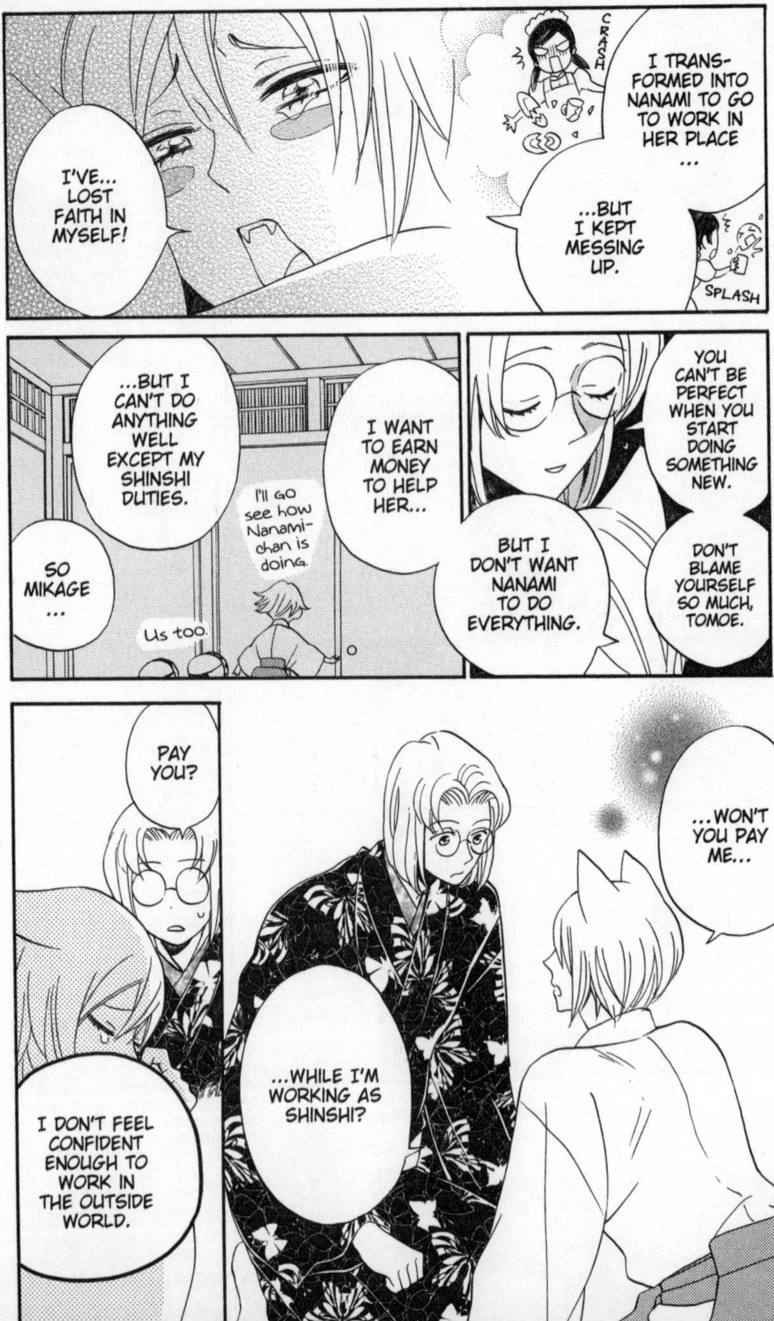
CRASH
I TRANSFORMED INTO NANAMI TO GO TO WORK IN HER PLACE...
...BUT I KEPT MESSING UP.
SPLASH
I'VE... LOST FAITH IN MYSELF!
YOU CAN'T BE PERFECT WHEN YOU START DOING SOMETHING NEW.
DON'T BLAME YOURSELF SO MUCH, TOMOE.
BUT I DON'T WANT NANAMI TO DO EVERYTHING.
I WANT TO EARN MONEY TO HELP HER...
...BUT I CAN'T DO ANYTHING WELL EXCEPT MY SHINSHI DUTIES.
I'll go see how Nanami-chan is doing.
SO MIKAGE...
Us too.
...WON'T YOU PAY ME...
...WHILE I'M WORKING AS SHINSHI?
PAY YOU?
I DON'T FEEL CONFIDENT ENOUGH TO WORK IN THE OUTSIDE WORLD.

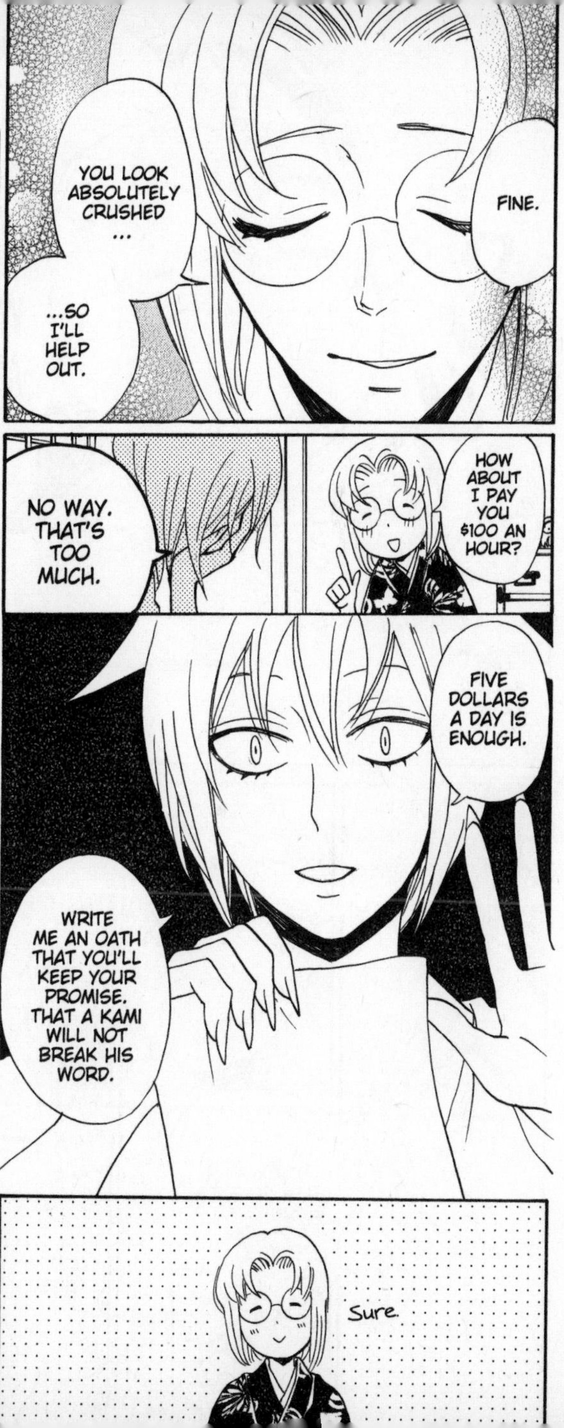
YOU LOOK ABSOLUTELY CRUSHED ...
FINE.
...SO I'LL HELP OUT.
HOW ABOUT I PAY YOU $100 AN HOUR?
NO WAY. THAT'S TOO MUCH.
FIVE DOLLARS A DAY IS ENOUGH.
WRITE ME AN OATH THAT YOU'LL KEEP YOUR PROMISE. THAT A KAMI WILL NOT BREAK HIS WORD.
Sure.

Thank you for reading this far!

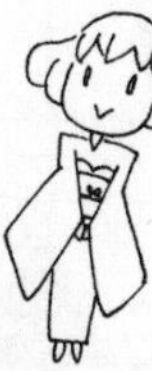

Volume 25 will be the final volume, so I hope you read it too.

If you have any comments and thoughts about volume 24, do let me hear from you!

The address is...

Julietta Suzuki
c/o Shojo Beat
VIZ Media, LLC
P.O. Box 77010
San Francisco
CA 94107

Now then.

I hope we'll be able to meet again in the next volume! ♡

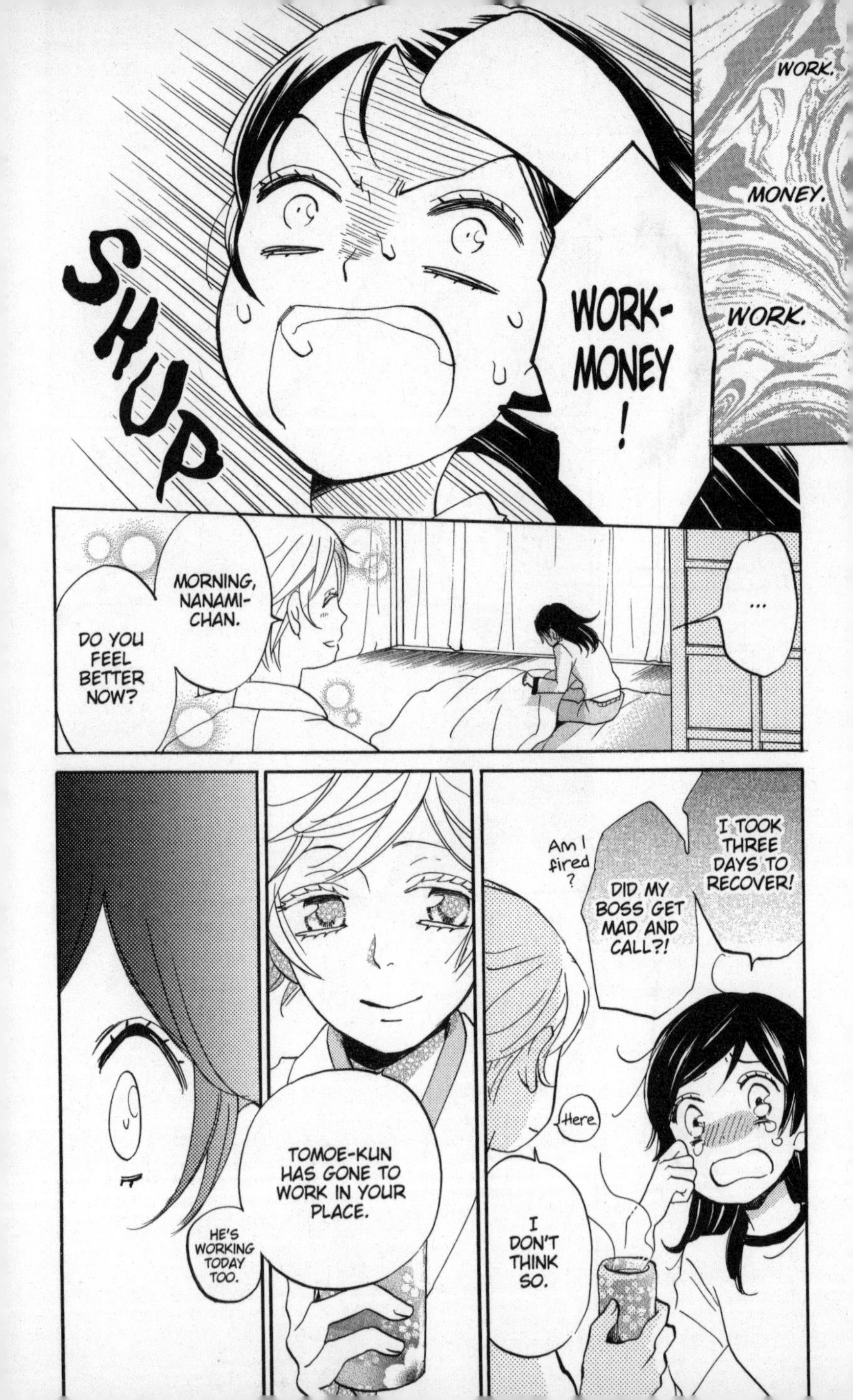
WORK.
MONEY.
WORK.
WORK-MONEY!
SHUP
...
MORNING, NANAMI-CHAN.
DO YOU FEEL BETTER NOW?
I TOOK THREE DAYS TO RECOVER!
DID MY BOSS GET MAD AND CALL?!
Am I fired?
Here.
I DON'T THINK SO.
TOMOE-KUN HAS GONE TO WORK IN YOUR PLACE.
HE'S WORKING TODAY TOO.

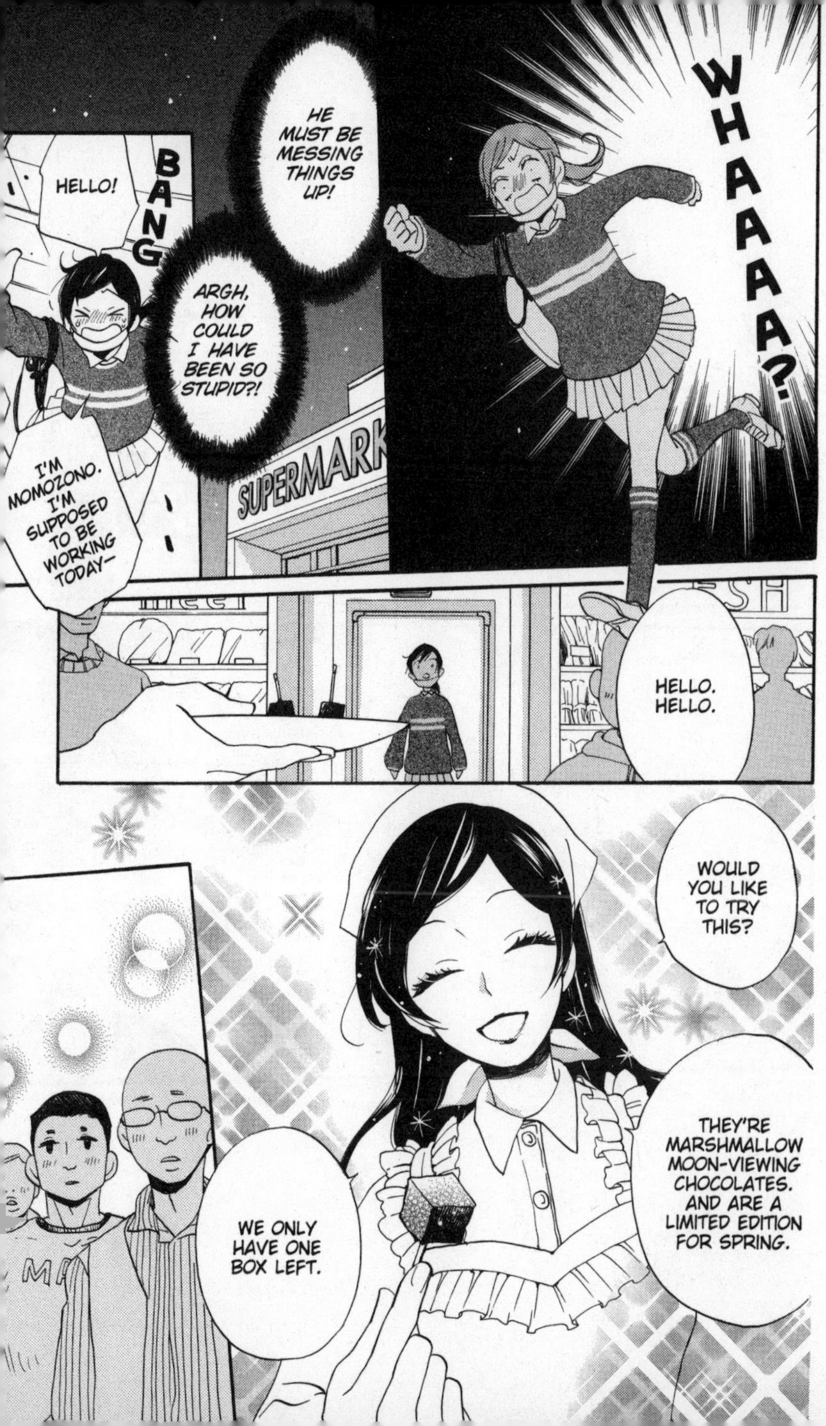
WHAAAA?!
HE MUST BE MESSING THINGS UP!
ARGH, HOW COULD I HAVE BEEN SO STUPID?!
SUPERMARK
BANG
HELLO!
I'M MOMOZONO. I'M SUPPOSED TO BE WORKING TODAY—
HELLO. HELLO.
WOULD YOU LIKE TO TRY THIS?
THEY'RE MARSHMALLOW MOON-VIEWING CHOCOLATES. AND ARE A LIMITED EDITION FOR SPRING.
WE ONLY HAVE ONE BOX LEFT.

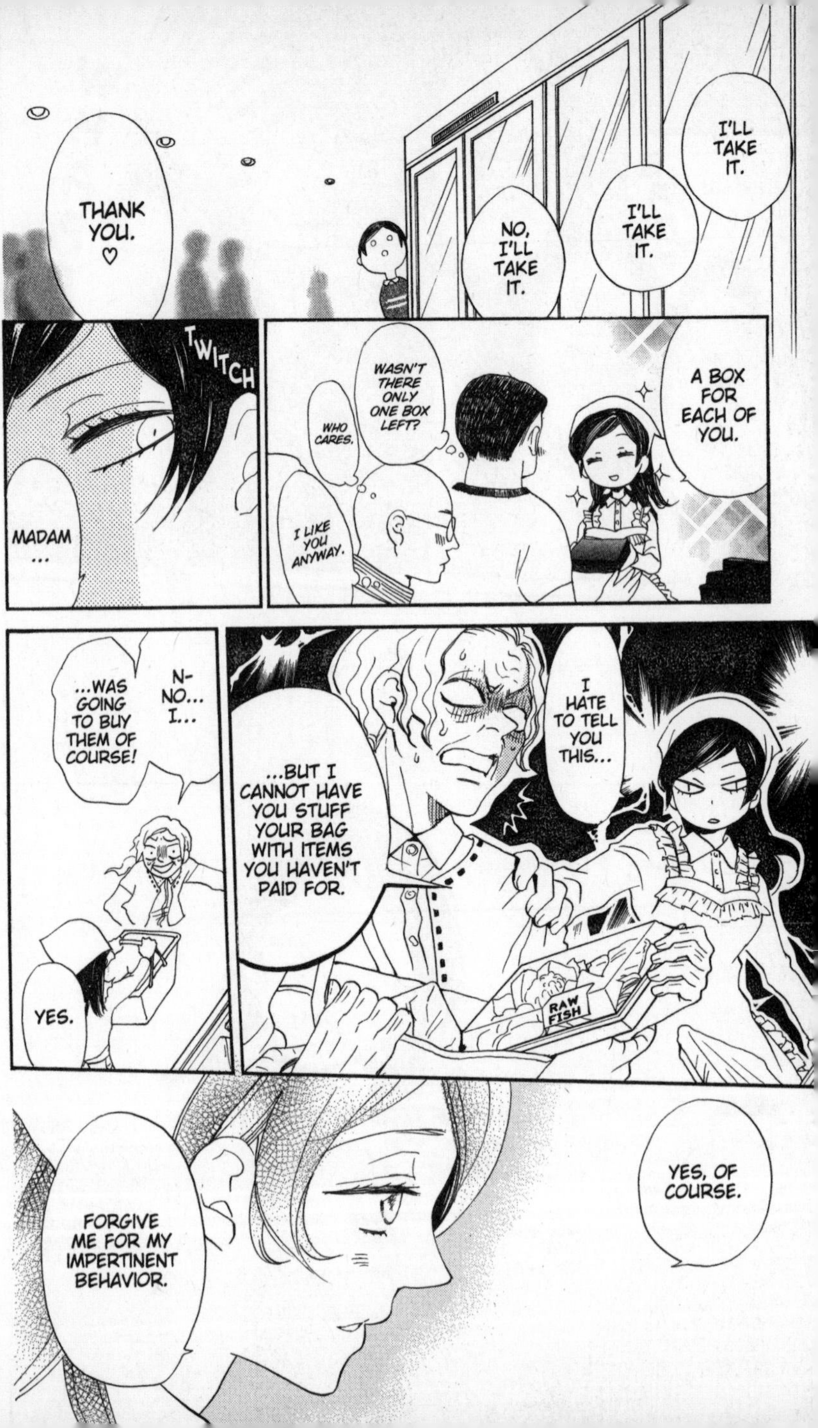
I'LL TAKE IT.
I'LL TAKE IT.
NO, I'LL TAKE IT.
THANK YOU. ♡
A BOX FOR EACH OF YOU.
WASN'T THERE ONLY ONE BOX LEFT?
WHO CARES.
I LIKE YOU ANYWAY.
TWITCH
MADAM ...
I HATE TO TELL YOU THIS...
...BUT I CANNOT HAVE YOU STUFF YOUR BAG WITH ITEMS YOU HAVEN'T PAID FOR.
RAW FISH
N-NO... I...
...WAS GOING TO BUY THEM OF COURSE!
YES.
YES, OF COURSE.
FORGIVE ME FOR MY IMPERTINENT BEHAVIOR.

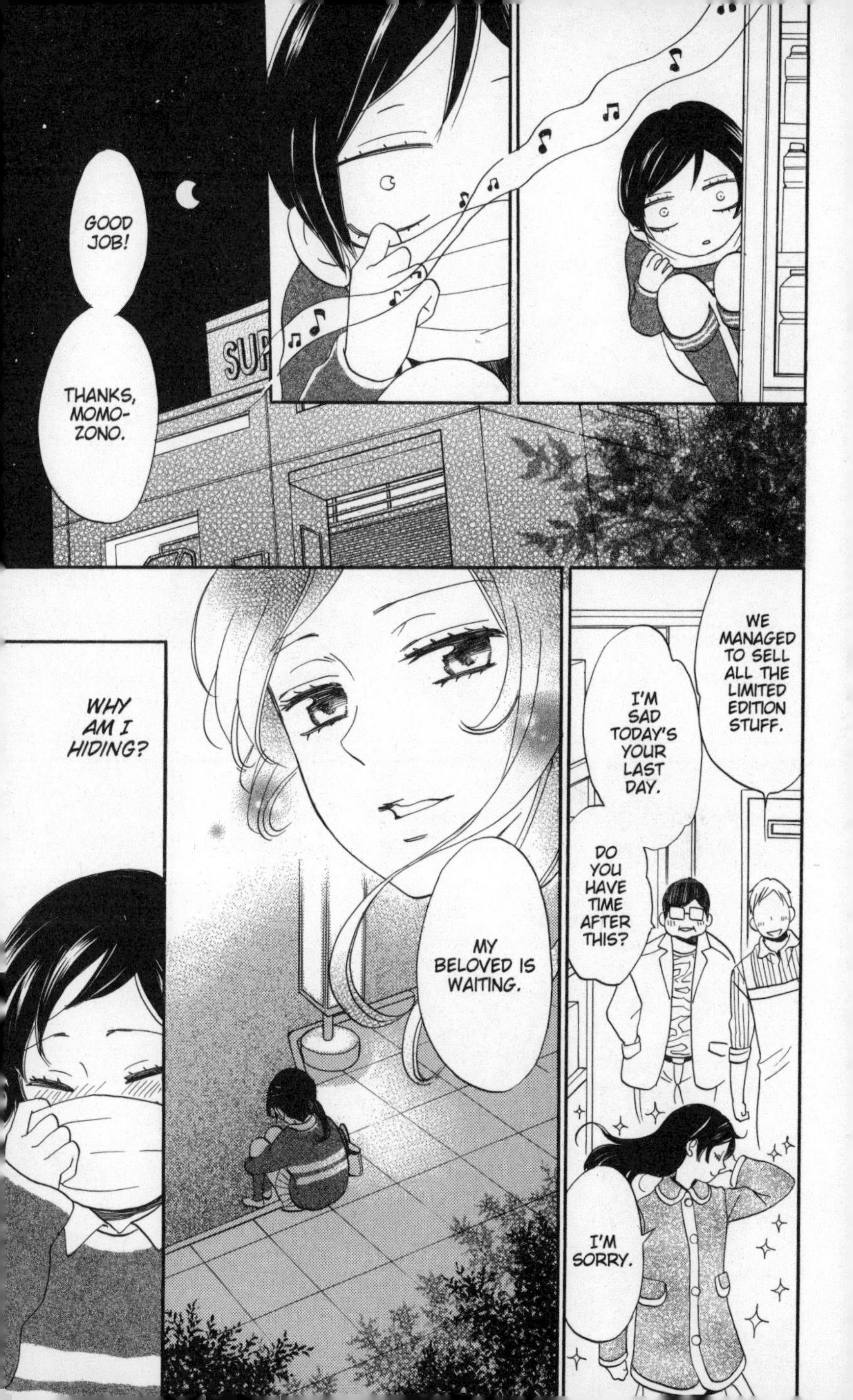
GOOD JOB!
THANKS, MOMO-ZONO.
SUP
WE MANAGED TO SELL ALL THE LIMITED EDITION STUFF.
I'M SAD TODAY'S YOUR LAST DAY.
DO YOU HAVE TIME AFTER THIS?
I'M SORRY.
MY BELOVED IS WAITING.
WHY AM I HIDING?

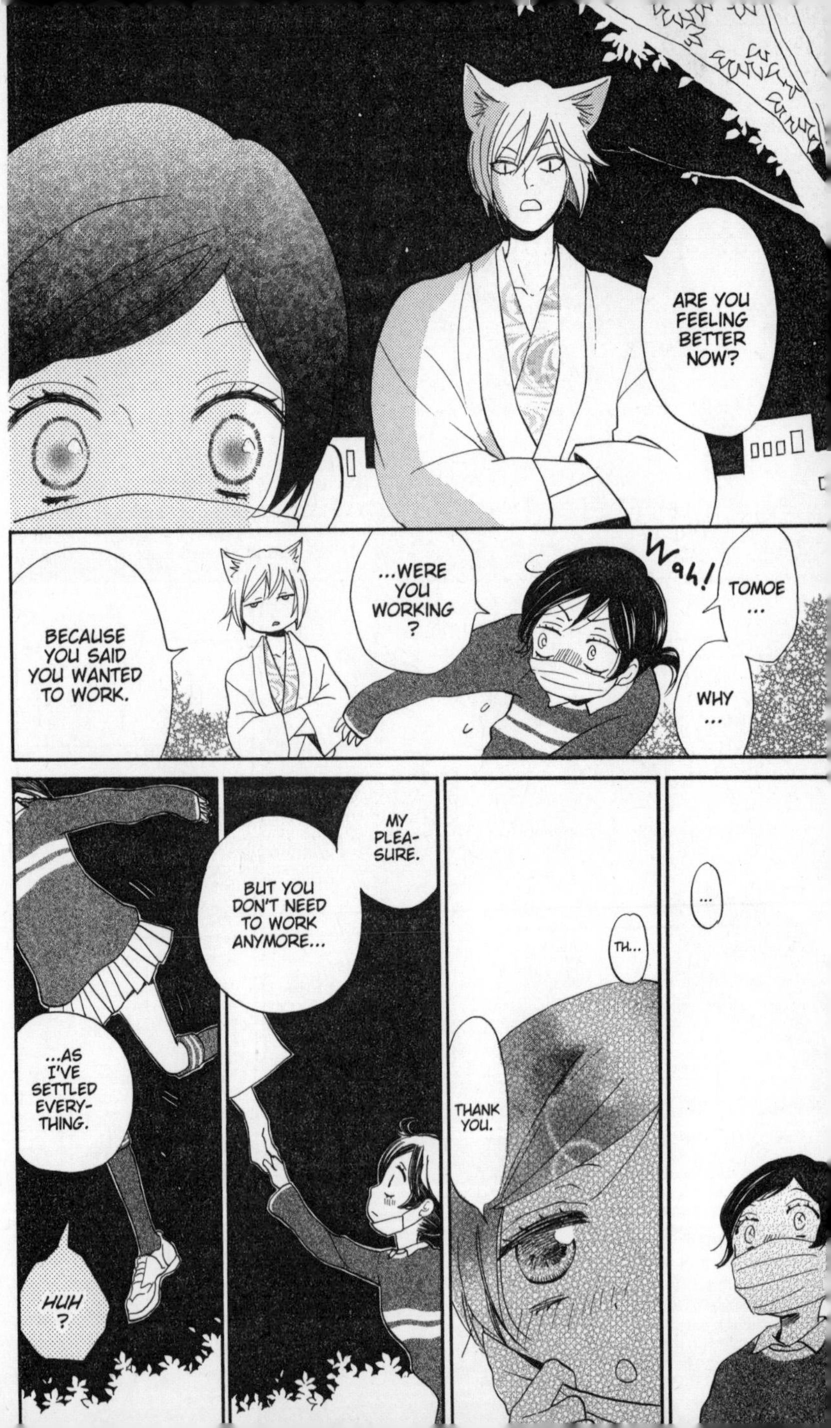

ARE YOU FEELING BETTER NOW?
TOMOE ...
WHY ...
Wah!
...WERE YOU WORKING?
BECAUSE YOU SAID YOU WANTED TO WORK.
...
TH...
THANK YOU.
MY PLEA-SURE.
BUT YOU DON'T NEED TO WORK ANYMORE...
...AS I'VE SETTLED EVERY-THING.
HUH?

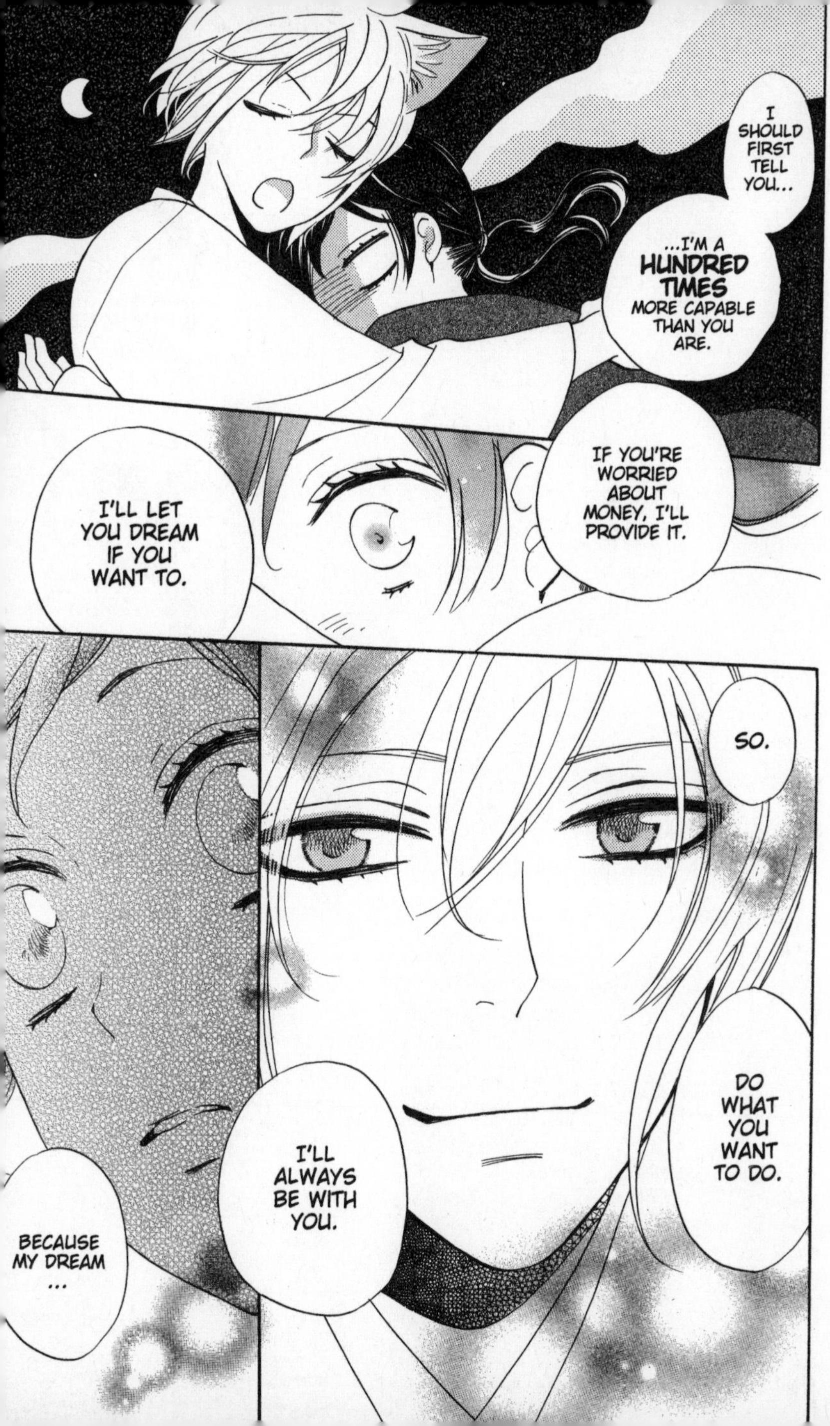
I SHOULD FIRST TELL YOU...
...I'M A HUNDRED TIMES MORE CAPABLE THAN YOU ARE.
IF YOU'RE WORRIED ABOUT MONEY, I'LL PROVIDE IT.
I'LL LET YOU DREAM IF YOU WANT TO.
SO.
DO WHAT YOU WANT TO DO.
I'LL ALWAYS BE WITH YOU.
BECAUSE MY DREAM
...

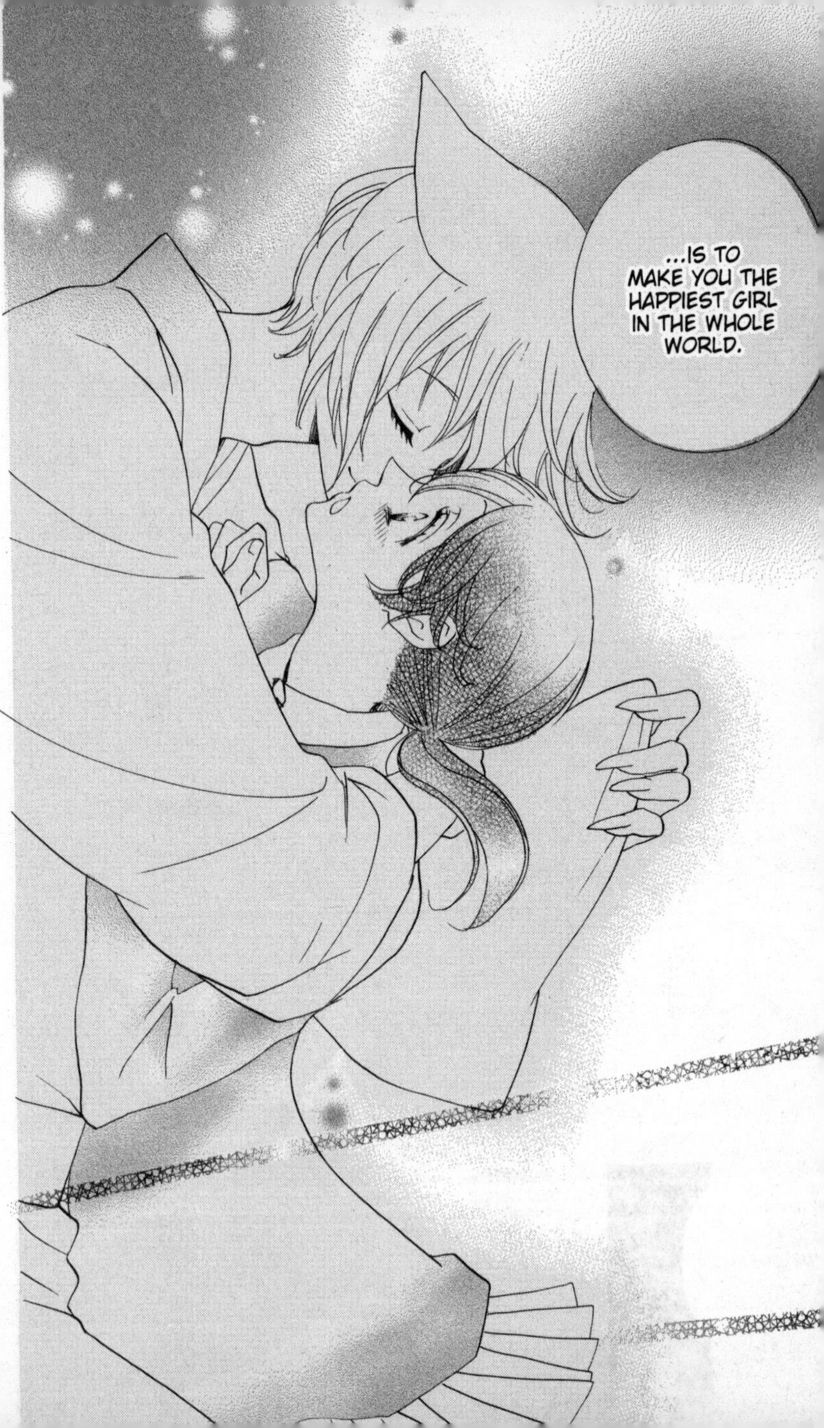
...IS TO MAKE YOU THE HAPPIEST GIRL IN THE WHOLE WORLD.

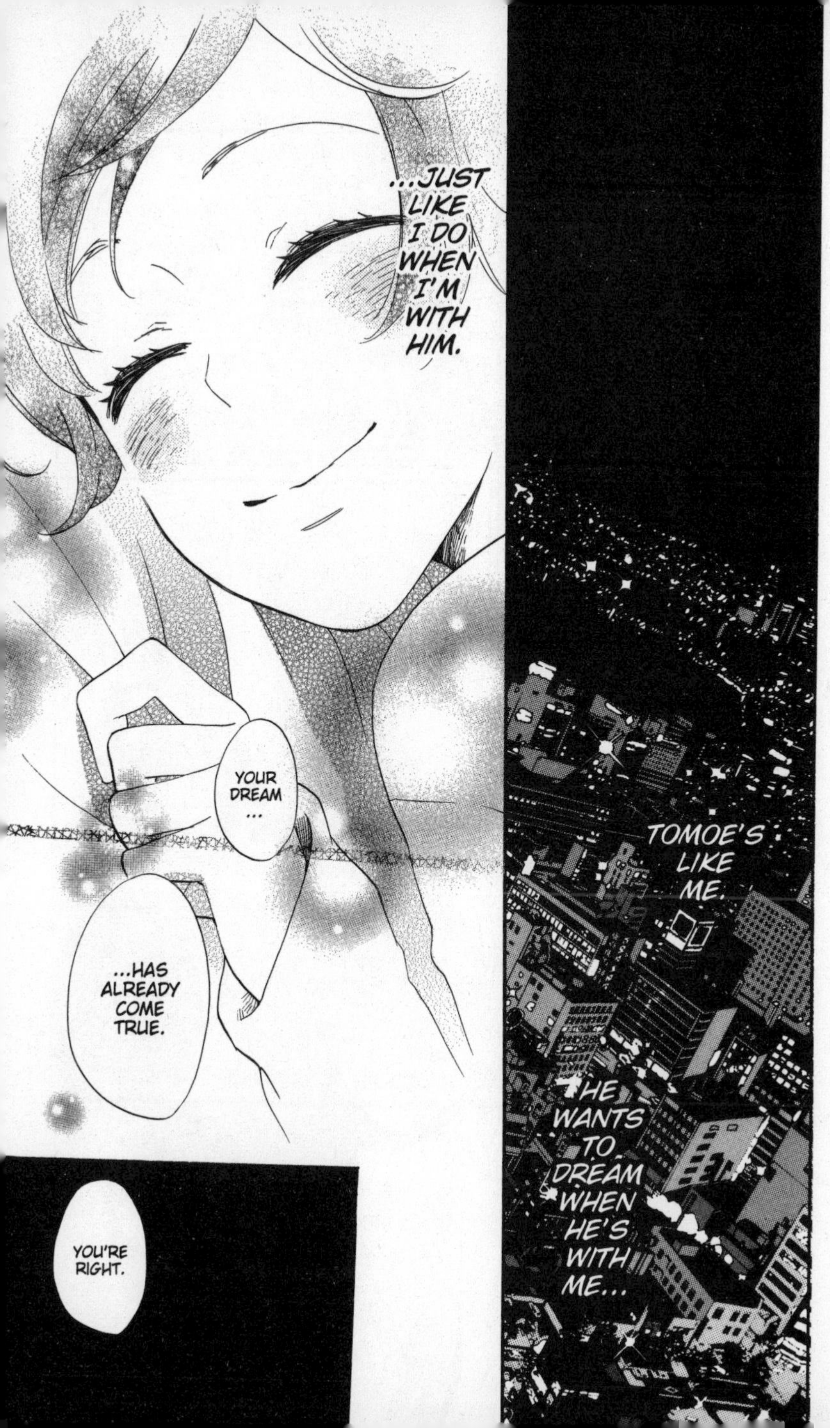
TOMOE'S LIKE ME.
HE WANTS TO DREAM WHEN HE'S WITH ME...
...JUST LIKE I DO WHEN I'M WITH HIM.
YOUR DREAM...
...HAS ALREADY COME TRUE.
YOU'RE RIGHT.

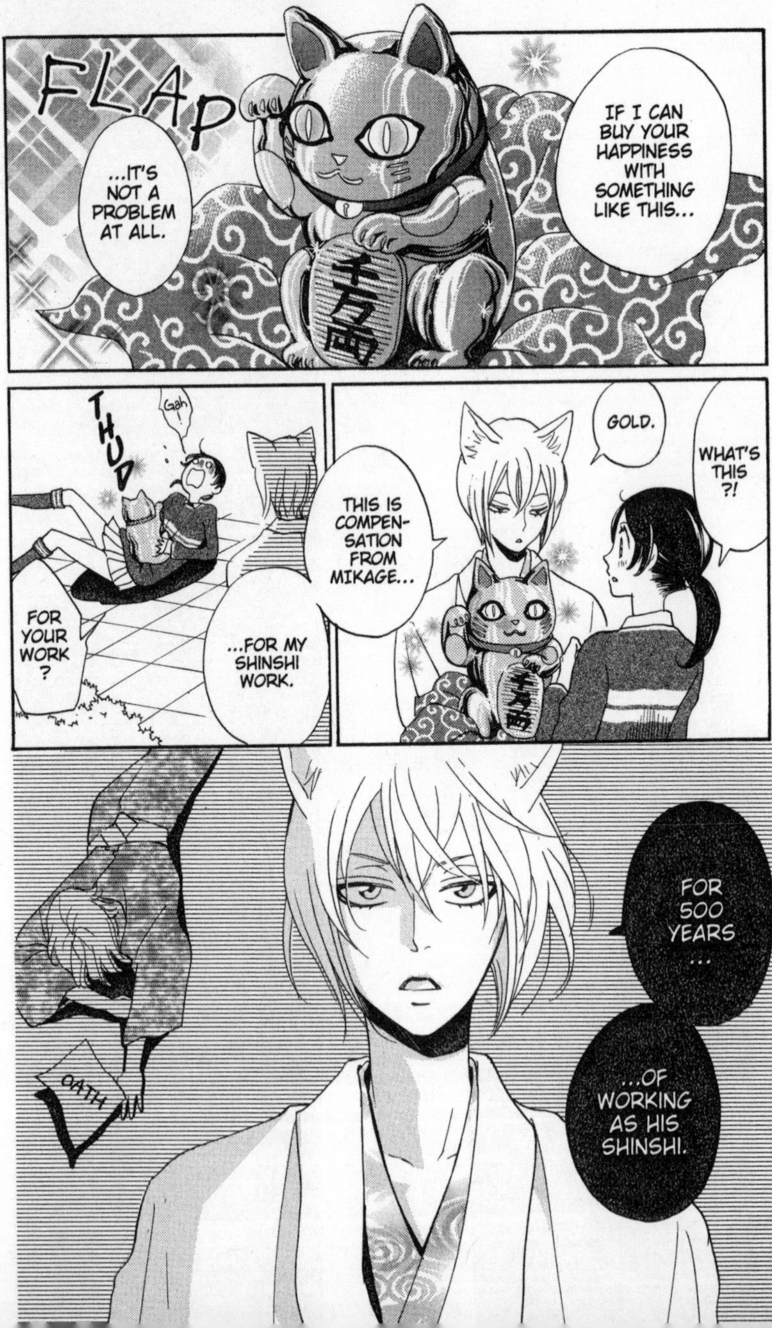
IF I CAN BUY YOUR HAPPINESS WITH SOMETHING LIKE THIS...
FLAP
...IT'S NOT A PROBLEM AT ALL.
WHAT'S THIS ?!
GOLD.
THIS IS COMPEN-SATION FROM MIKAGE...
FOR YOUR WORK ?
...FOR MY SHINSHI WORK.
Gah !
THUD
FOR 500 YEARS ...
...OF WORKING AS HIS SHINSHI.
OATH

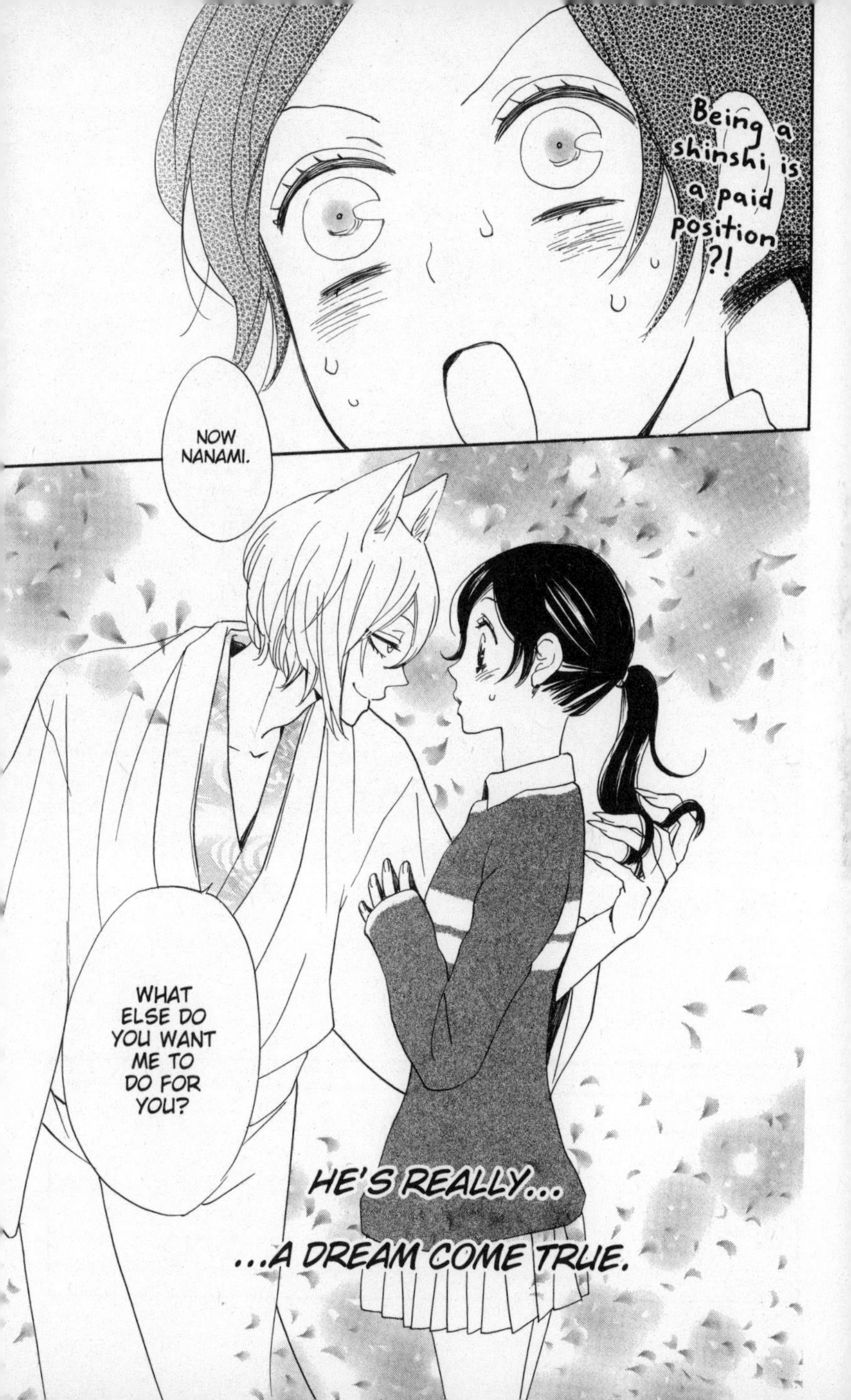
Being a shinshi is a paid position ?!
NOW NANAMI.
WHAT ELSE DO YOU WANT ME TO DO FOR YOU?
HE'S REALLY...
...A DREAM COME TRUE.

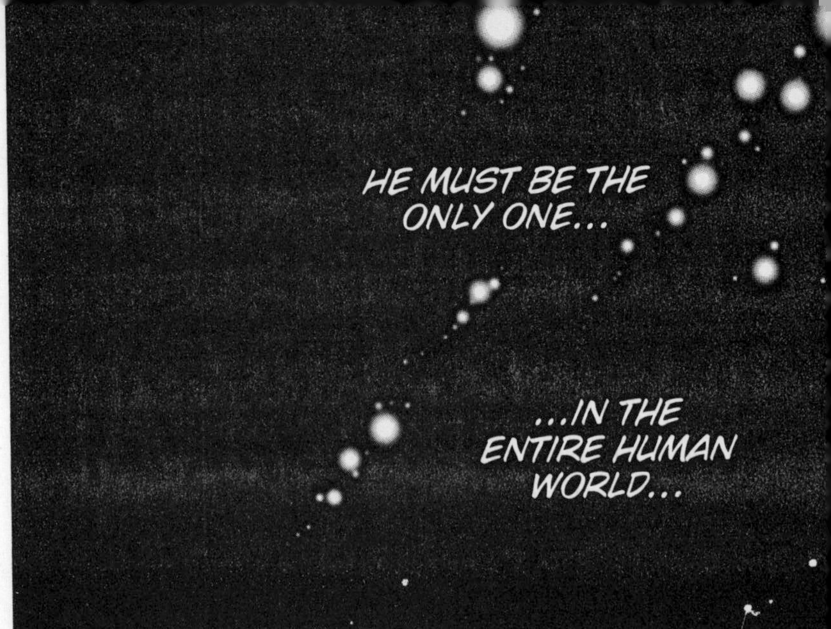
HE MUST BE THE ONLY ONE...
...IN THE ENTIRE HUMAN WORLD...
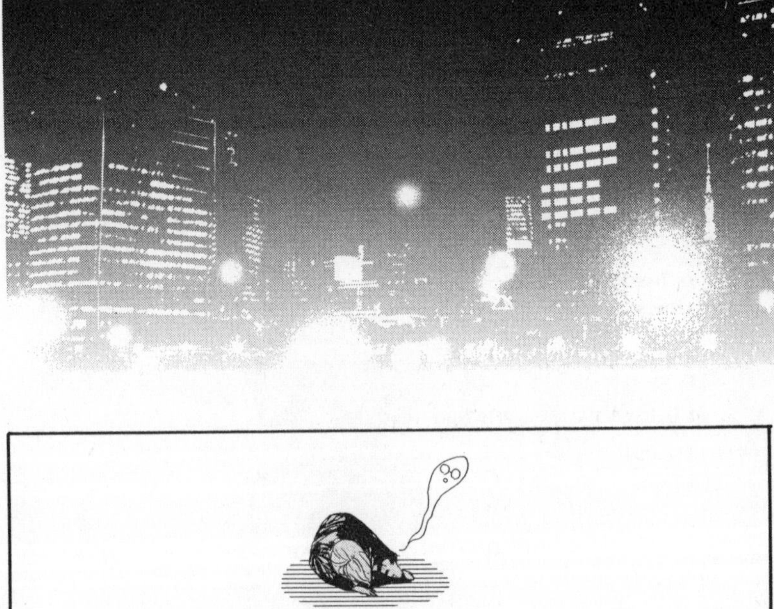

The Otherworld

Ayakashi is an archaic term for yokai.

Kami are Shinto deities or spirits. The word can be used for a range of creatures, from nature spirits to strong and dangerous gods.

Onibi-warashi are like will-o'-the-wisps.

Shikigami are spirits that are summoned and employed by onmyoji (yin-yang sorcerers).

Shinshi are birds, beasts, insects or fish that have a special relationship with a kami.

Tochigami (or *jinushigami*) are deities of a specific area of land.

Yokai are demons, monsters or goblins.

Honorifics

-chan is a diminutive most often used with babies, children or teenage girls.

-dono roughly means "my lord," although not in the aristocratic sense.

-kun is used by persons of superior rank to their juniors. It can sometimes have a familiar connotation.

-san is a standard honorific similar to Mr., Mrs., Miss or Ms.

-sama is used with people of much higher rank.

Julietta Suzuki's debut manga *Hoshi ni Naru Hi* (The Day One Becomes a Star) appeared in the 2004 *Hana to Yume Plus*. Her other books include *Akuma to Dolce* (The Devil and Sweets) and *Karakuri Odette*. Born in December in Fukuoka Prefecture, she enjoys having movies play in the background while she works on her manga.

KAMISAMA KISS
VOL. 24
Shojo Beat Edition

STORY AND ART BY
Julietta Suzuki

English Translation & Adaptation/Tomo Kimura
Touch-up Art & Lettering/Joanna Estep
Design/Yukiko Whitley
Editor/Pancha Diaz

KAMISAMA HAJIMEMASHITA by Julietta Suzuki
© Julietta Suzuki 2016
All rights reserved.
First published in Japan in 2016 by HAKUSENSHA, Inc., Tokyo.
English language translation rights arranged with
HAKUSENSHA, Inc., Tokyo.

The stories, characters and incidents mentioned
in this publication are entirely fictional.

Printed in the U.S.A.

Published by VIZ Media, LLC
P.O. Box 77010
San Francisco, CA 94107

10 9 8 7 6 5 4 3 2 1
First printing, June 2017

VIZ
MEDIA
www.viz.com

Shojo
Beat
www.shojobeat.com

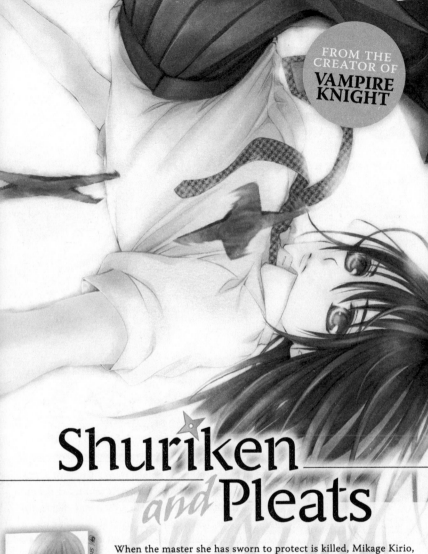

Behind the Scenes!!

STORY AND ART BY BISCO HATORI

Ranmaru Kurisu comes from a family of hardy, rough-and-tumble fisherfolk and he sticks out at home like a delicate, artistic sore thumb. It's given him a raging inferiority complex and a permanently pessimistic outlook. Now that he's in college, he's hoping to find a sense of belonging. But after a whole life of being left out, does he even know how to fit in?!

RATED FOR TEEN
ratings.viz.com

VIZ MEDIA
www.viz.com

Shojo Beat